A Race at Bay

A Race at Bay

New York Times Editorials
on "the Indian Problem,"
1860–1900

Robert G. Hays

With a Foreword by Paul Simon

Southern Illinois University Press

Carbondale and Edwardsville

Printed in the United States of America
Designed by Hillside Studio Inc.
00 99 98 97   4 3 2 1

Library of Congress Cataloging-in-Publication Data

Hays, Robert G.
    A race at bay : New York Times editorials on "the Indian problem,"
1860–1900 / Robert G. Hays ; with a foreword by Paul Simon.
      p.   cm.
Includes index.
      1. Indians of North America—Public opinion. 2. Indians of North
America—Government policy. 3. Indians of North America—History—
19th century—Sources. 4. Public opinion—United States. 5. New York Times.
6. American newspapers—Sections, columns, etc.—Op-ed pages—History.
I. Hays, Robert G. II. New York Times. III. Title.
E98.P99H39 1997
973'.0497—dc20   96-22191
ISBN 0-8093-2067-3 (cloth : alk. paper)   CIP

The paper used in this publication meets the minimum requirements of
American National Standard for Information Sciences—Permanence of Paper
for Printed Library Materials, ANSI Z39.48-1984. ∞

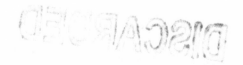

Indians of the far North-west have been nearly driven to the wall by the advancing tide of white civilization, and their attitude is that of a race at bay. The "irrepressible conflict" between their roving mode of life and the demands for strictly prescribed bounds made by civilization is leading to a final struggle in that region, before the red race, hopelessly worsted, sinks beneath the power of the white.

—*New York Times*
July 12, 1878

Contents

Contents

Contents

Contents

Contents

Foreword

I first met Bob Hays more than twenty years ago, and I found him to be a thoughtful and sensitive person. The reader of this volume will come to the same conclusion. But "thoughtful" and "sensitive" are not words that can be applied to the policy of the United States toward American Indians.

No nation has an unblemished record. U.S. history cannot be changed, but our future conduct can be improved. And we can—yes, we can—learn from our history. That is true as we look at our history of much too much insensitivity to the plight of African Americans; our failure to speak out vigorously against Hitler's oppression of the Jews, against the Turkish massacre of the Armenians, and against Stalin's policies that caused death to millions of Ukrainians; and our shipping 120,000 Japanese Americans who had committed no crimes from their homes in California, Oregon, and Washington to camps in the interior of the United States in 1942. But one of the least glorious parts of U.S. history is our treatment of Native Americans.

By focusing on one newspaper that wrote a remarkable amount about American Indians, considering its physical location, Bob Hays helps us to understand our heritage better and, I hope, motivates us to improve our conduct and our policy. In looking at this era of the *New York Times* editorials before the Ochs family bought that newspaper, Bob Hays holds up a mirror of the nation—sometimes at its best and sometimes not. The editorials show both insensitivity and compassion. One week the newspaper would refer to American Indians as "savages" and a few weeks later would have a remarkably enlightened editorial.

You will cringe when you read that a committee of the Colorado legislature approved a bill "for the destruction of Indians and skunks," with a $25 bounty to be paid out of the Colorado state treasury on the presentation "of such scalp, or scalps, with the ears entire." The *New York Times* was not the only journal outraged, and the measure did not pass. The *Times* suggested, tongue in cheek, that the name of the chief sponsor should be added to the list for whom a scalp bounty would be paid. It is worth noting that today Colorado is represented in the U.S. Senate by an able legislator, Senator Ben Nighthorse Campbell, a Native American.

Those who have a sensitivity to the church/state conflict over the school prayer issue will note with interest that, more than a century ago, Indian agents were appointed by the federal government upon the recommendation of religious bodies. On May 30, 1870, the *Times* admonished the religious community: "The churches have done almost nothing [for the Indians], being so much occupied with the foreign heathen that they have almost utterly neglected these wards of the nation."

In commenting on January 8, 1878, about "a great official scandal," the *Times* called for protecting Indian trust funds more carefully, a call that would be timely today. Other *Times* commentaries are equally current, including the observation "The Senate dearly loves to talk" (February 19, 1881). At other points, the *Times* demonstrated a limited vision. On May 20, 1879, the newspaper noted editorially, "The decision in the Ponca Indian case has been misunderstood by many as clothing Indians with certain civil rights."

Even the titles of the editorials are instructive: "Taming the Savage" (April 15, 1875) was followed a few years later with "What Will We Do with Them?" an editorial suggesting that responsibility for American Indians should be shifted from the Interior Department to the War Department (now the Defense Department).

One thing has changed. On May 20, 1866, the *Times* noted that "this unhappy race . . . has no champion on the floor of Congress." While much remains to be done, Senator Daniel Inouye of Hawaii has devoted a great deal of time to chairing the Senate Select Committee on Indian Affairs and has been both effective and eloquent on their behalf, and he has received virtually no public commendation for his efforts.

The problems of the nineteenth century are still not adequately addressed today. Native Americans on reservations have accumulated an appalling set of statistics on unemployment, infant mortality, suicide, crime, alcoholism, and almost every other index of quality of life—including the percentage of homes without electricity and running water. If the federal government were to have a genuine welfare reform program that included job guarantees—and nothing short of that will be *real* welfare reform—the life of the reservation Indian would markedly improve. Unfortunately, their brothers and sisters in urban America are generally not much better off, with one exception: The measure that permitted the establishment of community colleges on reservations is already showing signs of lifting the lot of those who seize this opportunity. And many of the better-educated Native Americans living off the reservations are now doing well. The profits from casino gambling are also helping some Indian reservations temporarily, but the fast-buck glitter brings with it problems, and if earlier American history is a fair guide, the appeal will fade as quickly as it has ascended. Indian reservations should not have to rely so heavily on this source of revenue.

One final observation: Bob Hays lives in Champaign, Illinois, home of the University of Illinois. While Dartmouth, Stanford, and other colleges have dropped their American Indian mascots, the University of Illinois has not. This is an affront to Native Americans. That the dance done by Chief Illiniwek is a religious dance, carefully learned from Indians, makes it even worse. Can you imagine our tolerating a Catholic priest dancing around at half-time at a football game, wearing his vestments, carrying a chalice? Many of the University of Illinois alumni get incensed when the subject is mentioned, which suggests that some of them did not learn much racial sensitivity during their years at the university.

That college is not alone, of course. We still have the Washington Redskins professional football team, for example, along with the Chicago Bears, St. Louis Rams, and other animal mascots. A British publication a few years ago called the naming of athletic teams for American Indians a last vestige of overt racism in the United States. That may be an exaggeration, but our insensitivity is as appalling as some of those old editorials in the *New York Times*. A few years ago, Naperville (Illinois) Central High School changed its nickname from the Redskins to the Red Hawks, and my guess is that, in the process, that school's student body and parents learned a little of our history and not-so-good traditions.

Through this study of four decades of *Times* editorials, Bob Hays reminds all of us of some of our history and not-so-good traditions.

—**Paul Simon**

Preface

When I was a graduate journalism student at Southern Illinois University, one of the courses I liked best was a seminar in journalism history taught by Professor Jim A. Hart. I came away from that seminar with an immensely greater appreciation for the role of newspapers in early America, particularly during the last half of the nineteenth century. It seemed remarkable to me that the Civil War was so well reported. And I was fascinated by the editors and reporters who shaped the newspapers of that day; these were men, and occasionally women, of stature, despite the well-known excesses of some of them.

Yet with all the interesting literature we read, or heard reported by others, one article stood out in my mind. It was an 1870s battlefront news story, published in the *Chicago Tribune* as I recall, from one of the many Indian wars that disgraced that period. I had in my hands the exact story that readers at the time had had in theirs, written by a war correspondent who was a firsthand witness to the combat. And I wondered how extensive such reporting had been, how much the general population knew about those bloody skirmishes on distant frontiers and about the circumstances that led to them. I knew then that I wanted to write a book on the topic. That idea lay dormant, on a list of things to do, for many years.

Then, some years ago, while working on a research paper in the University of Illinois newspaper library, I happened on an article in the back files of the *Washington Post*. That brief piece, published in February 1988, was headlined "New Sioux War Chief." It reported that the Sioux Nation had named its first war chief in more than a century and charged him with leading a battle to recover the sacred Black Hills of South Dakota from the federal government. The time had come for me to put other things aside; the work that became this book took its place at the top of my list of things to do.

My main interest, to revive and paraphrase a cliché from the more modern era of Watergate and other Washington scandals, was, "What did people know and when and how did they know it?" I looked at the contemporary press and found that the *New York Times* offered the best promise to answer that question. The continuity the *Times* provided in tracking what it commonly called "the Indian problem" was astounding. Further, the editorial pages afforded an exceptional combination of information and opinion. My task was principally one of selection.

If I had any doubts that I was on the right track, they quickly vanished in the spring of 1994 as I sat in a Washington hearing conducted by the Senate Committee on Indian Affairs. In that hearing, chaired by Republican Senator John McCain of Arizona, the ranking minority member, representatives of scores of Indian tribes and Indian support organizations from Mississippi to Alaska testified as to difficulties they saw blocking progress toward Indian self-determination. Their testimony focused primarily on problems in the Indian Health Service.

I was amazed. I was hearing restated, in a Senate committee room in the national capital in 1994, virtually the same arguments I had just read in a *Times* editorial published in 1891! The *Times* had complained then that a single government doctor serving a tribe of 13,000 scattered over a reservation of 12,000 square miles was insufficient. The Indians testifying in Washington more than a century later might have been following the same script.

If I have learned anything from this work, it is the simple fact that many of the problems faced by Native Americans today already were widely recognized in the 1800s. We seem to continue through repeated cycles in which issues remain the same and problems rarely are fully resolved. The roots of these challenges lie deep in our national history.

When Dee Brown's marvelous book *Bury My Heart at Wounded Knee* was published in 1970, it stunned the nation. Brown traced the tragic history of what the *Times* called the Indian problem through the Indians' point of view. It must have seemed to readers that this story had not been told before. But it had. Nearly a hundred years earlier, Helen Hunt Jackson had told it in her exceptional work, *A Century of Dishonor*. And much of it had been told, as it was happening and with varying degrees of accuracy and comprehension, by the American newspapers.

This is a story that bears repeating today, for better or worse, precisely the way it was told to Americans then. That is the intent of this book. I hope the retelling adds something to our understanding of why things are the way they are. If we understand better how we got here, we may be better prepared to decide where we ought to go next.

It will sound trite, but I should first thank the anonymous writers whose work filled the editorial columns of the *New York Times* from 1860 through 1900. They helped write the history of our country. In the present world, Jane Wiles and her staff in the University of Illinois newspaper library deserve great thanks for collecting and preserving those early journalists' work. I am grateful to Senator Paul Simon, himself a journalist and historian, for taking time from his busy schedule to write a reflective foreword. At the Southern Illinois University Press, Director John F. Stetter voiced strong support for this book from our first contact. I appreciate very much the work he and his staff did to bring it to fruition. I am especially grateful to John K. Wilson, the project editor.

Finally, I am indebted most of all to Mary Hays, my wife and research assistant, who contributed countless hours in a dark and often uncomfortable library nook poring over microfilm, checking indexes, and evaluating and taking notes on *Times* editorials. Without her devotion to our work and her critical insight into what is, and what is not, important, this book would have been years longer in the making and not nearly as good.

While I am grateful to all of the above, I take full responsibility for the content of this book. If there are errors of fact or judgment, they are mine alone.

Introduction

Charles Merz, editor of the *New York Times*, wrote more than a half-century ago that the editorial page "is not written to make chapters in a book." Ironically, his statement appeared in the introduction to a book, a collection of *Times* editorials published in 1941. That book, *Days of Decision*, effectively traced the newspaper's editorial positions relative to the war raging in other parts of the world—a war that *Times* editors perceived must eventually engage the United States.

Merz clearly did not intend to diminish in any way the importance of newspaper editorials. He wanted to emphasize their value as a reflection of contemporary events. The editorial page, he said, is written "for tomorrow's readers in terms of the day's news." He left to passing years the privilege of "shifting the focus on what happened yesterday and of picking holes in last week's arguments."

In this view, Merz mirrored a position set forth by earlier *Times* editors. In a foreword to the first *Times* index, covering the period from September 1851 through December 1862 and published by the newspaper, the case was stated succinctly: "The newspaper is one of the most valuable sources in the study of history, and is the only source that gives a day-to-day account of events and trends from a truly contemporary point of view."

And so the book that Charles Merz felt obligated to introduce with a disclaimer about the role of the editorial page is valuable today for reasons that go well beyond its insights into an influential newspaper's editorial leanings; it is a useful history of events and situations that preceded American entry into World War II. But at the same time, its greatest usefulness may lie in a contribution somewhat less obvious. Preserved within it is a remarkable sampling of the information and ideas to which *Times* readers were exposed during that period of American history beginning in 1938, when the war in Europe must have seemed far distant, and concluding with American entry into that awful conflict. What an informed public knows at any point in history is a critical aspect of that history, yet one that often is overlooked.

In a free society where newspapers are readily available, the editorial pages serve as an irrefutable guide to the things that matter. Events, situations, or ideas that are of little or no intrinsic importance may be of dramatic consequence if the public perceives them so. And at the same time, those things that rightfully should be of concern may go unnoticed until the editorial writers call them to public attention.

Newspaper editorial pages gain strength with conviction; great newspapers are expected to stand for something. Charles Merz noted that while much of the editorial writer's work might be perishable, the writer has an important ally not so easily dismissed: his or her own deep sincerity and loyalty to the ideals of the newspaper in which the work appears. On a large newspaper such as the *Times*, there typically is a team of writers contributing to the editorial columns. Today, editorial writers are expected to reflect a common view; the writer and the newspaper as an institution are indistinguishable to the reader. The editorial "we" prevails. Individual editors and writers come and go, but the editorial voice continues uninterrupted, its influence undiminished.

Although that consistent institutional voice has not always been the common editorial-page pattern—as readers of this book will see—the role of an important national newspaper over a period of history ought not to be underestimated. What the newspaper chooses as editorial subject matter at times may lead public opinion and at other times may follow, but it stands as a valid measure of what people care about—or should care about—during any particular span of years. This is an easy read in times of long-term but momentous and overarching conditions such as war, or immediate national tragedies such as political assassinations. It is less clear as it relates to long-term and less dramatic social movements or conflicts, or developing conditions that barely inch their way into the public consciousness—changing race relations, for example, or shifts in economic patterns that may go undetected for years. But even these have a way of bursting forth in dramatic fashion in some climactic event that has been years in the making. And when that happens, although many are taken by surprise, the best-informed people at least know they were forewarned through the editorial pages.

American historians tend to focus most sharply on easily classified periods: presidential administrations, wars, economic depressions, and the like. That is a rational approach. Through it, our history is developed layer on layer, one span of years compared and contrasted with another. One of its best advantages is that it allows us to build on what is there; we need not bother to repeat what already has been written unless there is new information or a new interpretation. The traditional historian builds and the revisionist tears down, often from the same record.

The record itself deserves our attention. It is that "day-to-day account of events and trends" that we can always look at with fresh vision, that point of view expressed by contemporary writers that we can reexamine in the light of passing decades. There are instances in which that record, simple and unadorned, is revealing in its entirety in ways that might never be apparent when viewed piecemeal.

One of those instances is represented by this book, which brings together a collection of remarkable editorials from the *New York Times* over a forty-year period. Viewed as whole, these editorials can help us understand not only the events and situations that made up what *Times* editors commonly called "the Indian problem," but they also can provide important insight into what people knew, or at least could have known, at the time. Public images of the Native Americans and public understanding of the issues that surrounded them may not have been shaped by the *Times*—not nearly as influential then as it is today—but clearly the *Times* editorials stand as an authentic contemporary record of events and ideas that helped forge the informed public opinion of the day.

During much of the period covered by this collection, editorials offered a more reliable account of frontier news than did the news columns of the *Times* and other newspapers in the East. News columns too often included reports telegraphed by irresponsible or prejudiced correspondents, or stories based on accounts from papers in the West or letters from misinformed travelers and biased frontier residents. These frequently proved to be exaggerations at best, or in more serious instances, rumor-based and unfounded. One day's massacre was another day's retraction. News stories that otherwise proved to be accurate sometimes appeared more than once, having been received from different sources and assumed to be accounts of different events. The editorials were more likely to be based on verified information. Unlike news editors, the editorial writers had the advantage of time. Their editorials commonly were as informative as they were persuasive.

Each editorial included in this collection was selected for two vital reasons. First, and most important, it offers significant insight into the complex and often bitterly divisive issues surrounding the place of Native Americans in a nation bent on expansion. Second, it demonstrates the breadth of specific topics the *Times* dealt with that related to these issues. In no sense is this collection offered as "the best" of the *Times* editorials of the period; the quality of writing is somewhat irregular, though most are well written. Rather, it is intended that readers will gain an accurate sense of how pervasive and permanent "the Indian problem" appeared to those who believed that it mattered. This sense comes best from considering the collection as a whole. But at the same time, most of the editorials included are of such power as to merit individual attention.

The goal of presenting a comprehensive view led to the chapter organization. During the four decades covered by this collection, there were enough *Times* editorials on the unremitting search for the "correct" national policy toward the Indians to fill this volume. The same could be said of editorials about the corruption among those charged with carrying out policy at various levels, or about the so-called Indian wars. Powerful as these might be, however, they would miss critical aspects of the overall picture presented in this collection.

For example, editorials on individual chiefs—some held forth as heroes and some bitterly denounced—and their qualities as spokesmen and leaders would be missing. So might those editorials included here that reveal the depths of public opinion and the role of the press, those devoted to the Indians' own culture and politics, and those that demonstrate the irrepressible conflict between the Native American way of life and encroaching white civilization. The powerful *Times* editorials on depredations upon the Indians by white settlers and the endless chain of commitments made and broken also might be eliminated.

The editorials selected are presented as they appeared, without editing or editorial comment. Antiquated style and spellings are retained. These may appear to be inconsistent, since common usage tends to change over time. Unusual spellings of proper names—particularly, Native American names—also are kept. Like grammar and style, these too vary over time in some instances. Conventional grammatical construction a century ago differed a good deal from that which readers are accustomed to today; editors used commas superfluously and hyphenated most compound words. These also are preserved. In the rare instances where typographical errors or other simple mistakes occurred, these are indicated in the text. But these things need not distract the reader, and none lessens the impact of the editorials in which they might appear. On the whole, the writing remains crisp and clear and in many cases dramatic.

A final point: Given the nature of this collection and the time frame represented, it is inevitable that the *Times* editorial writers made reference to numerous people, events, and situations not familiar to the modern reader. No effort is made to clarify these; such clarification would add little to the understanding and the impact of the editorials in which they occur. If readers at times are left curious and are led to seek more information, so much the better. Even the casual reader will recognize that many of the issues surrounding the treatment of Native Americans in the nineteenth century are issues that even today are yet to be resolved.

A Race at Bay

1 The *Times* and "the Indian Problem"

Many of the Western settlers are very anxious for a war of extermination against the Indians, and assert that outrages and atrocities will never cease until this is adopted and ended. But this in itself would be an atrocity of the most gigantic and inexcusable character. Moreover, it would not be near as simple or easy a matter as these exterminators suppose. We believe it would be a war thrice the length of that lately waged against the Southern Confederacy, and would entail great bloodshed on our side as well as the other, and also enormous expense.

—*New York Times*
September 15, 1865

IN 1860, the *New York Times* devoted two dozen news stories to what it would commonly refer to over the next forty years as "the Indian problem." The sources of information were wide-ranging. Longer reports from the West Coast were weeks out of date, having been delivered by way of slow steamship. A January report from the West cited anti-Indian sentiments among white Californians. It noted that what the white settlers really wanted was "the Indians exterminated." There were concerns about the Apaches in the Southwest, as well, and by April the news centered on the Comanches in Texas. A brief West Coast dispatch in May reported the murder of a Pony Express rider by Indians; this later proved to be untrue. July brought reports of difficulties with the Cheyennes, Sioux, and Pawnees in Nebraska. In early August, the newspaper carried an extensive story on various tribes situated in the upper Missouri River valley and the military forts located in that region. A front-page report in late October concerned the massacre of white settlers across the Canadian border in British Columbia by Snake Indians. Two weeks after that, the news included reports on the use of United States military troops on Cherokee lands.

The *Times* and "the Indian Problem"

The *Times* published the annual report of Commissioner H. B. Greenwood of the Bureau of Indian Affairs in early December. Greenwood wrote that the government had negotiated eleven treaties with various tribes since March 1857 and had gained more than thirty million acres of land in the process. The $3,726,880 the government agreed to pay for the land would be held in trust for benefit of the Indians. (How this money was spent—or not spent—was the subject of numerous editorial complaints in later years.) Commissioner Greenwood expressed enthusiastic support for the nation's policy toward the Native Americans—often "aborigines" in the news and editorial columns of the *Times*—and claimed that "the problem as to the Indians' capability of elevation in the social scale has been satisfactorily solved." He stated full confidence that "the experiment of engrafting the habits of civilized life upon the wild stem of savage existence has been a success" and needed only further development "to insure its complete triumph." That, of course, would require additional appropriations by Congress.

But the news reports in the *Times* already had offered ample evidence that the commissioner's hopes of elevating the Native Americans needed to be balanced by somewhat greater awareness that "civilized life" remained an elusive goal among some white citizens as well as Indians. The Indian problem, it was clear, involved aggression on both sides.

For example, the troops called into service on the Cherokee lands had to forcibly remove illegal white squatters bent on occupying Indian territory. And correspondence from the West eventually sketched in vivid detail a massacre of some two hundred peaceful Indians at a settlement near Eureka, California, called Indian Island. Although that slaughter of innocent men, women, and children apparently was carried out by a band of desperadoes, the California correspondent for the *Times* reported, the murderers clearly had to have been aided and abetted by local farmers and ranchers. The correspondent found no reason to doubt information that the intruders knew the Indians were without weapons and therefore defenseless and that, "entering lodge after lodge, they dirked the sleeping, and with axes split open and crushed the skulls of the women and children."

Editorially, the *Times* demonstrated little clear direction as yet relative to the Indian problem. It expressed concern in March about frontier posts that created business for "thieving, murdering Indians," who in turn were sheltered, armed, and fed by the Interior Department. An April editorial warned of the danger that Indian problems in Texas were being used as a flimsy pretext to put troops on the border as a prelude to war with Mexico. And near the end of the year, an editorial expressed the newspaper's ire over the high cost of the government's Indian policy—without much attention to the policy's relative success or failure.

Inevitably, attention to the Indian problem diminished as the nation moved closer to civil war. In January 1861, the *Times* reported that Catawba Indians in South Carolina were involved in the secession movement. A later story dealt with an alliance between Missouri Cherokees and the Confederate Army, while the editorial page denounced the secession of Texas tribes. Some of these Indians held slaves, the *Times* noted, and their loss was good riddance. But a September editorial, "The Indian Allies of Secession," implied that the Confederates were taking advantage of ignorant savages; it expressed concern that "Southern civilization" might enslave them and wipe them off the face of the earth.

Despite the news and editorial columns' concentration on the war over the next several months, however, circumstance assured the Indian problem a continuing share of space. Early 1862 brought stories on conflicts in Kansas, Colorado, California, and Utah. Then, in August, a disagreement between the Sioux and white settlers in Minnesota turned violent and bloody, leading to hundreds of deaths. The *Times* editorially called for aid to the "massacre victims" and lauded New Yorkers for their fund-raising efforts. It demanded that the Sioux be exiled from Minnesota but saw in this an act of mercy. It noted that not all the Sioux were guilty of crimes against the whites and argued that removing those not guilty was the best way to protect them from potential white mob action.

When three hundred Sioux were convicted of murder and sentenced to hang, the *Times* supported President Abraham Lincoln's pardon of all but thirty-nine of those convicted. Although the atrocities had been cold-blooded and shocking, it contended in follow-up editorials, the execution of three hundred Indians would be "an awful event," an event "without example . . . in any Christian nation."

Barely emerging was a general *Times* editorial policy on the Indian problem. Over the next several decades, the *Times* would support the cause of the Native Americans on most fronts. *Times* editorials would give the Indians the benefit of the doubt in questions of aggression, assuring readers that virtually every instance of open conflict could be found to have originated with injustices by whites. They would praise the oratorical abilities of the chiefs and commend the patience and forbearance of tribes that suffered the consequences of what the *Times* saw as misguided, inconsistent, and deceitful government policy. They would express open and sincere admiration for the skill and courage of Indians as warriors. And they would be tenacious in their utter contempt for the provocative and unceasing drumbeat of a complex war machine of commercial interests that stood to benefit financially from armed confrontation on the frontier.

In the coming months and years, the *Times* editorial columns would hammer at the failure of presidents and Congress alike to develop a rational and humane national policy toward the Indians and would attack with some vigor the corrupt public officials responsible for mismanaging the policies that did exist. The newspaper would be unwavering in its insistence that promises made to the Native Americans should be kept, that reservation lands set aside for them should be inviolate. It would maintain that, because white encroachment had robbed the Indians of their ability to survive by hunting and made them "wards of the nation," the government had an obligation to help educate and train them so they could make their way in the menacing world of the whites.

But at the same time, *Times* readers would almost certainly notice a marked ambivalence in the tone of editorials on the Native Americans. The editorials would never deal with the Indian problem from the perspective of objective commentary; instead, the writers would steadfastly couch their views in terms of "we" and "they." Their personal passions often would seem paradoxical and sometimes at odds with the general institutional views of the *Times*. Editorials expressing positions fortuitous to the Indians still were likely to be laced with derogatory terms; the "aborigines" also might be "red-skins," "greasy red men," "copper-colored inhabitants of the plains," or "dusky savages" described as lazy and shiftless, particularly vulnerable to the ravages of whiskey. In addition, *Times* writers perpetuated vicious and stereotypical images in satirical editorials not specifically intended to touch on the Indian problem. Intended or not, a common image of the Indians portrayed by the *Times* would be that of an inferior race decidedly less advanced than white citizens. When one band or tribe did well, the editorial writers might imply that this group was exceptional and, somehow, ahead of others in its progress toward civilization.

There was an inherent mystique surrounding the Indians that clearly would influence the *Times* editorial columns and that the editorial writers never would be able to dispel fully. Sometimes they would attempt to demystify the Native Americans with editorials of the "Where did they come from?" and "What do they want?" variety. At times they would treat the native cultures with dignity, at times with contempt.

But in this earlier time, even as the eyes of the nation were fixed on the Civil War—and before clear editorial-page trends were apparent—the news pages of the *Times* showed one factor that would be constant: So long as the Indian problem was important to the *Times*, there would be no shortage of targets onto which it might lock its editorial sights.

Military action against the Indians in the West continued. A majority of *Times* stories on the Indian problem during 1863 related to campaigns in Utah and the northern Great Plains. Bands of Sioux, Winnebago, Bannocks, and Shawnee bore the brunt of white military might. A year that began with the execution of the thirty-nine convicted Sioux in Minnesota ended with reports of General Alfred Sully's expeditions against Sioux bands across the upper plains—a campaign that extended through the coming year.

Action against Navajos and Apaches in the New Mexico and Arizona territories dominated early news reports in 1864. But summer brought more skirmishes to the north; the names of army outposts such as Fort Laramie and Fort Larned became painfully familiar to *Times* readers. Indian uprisings in Kansas and Nebraska were reported as well. The *Times* gave increasing amounts of news space to army accounts of activities across the vast western frontier, from Mexico to Canada.

Times opinion columns, meanwhile, explored a notable new element of the national policy toward Native Americans: the proposed relocation of the "semi-civilized" tribes onto the Indian Territory in the Southwest, which region was to be held "inviolate forever." In an August editorial, the *Times* said the proposal's greatest promise lay in its prospects for abolishing the tribal system and boldly suggested that it might lead, eventually, to citizenship for the "civilized Indians." To those who feared the Indians were not ready for voting rights, it asserted that "the loyal members of these nations [the tribes] are fully as capable of intelligently using the ballot as are the majority of the white men of Arkansas and Missouri."

The latter statement was typical of a chauvinistic attitude that recurrently crept into *Times* editorials. Time and again, the editorial writers contrasted what they saw as a more enlightened view of the Indian problem on the part of Easterners with a less generous frontier mentality they contended was common in the West. But they also pointed out that contemporary treatment of the Native Americans in the West simply paralleled what had begun on the East Coast a century earlier.

Times editorials on the opening of the Indian Territory also emphasized another view that by now had become a fixed stand for the newspaper. There was no logic, the *Times* insisted, in dealing with Indian tribes as though they were sovereign nations. Although it had rigidly insisted that treaties with the Indians should be honored—and maintained that they never were—it questioned any policy that attributed elements of separate nationality to the Indians in the first place. "At some day, not far distant," another August editorial said, "the quasi-sovereignties of the tribes must terminate, the system of communal land-holding be abolished, and the Indians prepared to take their place among American citizens, or to pass away and be forgotten." This position would be stated a great many times during the coming years.

Peace on the plains, it now had become apparent, was not to be achieved easily. New reports of hostilities pervaded the news pages of the *Times* in the early weeks of 1865. During that year and the following one, scarcely a week passed without at least one story of conflict between the Indians and white settlers or Indians and military forces. Readers learned to accept as regular fare such tribal names as Choctaw, Chickasaw, and Cheyenne.

On its editorial pages, the *Times* expressed grave concern about calls for a war of extermination. Troublesome reports of Indian brutalities all along the frontier made such a view understandable, an April 1867 editorial admitted. But it also complained that contact with whites had "opened the doors to debauchery, intemperance and wretchedness to the Indians, giving them in homeopathic doses the veriest attenuations of morality and virtue."

The editorial blamed "the belligerent army officers and corrupt traders of the [Indian] Bureau" for making it even more difficult to get a true picture of conditions in the West. That comment represented a *Times* view that changed over time. Corrupt traders almost always showed up on the editorial writers' lists of villains who could be blamed for the Indian problem, but in later years army officers usually got high marks. The *Times* wavered in its position on transferring the Indian Bureau from the Interior Department back to the War Department (where it once had been), at times opposing the idea outright and at other times seeing it as a positive move. It also would come to give great weight to the views of military officers and to generally express confidence in their evenhandedness in dealing with the

Native Americans. But it had learned early to draw clear distinctions between the behavior of volunteer militiamen and regular army troops. For years after Colonel John M. Chivington and his Colorado volunteers slaughtered hundreds of innocent Cheyennes and Arapahos in the Sand Creek massacre of 1864, the *Times* continued to cite that butchery as one of the darkest stains on the nation's history.

The end of the Civil War freed some of the army's most prominent military commanders for service on the frontier. Familiar warriors such as General William T. Sherman and General Phil Sheridan now were to be associated with the Indian problem. But *Times* readers also would grow accustomed to some new names: Red Cloud, Satanta, Captain Jack, Sitting Bull, Joseph, and Geronimo, among others. *Times* editorials would laud Red Cloud and Joseph, express grudging admiration for Satanta. But Sitting Bull and Geronimo were treated with outright contempt, while lesser chiefs drew little more than passing notice.

The outspoken Sherman, never friendly toward the Indians, nonetheless had great respect for their ability as fighters. The *Times*, in an early 1871 editorial on President Ulysses S. Grant's efforts to promote peace with the Native Americans, praised the president for taking a high moral ground. But lest readers forget the more pragmatic reasons for avoiding further clashes with the Indians, it reminded them that "Gen. Sherman has placed his opinion on record that fifty Indians could check-mate three thousand soldiers, and we need not go very far back in our history to discover the fact that Indian wars are the most expensive and utterly barren of result of any military undertaking in which we can possibly engage."

Given its Republican leanings, the *Times* commonly needed but little excuse to express its ardent support for the policies of Republican presidential administrations. It saved its most strident editorial voice for blasts at both Democratic political figures and rival Democrat editors. But when it came to national Indian policy, the editorial writers seldom exercised restraint in assailing the strategies of either party. President Grant—despite the various scandals during his administration—got significantly higher grades from the *Times* than most chief executives of the period on this front. But the editorial columns found a great deal to fault in the way policy was carried out by lesser officials in the Interior Department.

The *Times* praised Grant's "peace policy" toward the Indians. It steadfastly maintained that the problems arose from faulty execution of the policy and not the policy itself. Simply put, Grant's policy called for religious organizations and other philanthropic agencies to join with the government in efforts to staff the corrupt Indian service with dedicated people who would run it honestly and humanely. When that policy came under fire in later years, the *Times* claimed that it had "never been reserved" in its criticisms of Grant's appointments or his public policy. But in the case of his peace policy toward the Indians, it defended that initiative as "a bold expedient" by which the president had "resolved to gain the co-operation of the moral and reformatory elements of our population, and to go for his workers where he would be most likely to get honest men." The Grant policy brought a number of Quakers, among others, into the Indian service. Their influence would be seen for years to come.

And yet there would be no respite from the Indian problem. The *Times* expressed concern that conditions on the frontier were growing more dangerous, President Grant's peace policy notwithstanding. There were new Kiowa, Comanche, and Osage outbreaks, and the army's forces were spread too thinly in light of the Indians' strength, it suggested in an August 1874 editorial. It feared that General George Custer, camped in the Black Hills, was vulnerable and in danger of attack. It noted that "chiefs who are organizing forces for the war-path boast that they can bring four thousand warriors against his little expedition." The *Times* still supported the peace policy but decried weakened military strength that it feared would leave the army ill-prepared for a concerted Indian attack.

In the first week of January 1875, the *Times* news columns carried stories of attacks on whites by the usually peaceful Cherokees. The next two months brought new accounts of conflicts with Cheyennes, Apaches, and Kiowas. Summer brought no lull. Hostilities were reported on the Kansas frontier, along the Klamath River in Oregon, and elsewhere. The newspaper paid a great deal of attention to negotiations that brought chiefs Red Cloud, Spotted Tail, and others to Washington and led the Sioux to relinquish claims to extensive lands in Nebraska.

Even so, according to a bitter *Times* editorial in May, newspaper readers were becoming bored with stories relating to the Indians. The public, it indicated, cared little for either the present or future condition of the "red man." It questioned whether any race on the face of the earth ever had been treated worse than the Native Americans. It condemned shallow editorial writers who considered it clever to refer to the Indian as "Lo" but took some solace in the fact that, "If Spotted Tail and Red Cloud could read *The Times* they would find out by and by that we, at least, have not told them lies. . . ." (Ironically, it was only a matter of time before *Times* writers added "Lo" to the vocabulary of their Indian editorials. An editorial just three years later compared the status of the Indian and the Negro: "Lo is now predicted to be, like Sambo, permanently a member of the American community.")

The apathetic public the *Times* had been concerned about was jarred awake by the annihilation of General Custer and his troops by the Sioux on the Little Big Horn in Montana in the early summer of 1876. The setting closely resembled that which the *Times* had warned of more than a year earlier. But *Times* editorial writers, responding to the shock of Custer's loss, assumed that "so few newspaper readers have followed the course of the Indian warfare" that most of them would be astonished and alarmed. "We have latterly fallen into the habit of regarding the Indians yet remaining in a wild or semi-subdued state as practically of very little account," noted a July editorial. But an event such as the Little Big Horn battle, it contended, should make people realize the difficulties of the Indian problem yet to be resolved.

Custer's defeat once again left the *Times* in the position of having to defend the Grant peace policy. It was not that policy that outraged the Sioux, the newspaper argued, but the fact that the government for years had been systematically cheating the Indians out of their lands. After expressly assuring the Indians by treaty that the Black Hills would be left to them, it noted, "our people burst into the Black Hills region" and the Indians were told they must move. The *Times* then took a bold editorial position: "The wild leaders, embittered by a sense of their wrongs, burst into war, or more correctly resisted invasion—and on the late occasion only too successfully."

In the editorial columns of the *Times*, General Custer became something of a tarnished hero. The *Times* editorial writers paid appropriate homage to his courage and mourned his loss but nonetheless called attention to his brash and reckless military maneuvers that virtually assured his own devastating defeat. At the same time, the newspaper's treatment of events on the Little Big Horn and their aftermath demonstrated fully how troublesome the Indian problem was as an editorial issue for the *Times*. It held Sitting Bull responsible for what it considered an unnecessarily brutal battle. And while for a time it effectively rationalized the Sioux chief's behavior as simply that to be expected of any enemy during war, it never again was able to treat Sitting Bull with less than unequivocal contempt. He was the subject of scathing editorial comment for the rest of his colorful life and even at his death was the target of one final *Times* insult.

Months after Custer's defeat at the hands of the Sioux, an anonymous *Times* writer's scorn for Sitting Bull led to a striking example of the type of editorial-page paradox referred to earlier. "He [Sitting Bull] knows that no race of men on the face of the earth are so petted and pampered as the North American Indian," that writer said, ignoring the abundant evidence to the contrary presented regularly by the newspaper's own news and editorial pages.

Throughout early 1877, reports of Sitting Bull, Crazy Horse, and Spotted Tail were prominent in the *Times*. Sioux war battle sites such as Greasy Grass Creek, Rosebud Creek, Slim Butte, and Little Muddy Creek were introduced to readers in the East. But this would be a short-lived war; April brought the story of Spotted Tail's surrender; an "official report" of Crazy Horse's capitulation was published on May 15; and by mid-June, even the dogged Sitting Bull was said to have been subdued. Yet another story detailed the surrender of the Cheyennes under Dull Knife and Standing Elk.

And the *Times* would not allow memories of the fatal clash on the Little Big Horn to fade. It continued to recount that battle through reports by Native Americans who told the story from their own points of view. A front-page story in May announced plans to erect a monument on that remote Montana battlefield to memorialize the soldiers who had given their lives there.

The Sioux were not the only Native Americans to occupy the nation's military forces during that eventful season. The *Times* also reported on a series of events in Idaho that culminated in a desperate and bloody war with the Nez Percés under Chief Joseph. That conflict would continue through early October, when Joseph surrendered to General Nelson A. Miles. In November, the *Times* carried a front-page story on Joseph's heroic and emotional surrender speech—just two days after it reported Sitting Bull's account of the Custer massacre on the Little Big Horn.

Even as it continued to vilify Sitting Bull, the *Times* all but venerated Chief Joseph. Editorials, as the Nez Percé war progressed, praised the military tactics and combat skills demonstrated by the overmatched Joseph and his warriors. Theirs was one of the most gallant and stubborn fights in the history of the Indian wars, the newspaper noted. As usual, it praised the army troops responsible for bringing the campaign to a successful conclusion; and in the

Nez Percés, it suggested, they were "met with an energy as tireless, and a bravery even more desperate, than their own." The Indians had inflicted heavy losses on the army before finally giving up. But they were fighting for their homes, the *Times* pointed out, and for what they believed to be their rights.

The *Times* made no bones about its belief that the Nez Percé war never should have been fought. It was "an unpardonable and frightful blunder" and a crime on the part of the government, the *Times* said in an October editorial. The victims, it said, were both the gallant officers and men of the army and "the peaceful bands who were goaded by injustice and wrong to the warpath." The editorial expressed regret that immediate responsibility for the war could not be fixed. But as so often was the case in conflicts with the Native Americans, that responsibility was too obscurely distributed to allow anyone to be brought to account at the bar of public opinion. This facet of the Indian problem never seemed to change.

Sitting Bull, now in self-imposed exile in Canada, continued to draw the attention of the press. In the first ninety days of 1878, the venerable Sioux leader commanded no fewer than ten stories in the *Times*, most of them on the front page. But on the editorial pages, the newspaper was focusing more sharply on fraud and mismanagement at various levels within the government Indian service. A January editorial called attention to a scathing report generated by an investigation into activities in the Indian Office of the Interior Department. In April, the *Times* questioned why the tribes in the Indian Territory needed to maintain an expensive delegation in Washington to protect their interests. There would be little surprise, it concluded, if time should prove that "certain enterprising white men" were interested in keeping control of a large slice of the tribes' revenues in Washington.

The *Times* at this point finally had come to the position that the needs of the Native American cultures and the demands of encroaching white civilization might be irreconcilable. Citing the recent Bannock uprising in the Northwest, it suggested that the troubles went beyond the unfulfilled treaties, broken promises, agency frauds, and threatened coercion that had led to so many difficulties with various tribes in the past. Otherwise, it said, conflict still might be avoided. But the current problems in Idaho, Montana, and Oregon seemed to *Times* editorial writers to lie deeper; the Indians at last had been driven to the wall by the advancing tide of white civilization. The writers saw an irrepressible conflict between the roving way of life preferred by the Native Americans and the "prescribed bounds" essential to the whites' society—a conflict that in the end the Native Americans were destined to lose. And while the *Times* did not question the Indians' commitment to the justness of their cause, nor their willingness to fight for it, the newspaper now asserted that it would be "but a slender favor" to attempt to preserve the Indian way of life any longer. Henceforth, it would seldom waver from its conviction that it was in the best interests of the Native Americans to bring them into the national fold as participating citizens.

The *Times* had persisted for some time in the belief that it was illogical to sign treaties with the various tribes, thus treating them as foreign nations. But it generally had embraced the idea of segregating the Indians on reservations and preserving these from white invasion. Now it would move more consistently toward a position that favored the ultimate breakup of tribal organizations and promoted individual land ownership among Native Americans instead of tribal lands held in common. Like white squatters, the *Times* asserted, Indians who proved to be successful landholders could and should be good citizens. The alternative, continuing to place the Native Americans on reservations and supplying them with government rations, it said, would institutionalize their pauperization and make them permanent wards of the nation.

But in the meantime, the *Times* would continue to emblazon its editorial pages with outrage over the injustices it had come to expect as part of the Indian problem. Never did there seem to be a shortage of topics. One long-running case followed closely by the *Times* was that of the Poncas, who had been forced to move from their reservation in the Dakota Territory in 1876 to the Indian Territory in the Southwest. The relocation had deadly effects on the Poncas, who, the *Times* asserted later, "sickened and died like pestilence-stricken sheep." After their pleas to Washington went unheeded, a number of Poncas deserted the territory and struggled back to their homeland—only to be taken prisoners by the army.

Thanks in part to *Times* reporting, the Ponca case drew a great deal of national attention. A number of people helped raise funds to pay for legal assistance, and when a federal judge eventually ruled in the Poncas' favor, the Indians gained new standing in court. But the situation never would have developed in the first place, a *Times* editorial implied in December 1879, had it not been for "the evil genius which is forever stirring up the never-settled question of the relation of the red man to the Government of the United States. . . ."

The *Times* treated with similar gravity the situation of the Utes in Colorado. That tribe, following a stubborn dispute over government efforts to force it to replace its traditional hunting culture with agriculture, rebelled at last and had to be overcome by military force. Here, again, stated a *Times* editorial, was an inevitable collision between the Native American way of life and white civilization. "Nobody appears to have known how deep in the Indian breast was the hostility to the so-called improvements of the white man," it said. But from the outset, it argued, the Utes' struggle was futile. They were no match for the power of the United States government; nothing but certain overthrow awaited them. "Perhaps this is destiny," the *Times* editorial concluded, "as hurried on by the American people. But it is impossible not to feel at least a passing pang of commiseration for a tribe thus systematically improved off the face of the earth."

Overall, the magnitude of the Indian problem appeared to be undiminished—at least as measured by attention from the *Times*. More than four dozen stories on the Indians appeared in the news columns of the paper through the first six months of 1880, and there were nearly a hundred stories during the remainder of the year. The ubiquitous Sitting Bull was the subject of a number of these between mid-September and the end of the year. In the Southwest, a small Apache band under Victorio was proving to be a serious headache for the army. Victorio soon met his death. The *Times* extended no sympathy over his loss. But, stating a position now familiar to readers, it noted that "ordinarily competent and honest management" on the part of white authorities could have prevented his taking to the warpath to begin with.

It was another Apache leader, Geronimo, for whom the *Times* saved its true wrath. Next to Sitting Bull, Geronimo, among all the native chiefs, was the target of the newspaper's most ardent vilification. He and his warriors were front-page news in the *Times* through much of 1885 and into early 1886. Geronimo's trail, an early 1885 editorial lamented, was marked by the "mutilated bodies" of his victims. The editorial suggested that if any of his small band escaped the soldier's rifles, "we do not see why those who may survive should not be hanged." Even as they expressed their outrage, however, the *Times* editorial writers were careful not to paint all the Apaches with the same brush. They assured readers that there were thousands of Apaches who remained peaceful and "who know that Geronimo's deeds only deepen the settler's hate for every being that has copper-colored skin." Following Geronimo's eventual capture, the *Times* supported the decision to imprison him rather than put him to death as had been demanded by many on the Southwest frontier. Just to be rid of Geronimo and his followers, it said, was what mattered to the settlers in the long run.

Close after Geronimo's capture and imprisonment came the death of Sitting Bull in 1890. Insofar as the Indian problem was concerned, the open conflict era was virtually ended. The Native Americans, as the *Times* had pointed out more than a decade earlier, had been in a losing struggle against the overwhelming forces of white civilization. Now they were very much at the mercy of a national government they had opposed but whose protection was their best hope. It would be their lot, during the last decade of the nineteenth century, to watch helplessly as much of their remaining land was divided among white settlers and to face renewed efforts to force them to give up the final vestiges of their ancient cultures.

The most savage scenes of Indian warfare, the *Times* pointed out, now might be seen in Buffalo Bill Cody's Wild West Show. And Indian warriors now would wear the uniforms of the United States Army. But the *Times* never lost sight of the fact that the Native Americans had made vital contributions. The Iroquois League, it pointed out in an 1893 editorial, predated European settlement of the North American continent. With no model to follow, the Iroquois had created a formidable federal system—an ancient federation that endured for perhaps five hundred years—"out of their own minds and experience," it said.

The Indian problem had not disappeared. The nature of issues had changed, in some ways becoming more complex, but more than a century of strife had left a bitter divide. The *Times* now turned its editorial sights on conditions surrounding the transition of the Native Americans into the white world, under the whites' conditions. Insistent and mundane matters such as the Indian Bureau's authority to prohibit the sale of beer on the reservations gained passing attention by the *Times*. But the *Times* editorial writers were more concerned about vital issues such as Indian education. They strongly endorsed schools on the reservations as an alternative to forcing Indian children to be removed to distant institutions. They were alert to continued graft, corruption, and incompetence in the government Indian service. They argued the advantages of training in trades and industry for the Indians, as a means to the "throwing down of reservation barriers." The reservation system, the *Times* now insisted, restricted the Indians' progress to full participation as citizens.

The *Times* warned against the false economy of a move to eliminate the long-standing Board of Indian Commissioners. The knowledge and vigilance of the unsalaried commissioners, it said, helped prevent waste and corruption in the Indian service that not only was a fraud on the taxpayers but also could be cited as a direct cause of much of the bloodshed of the past.

White civilization, the *Times* continued to point out, came at a high price to the Native Americans. In the spring of 1897, it detailed action by which Coconino County, Arizona, authorities drove out sixteen peaceful Navajo families through an outrageous demand that they pay an exorbitant tax on their livestock or flee the county. "The whole business," stated a *Times* editorial, "was in the whites an outbreak of savage envy and hatred." It called on the federal government to investigate "an outrage so cruel and contemptible" and to protect the Indians by all necessary force. Clearly, in the eyes of the *Times*, the Indian problem remained a serious issue on the national agenda.

At about that same time, the newspaper paused to pay a closing tribute to Chief Joseph of the Nez Percés. Joseph was making his first trip to the East, where, among other things, he would appear in New York's Grant Day parade. The *Times* deemed it an honor to welcome the chief who, twenty years earlier, "was so determined and so fair a fighter" and who had kept his pledge to fight no more. In Joseph it also saw a somewhat melancholy end to the Native American image it had endeavored to make familiar to its readers during the past half-century. "The American bison," said the poignant *Times* editorial, "is scarcely more completely extinct than the savage, unspoiled by civilization, of which the chief of the Nez Percés is a very typical specimen."

At the turn of the century, the *Times* had come full circle in its philosophy concerning the Native American as ward of the nation. The Indian problem, to the *Times*, now manifested itself through innumerable barriers to full Indian participation in national life as citizens. It continued to assail the policy of government handouts that it believed promoted Indian pauperism and complained in a November 1900 editorial that annuities were an obstacle to civilizing the Indians and should be ended. But the editorial writer qualified this hard position with a familiar disclaimer: "As we are responsible for having brought the Indian to his present condition, any plan of reformation that is to be adopted ought to be tempered with mercy and persisted in with firmness and common sense."

The *Times* editorials during this entire period were written anonymously—like those in most newspapers then, as now. There is no sure way to know who penned those most impassioned pleas for justice and humanity toward the Native Americans, those thoughtful expositions on national policy gone awry, or those occasional ugly attacks on the Indian character. However, a newspaper's editorial policy is set by its management. Throughout the decades during which the Indian problem was a matter of high priority, the *Times* management enjoyed reasonable continuity. The scholarly Henry J. Raymond, who established the newspaper in 1851, continued as publisher until his death in 1869. Under his leadership, the *Times* early on gained a solid reputation for accurate and fair news reporting and for editorials of insight. George Jones, Raymond's business partner, took over the newspaper after Raymond's death. Jones relied heavily on his editor, Louis J. Jennings, and assistant editor John Foord. John C. Reid served as managing editor from 1872 until 1889.

After George Jones died in 1891, the *Times* was bought from his family by a group headed by Charles R. Miller and Edward Cary. Both were old hands at the *Times*, Miller having been editor since 1883 and Cary having worked for Jones as associate editor. This team managed the newspaper until 1896, when Tennessee publisher Adolph S. Ochs scraped together a business deal that permitted him to buy the *Times*. Ochs immediately named Henry Loewenthal, a staff veteran, as his managing editor.

These were the men who set the course of the *Times* during the decades under consideration. The newspaper's influence as an opinion leader varied immensely at times during that period, and its circulation was a good deal smaller than that of some of its more colorful rival publications. But there was never a point between 1860 and 1900 at which the *Times* failed to serve as an important source of information and opinion for a significant segment of the public and a forum for the discussion of important questions. Then, as now, what the *Times* reported and what editorial positions it took mattered a great deal to many among the best-informed.

The latter half of the nineteenth century, particularly after the end of the Civil War, was a period of rapid national expansion. Settlers on the ever-moving frontier may have faced regular and frequent reminders of the native tribes they sought to replace on the vast territories, but the distant conflicts to the west could easily have gone unnoticed by their compatriots in the East—on the whole, little affected by the Indian problem. But this was a struggle the *Times* would not let them ignore. Treatment of the Native Americans, in the eyes of the *Times*, became a matter of national honor. Injustices on some distant frontier, remote and otherwise unknown to readers in New York, were brought home to them regularly through the news and editorial pages of the *Times*.

From 1860 through 1900, the *Times* ran nearly one thousand editorials on topics related to the Native Americans. Although the newspaper's general editorial position at times was inconsistent, many of its editorials were masterfully crafted and written with power and passion. *Times* editorial writers kept the subject alive, focusing on topics as narrow as minor frontier incidents or as broad as failed national policy. The questions to which the *Times* sought answers were persistent ones; in its columns, such questions would not be allowed simply to go away without explanation. If the Indian problem would not go away, neither would the attention paid it by the *Times*.

Such attention was manifest in the paper's news columns, of course. But it was reflected most vividly on the *Times* editorial pages. Through the editorial columns, particularly as viewed over a period of years, readers were reminded of the magnitude, complexity, and difficulty of issues that collectively constituted the Indian problem.

2 The Status of the Indian

President Grant has simply kept in view the facts that there exist
three hundred thousand people of Indian race within the Union,
that they have certain rights as human beings and as original settlers which the Government of a free people is bound to respect,
and that the largest measure of civil equality which they manifest
an ability to appreciate ought to be extended to them.

—*New York Times*
February 5, 1871

O F ALL THE SEPARATE DILEMMAS that, collectively, made up what the
Times referred to as the Indian problem, none was more persistent than
the question of Indian status. It was commonly accepted that the Indians
were not citizens of the United States, routinely subject to the jurisdiction
of the national government. Neither were they ascribed citizenship in any
individual state or organized territory. When Congress passed a post–Civil
War civil rights bill in 1866 designed to negate the "black codes" and assure
citizenship to freed slaves, it specifically exempted the Indians. The legislation declared that all persons born in the United States were citizens—except
untaxed Indians.

But if the Indians were not citizens and if, as the *Times* insisted, the Indian
tribes were not themselves sovereignties, then what was the legal affilia-
tion of individual tribespeople? What was their relationship to the national
government? To the governments of various states or territories in which
they might be located? What rights and responsibilities, under law, did they
have or should they have? The *Times* editorial columns persistently raised
these perplexing questions and rarely came to satisfactory conclusions. The
overriding circumstance, and thus the starting point for *Times* editorial writers, was simple: Because the Indians were not citizens, their legal status was
one of virtual limbo. For the *Times*, this meant that it was much easier to

pose questions than to posit answers. It also meant that the broad issue of Indian status was one ripe for editorial opinion.

Nationally, the discussion of Indian status generally centered on one of two concerns. Control of the Native Americans got the most attention, while any regard for their rights generally was relegated to lower priority. The responsibility for control commonly fell on the War Department, to be carried out by the United States Army. The rights of the Indians would be the province of the Department of the Interior; within it lay the Indian Bureau, with day-to-day responsibility for administration of national Indian policy.

The *Times* soon took issue with the national government's confirmed policy—rooted in decades of tradition—that conferred virtual sovereignty on the tribes. This had permitted government agents to negotiate treaties with the tribes and may have been practical in the early national experience. But it made little sense in 1870, by which point the *Times*, along with others, had come to suggest that it was more reasonable to make the Indians citizens. The *Times*, no doubt reflecting the sentiment of the day quite accurately, was willing to grant the Indians the rights of citizens if they made adequate progress toward "civilization." Civilization, obviously, was defined in the whites' terms.

Citing reports by Quakers who had been working with the Indians, the *Times* suggested in a brief editorial note in early 1871 that the Friends' society had done "exceedingly good and promising work" among the Winnebagos by awakening in them a sense of the advantages and duties of civilized life. Among other accomplishments, an anonymous *Times* editorial writer said, the Quakers deserved credit for the "successful deposition of chiefs opposed to civilization and their replacement by more progressive ones." Many of the young men of the tribe, it was noted, had voluntarily assumed the costume and customs of the whites. Surely this was advancement.

The *Times* expressed its encouragement over an Interior Department report at the end of 1872 that it believed demonstrated progress toward civilizing the Indians. Of the 300,000 Native Americans living in United States territory, exclusive of Alaska, the newspaper noted, "97,000 are civilized, 125,000 are semi-civilized, and 78,000 are wholly barbarous." It said that while twenty nomadic tribes had increased in number, "they are being led into industrial pursuits and peaceful habits."

One principal element of white civilization, of course, was the judicial system. But Indians generally had been excluded from this system. Tribes might be held responsible for criminal acts of individuals, with the administration of justice often left to military authorities. Tribespeople might appear as defendants in criminal court, where they were nearly certain to be convicted. The notion of protection under the whites' law was alien to the Indians, however. They had no standing in the whites' court.

But this convention was jolted by a dramatic case brought on by the detention of a handful of peaceful Indians by military authorities in the spring of 1879. The small band of Poncas led by Standing Bear was arrested in Nebraska after refusing permanent relocation in the Indian Territory. When Standing Bear and his followers sought to be released on a writ of habeas corpus, the government contended that only citizens were entitled to such protection. Judge Elmer Dundy, presiding over the U.S. District Court in Omaha, disagreed. The law defined applicants for writs as "persons" or "parties," he declared, not as citizens. He freed Standing Bear and his followers.

The *Times* followed the proceedings in Omaha closely. It initially suggested that that decision was important only because the Indians were granted "standing" in court. But in coming weeks, it would read a good deal more into the case. "Congress," the *Times* explained in a June editorial, "intended to give to every person, native, foreigner, citizen, or Indian, who might be unlawfully restrained of liberty under color of authority of the United States the right to the writ and a discharge under it." Further, it noted that Judge Dundy's ruling extended to the broader issue of military authority over peaceful Indians. "It was not denied that in time of war the Government might remove hostile Indians to a place of safety, and detain them during the existence of hostilities," the *Times* explained. "But, in the opinion of the court, this is a war power, which cannot be lawfully exercised in the case of Indians whose tribe is at peace with the Government."

Judge Dundy's decision in the case of Standing Bear gained a great deal of notice nationally, in part because of the amount of attention paid to it by the *Times*. Helen Hunt Jackson, one of the most influential writers of the day, contended that relative to acts of emancipation, Judge Dundy should take a place in history alongside Abraham Lincoln. Mrs. Jackson included a *Times* editorial on Standing Bear's case in her remarkable 1881 book on white America's treatment of the Indians, *A Century of Dishonor*. That editorial, "Civil Rights in Acres," is included in this chapter.

Passage of the Fourteenth and Fifteenth Amendments, designed to assure citizenship and voting rights without regard to race or color, had made the question of Indian citizenship more pressing. But the courts had held, as the

Times had predicted they would, that Indians were not born subject to the jurisdiction of the United States and therefore were not citizens. Following one such ruling in early 1880, a *Times* editorial asserted that a state might permit any Indian to vote or the United States might make any Indian a citizen—thus assuring the right to vote under the Fifteenth Amendment. "But an Indian cannot make himself a citizen of the United States without the consent and co-operation of the Government," the editorial concluded. "The fact that he has abandoned his nomadic life or tribal relations and adopted the habits and manners of civilized people may be a good reason why he should be made a citizen of the United States, but does not of itself make him one." The status of Indians under the Fourteenth and Fifteenth Amendments, the editorial suggested, was one of the most difficult questions the federal courts had to decide. It also suggested that the question was among the most important.

Citizenship eventually was brought into relatively easy reach of Native Americans by the Indian Severalty Law of 1887. But it came at a high cost. For many, to accept land in severalty was to deny their culture—a price the *Times* never seemed fully to appreciate.

By the 1890s, the newspaper's editorial columns finally were liberated from regular observation of the status of the Indians, though there would remain an occasional passing glance. The *Times* could not have given the decades of attention it did to the Indian problem without a gallant struggle to make sense of the status dilemma. Some important examples of that heroic effort form the remainder of this chapter.

↤ The Indian Territory

August 13, 1864

The Secretary of the Interior, in his last annual report, uses the following language in relation to the present status of the Indians. It deserves consideration:

"It may well be questioned whether the Government has not adopted a mistaken policy in regarding the Indian tribes as quasi-independent nations, and making treaties with them for the purchase of the lands they claim to own. They have none of the elements of nationality; they are within the limits of the recognized authority of the United States, and must be subject to its control. . . . Indeed, whatever may be the theory, the Government has always demanded the removal of Indians where their lands were required for agricultural purposes by advancing settlements."

Two or three projects have been mooted. Senator Pomeroy, of Kansas, submitted a proposition to remove all of the semi-civilized tribes in Kansas and elsewhere in the West, to the Indian Territory, and then, abolishing the system of tribal agencies and traders, control all the nations by one general superintendency, holding the country inviolate forever. This project has been approved, to a certain extent, by the Indian Bureau and Congress, and an appropriation was made to aid it. Commissioner Dole was West during last Summer for the purpose of perfecting arrangements. Treaties to this end were made with one or two Kansas tribes.

Much can be said in favor of this plan, if it can be thoroughly carried out. It is open to the objection of not taking into consideration the future relations of the Indians to our civilization. At some day, not far distant, the quasi-sovereignties of the tribes must terminate, the system of communal land-holding be abolished, and the Indians prepared to take their place among American citizens, or to pass away and be forgotten. A plan, like the foregoing, which would also offer representation and citizenship to the civilized Indians might be the most desirable to adopt.

Another has been mooted. It would be more likely to meet the views of the Western people, whatever might be said of its justice. It is to abolish the tribal system altogether; secure by some equitable arrangement to the Indians, each individual's proportion of the funds belonging to them held by the Government; give to each person a certain amount of land in severalty, and then make them citizens of the United States, throwing open the unoccupied lands to the white settler. This would give us a new Free State to the Union. This plan will meet its chief objections from the agents and traders who live out of the present system; and its most strenuous opposition from prominent Indian leaders, like the Rosses, who naturally desire to preserve their great personal influence. Other objections might be urged against the voting proposition. To this it can be truly replied, that the loyal members of these nations are fully as capable of intelligently using the ballot as are the majority of the white men of Arkansas and Missouri. It is certainly more in accordance with the spirit of our institutions, that so far and fast as practicable, those who are part of our population should be elevated to and accorded the privileges of American nationality.

↩ The Indian Appropriations

March 23, 1869

The Indian Appropriation bill which passed the House is the one which passed that body at the end of the Fortieth Congress, and which, being sent to the Senate, was overloaded with amendments until it sank.

It appropriated the sum the House Committee called for—namely $2,413,816; this the Senate nearly *trebled* last session by adding items amounting to $4,341,902. It now remains to be seen whether the same disagreement will again occur. The difference in view is this: The House bill proposed only to pay the amounts stipulated for in existing Indian treaties, while the Senate added those necessary for the treaties made since last August by the Indian Peace Commission. The House action has the advantage of providing at once for an expenditure about which there cannot be a dispute. The Senate action has a certain show of reason in precipitating the general question of our Indian policy—a most important question, involving the whole matter of Indian treaties, Indian government, Indian agents, and Indian wars.

There should be no objection, apparently, to considering these two matters separately—that is, adopting the House theory, to appropriate forthwith what money is actually, indisputably and urgently necessary, and then debating the later Indian treaties, and our Indian policy as a question by itself. The spirited preliminary discussion in the House, though premature, was sufficiently indicative of the feeling of Congress and the country upon the present Indian system. What we call our "Indian policy" is only a vast quagmire, into which contractors tumble annually millions of appropriations, making it, however, only more hopeless than ever.

When Mr. Wood denounces the treaty system as "a fraud on the Treasury and an injury to the Indians," he keeps within the bounds of fact. Mr. Lawrence publicly declares not only that "the whole Indian Bureau is rotten and a mere den of thieves," but that "treaties have been put through the Senate when there were not six Senators present;" and the recent abuse of the treaty-making power in regard to the Indians, is matter of history. At the very start, the question comes up, are the Indians foreign Powers? If not,—and certainly, while inhabiting our territory, subject to our laws, they are not,—the very word "treaty" is a misnomer. Yet that word has been used of late years, and under cover of it, what is really a contract or agreement, and, as such, a matter of legislation, has been exalted to the super-legislative character of a treaty.

We admit that difficulties surround the subject; that the *status* of the hostile tribes especially, is anomalous; that it might be as unsatisfactory to call them "insurgents" or "rebels" as foreign enemies; that there is something of the nature of a treaty hanging about our compacts with them. Nevertheless, there is no such anomaly or confusion as justifies the subordination of the treaty-making power to the legislative power in Indian matters, so as to justify the former in buying and selling public lands through treaties with Indian tribes. Mr. Julian tells us that the new Administration opposes this latter practice, and is anxious to break it up. It is clear, at all events, that with nearly a dozen new Indian treaties pending, and the appropriations required so large, it is worth while to see on what general principles we shall proceed, what claims the Indians really have on us, and how these claims may best be satisfied.

↜ Improving the Indians

November 5, 1869

"What to do with the Indian" has become a pressing problem, now that civilization has found a grand highway between the Atlantic and Pacific, along which already pours a mighty stream of travel and traffic. Our new and intimate relations with the red men will no longer suffer us to continue our Podsnappian policy of "waiving them nay." So long as there were vast untenanted, uncultivated regions of the continent to which the Government could transfer the Indians,—beyond the bounds of travel and trade,—our fathers solved the Indian problem by simply moving the savages themselves out of the way. But there is no longer now—or very soon will no longer be—any "out of the way" to banish them to. The westward tide of commerce and civilization has met an eastward tide from the Pacific, and the two are now broadening over the vast region where the Indian once was substantially his own master. The conflicts between the red men and the white, already bloody, will be likely to grow more bitter, as the weaker goes gradually to the wall. Here and there, as now in Montana, the red men threaten to drive the whites from the Territory. We know very well that they can do nothing of the kind; but the difficulty is in their thinking they can do so. We cannot afford, for lack of a definite Indian policy, to imperil the lives of our own frontier people.

In answer to the question, "What to do with the Indian?" the Western pioneers and settlers say very promptly and decidedly, "Exterminate him!" and the London *Times* admits that this is, though a disagreeable, yet a probable and an excusable upshot of the problem. Fortunately, however, for the red men, fortunately also for the white, and fortunately for our national honor, this "remedy" for the Indian evils is gradually dropping from the range of possibilities. The present Administration came into power with different ideas on the Indian question from any that had preceded it—ideas less sentimental, but more humane. They were the ideas of our army officers, who are familiar with Indian character, and whose view is, in brief, to treat hostile tribes with severity, friendly tribes with generosity, and all with perfect frankness, honesty and justice. As "extremes meet," what was more natural than for the "Quakers," or friends of peace, to coalesce with the soldiers, or "men of wrath," in this matter?

At all events, the coalition was made, and thus far the troops have had the hearty co-operation of the Friends in efforts to ameliorate the condition of the Indians. The recommendations of the Quakers to the Indian Bureau, which we noticed yesterday, are evidently based on the grand idea of altering the *status* of the Indian from that of an enemy or outlaw to that of an American citizen. Such, for example, are these:

"Industrial schools for the education of all the children.

"Teaching the English language, prominently, in order to qualify them for citizenship.

"That the Indians be supplied liberally with teams and tools to break up all their prairie lands, haul timber and lumber to build houses, work their land and perform all their work, which it is necessary to do on their farms, and have competent, judicious persons for a time to encourage them therein, and give them the needful instructions."

Evidently the design of these provisions is to make the Indian an object not for extermination, but for respect—to raise him, in time, to the full grade of citizenship, and to add him as an element to our nationality.

It is a striking experiment, and one whose results can hardly be forecast on mere theory. What we know is that the Administration and the Friends have thus far been in accord, and that any reasonable scheme which the latter propose will have a fair opportunity for trial.

✍ Fair Play for the Indian

December 17, 1869

It looks as though the Indian might receive fair play, now that the army officers have so strenuously taken his part. Though, to say the truth, it is not the soldiery, but the settlers and the sutlers, that have been the Indian's worst foes. Our troops have fought the savages continually, but they have never deceived or defrauded them. It is rather the peddlers and traders who have done most to "demoralize" the red men; and with them have been allied the frontiersmen, who have counted the Indians fair prey for fraud, and good food for powder. The ranchman or squatter, like the traditional backwoodsman of Cooper's novels, "hates an Injun like pison," and is usually free to announce his creed regarding the Indian, which consists of one line—"I believe in shooting a redskin on sight."

It is out of this bloodthirsty and lawless frontier morality that half the Indian wars have arisen. We are forever reciting raids and rascalities of Sioux and Arapahoes; but, if the truth were known, many of their depredations would be found to be only return blows for some crime committed by our settlers. An Indian massacre is often preceded by a white man's murder. The Indians have no press, no telegraph, no means or disposition of making known their wrongs received at our hands; and as for our far-West communities, Indian shooting is hardly rare or extraordinary enough among them to be mentioned even for eulogy—and anything but commendation it would not receive.

What is the result? Precisely what Generals Ord and Thomas and Sherman tell us now, and precisely what Generals Pope and Schofield and Augur and Hancock and Harney and Hazen and Sheridan, and all other officers who had previously written on the subject, had said before. General Ord speaks of a case in which a harmless Pinto boy was murdered in cold blood by a worthless vagabond, within a stone's throw of Camp McDermott, and "other similar murders" he reports in Arizona. Is it any wonder that Arizona is infested with lawless Indians, and that life and property are more unsafe there than anywhere else in the Union, unless, perhaps, in New Mexico? The State or Territorial authorities, says General Ord, are either powerless or indifferent to the killing of Indians by the whites, so that the murderer almost always escapes. But how is it if, in retaliation, an Indian kills a white? Why, all the white people demand that the whole tribe shall be held responsible, and war declared. The Indians, of course, retaliate in the best and only way possible, and then we have a war. Generals Thomas and Sherman affirm the facts and views of General Ord in the strongest terms. The former said he was a personal witness to the excitement created in the camp of the peaceful Pintos by the unprovoked and unpunished murder of the Pinto boy. General Sherman indorses the batch of papers on this subject in this remarkable language:

"This case illustrates the origin of most of the Indian wars on our frontier. A citizen may murder an Indian with impunity; but if the Indian retaliates, war results, and the United States must bear the expense."

Such being the wrong, what is the remedy? On this point all our army officers, as usual, concur. It must consist in giving the Indians some of the privileges and safe-guards of citizenship. We sometimes ask the Indian to perform the obligations of citizens—let them, then, be invested with their rights. The great mistake of all our Indian legislation hitherto has been, that we have regarded the Indians as a sort of hostile power circumscribed within our own national domains. We made *treaties* with them—a confusion of relations at once; we declared war and made peace with them, like any other belligerents—though they were a part of our population. The new view is not to exterminate, but to civilize the Indian; not to consider him as beyond the pale of law, but to bring him upon reservations where he will conform to law; not to deprive him of human rights, but to throw before him the aegis of citizenship, and so teach him to prize and not to spurn it. General Ord declares that these are the views of army officers; and that it would act as a preventive if, in such cases, the murderers could be arrested by the military and held, or turned over for trial by the nearest United States Court; and it would give the Indians some little show of equal justice. General Thomas says that he sees no better method than to extend civil authority over the Indians now within the settlements, and to enable them to appear as witnesses in all cases affecting their own interest and that of the whites toward them. All this can be accomplished by Congressional legislation, which, we doubt not, will be promptly provided.

A New Way with the Indian

January 26, 1870

The President made a remarkable speech the other day while conversing with the chiefs of the Cherokee and Creek nations. Here is the debate:

Indian Chief—"Mr. President, we call here to-day to offer our fealty to you as our recognized guardian and ward, and to pray you, Sir, to continue our good friend and father."

The President—"You are welcome, and in reference to continuing your 'good father,' as you say, I must answer that I have long thought that the two nations which you represent, and all those civilized nations in the Indian country, *should be their own wards and good fathers. I am of the opinion that they should become citizens*, and be entitled to all the rights of citizens,— cease to be nations and become States."

This is the boldest and bravest thing that has been said on this sad question. We can never reform a people without elevating them. We have had two policies with the Indians:—extermination or apathy. The Government has never interfered with them except to make war when they were unruly and plunder them when at peace. The President proposes to treat them as men, and his conclusion is a riper result than we have seen in any discussion. We must in some way atone for our crimes as a nation, for it will be written that we enslaved the African, persecuted the Chinaman, and massacred the Indian! In dealing with a question like that of the Indians we are apt to be sentimental, and this is why we are so rarely practical. We owe something to the men of the frontier who go into new countries upon assurances of protection and yet live in fear of the scalping-knife. We must pardon something to the feelings of a man who stands over the bodies of his murdered wife and children. Justice comes with law, but law's first element is peace. We cannot compromise with disorder, nor reason with murder and assassination. This was the error of Mr. Phillips when he applauded the Cheyenne warriors for pulling up the railway track in Kansas. The Tipperary bog-trotter who "tumbles" a land agent cannot plead the atrocities of Strong-Bow and Cromwell. Yet in discussing the causes of his crime and the true remedy, it would be competent to make such a plea in Parliament. Justice is due to the Indian, protection to ourselves. Can we not give both? We believe so, and feel that the President shows us the way.

It was well for the President to send agents among the Indians from a society whose members are generally known for their wisdom, patience and charity. An Indian is not so wild but he can tell the difference between a border ruffian and a Quaker gentleman. Other Administrations have remitted him to scoundrels and adventurers, who first robbed, then murdered him, and sent the Government a claim for damages. Something of this came from regarding the Indian as simply a ward, with unavoidable weakness and necessities, many simple wants—needing every encouragement—rude, savage, uncouth, with a rigid notion of right and wrong and good and evil that generally appealed to the tomahawk or rifle when adjudication became necessary. This sentiment we are apt to construe as an absence of all honor, truthfulness, humanity and mercy. How much of that is in the Indian nature we do not say. But what evils, what stern, savage, cowardly sins may not be fostered in every ignorant nature by an example like that we have given the Indian. In our wickedness and pride we have taught him that truth was a dream, virtue a fiction, all manly honor and right of property the merest fancy. We have robbed him, despoiled his lands, degraded his women, taught him drunkenness, gambling and all uncleanness,—we have taken from him his trinkets, his minerals and gems, his annuities, even his food and clothing. Is it any marvel that this teaching should bear black and deadly fruit?—that his savage nature should execute the villainy we have taught?

Shall it be death or peace? The President says peace. We have had enough of tutelar and patriarchal traditions and "nations" and tribal wars and strifes. The "Indians should be their own wards and good fathers," says the President. Let us have an end of any subordinate relation. Let the Indian be as other men. Protect him, punish him, teach him! The law of the beginning should be a law to him, even as to men of a paler face. By the sweat of the face should he eat bread. These slowly-festering Indian wars are political ulcerations. We cannot call the policy war, but extermination—the common law custom of offering a prize for every wolf. We must protect the settlers against indiscriminate vengeance. We must restrain and educate the Indian and allow him a chance to educate himself. There is no better doctrine in some respects than the homely lesson, "Root, hog, or die!" We believe that all things are possible to a race which has given us Logan and Tecumseh and Red Jacket—which has placed in the Presidency of Mexico the only statesman of the Mexican race worthy to be named with Washington. It was said if the negro were freed he would starve and die; but we find that freedom has only brought him many blessings. It is said if we remove the Indian from a condition of tutelage he will also starve and die. We cannot believe it, and even if such a fate came to him it would not be worse than his present hard destiny. We claim to guard the Indian, but we only invite him to war and destruction. Let us simply open the way to citizenship, that in time he may be his own "ward" and "good father."

We honor the President for this declaration! The Indian question has been our nation's shame,—its burning, bitter shame. And in their weakness men cry for extermination. To speak such a word is not only a crime, but a degradation. It means we are too weak to be honest and just—that we are cowards. When we say that we must destroy to live, it means that we can dare nothing for justice, that we are too sordid for a liberal, generous, magnanimous policy. "Let us no longer have tribes, but citizens, and no longer nations, but States—no longer savages, but men." We may not realize this hope, but we can labor for it. We owe the Indian justice! Let us grant that, and permit him to work out his own political and social salvation.

∽ The Wards of the Nation

May 31, 1875

There is now going on at Washington what is styled—in diplomatic language possibly—a negotiation between the United States, and the chiefs or principal persons of the Indians recognized as having a right to the reservation in which the Black Hills are situated. Red Cloud, Spotted Tail, and other Indians of picturesque names, are supposed to be one of the equal parties to this negotiation; and we again call attention to the attitude of our Government toward these Indians, as an illustration of our method of dealing with these so-called wards of the nation.

So far as negotiating for a sale of the Black Hills country is concerned, it is evident these Indians did not come to Washington of their own accord, although, no doubt, they like well enough to visit the National Capital. The Secretary of the Interior, not the Indians, moved in this matter, and behind the Secretary were various persons, official and unofficial, from the States and Territories more immediately affected by the reports of gold deposits in the Black Hills. Theoretically the Indians are the rightful possessors of that country by a title as perfect as that of Mexico to the territory across the Rio Grande; and we have made treaties with them upon the theory that they are an independent and sovereign people, as much so as the people of Mexico. Following up this theory, there is no more propriety in summoning these chiefs to Washington, and really by force bringing them there—for they understand that an invitation from the United States is a command—than there would be in summoning the President of Mexico there in a similar way and for a similar purpose. In fact, however, this pretense that they are a sovereign people deceives nobody, its only use, if it has any use whatever, being to keep up the monstrous imposition in every way practiced upon these helpless Indians.

All the talk now going on has little significance except to show that the solemnity of dealing with these Indians as though they possessed any rights, as tribes or individuals, is the most evident farce, ending, however, we are sorry to say, often in the ugliest tragedy. The United States make the trade, or treaty, or whatever the result of the negotiation is called, and the Indian, as a matter of course, is obliged to assent to it; if persuasion or management does not secure his approval, what practically amounts to force, or what in law is known as duress, is resorted to. They have just the same freedom of choice, in fact, that a slave has; that is, none at all. The United States are the master, while the Indian, powerless as an independent power, has not for his defense the protection of the Constitution or the rights of a citizen. He is not a foreigner; he is not regarded as a citizen; he only holds that nondescript relation which, for want of a better name we suppose, has been called the "ward of the nation." Unhappily for the poor ward, our guardianship has been one from whose absolute power there has been no escape, and from which there has been no appeal except to a public opinion that has generally slept quietly while the Indians were robbed and exasperated to savage violence, and has then found a moment of wakefulness sufficient to curse the savage who stands in the way of the march of white civilization.

The reports from Washington show, in a sad way, this melancholy condition of the Indian. Red Cloud evidently doubts whether he has any friends. He came thinking to appeal directly to the President, and doubting every one else. He distrusts the Government interpreters. He complains of his rations alike at Washington and on the reservation. He has brought with him, and seems to listen to the advice of, white men who have traded and lived among the Indians. He says the Secretary and Commissioner have not kept their word. He is losing what little faith he ever had in treaties. He sees his own weakness, yet he knows enough of what ought to be his rights, to make no haste in surrendering them. Yet he, like all the other Indians, is practically friendless and helpless. On the frontier, between the settlers and the adventurers, closing in on them alike from the West and the East, and with the treatment they are sure to receive from the Government, the Indians might as well be between the upper and nether mill-stones. They are sure to be ground to powder. The trader is no more their friend than the agent; they are both interested in the Indian to the extent of what they can make out of him, and neither cares for him beyond that.

The difficulty is and has been that the Indian has always and everywhere been compelled to surrender every desirable place he has occupied to the white man. He has not had the art, the wit, or the power to resist these aggressions. If, instead of driving him before civilization, and keeping him in contact with only the worst phases of it, he had been left to his possessions, and his rights had been protected, like white men's rights, by statutes and the courts, he might have been as inoffensive as the Indians in New-York or Canada. It is possible the red man would not, even then, have survived; the peaceful influences of civilization might have proved too strong for a race which consisted for generations of only warriors and hunters. But we might have escaped the reproach which impartial history must now cast upon us, that we have really destroyed a people powerless to resist us, and whom every sentiment of humanity and every feeling of national pride commanded us to protect.

ᘓ Decrease of the Indians

June 24, 1878

The well-informed persons who suppose that the Indian race in the United States is declining, and destined before long to become extinct, are diminishing in number faster than the Indians are. Such an idea has been prevalent, and has fostered apathy toward the red man. But recent investigations lead to a different opinion. Lo is now predicted to be, like Sambo, permanently a member of the American community. For centuries, very probably, his peculiarities and needs will require the Government to maintain an "Indian policy."

Three considerations are urged against a belief in any rapid decrease. One is that our impressions as to the original number are probably exaggerated.

The Status of the Indian

No real knowledge exists. Neither Government nor commerce, at the date of colonization, nor the ethnologic science of that day, preserved any statistics. There was no census, nothing like an enumeration. We possess only vague and general estimates, and they are intrinsically untrustworthy, coming from sources whose natural tendency would be toward overstatement. Some of these estimates are from Indians; but an Indian brave describing to white visitors the number of his tribe, would be likely to exaggerate. Some are from whites reporting to their own people the results of some contest with Indians; but warriors are prone to overrate the number of the enemy, for to magnify the opposing force enhances the glory of victory; mitigates the mortification of defeat. Some are from the Jesuit fathers, laboring as missionaries among the native tribes; but they might easily place the number needing their labors above the actual fact. Some are from adventurers on their return to Europe; such persons are always apt to swell the accounts of what they have seen and heard. In one word, our idea of the ancient number of the Indians hangs upon the guesses of people whose interest and tendency was to guess large. Hence, we may well have been led to overestimate the decrease.

The same point is reached by another road. If one should visit Saratoga in October, and find hotels and lodgings all full, he would know that the number of guests had not diminished much since July or August. Lieut.-Col. Otis, who has written, recently, with fullness and candor upon this whole subject, reasons in a similar way about the Indians. He considers that the present number is about as many as could have subsisted in the country in aboriginal days. Bear in mind that when the country was covered by the primeval forest, only parts of it were available for Indian support; only the streams which could be fished and the traversable forests which sustained and sheltered game, could maintain fishing and hunting savages. He urges that Indians living wild, and untaught in the arts which promote compact dwelling, require, on the average, about six thousand acres of the wilderness apiece, to support the game and fish required for their food in such quantity that what the Indians kill and eat yearly is replaced by natural increase. If twenty thousand in a tribe live by hunting the buffalo, for instance, they cannot subsist permanently within less territory than will feed say a herd of a hundred thousand, for when the young buffaloes of the year do not replace all losses, including that by hunting, food fails, and the tribe must move or perish. They have no game laws to preserve the game; no fish commissioner to restock exhausted waters. Taking the aggregate territory at about twenty-four hundred million acres and the existing number of Indians at nearly four hundred thousand, he computes that nearly as many now live as could sustain themselves throughout the whole land if they were deprived of all support from the whites and of all the whites have taught them, and remitted to aboriginal conditions and to a dependence on hunting and fishing as a chief subsistence. If the premises are sound, the inference is irresistible that there has not been much decrease.

A third consideration, looking more toward the future, is, that there are not now in operation any causes adequate to produce extinction. The wars from which the tribes now suffer, are not wars of extermination. Pestilence and famine are so far counteracted by the resources of science and humanity, that they are not probable causes of the destruction of a whole race. The Indian suffers much injustice and privation at the hands of the white man, but he receives liberal supplies from the white man's Government, and thrives, rather than pines and dies, upon the support he receives. It is known, indeed, that single and noted tribes have waned and become extinct; but many hold their own in numbers, and some have actually increased. Thus there is no reason to say that the Indian question will lose interest or importance by the extinction of the race.

∽ Indian Civil Rights

May 21, 1879

The decision in the Ponca Indian case has been misunderstood by many as clothing Indians with certain civil rights. It has been asserted that the well-known phrase employed in United States statutes, "Indians not taxed," will be rendered obsolete by a decision given by a United States District Judge. Evidently, the circumstances under which Judge Dundy gave his dictum have not been understood. The Ponca Indians, a small remnant of a once-powerful tribe, were removed from the frontier to that part of the Indian Territory which the Government has reserved for temporary uses. That part of the Territory was purchased of the Five Nations, and the title reverted to the United States, from whom it was originally conveyed to the individual tribes comprising the Five Nations. The Northern Cheyennes, the Modocs, the Nez Percés, and remnants of several other tribes, including the Poncas, have been placed on these lands by Executive order. The Poncas were not captives of war, as were the Nez Percés and Modocs, for example. But they were gathered up by a military force, and were forcibly detained on the land allotted to them in the Indian Territory. It should be borne in mind, also, that not one acre of the land in the Indian Territory, owned by the United States, has ever been set apart as a reservation for any tribe by act of Congress. The Modocs, it is true, although held as prisoners of war, so to speak, are allotted a certain tract, which they cultivate and otherwise use for purposes of their own. But the so-called reservation is simply leased land, which the Indians occupy temporarily, and from which they may be dispossessed by the Government at any time. It was probably intended that the Poncas should be taught to imitate the Modocs, and be encouraged to make for themselves permanent homes and farms on the lands where they had been placed by such force as was necessary to move them.

But the Poncas are not broken-spirited, as the Modocs are, and they refused to stay on the tract assigned to them. They escaped, just as the Northern Cheyennes escaped, last Summer. But the Poncas did not, like the Cheyennes, signalize their return to a wandering life by butchery and plunder. Latterly, indeed, they have been peaceable and as well behaved as a roving Indian ever can be. After their departure from the Territory, an armed force was sent out to reclaim these ungrateful prodigals and bring them back to the protection of a paternal Government. The people of Nebraska evidently sympathized with the fugitives, who did not make bloody resistance, as the Cheyennes did on a similar occasion, but surrendered at discretion. While they were thus held by the military force, a writ of habeas corpus was sued out in the United States Court, and the Poncas were brought before Judge Dundy, in order to ascertain why they were thus deprived of their liberty. It was shown that the Indians were not prisoners of war, taken while engaged in active hostilities. Neither were they "treaty Indians," confined upon a reservation under the provisions of a convention with the United States. They were illegally detained on certain lands of the United States, restrained of their liberty, and that without any pretense that they were offenders against law or treaty-obligations. The Judge accordingly ordered the release of the prisoners, who have gone to their friends, the Omahas, where they were promised assistance in taking a new start in life. Gen. Crook liberated his prisoners, probably very gladly, though he may have felt that the next time he has occasion to detain them it would be as prisoners of war, captured in arms. The Indians, however, appear to have realized the importance of this act of deliverance. Their volunteer attorneys were rewarded with such poor gifts as the band had to bestow, one of the lawyers being richly endowed with a war-bonnet whose great antiquity would enhance its value more to a Ponca than to a white man.

The only novelty about this whole proceeding was the fact that the Indians had any "standing in court." To be sure, Indians have often appeared as defendants in criminal cases; and it may be added that they have uniformly been convicted. But the Poncas before Judge Dundy were in the attitude of petitioners in civil proceedings; and what is more, their civil rights were granted them. Gen. Sheridan, having made one of his characteristically hasty criticisms regarding this decision, Judge Dundy has explained that there is no law creating a reservation in the Indian Territory, none for removing Indians thither, and none for keeping them there. This is the whole case. It is not insisted that Congress might not make a treaty with an Indian tribe the conditions of which should require the Indian party to the agreement to remain on a reservation, or that such a treaty could not be enforced by all the power of the United States in case the Indians should leave their reservation. But, until some such treaty is made with the Poncas, or until they may be taken in active hostilities, they are as free to go and come as any white law-abiding citizen of the United States. The fact that they are "Indians not taxed" does not make them vagrants, liable to arrest and detention by the United States authorities. The Poncas by this time understand that "the Indian is just as good as a white man, as long as he behaves himself."

ᕦ Civil Rights in Acres

February 21, 1880

As most of the readers of *The Times* already know, friends of the Ponca Indians are endeavoring to have the tribe restored to their old reservation in Dakota. Or, more strictly speaking, it is proposed that their reservation shall be restored to them. The lands occupied by the Poncas were ceded to them by the United States by solemn treaty. By a cruel and wicked blunder, which no man has attempted to explain, those lands were ceded to the Sioux. But the Sioux did not want the lands, and they have never occupied them unto this day. To this robbery of the tribe was added the destruction of their houses, movable property, and farms. A citizen of the United States would have redress in the courts for such an outrage as this. An Indian has no legal status. He is merely a live and particularly troublesome animal, in the eye of the law. But, while the Poncas were trying to get back on their lands, they were arrested by order of the Secretary of the Interior, on the charge of running away from the agency to which they had been sent by the Government when their lands were taken from them. It is not necessary to add words to intensify this accumulation of criminal folly and wrong. Certain citizens of Nebraska, hearing of the injustice which was being perpetrated on the Poncas, raised funds and had the chiefs brought before United States District Judge Dundy on a writ of habeas corpus, to inquire why they were thus restrained of their liberty. Judge Dundy decided that an Indian was "a person" within the meaning of the Habeas Corpus act, and that these persons were unlawfully held in duress.

It was thought that the United States would appeal from this dictum, but no appeal was taken, much to the disappointment of the friends of the Indians, as it was hoped that a decision could be reached to show whether the Indian was or was not so far clothed with the privileges of a citizen that he could have a standing in the courts of law. Accordingly, the public-spirited and philanthropic persons who had espoused the case of the Poncas, resolved to make up a case, which, carried to the United States Supreme Court, should determine once and forever this moot point. To this end, money has been raised by subscription, by special gifts, and by contributions taken at public meetings in various parts of the country. A lady residing in Boston, moved by the pitiful condition of the Indians who try to struggle toward civilization, offered to supply all the money which was lacking toward the expenses of the suit, provided Secretary Schurz would give some public assurance that he favored this manner of determining the case, or would give his reasons against this attempt. The lady's proposition was sent to Mrs. Helen Hunt Jackson, whose disinterested and efficient labors in behalf of the deeply wronged Poncas had already attracted attention. Mrs. Jackson forwarded to Secretary Schurz the whole statement. Thereupon an interesting correspondence ensued. This correspondence has been printed in the Boston papers, presumably by direction of Secretary Schurz.

In reply to the request to say whether he approves of the movement to carry the Ponca case to the Supreme Court, in order that the tribe may recover their old reservation, the Secretary says that this would be useless, as the courts have repeatedly decided that an Indian tribe cannot sue the United States. Unfortunately, Mr. Schurz does not cite these cases, but we must take it for granted that he knows what he is talking about. He adds that he has taken the advice of lawyers, who coincide with him in this opinion. As a suit cannot be brought at all, according to the Secretary and his eminent legal advisers, it would be idle to collect money for this purpose, and the Secretary suggests that if the disinterested friends of the Indians had consulted lawyers before they began their work, they would be of his opinion as to the futility of the attempt. This, of course, leaves the impression that the Secretary withholds his approval of the movement to secure legal rights for the Poncas, though he does not say so in express terms. His reason for not approving the attempt is that it will do no good. His solution of the Indian problem, as it is vaguely called, is to settle the Indians in severalty, breaking up their tribal organization, and giving to each individual his lands in fee simple. This, the Secretary thinks, will enable them to hold their lands by the same title as that by which white men hold theirs, and, "as a matter of course, they will have the same standing in the courts" as white men. It is to be regretted that the Secretary did not pause here long enough show how the giving to an Indian of 160 acres of land can clothe him with civil rights which he does not now possess, and which the Secretary thinks that the courts cannot give him. For this reason, however, Mr. Schurz is greatly in favor of legislation providing for the settlement of the Indians in severalty, various bills to accomplish which, he says, are in preparation. As for the money raised already, the Secretary suggests that since, in his opinion, it would be misspent in obtaining judicial decisions, it might be used in the education of Indian children.

Replying to this, Mrs. Jackson asks if the Secretary would be in favor of the Poncas recovering their lands by process of law, provided that could be done. To this direct and very important inquiry we regret to notice that the Secretary finds himself unable to reply; although, in a letter immediately following this, he does say that if an Indian tribe could maintain an action at law in the courts to assert its rights, he would no more object to it than he would to a white man's doing the same thing. As to the suggestion that the money collected for the expenses of legal proceedings be used for educational purposes, Mrs. Jackson asks the Secretary how it would be possible to take money given for one specific purpose and use it for another and wholly different purpose. Mr. Schurz rejoins that the consent of the donors may first be obtained. But he forgets that it would be impossible to canvass the country to ascertain the wishes of thousands of unknown givers to this fund. Referring to the intimation that the friends of the Indians had not taken legal counsel in this matter, and that the Secretary had, Mrs. Jackson observes that they did take such counsel, and that an omission to do so would have been indeed foolish.

It will be observed that the Secretary's objection to the attempt to secure civil rights is its futility; and, in answer to Mrs. Jackson's statement that the friends of the Indians have sought the opinions of lawyers in this case, he replies that one "can find lawyers of skill and standing to undertake for a good fee, any case, however hopeless." To those who might think that this is unjustly severe on the legal profession, it should be said that Mr. Schurz has been by profession a lawyer, and should know what he is talking about. And we must presume that Mr. Schurz's profound knowledge of the law, which is fortified by the opinions of eminent legal men, induces him to consider the whole case closed, in advance of its submission to the courts. It would be interesting, however, to know if the Secretary's lawyers of skill and standing are less easily influenced by the prospect of "a good fee" than the lawyers of skill and standing consulted by the friends of the Poncas. The exceedingly able opinion of Secretary Schurz, we find, is that it is useless to give the Indian a standing in the courts through judicial decisions, as he can readily secure this by accepting from the Government of the United States a deed of 160 acres of land.

ᙍ Qualifications for Citizenship

March 13, 1880

It is agreed that a Republic like our own must be very cautious in the selection of its new citizens. We have always been rigorous in this regard. In this City, for example, we seldom elect a man to office until he has been naturalized. When Mr. John Kelly, last year, gave us a County ticket almost exclusively composed of foreigners of Irish birth, some of the weaker brethren were disposed to murmur. It was complained that it was hardly fair to govern an American city by foreigners exclusively. But Mr. Kelly assured us that every one of his nominees had been duly and legally adopted into American citizenship, and were, consequently, superior to those who had accidentally been born on American soil. And it is conceded that almost all of our adopted fellow-citizens know how to vote; and if they do not know this first duty of an American freeman, they are sufficiently teachable to vote as they are told. Mr. John Kelly kindly tells them. Whatever qualification of citizenship we may exact, we do not ask of our new citizens that they shall prove a good moral character and an ability to control their own private affairs. If we did establish this test, there would be an alarming falling off in the vote of all our large towns and cities. But it is proposed by a bill now before Congress to make citizens of native Americans—that is to say, American Indians—provided each applicant for this high honor shall be able to prove "that he has sustained a good moral character for two years, and that he is of sufficient intelligence to control his own private affairs." Precisely what constitutes a good moral character is an open question. In this country the standard of morality varies very much. In Connecticut, for example, the moral standard of the people is considered to be higher than in Montana, although it is barely possible that, while three-card monte, horse-racing, and profane swearing are not so openly countenanced in the Land of Steady Habits as in Montana, the Territory does have the advantage over the State in the matter of poisoning and wife-murder.

But the moral qualification of citizenship, as applied to our Indian wards, probably refers to that abstention from the savage practices which, in the eyes of civilized men, ought to constitute Indian immorality. If the bill now before the Senate shall become a law, the Indian applicant must prove that for two years he has not killed anybody, has taken no scalps, has not beaten his wife, and has been faithful to his only wife. When a young Indian brave prepares himself for the duties of manhood, he goes through an ordeal which would break down an ordinary white man. He passes days and nights in a "medicine lodge," the object of terrifying incantations, bearing with unblenching fortitude a series of tests of his powers of endurance, and solemnly swearing, under the most awful penalties, that he is honest, chaste, insensible to fear, and strictly temperate in spirit and body. For him to be able to prove that he has sustained a good moral character for two years, as a qualification for the duties of an American citizen might possibly be an easy matter. But when it comes to a question of the white man's morality, it is not unlikely that he would fail. It is well known that there is a wide difference between Indian morality and the article most in favor with white men. Naturally, if an Indian candidate for citizenship had passed successfully the test of murder, scalping, and horse-stealing, we should attack him on the subject of truthfulness. This would be a delicate matter. We might find it difficult to show an Indian that he must keep his word before he can have a vote and obtain a standing in the courts of a people who have never kept one of the numerous treaties which we have made with Indians. How can we teach truthfulness to a race which has suffered from our national habit of lying to the Indians for an entire century? If it is immoral for the Indian to lie and steal, it ought to be immoral in a nation of white men.

Of course, every citizen of the United States should have "sufficient intelligence to control his own affairs." All citizens of this intelligent Republic control their own affairs. There may be a few exceptions. Some fashionable young gentlemen in this City, who have rich relatives, have no affairs to control. They neither toil nor spin, but their sustenance is paid for very much as our paternal Government has paid for the maintenance of its "Indian wards" ever since we instituted the present system of pauperization. Then there are a few hundred thousand men in jails and penitentiaries who are so notoriously incapable of controlling their own affairs that the safety of society compels them to be kept under lock and key. But it is only in extreme cases that they lose their right to vote; and nothing can take away from them the citizen's standing in the courts. A native American with a red skin cannot sue a white man in the courts until he has proved that he has lived a moral life for two years past, and that he is capable of managing his own private affairs. Heretofore, the Indian, like the curled darling of the city, has had no private affairs to control. It has been the aim of a beneficent and paternal Government to reduce him to a condition of pupilage, and to keep him there. But when we do take our foot off him, we demand that he shall show a certificate of good moral character and a fair business knowledge. We should be thankful that this new qualification of citizenship is not retroactive in its application. If no man could vote unless he could prove a good moral character and an ability to control his own private affairs, what a falling off there would be in the Democratic vote of the Republic. What would become of the political influence of Mr. John Kelly? Or the local support of Congressman S. S. Cox? If no man could vote for State or City officers unless he showed a certificate of two years of moral conduct, naturalization papers would no longer have much value. But we must have no half-way measures with our intending Indian fellow-citizen. Before he swears to his morality and intelligence, let him prove that he subscribes to a daily newspaper, has a church-sitting, and wears trousers.

↩ Indians as Citizens

February 19, 1881

If the debate on the Indian Severalty bill, which is now pending in the Senate, simply delayed public business which might be reached later in the session, it would not be unprofitable. It has certainly served to place before the country in a very strong light something of the injustice and many of the eccentricities of the present policy of the United States Government toward the aborigines of this country. The debate has also developed the fact that, while Senators may differ as to the means to be adopted to give the North American Indian the rights of a citizen before the law, they are substantially agreed that this end must be reached sooner or later. But the pending bill is full of absurdities; and, while it is admitted that the work to be accomplished is environed with many difficulties, it is fairly claimed that the bill, should it become a law in its present shape, will postpone indefinitely the remedy which it seeks to provide. Instead of meeting the case manfully, the framers of the bill have shown so much timidity that the long-oppressed "wards of the Nation" will, under the operation of the law, be hampered by so many conditions that it is very doubtful if they will ever be able to avail themselves of the privileges which it is sought to confer upon them. Nevertheless, it is gratifying to see that a beginning has been made in a work of real reform.

But, as Congress has less than a fortnight left of its present session, and the bill cannot possibly pass the House, it is difficult to see where any good can be accomplished by continuing the debate. The Senate dearly loves to talk. The debate in that body, since the pending bill has been before it, has been as verbose and wordy as it could have been if this was the beginning of a long session of Congress, instead of the end of the short session, which terminates the official life of the Forty-sixth Congress. It is hardly probable that the bill will pass the present Senate; and, if it should, it must be reintroduced at the next session, and the discussion must begin again, with new men to participate in it, and new interests to be consulted in perfecting a measure of so great importance as this is conceded to be. Therefore, although the long debate has had its uses, we venture to express a very general desire that the Senate shall let the subject lie and address itself to matters of immediate concern. If Congress is to accomplish anything during this session which shall assist in the solution of the Indian question, the matters recommended to its attention by the President in his late Message on the Ponca affair will occupy all the time that may now be spared for any branch of this subject. And the President has expressed a desire that these matters shall be attended to during his term of office, now drawing to a close.

It is certainly a remarkable thing that we should have so long persisted in withholding from the Indian the rights which are unhesitatingly conferred upon every other human being living within the confines of the Republic. The practice of recognizing the tribal and communal relations of the Indians was the first great error in our policy. We have made treaties with bands of aborigines as if they were independent nations. And yet the individual Indian, the subject of the treaty-making power, has never had, in the law courts of the land, even the slenderest right of all those which have been granted to the most ignorant and depraved people of other lands domesticated upon our soil. This fact has been strikingly put in a single sentence by Horatio Seymour, who said: "Every human being born upon our continent, or who comes here from any quarter of the world, whether savage or civilized, can go to our courts for protection—except those who belong to the tribes who once owned this country. The cannibal from the islands of the Pacific, the worst criminals from Europe, Asia, or Africa, can appeal to the law and courts for their rights of person and property—all, save our native Indians, who, above all, should be protected from wrong."

And these errors have been persisted in with amazing pertinacity. When Congress, after years of supine indifference, was aroused to a sense of the absurdity of making treaties with these mere creatures, who are not admitted to be even "persons," it was solemnly enacted that the practice should cease. But, although no more "treaties" have been made, the custom is perpetuated under the name of "agreements." Precisely how far an Indian appreciates the difference between the old-fashioned treaty and the new-fangled agreement it would be interesting to inquire. It would certainly puzzle an astute lawyer to show that there is any appreciable difference in the results attained under either system. The indications are that the Indian is more completely at the mercy of Government officials now than he was when he was defended by the provisions of a solemn treaty which was only made to be broken. And, in strict conformity with the ancient superstition, which rigorously classed the Indian as a mere wild animal, every chapter of legislation relating to him discriminates against him as a being totally unfit for civilization, and incapable of taking care of himself. In the Pension bill, now before the Senate, there is a clause providing that the accrued pensions due to the survivors of a brigade of Indians, who fought in the late civil war, shall be dribbled out to them in installments, instead of being disbursed as money is to every other disabled soldier of the Union. These civilized Indians, although fit to serve the country and fit to be associated in the Army with citizens of the United States, are not thought fit, after all their long service, to be trusted with the few hundreds of dollars due them as disabled veterans, under the law which pays pensions, without question, to the most ignorant negro drawn from the cane-brakes of the South.

Nobody proposes to give to the Indian that charm which is supposed to clothe its possessor with a panoply against oppression—the ballot. It is proposed that he shall be permitted to own his land, in severalty, and under a title which he may defend in the courts of law. Even a Chinaman has this right. Under the present condition of things, if an Indian is robbed, he has no redress except what the indifferent or dishonest agents or the sluggish machinery of the Interior Department may furnish him. The maintenance of the tribal relation perpetuates a system of pauperism, makes forever impossible the individuality of persons, and facilitates every species of private and official robbery. The Indians are solemnly lectured as to their duty to apply themselves to the arts of peace; and they no sooner begin to learn their lesson than they are uprooted from their half-tilled acres, and are transplanted into the wilderness. It is unreasonable to complain of the tardiness with which the Indians adopt the ways of civilized life and become self-supporting under such a wretched system as this. Gradually, and with discreet management on the part of the Government, the Indian may be allowed to own his land, as other men own theirs, and be given the right to defend himself under the law, as other men defend themselves.

What Will We Do with Them?

June 18, 1883

Gen. Crook has brought back from Mexico nearly 400 captive Chiricahua Apaches—men, women, and children. These people were formerly "settled" on a reservation in Southern Arizona. They broke away in detachments and went to Mexico, and from thenceforth devoted themselves to robbery and murder. In what capacity have they been brought back? Having been captured by a military expedition into a foreign country, they might be called prisoners of war. If they are, they are entitled to the rights of belligerents. But as they have not made war upon the United States, but have committed very much the same sort of crimes as those which have furnished the regular industry of the cowboys of the South-west, they may be considered as merely thieves, brigands, and organized murderers. Under a regular law administration, even the banditti of the West are entitled to a fair trial, although the hurried course of justice has denied this to the James, Barber, and other "boys" of recent and sanguinary fame. High as popular passion may rise in Arizona, nobody will undertake to lynch the Apache captives. There are too many of them. Besides, there is Crook.

The fact is that Crook's prisoners are wards of the Nation, who have run away from our guardianship. They are also foreign enemies with whom we have made treaties, as we have made treaties with Great Britain, Russia, or any other foreign power. They are thieves and murderers, kidnaped in Mexico, without the aid of extradition papers or any other international formula. If they are tried in the United States, they might ask for a jury, witnesses, and an assignment of counsel. Of the hundreds brought back by Gen. Crook, a few men, like Nana, Loco, and Geronimo, are known to be guilty of crimes of which they might possibly be convicted. Others, less conspicuous, may be equally guilty, but their conviction would not be easy. A large number of non-combatants—women and children—would remain to be provided for if their natural protectors should be punished by death or imprisonment. To send any considerable number of the captives to a reservation, from which they would flee again on errands of theft and butchery, would indeed be folly. The policy of the Government in its treatment of Indians has been variable and shifting from year to year. No disposition of the captive Apaches could be made consistent with all the courses which the Government has heretofore pursued. The situation is a novel one. People generally would be satisfied to accept any solution that may be offered by Gen. Crook.

⌒ [Untitled]

July 31, 1892

The Presidential canvass of 1892 will have among its distinctive features that of the entrance of the red man into politics on a small yet notable scale. The Sissetons of what was lately the Fort Traverse Reservation, near Brown's Valley, in South Dakota, have their club and are harangued on the subjects of the time by white and red orators; and perhaps by this time they may have progressed far enough to be deep in the discussion of the McKinley tariff and the Force bill, to say nothing of subjects of more immediate interest to them. In Southern Kansas the prospective Indian vote is said to be the deciding factor in one or more counties. All this opens a new vista for the aborigine. The law distinctly provides that Indians who take their allotments in severalty shall become citizens, and there are also other ways in which citizenship may be acquired. The Sissetons have accepted this form of land holding, and so have tribes and individuals elsewhere. When, by conforming to State laws and to registration rules, the red men take their full share in elections, they will doubtless find some statesmen anxious to look after them and help them who have hitherto been but little concerned with poor Lo's grievances. The day, in fact, when Lo will take his place on the floors of Congress, representing white men as well as red, may not be very far distant.

⌣ [Untitled]

May 23, 1894

The decision of the Attorney General in regard to Indian rights of inheritance, reversing one which had been rendered by the Assistant Attorney General under Mr. Harrison's Administration, is justly spoken of as avoiding a world of possible trouble. The case was one of rival claims to the same severalty allotment tract, made by a Sioux Indian and by the daughter of a white father and a Sioux mother. The latter had recorded her choice first, but the question arose whether she was an Indian at all. She had married a white, who at first supported her and their family independently, but at length they moved upon the reservation, where she claimed and received her share of the tribal rations. The first opinion rendered in the case was against her, on the ground that by the common law the status of the children of free parents follows that of the father. However, this would have disturbed so many subsisting relations that the Interior Department suspended action on it; and now Attorney General Olney decides in favor of the woman, since among many Indian tribes the established line of descent is through the mother, and "mother's right" is recognized among others where the line is through the father, while the Sioux usages are to treat the mixed bloods as members of the tribe and entitled to a share of tribal property. The Government has, in fact, assented to this view in many of its compacts and dealings with Indians, so that a contrary decision would have unsettled many land titles and property relations.

∽ The Indians and the Game Laws

August 18, 1895

The underlying cause of the recent troubles between the settlers and the Bannocks has existed for a long time, and is not limited to the Indians of the Fort Hall Reservation. Nearly six years ago, on Nov. 1, 1889, the Indian Office notified its agents that complaints were frequently made that Indians, on leaves of absence from their reservations, "slaughter game in large quantities, in violation of the laws of the State or Territory in which they reside, and that, in many instances, large numbers of wild animals are killed simply for their hides." Last year, also, similar complaints were received, and then, as in 1889, the agents in six States, including Idaho and Wyoming, were expressly instructed to notify all their Indians that hunting was not allowed upon passes obtained for visiting only, and that those Indians that had treaty rights of hunting must use them for supplying their needs and not for mere purposes of amusement, or for "the slaughter of wild animals in vast numbers for the hides only."

Nevertheless, the very implication of the circular of 1889 and the instructions of last year is that where the treaty right of hunting does exist, it is not made subject to State and Territorial laws. It is part of a compact between the Federal Government and the Indians. The Interior Department has indeed decided that the privilege does not permit wanton destruction of game, this restriction being presumably in the interest of the Indians as well as of others. But the main point is that, in the circular of 1889, still in force, only those Indians who try to use mere visiting passes for hunting privileges are mentioned as being in danger of arrest under State laws. Indians who have the treaty right of hunting are responsible to their agents for the manner of its exercise; but the right itself has been purchased for good and valuable considerations, sometimes, perhaps, by the surrender of lands worth a thousand times more than the few elk and deer shot by them, and their rights to hunt are as legal as any that sportsmen in Pennsylvania or New-York have to the preserves they purchase and stock.

This is precisely the point which some of the settlers in Idaho and Wyoming apparently try to ignore. The old race hatred expresses itself in a refusal to concede that Indians can have rights which white men have not, in any matter of common interest. Accordingly we find, in Mr. Browning's report, already referred to, that his agents had informed him that white men were "killing game merely for the pleasure of hunting," directly around Indian reservations, and further that "the State officers, in some instances, said that they did not feel justified in prosecuting white men for violating game laws while the Indians were allowed to hunt." It seems to us that this last absolutely preposterous view may furnish the real clue to the events of the present Summer, in which we have seen arrests of Indians under State laws, as if no such thing existed as a treaty right to hunt, and then several men, a woman, and a child shot down like dogs on the ground that they were attempting to escape from an arrest whose purpose and end may have been to them utterly beyond comprehension.

As to the remedy against a repetition of this year's lamentable and disgraceful occurrences, perhaps it might be found in a purchase from the Indians of their right to hunt at all, if this can be effected without making them dissatisfied, and on reasonable terms. At least, such rights could be purchased as are not subject to local laws, leaving to the Indians only such hunting privileges as are in conformity with those laws, and making them liable to arrest for disobeying them.

3   The National Indian Policy

> From what has been discovered thus far we should say that it
> is likely that the reservation policy will be recommended more
> strongly than ever, as the basis of all Indian legislation and ac-
> tion; that the whole treaty system will be abolished, root and
> branch; that we shall never henceforth make diplomatic nego-
> tiations with Indians, as if they were foreign nations; and that
> certain attempts may be made, whether in connection with
> Territorial organization or otherwise, to connect them more
> directly with our republican system of government.
>
> —*New York Times*
> July 15, 1869

IN 1860, the principal interest of the *Times* insofar as the Indian problem
was concerned was the protection of white settlers on the frontier. It
was convinced that the two executive departments most directly concerned
with the Indians, the War Department and the Department of the Interior,
were working at cross-purposes. The various Indian agencies, supported by
the Department of the Interior, were charged with responsibility to aid the
Indians. The nation's military forces, meanwhile, were expending immense effort and resources to combat the Indians. From that time until the
turn of the century, the *Times* would find much to dislike in the national policy toward the Native Americans. It would maintain consistently that the national government was, in one way or another, responsible for many of the
most dismal elements of the Indian problem.

At the earliest period, the *Times* was outspoken in its condemnation of
policies it believed were too lenient on warlike tribes. The primary responsibility of the government, in the view of the *Times*, was the protection of
white settlers. It challenged the effectiveness of the army in this regard, even
though the hostile Indians at this point were the only significant enemy on

which the army had to focus. The Civil War soon changed that situation, however, and the newspaper's editorial tone toward the military became much more positive in time.

After the war, with the flow of white settlers to the West greatly magnified and white aggression toward the Indians much more prevalent, the convictions and the concerns expressed by the *Times* dramatically changed. It openly called on the government to treat the Indians—whom it now was inclined to see as essentially peaceful and defenseless—more fairly. It hailed the formation of the Indian Commission, charged by Congress with responsibility to secure a permanent peace with the Native Americans. But the *Times* worried about the negative influences that vested interests might bring to bear. In a July 1867 editorial, it warned that the new commission was bound to meet with a great deal of opposition. "The agents, traders, petty politicians and land swindlers who have stirred up the Indians to the existing state of war, will do all in their power to thwart the Commission," it argued. The government had been spending a million dollars a week making war against the Indians, it explained, and "the prairie sharks are sure to feather their nests with a good portion of such sum."

The Indian Commission never lived up to the full potential the *Times* saw for it. It was not long, in fact, until the editorial columns were aiming much of their ire at the commissioners. Near the end of 1868, a forceful editorial suggested that both the Indians and the white settlers had suffered because of the government's ineptitude and the general failure of the commission, which it charged with outright deceit.

The *Times* was firm in its conviction that a policy of "colonization" was the best solution to the Indian problem. By putting the Indians on reservations, its editorials held, the government could prevent the contact with white settlers that so often led to conflict. It accepted the fact that such a policy, to be successful, depended on maintaining the reservations as inviolate by whites and helping the Indians survive until their cultures could be transformed. Whether these changes were desired by the Indians rarely seemed to enter into the thinking of *Times* editorial writers, though in later years they did acknowledge that the level of the Indians' resistance had been underestimated. The position of the *Times* was modified over the years, of course.

The *Times* was adamant in its opposition to a national policy of "manifest destiny" toward the Indians. It contended that this approach meant only extermination of the Indians and expressed its confidence that the Indian problem could and should be solved by a humane policy. But in its editorial columns, the *Times* portrayed the national policy as one that was too inconsistent to be classified either way. The policy ostensibly was humane, the newspaper said, but in its application rarely provided even simple justice. Indians, the *Times* said in an early 1878 editorial, could hardly be expected to understand the workings of a complex government in which "sometimes superintendents are supreme, and sometimes soldiers." It said Indians were likely to find the words of either civil or military agencies falsified by the acts of the other and "the universal grievance of the red race is the double-dealing of the white." Congress also came in for its fair share of criticism in *Times* editorials on the Indian problem. In instance after instance, the newspaper faulted Congress for failure to enact legislation supporting a consistent Indian policy.

By the mid-1880s, the *Times* itself had moved somewhat more forcefully toward a position that called for full participation of the Indians as national citizens. The reservation system it had favored now seemed less attractive—especially given the fact that the government had proved unwilling or unable either to protect the Indians' lands from white encroachment or to supply the Indians with adequate food. The *Times* now believed the land should be owned by the tribespeople as individuals, rather than in common. It called for surplus Indian lands to be bought by the government, which in turn should help establish Indian farms and schools.

The *Times* continued to point out, however, that there was an immense backlog of injustices yet to be fully remedied. It lashed out at "agreements" that never had been agreed to by the Indians, including white seizure of the Black Hills after gold was discovered there. The treaty of 1868 that established the Sioux reservation, including the Black Hills, had promised that no non-Indians except government agents ever would be permitted to "pass over, settle upon, or reside in the territory described." But now, the *Times* reminded readers in an 1886 editorial, "On the west the Black Hills mining region is occupied by active settlers. On the east and south the farmer presses upon the boundary and two railways are waiting for the time when they can extend their lines through this Indian country." Having made the Indians wards of the nation through the reservation policy, the *Times* asserted, the government had failed miserably in its obligations to sustain them. The newspaper's editorial writers had little confidence that corrupt government agents would succeed in remedying this situation, no matter what the national policy.

The National Indian Policy

The *Times* always had taken the position that Indian tribal sovereignty was problematic. It supported the Indian Severalty Law, which provided for the awarding of lands to individuals instead of tribes, but nonetheless called for the views of the Indians to be heard. The law "which is designed to prepare the way for making the red men self-supporting citizens," the *Times* declared in a brief editorial in June 1887, "does not propose to enforce itself against the wishes of those who are meant to be its beneficiaries." But if the tribal loyalties prevented a "broader patriotism" and kept the Indians in isolation, it proposed, the gradual decline of tribal obligations and restraints would be of benefit to them.

By the end of 1890, the *Times* was able to claim that the "great work" of the year had been the government's purchase of surplus Indian lands. And while it was unfortunate that all the terms of the agreements had not been carried out, it said in a lengthy editorial, "the red man long ago became accustomed to such treatment."

Treatment received by the Indians at the hands of the national government was a topic that had occupied countless *Times* editorials by the turn of the century. The newspaper's editorial writers had energetically attacked policies they believed wrong, as well as the government agencies that carried them out. Nor had prominent individuals, from presidents to cabinet secretaries, been spared. At the same time, the newspaper's editorial columns had taken strong stands in support of favored policies. Many of its own positions had varied with changing circumstances, while others had remained intact. Given all the intricacies of the Indian problem, one permanent aspect was the government's enduring effort to find solutions through public policy. The *Times*, without fail, was watching. The editorials that follow represent an extensive cross section of the exposition and analyses of those efforts on the part of the *Times*.

↩ Our Frontier Policy

March 8, 1860

We notice that Senator Wilson has introduced a resolution instructing the Committee on the Militia to consider the expediency of transferring the control of the Indians from the Interior to the War Department.

The Indian Department was originally embraced within the War Department, and the transfer of the former to the Department of the Interior ten years ago has immensely augmented our frontier difficulties. The Secretary of War and the Secretary of the Interior are constantly working at cross purposes, so far as the Indians are concerned. The Secretary of War equips and sends out armies to fight Indians armed, equipped and rationed by the Secretary of the Interior. The move of Senator Wilson is very important, therefore, as it proposes to give the control of the Indians to the War Department, where it properly belongs.

But there are evils existing in our frontier arrangements greater and deeper than all this. Our entire system of management on the frontiers, both in the War and Indian Departments, utterly fails in the purposes for which they were instituted. The military affords no protection to the emigrant and frontier settler. Our frontier posts rather create business for thieving, murdering Indians, who in turn are blanketed, armed and fed by the Agencies, and allowed to roam at large without let or hinderance. In short, our frontier Military and Indian Agency systems are worse than useless, inasmuch as they fail to protect our own citizens or control the Indians; and furthermore, they are the prolific sources of corruption and all the worst vices to which both the white and Indian races are predisposed. If Senator Wilson will extend his inquiries, and procure an investigation of our entire frontier system, military and Indian, herculean as the task will be, a result proportionate to the labor will follow. Aside from the mischief that comes upon frontier citizens from our mistaken frontier policy, the cost entailed upon the country is enormous. The present expenses of the War Department, including that for Indian affairs, are $30,000,000 per annum, and these expenses, at the present rate of increase, will reach $60,000,000 in 1865. A subject of greater importance in our domestic affairs could not come before the Senate.

⤳ Our Indian Policy

December 8, 1860

Upon the presentation, last year, of the Annual Report of the Secretary at [*sic*] War, we took occasion to comment upon the rapid and inexcusable growth of expenditures in that department of the public service. From a fraction less than $12,000,000, as they existed in 1851, they had risen to a fraction less than $30,000,000; and, upon examining the objects upon which the money was lavished, we predicted that if the same ratio of progression continued, before 1865 they would reach the enormous sum of $60,000,000, or two-thirds of the entire outlay of the Government. We are happy to state that the tendency to increase has at least been suspended. The present report of Mr. Floyd indicates that the figures have fallen from $28,000,000, in 1858–59, to $19,000,000, in 1859–60—a saving of one-third. It is true, the expenditures for the three months ending Sept. 30, being the first quarter of the current fiscal year, ascend to about $6,500,000, prefiguring an enhanced aggregate for 1860–61; but before this year expires the present Administration will have retired from office, giving place to successors who will be bound by every consideration of self-interest to bring the expenses of the Government far within the limits indulged by the actual Cabinet. It is safe, therefore, to regard the growing extravagance of the War Department as arrested, and the policy turned in the direction of retrenchment and economy.

An inquiry into the conduct of the national military concerns shows that the great bulk of outlay is connected with the administration of Indian affairs. The Secretary remarks at the outset of his Report:

"In conformity with the policy which I announced to you in my last annual report, the troops available for service against the hostile Indians, and others that have become so since that time, have been engaged in campaigns of the greatest activity. This year the army has been constantly in the field, and upon an active war-footing."

It seems, therefore, that the entire military strength of the nation finds active employment in warfare with a half-dozen tribes of savages, inconspicuous in numbers, and only formidable for their ability to elude punishment by prompt dispersion, and to assemble for predatory purposes whenever the temptation to plunder is presented. With several of these tribes we have treaties, and annually furnish them with arms, money and other bribes to tranquility. With others no covenants have been made; and what is the most disagreeable feature of the business is, that the savages who are under no obligations to preserve peace, and who are most often in a state of hostility, frequent the regions through which our lines of communication with the Pacific shore are extended. Hence, the constant stories of attacks on overland mail coaches and the Pony Express riders; the frequency with which trains are plundered, and relay stations assaulted. The Apaches, the Camanches, the Navajoes, the Kioways, the Sioux, and the Pah-Utes, are always ready for a massacre, or a robbery; and in the pursuit and punishment of the slippery delinquents, an army twice the size of our entire establishment might have ceaseless occupation. The upshot of this state of things is a steady and exhaustive demand upon the Treasury, uncompensated by any advantage to the public service. Lives, as well as money, are squandered; the frontiers are insufficiently guarded; travelers are unprotected. And to mend the evil seems as hopeless a task as to fill Bunyan's Slough of Despond, into which "ever so many cart-loads of books had been cast," and the slime was deeper than ever.

It is needless to say there is something radically wrong in a system which produces no better fruit. What that error is, the Secretary of the Interior hints at in his Report. It lies in the unlimited range enjoyed by these nomade [sic] tribes; and the remedy is the extension of the system of reservations. The Secretary believes in a partial extension of the system. It should be universal. The experiment so triumphant in respect to the tribes in the Indian Territory, is the best evidence that the Indian, when confined to limits inconsistent with his vagrant habits, settles down quietly to agricultural and various industrial pursuits; and makes important advances in civilization. The majority of the wild aborigines of the Plains roam as widely as if the whole unbounded continent were theirs. Two or three of the tribes above named as especially troublesome, occupy territory five or six thousand square miles in extent, although the aggregate number of the savages does not exceed fifteen hundred warriors. Yet with the aid of their fleet horses, their knowledge of the country, and their acute sagacity in selecting points and objects of attack, this handful maintains a condition of terrorism over the broad region it scours, wholly irreconcilable with white colonization, and unsafe to the necessary traveler. Such paltry expeditions as are organized to punish these depredators, are generally unfortunate, and always useless. There is no glory in attacking an enemy ever ready for flight; and much damage from their skill in the use of their weapons, even when in retreat before lagging pursuers. The same reasons, indeed, as rendered the Roman legionary an indifferent match for the Parthian, affects the usefulness of our troops, when employed against the Apaches and Navajoes. Warfare of this sort will, of course, last as long as the Indians endure. With a better system, which should place the savage, subdued by the exhibition of overwhelming force, within the boundaries of well-guarded reserves, and there compel him to the abandonment of his wandering and thieving habits, and to the practice of honest industry, the present War budget would be diminished one-half; and the anomaly of a standing army retained upon a war footing year after year with no external enemy to oppose; and the further anomaly of a regularly increasing outlay for the preservation of order among tribes whose numbers decline in a far more rapid proportion, would no longer confound common sense.

It may seem absurd and untimely to discuss what the future policy of the Government ought to be, when the Government itself totters apparently on the verge of dissolution; and when, if it survive in any form the present crisis, it is impossible to say over how much of the actual surface of the country it shall prevail. Still, so long as War and Indian estimates figure before the eyes of Congress, and call for scrutiny and action, it remains a duty to discuss the wisdom of their application; and, if practicable, to indicate a sounder economy. The lesson, in any event, cannot be wholly profitless.

⌒ Indian Affairs and the Secretary of the Interior

December 23, 1865

We were glad to see the resolution, recently brought before the House by Mr. Doolittle, rendering assistance to Indians in the United States Territory. In general, the relation of the Anglo-Saxon race with inferior races, all the world over, is a most unpleasant matter to contemplate. Whether it is with the Hindoos, or the Australians, or Jamaicans, or on this side with Californian Chinese, or negroes, or Indians, the uniform habit and tendency of this "imperial race" is to crush the weak.

Whatever Christianity has done in the world, it has but in the faintest degree modified the tyrannical and grasping spirit of our race toward all lower and weaker races. Our progress and the English progress is continually over the ruins of nations less skilled and with less of our pertinacious energy. The dealings of this nation toward the Indians form one of the most disgraceful chapters in modern history. We first drive them from their lands, and then suffer them to be poisoned with our diseases and debauched with our vices. They are steadily driven back to the region of the buffalo, and now even in the wild mountains bordering on that region, the miners are destroying the game and breaking up the solitude, on which their support as hunters depends. This result, of course, cannot be avoided, but what could be done, should be the preparation by education and the facilities of civilization of the friendly Indians for something better. It seems to be generally admitted that many of the "Indian Agents" who have hitherto been the carriers of civilization to them, have been the worst enemies these poor people ever had.

The Secretary of the Interior proposes in his recent message, "a civilization and educational fund" to be provided by Congress, and disbursed in cooperation with benevolent organizations of private individuals. He thinks that the churches of all denominations would then attempt to occupy this missionary field, and that the Indian tribes would thus be brought into contact with a class of men and women "conforming to a higher standard of morals than that recognized as obligatory by too many of the present employes of the government." He hopes that thus they would be gradually elevated, and led to adopt agricultural and pastural pursuits.

There are now three hundred and fifty thousand Indians within the jurisdiction of our government. It is satisfactory to know that the calamities which have recently been brought upon some of the tribes, are not directly our own fault. They broke their treaties, and taking advantage of our troubles, as well as instigated by rebel emissaries, attacked our peaceful settlements, perpetrating the most horrible barbarities, and entering on an unprovoked war. The result was, of course, disaster and ruin to themselves. Their country was laid waste, vast amounts of property were destroyed, and the inhabitants were reduced to a state of the utmost destitution, so that this Winter thousands will die of starvation, unless assisted by the government.

The political result of the war has been the abolition of slavery among the conquered Indians, the cession of some of their lands for Indians who had been on reservations elsewhere, and the establishment of civil government among them.

If no other argument were needed for civilizing instead of exterminating these wild tribes, it would be found in the immense expense of such a cruel proceeding. Each regiment sent against them costs the country $2,000,000 per annum, and the warfare might be waged with no apparent result for a generation; while the effect would be to break up or endanger all our chains of connection between the Atlantic and Pacific.

We are glad that the Secretary of the Interior has the independent judgment and the humanity to protest in advance against such cruelty, and to recommend that "stringent legislation be adopted for the punishment of violations of persons and property of numbers of Indian tribes who are at peace with the government."

Some such measure as the establishment of an "educational fund," to be disbursed in cooperation with private societies, will have to be adopted, if we would not have the Indians of the plains perish from starvation or become utter beasts of prey.

There is no doubt that our churches have been too much absorbed in the heathen of Asia and Africa, and have thought too little of the heathen whom the conquering Anglo-Saxon race were trampling under foot.

It ought to be a matter of the most absolute duty for our humane and religious community to raise up and civilize the Indians. It is a matter of national honor that these wild owners of the soil, ruined by our success, should receive exact justice in the desolate regions yet abandoned to them.

ᔕ A Friendless Race

May 20, 1866

We do not suppose there is any likelihood of getting a Congressional Committee to investigate the butchery of sixteen friendly Indians, fourteen of them women and children—a report of which has been forwarded to the authorities by the Governor of Idaho. The Governor speaks of the "depraved moral sentiment" which is evinced by the whites toward the poor Indians, defenceless and peaceable; and says that the excitement runs so high that he finds it hard to carry out his instructions for their protection. We mention this matter, here, however, only for the purpose of calling attention to a single remark of the Governor of Idaho which confirms in a striking way a point which we have urged in the *Times*, and which furnishes a fit comment on the late savage letter of Sylvester Mowry, offering to exterminate an Indian tribe which had been accused of an assault on one of our garrisons. We wrote in the *Times* of Wednesday, in commenting upon our Indian policy: "It is on record, as the experience of all those most familiar with Indian affairs, that the aggressors in nearly all quarrels, and the beginners of nearly all outrages, are the whites—rarely indeed the Indians." Two days after we had the official dispatch of the functionary already referred to, who closed with the words: "In no case that I have examined have I found the red man the aggressor; but invariably the trouble springs from some fiendish outrage of bad white men." This statement of ours, thus endorsed, is one which should never be lost sight of in regulating our policy and action toward the Indians. This unhappy race, less fortunate than the negro, has no champion on the floor of Congress, but, on that very account, the authorities should be all the more vigilant to see that the paternal government which it ostensibly exercises toward them does not furnish a pretext for cruelty and wrong.

⌒ Our Indian Policy

May 26, 1867

The tenor of the letters and dispatches forwarded for publication from the Indian country indicate a desire on the part of our military authorities to have the Indian Bureau transferred from the Department of the Interior to the War Department. We are informed that the army officers are unable to do as they wish regarding the Indians because of the interference of the civil officers of the Indian Bureau. The line of policy which the War Department would adopt toward the Indians has been indicated during the past few years in a manner which does not commend itself to the humane portion of our people.

The destruction of Indian villages, the slaughter of Indian men, women and children, repeated threatenings of severe punishment for trivial offences, and the too frequent execution of such threats, do not mark a line of conduct calculated to win the red men to peaceful pursuits, or to secure their good will and respect.

The troops, and the border settlers also, (encouraged by the example of the troops,) seem to have acted upon the belief that "Indians have no rights which the white man is bound to respect." The example set by Col. Chivington, in massacring in cold blood, without provocation, and without subsequent rebuke, a whole camp of Indians, old and young, male and female, has given the cue to settlers and others, until an Indian has come to be regarded by them as of no more account than a prairie dog or a coyote, and to be shot down with as little reluctance. These settlers are anxious that the military authorities should control Indian affairs, for the reason that they believe that force is the only argument to be used in dealing with them.

The management of Indian affairs certainly could not be much worse than it has been of late, but it may be doubted whether any improvement would be effected by giving the War Department and army officers supreme control. Should this be done, the policy would be simply to prevent the Indians from pillaging and murdering, and to retaliate where prevention was impossible. No thought of civilizing or improving their condition would enter into the heads of those having authority, nor would it be expected of them. They would be sufficiently occupied in caring for their troops, without attending to the education of squaws and papooses. But that this can be done, and the condition of the Indians so improved as to render them inoffensive, if not useful, is abundantly proved by experiments already made. There are tribes in both the Eastern and Western States, who are living quietly upon their own reservations, devoting themselves to agricultural pursuits, and to such other branches of industry as they are qualified to pursue. They have their educational institutions, and are training up their children to be useful members of society. They are no longer looked upon as beasts of prey, but are respected by their neighbors, and held in high esteem by all who have dealings with them. Even upon the wild prairies of the Indian Territory, several tribes, of their own will, have abandoned their roving habits, and have made long strides toward civilization.

The Cherokees, for instance, numbering 14,000 souls, own 4,000,000 acres of land, and are quietly settled upon their property. They own immense herds of cattle, and many of them have acquired large fortunes by sales of stock. Individuals own from 300 to 15,000 head of stock, horses and cattle, and these roam the prairies, requiring no other care than simple herding. They had, before the war, good schools, and many of them were well educated, not a few having graduated at Eastern colleges. They had a republican form of government of their own, and under it were thriving and growing rich. When the war broke out they were divided in sentiment, and as some of them owned negro slaves, they sympathized largely with the South, and suffered in consequence. Beef contractors for the Western armies entered their preserves and "confiscated" cattle without stint, while numbers of their young men were killed in Confederate uniforms. With the dawning of peace, however, these Indians set to work to repair damages, and are now rapidly recovering from the effects of the war. This tribe has on deposit in the hands of the Government $1,000,000, for which they are paid interest. The tribes of Creeks and Seminoles are similarly situated, owning large herds of cattle, and cultivating the soil. They raise wheat, oats, corn, cotton, tobacco, have many fine orchards containing fruit trees of all kinds, and realize large sums annually from the produce raised by their own industry. They have numerous schools, a liberal school fund, and are striving to obtain a respectable social position.

These tribes have done all this with comparatively little assistance or direction from the Government. How much greater progress they would have made had they been properly encouraged and honestly dealt with at all times it is impossible to conceive. But that the Indian is susceptible of civilization is abundantly proved by their experiment. If one tribe can flourish and do well, be rendered not only inoffensive but useful, why cannot all the others? How much more to the credit of the country and this generation would it be if, instead of killing off these red men because they do not think and live and do as we do, we undertook their education and civilization. The money expended annually in supporting troops upon the border would build school-houses, dwellings, mills, &c., and provide all that is necessary to locate each tribe comfortably upon its own reservation, and give them a good start in the world. Such a course would not only be a saving of money to Government, but a humane proceeding which would save the lives of many white men as well as Indians who must necessarily fall if our present policy is persisted in.

⤸ Indian Colonization

July 7, 1867

We published on Friday a lengthy letter written by Gen. Hazen, and addressed to Senator Henderson, Chairman of the Senate Committee on Indian Affairs. Gen. Hazen discusses at considerable length the Indian question, and concludes by suggesting, as a plan for the future treatment of Indians, a course which we have persistently insisted upon, viz., their colonization. No other plan for the settlement of our present Indian troubles seems to him or to us practicable. Locate the different tribes upon separate reservations, keep traders and agents away from them, instruct them in agriculture, establish schools for their children, and above all, treat them humanely and keep faith with them, and we may expect in future perfect immunity from Indian depredations.

While we agree entirely with Gen. Hazen in regard to his plans for the future treatment of Indians, we disagree with him quite as essentially in regard to his estimate of them and of their rights. He says that they are an "inferior race," and that "A wise Nature has made it one of her most imperative laws that her strongest and best kinds shall prevail, and destroy the effete, the weak and the unproductive. . . . So it is with the Indians. When by the natural flow of population a thousand civilized men require for their homes the place roamed over by one Indian, it is justice to all men that he should give way; yet, he is always invited to adopt our habits and remain upon as much of *his* ground as he may require in a state of civilization."

Thus, while admitting that it is "his" ground, he is to be crowded out by the stronger white race without so much as saying "by your leave." In civilized communities when the general good demands that the property of an individual shall be appropriated, the individual is amply remunerated for his loss—he is not forcibly robbed of his rights, and then scalped for grumbling. Why not treat the Indian as we do white men? When we run a railroad though a white man's farm we pay him a good round sum for the privilege, yet we lay rails all over the Indian's territory and shoot him if he objects. By what right do we thus practically ignore his claims to the soil he occupies, while theoretically we admit it? The Indian reservations are as much the property of the Indians as are the grounds at the National Capitol the property of the nation, and until we recognize this fact and treat the owners accordingly, we shall have our occupation of such lands resisted by force.

It is scarcely probable that much progress can be made in civilizing the present generation of Indians; but that they are incapable of being civilized, as Gen. Hazen asserts, is most satisfactorily contradicted by what has been done. Children of the red men have graduated with honor at our colleges, and, returning to their people, have exerted a most beneficial influence over them. Make it for the interest of the present generation to live at peace with us, educate the rising generation, and in a few years the red men will be found to be as good citizens, as intelligent and industrious, as any other class. The civilization of the nineteenth century demands that while we restrain the present savage we should look to the welfare of his children, and endeavor to elevate them in the social scale. This can scarcely be done by putting bullets through them and depriving them of their scalps afterward.

The whole Indian question is a perplexing one at best—more perplexing on account of the utter disregard of the rights of the red men which prevails at the West—and it will require careful treatment to avoid injustice and to prevent long-continued hostilities. We again cordially indorse the policy indicated by Gen. Hazen, and trust that Indian colonization may soon become as general as it is feasible.

✐ The Indians—What Policy Shall We Pursue?

January 19, 1870

The question whether we shall extend to the Indians the sword or the olive branch is fast narrowing to a practical decision before Congress. To that body have just been presented two papers,—one a report of Governor Harvey's Kansas Commissioners, the other the memorial of the Friends' Social Union, adopted at the Twenty-seventh-street meeting in this City; the former furnishing specific facts, the latter general principles. The Governor has been investigating claims for Indian depredations, and has, of course, visited the main scene of the outrages on Solomon and Saline Creeks—Ellsworth, Saline, Ottawa, Cloud and Mitchell Counties, in Kansas, the familiar stamping grounds of savage warfare. There, naturally, Governor Harvey's Commissioners find good ground for damages in the stock stolen, the houses and ranches ruined, the frontier fields laid waste, the goods captured. They find that many settlers have left homes and claims, deserting fields which had been for years profitably cultivated. They report that the wanton cruelties of Indians who intrude upon the settlers under the cover of pretended friendship "call loudly for measures to prevent any and all Indian tribes from coming within the borders." They believe that now the settlers are not safe in going for a bucket of water without arms for self-defence. Such is the pith of their report.

But on the other hand, all this means only that the policy of "reservations," which is the distinctive demand of every officer, without exception, who knows anything of Indian campaigning, must be enforced. That policy, which has been formally adopted by the Administration, and, to some extent, by Congress, is now partly established, and only needs time and patience for effective operation. Whether the 120 claims of Kansas settlers, ranging from $5 to $5,000 each, be passed or not, has little to do with our new policy. These outrages occurred during the years 1867 and 1868—none of them in 1869. That we admitted the extent of the Indian atrocities then, was made evident by the great mid-Winter campaign of Sheridan, a twelvemonth since, and the penalties extracted of the Indians by the squadrons of Carr and Custer. The Saline River raid, in the Spring of 1869, was the only important Indian demonstration in Kansas during the past year.

The Friends' memorial makes a strong plea in behalf of civilization and citizenship for the Indians. And—as if to illustrate that "extremes meet"— these advocates of peace declare their heartiest friends in this matter are the men of the sword—General Grant, General Cox, the Secretary of the Interior, and General Parker, the Indian Commissioner. They hold that we must now do for the Indian what we have done for the negro, namely, abolish distinctions of race, color and condition. They demand that a civil territorial government shall be given to the Indians, and that the Sheriff's posse shall carry into effect the justice meted out by Courts. They declare that the dilemma is civilization or extermination, and that as between these there can be no doubt which policy we should pursue.

For ourselves, we hold firmly to the doctrine that for the present the reservation system is the key, and the only key, to the Indian problem. So long as the Indian, nomadic by nature, is free to wander far and wide over the continent, so long it is idle to talk of civil government. Civilized he certainly must be; we accept the alternative proposed by the friends, and, despite the very liberal excuse proffered by the London *Times* for extermination, we believe that citizenship will be the true solution of the problem. But first we must give the Indian a "local habitation." So long as he is plied with rum by traders, and wronged in his bargains by sutlers, and defrauded of his dues by selfish speculators, we cannot manage him. Bishop Clarkson, of Nebraska, tells us that now "it is a disreputable thing to cheat an Indian in Nebraska." If so, a revolution has already come about. He tells us the Indians now receive every dollar of money, every pound of subsistence, and every yard of goods they are entitled to—a thing "beyond the memory of the oldest inhabitant." He rightly ascribes the credit to the Friends who have astounded "the sneak thieves that have fattened for years upon the meanest of all garbage, Indian stealing." But the Quaker agents are strongly in favor of the reservation system, because by that alone they can get at the Indians; and only in this way, too, can Indian traders be kept off, the red men governed, and the white men made secure. With the reservation, if a white murders an Indian or an Indian a white, he can be tracked and punished; but without it war is waged against a whole tribe, at vast expense, to avenge the iniquity of a single lawless man, whether white or red.

We need also to abolish the senseless policy of making "treaties" with the Indians. The very name involves a contradiction in ideas. Treaties are made with foreign States. Do we admit that the Indians constitute a foreign nation? This matter has been the vice of all our legislation. We should treat the Indians as "wards of the nation," not as strangers. Whether force shall or shall not be used depends on their own conduct.

⌒ The Oldest of American Difficulties

May 22, 1870

A Convention of the United States Indian Commission has been held in this City, for the purpose of discussing the progress which had been made in civilizing and protecting the Indians, and the work which still remained to be done in order to save them from total extermination. More light was thrown on the matter by a letter from Secretary Cox than came from any other source. He said that the object of the President in appointing the Commission was to bring the Government officers specially charged with the care of the Indians, into closer relations with "those citizens who are in earnest in their wish to make our Indian policy one of which a civilized nation need not be ashamed." He said, too, that the appointment of Quakers to the various Indian agencies was a step in the same direction, and that through this appointment "the Government held out its hand to the moral and religious people of the country, and invited closer co-operation, and a more intimate mutual understanding, in the efforts to save from destruction, both physical and moral, the remnant of the original inhabitants of the land." He reports, however, that the result has fallen far short of what was hoped for, that the public has shown little or no interest in the subject, and that the only particle of co-operation which has come from any quarter, outside the Society of Friends, has come from the Santee Sioux Mission.

Letters of greater or less interest were received from other sources, but few of them possessed any value, except for the light they threw on the character of the writers. Wendell Phillips', for instance, was an intemperate attack upon Sheridan and other army officers employed on the frontier, whom he generously accused of cowardice. Gen. Sherman, however, in a short, tart, and not altogether courteous epistle, which called down on him severe castigation from several members present, really touched the root of the difficulty. He wrote: "The Indian question was a practical one, and not one of mere feeling," and can only be discussed where the Indians are, "and that if they would adjourn to Fort Sully, Fort Rice or Fetterman, where they could see the Indians themselves," he would feel strongly inclined to attend.

The fact is, and the public apathy about the matter is due largely to the popular appreciation of it, that the question is one so practical, as Gen. Sherman says, and is mixed up with so many other questions that lie at the very basis of our whole social and political organization, that mere philanthropy or kindly feeling can do little or nothing toward its solution. If Mr. Garrison or Mr. Phillips were sent out to the frontier to embody their vituperative letters in action, there is hardly a doubt that they would, no matter what powers the Government armed them with, make as helpless and hopeless a failure as ever was seen. The reason is simple. There is a white problem to be dealt with along the whole of our vast frontier, in order even to get at our Indian problem, and toward dealing with the white problem our moral and religious volunteers can do nothing, or next to nothing. The reason why the Russians and French and English have always succeeded better with the Indians than we have, is, not that they are more humane or more just than we are, or have more tenderness for the red race than we have, but that their system of governing the white race is different. They do not give up their public lands in such vast bodies to adventurers of all kinds as we do, and have done for a long time past; and they do not permit the sparse and half-civilized communities which collect on their frontier to govern themselves as we do under our Territorial system. No Englishman, Frenchman, or Russian is ever allowed to wander far from the eye and hand of the Central Government. The soldier or policeman is constantly behind him. The consequence is, that their frontier population is always more orderly, law-abiding, and peaceable—though far less enterprising and progressive—than ours, and the Indian gains both by their submissiveness and their sluggishness.

Under our system, not only are these immense tracks [sic] of land flung open to all comers, but the large, lawless, and adventurous population which settles on them is left to govern itself as best it can. We give them absolutely no protection for life or property, and it is a notorious fact that during the first few years of the history of every Territory in the Union, large bands of cut-throats have ridden over it rough-shod, and no man has enjoyed any safety except such as his revolver could give him, until the accumulation of property, and the growth of settled habits have led to the organization of vigilance committees; and this state of society has existed, and actually does exist at this moment, along a tract extending though eighteen degrees of latitude. Considering what the condition of the peaceable, inoffensive, and timid white man is at this moment in Montana, or Idaho, or Arizona, or New-Mexico, there is really something strange in the lamentations over the condition of the Indian. That he should be robbed, cheated, and maltreated in all sorts of ways, and that religious and moral people should be able to do little or nothing for him, is a matter of course. In fact, to secure peace and protection for the Indian, while leaving him his liberty, we should have to reform our whole frontier society, and abolish our Territorial government, and set on foot a vast police force.

We shall of course do nothing of the kind. What we must do, if we mean to save the remnant of the Indians, is to gather them all into a small district which we can really police and protect, and there teach them the arts of civilized life. Scattering Quakers among them as Indian Agents, while leaving them in daily contact with some thousands of ruffians, who fear neither God nor man—the Indians themselves being neither very moral nor very religious, and mighty "quick on the trigger"—is like trying to put out a great fire with a gardener's watering-pot.

ᔪ Taming the Savage

April 15, 1875

There are two methods of dealing with the Indians. One is what may be called the manifest-destiny policy. This policy concedes to an Indian no rights which a white man or a white man's Government is bound to respect. It does not once say "turkey" to the Indian; it hardly is willing, in any division of the spoils of this continent, to give the red man the buzzard. It looks to no future for him but extermination. It remorselessly appropriates his hunting grounds, wantonly kills the game upon which he subsists, civilizes him enough to make him appreciate whisky, and then gets him drunk and swindles him out of every valuable he possesses; gives him Government annuities, blankets, and rations, in order that contractors and agents may grow rich by spoiling him; trespasses on his reservations, and when he resents it, declares war against him; closes in upon him on every side, and leaves him no resource but that which the wild beast has, who turns at last upon the dogs mercilessly pursuing him. It then calls him a savage, declares him incapable of civilization, and leaves him to the fate which an unfriendly and dominant race seem ever ready to believe is the destiny of an inferior people.

The other policy is that of humanity. It treats the Indian as a human being having rights clear and indisputable as an original inhabitant of the continent. It concedes to him a portion of the territory once occupied wholly by him. It recognizes his right to be governed by laws, and to have a chance at the real civilization of this century. It would keep faith with him—all the more rigorously because he is not able to make good his own claim to justice. While understanding that he is not always nor often the ideal red man of romance or imagination, it does not forget that he is a "man and a brother" as much as the darker-skinned race, over whose wrongs Congress legislates, parties divide, and armies are moved by an Executive vigilant in executing the laws. It does not see in him now the qualities of the model citizen, quiet, industrious, thrifty, intelligent; neither does it believe that his savagery is wholly his fault, or wholly incurable. It knows he has had small chance to be anything other than what he is; that white men, subjected to similar treatment would have developed some traits of a civilization characteristic of their remote ancestors; that Indians treated more like men with rights to be respected, have shown qualities of manhood and genuine progress in modern civilization; and it believes that, after all, the real ground of success in dealing with any man or race, in the long run, is to be found only in a respect for absolute justice.

It cannot be said that our Government has adopted either of these lines of policy. In theory it has professed to deal justly, even generously, with the Indian; in fact, it has generally treated him as an incumbrance to be got rid of in as summary a manner as possible consistent with our reputation as a nation. Pushed, driven, removed from reservation to reservation, the Indian has only known our border civilization, which we have no reason to believe is of the pious, missionary type, or that finds its highest enjoyment in temperance and peace. The contractor has not taught him honesty, the frontiersman has not instructed him in the art of agriculture; indeed, he has had more opportunities of learning from his white neighbors the mystery of draw-poker and the stimulating qualities of cheap and nasty whisky, than the arts of a peaceful, industrious people. And thus it happens that while the Government is paying six or eight millions annually to the small fraction remaining of the race once scattered over the territory now called the United States, only small numbers of these Indians are less savage than those who hunted in the unbroken wilderness of three centuries ago. To-day the Indian problem confronts us with difficulties much the same as those encountered by the colonies at Plymouth and Jamestown.

Gen. Custer's expedition to the Black Hills last Summer is likely to give a new illustration of our method of dealing with the Indians. That expedition, by its reports of the wonderful mineral richness of the country visited, has stimulated every daring adventurer, and already men accustomed to make good with the knife or the pistol their right to any pretensions they may make are mining in the Black Hills, or are on their way there with a miner's outfit—an outfit which, whatever else is forgotten, is never noticeable for the absence of a breech-loading rifle. Not unexpectedly, the Indians, who think that by treaty they have a right to the undisturbed possession of the country, are uneasy and meditate violence; and at Washington the situation is looked upon as possibly portending an Indian war. The Army, it is said, is at once going to remove these trespassing miners; the Interior Department is to send a geologist to examine the mineral deposit in that region; and we are told that, probably, a treaty will be made by which the Indians will sell to the United States this newly-discovered gold-bearing territory.

It is plain what is to come of this. Whether there is an Indian war or not, if the Black Hills prove rich in gold, the red man will be bought out or driven out, and the white man will take possession. This is not justice, but it is destiny. It would take an army to keep the gold-hunters out of that country. They would not, and probably could not, understand that our Government would respect the Indians' rights, or the stipulations of treaties. Even if they suspected such a purpose at Washington, they would make a different policy or an Indian war inevitable. Deplorable as this state of things is, and hopeless as it leaves us of any solution of the Indian question not utterly repugnant to what ought to be the moral sense of the nation, the wretched policy of the Government hitherto not only makes this result probable but almost inevitable. It is the fatal inheritance of years of wrong-doing; yet it is now clamorously justified by the representatives of the whole Western frontier; and the great body of the people, although their blood can be brought to fever heat over the demand for equal rights to a race recently enfranchised, look with utter indifference upon this "struggle for existence" of the race once without a rival possessing the lands now embraced within the boundaries of the Union. It is too late, no doubt, to expect a different policy; it is not too late to point the moral of the one too long followed.

ᓚ Gen. Grant's Peace Policy

July 30, 1876

The opposition papers are making use of our recent disasters in the Indian struggle as a new argument against the Republican Party, and a fresh charge in the indictment against Gen. Grant. Even the *Nation*, which is usually candid in such matters, speaks of the recent peace policy of the President as "committing the wild tribes to the care of missionaries and like pious persons in search of employment of any kind at small wages," and alludes casually to the late Indian Commissioner, Mr. E. P. Smith, as having "fallen a victim to cunning and unprincipled men." As is well known, we have never been reserved in these columns in our criticisms of Gen. Grant's appointments or public policy. We venture to say, then, knowing how soon Gen. Grant and his policy will have passed to the region of history and its more severe discussion, that posterity will find no act of his Administration which arose from higher motives or was more rationally founded than his much-abused "peace policy" toward the Indians. He found, as is well known, the Indian service more full of abuses than any branch of our civil service. The funds which the nation readily and generously contributed to repair the wrongs done to these unfortunate tribes, and to preserve them from extinction, had become a "campaign fund" of the worst description. Every President, or his political followers, had made use of it in the far Western States for election purposes. The Indians were cheated and robbed without stint or mercy. The wrongs they suffered were continually kindling new wars. And the whole question was in a muddle and confusion which was a disgrace to the administrative ability of the nation. The conscience, too, of the best part of the people was aroused, for they could not take the convenient view of the *Nation* that the Indians had no rights to the lands they occupied in the sense of "civilized jurisprudence," and they felt that their past treatment of these wild tribes was a shame to civilization and the Christian name.

Gen. Grant could not break up the treaty system with the Indians, or seek to incorporate them as individuals with the nation, for Congress had long since decided otherwise. Indeed, when we take such roving tribes as the

Sioux and Dakotas of the Plains, it is difficult to see how this could be done. Our previous policy had been to gather the Indians on "reservations," and to seek to civilize them, or, at least, to elevate them. This had not been a complete failure, as the *Nation* intimates. Numbers of tribes in California, Nevada, Minnesota, and other districts had begun to be tillers of the ground and industrious human beings. To carry out this policy more effectively, Gen. Grant used just one of those means which, if employed in other branches of the civil service, would have reformed our whole administration. As the work was to be mainly moral and reformatory, and as it had been disgraced by corruption, he resolved to gain the co-operation of the moral and reformatory elements of our population, and to go for his workers where he would be most likely to get honest men. It was a bold expedient to imitate action of government in the war in the sanitary field—to unite the best individual labor with official inspection—the co-operation of Government and private associations. A kind of board, corresponding to the board proposed by Mr. Curtis for his competitive examinations, was appointed by the President and Congress, composed of some of our best citizens, serving gratuitously, to inspect and partially manage the whole Indian service. These gentlemen decided on all the contracts and important disbursements. To secure agents fitted to carry on the work of teaching and reforming the Indians, each prominent religious association or body was called upon to nominate agents. They naturally picked out their best and most educated men, fitted for such labors, and, on the least suspicion of their characters, changed or recalled them. These men were by no means poor creatures, seeking any wages, but often devoted missionaries of much ability. Thus the "Indian fund" was taken out of politics, and all the appointments and expenditures put under the most honest and respectable control which the best moral organizations of the people could furnish. The thing worked well in many parts of the country, and many tribes were improving rapidly. But it is fair to the President and the Indian Commission to say that they both saw the absolute necessity of the new policy working in combination with the Army—that is, where education or religion could not control, law must enforce. And there was in it all, what the *Nation* has well called attention to, a pauperizing tendency, for which neither the board nor the President was responsible.

The new outbreak does not arise from the peace policy, or the misuse of Indian agencies. It is not chargeable on Gen. Grant or the Indian Board or the Republican party. It may be hard to confess, in the presence of the heroic dead, but they were killed because the nation, in its greed, had cheated these savage tribes. The wild men and chieftains, who fought as brave men fight everywhere for the last few miles of land they can call their own, never agreed to the treaty of 1868, removing them from the country west of the Missouri. It is well known that Sitting Bull and his chiefs never would consent to that treaty. Moreover, that treaty expressly excepted the Black Hills country, and pretended to guarantee the region of the buffalo, which last is an absolute necessity to the savage. Our people burst into the Black Hills region, and our railroad explorations and military expeditions have frightened away much of the buffalo herds, and thus threatened the savages with starvation. We disregarded these wrongs, though the other side had not assented to the treaty. We notified the chiefs that they would be treated as enemies unless they removed to the new reservation. The wild leaders, embittered by a sense of their wrongs, burst into war, or more correctly resisted invasion—and on the late occasion only too successfully. Had the peace policy never been heard of, we do not see that this collision would have been prevented. It belongs to no party or President; it is one of the fruits of a long course of rapacity and injustice by the nation. In the allusion to the late Indian Commissioner, our contemporary does a bitter injustice to an honest and faithful official who was entirely acquitted, and whose only misfortune was that he attempted to serve the public under an Administration which, in other directions, has fallen under severe and just criticism.

↩ Congress and the Indians

October 7, 1879

The war with the Utes brings us, once more, face to face with the Indian problem. This is a question which is invariably postponed. Rash and unthinking people blame the Army, the Indian Bureau, and the bad men who are sent out to act as agents. It may be admitted that all of these, at one time or another, are to blame for the frequent collisions which occur between the red men and the settlers—collisions which begin with savage massacres and end with massacres of the savages. But behind all these lies the general and unsettled policy of the United States. This policy is determinable only by Congress. What has Congress ever done to define the course of conduct which should be pursued toward the Indians? When did either branch of Congress (which has occupied days and weeks in the discussion of abstract political questions) ever consume one whole day in a debate directed to the settlement of the general policy which our Government should pursue to the wild Indians? The President, the Secretary of War, the Secretary of the Interior, and the Commissioner of Indian Affairs, may each have his private opinion as to what shall be done with the non-civilized tribes of Indians. But where is the statute which embodies any Congressional opinion upon this subject?

Take the case of the Utes as a fair example. They were granted an ample reservation within certain well-defined boundaries. The Senate confirmed the treaty by which this land was ceded to the tribe, and the House voted an appropriation to carry out that treaty. Thus both houses were committed, to a certain extent, to a policy which would confine the Utes to certain limits and furnish them with means of sustenance. Beyond this, however, Congress did not go. How these Indians were to be treated, whether as beings susceptible of motives which might influence their choice, or as creatures, who were to be handled like dumb, driven cattle, nowhere appears in any law or in any report of Congressional debate. Having voted money and ratified the treaties, as requested by the Department of the Interior, the responsibility of Congress is supposed to be at an end.

So far as the action of Congress is concerned, nobody knows whether it was, or is, or has been in favor of the wildest sort of freedom to the Indians or of civilization and agricultural pursuits for those long-neglected tribes. Obviously, it would be impracticable for Congress to adopt a settled and "cast-iron" policy to be pursued toward all the tribes. Lincoln's failure to approve of the reconstruction scheme as prepared by Henry Winter Davis and B. F. Wade was based on reasons which might well deter the National Legislature from adopting a plan to be similarly and indiscriminately applied to all Indian tribes. "This plan," said the good President, "is like the bed of Procrustes. If a man was too short for it, he must be pulled out; if he was too long, he must be chopped off to fit it." In like manner, it might be said that the treatment which would suit the peaceable and well-nigh civilized Pottawattamies would be utterly unfitted for the warlike Comanches. Nevertheless, Congress has failed to originate and formulate any policy which should be pursued by the Executive Department toward any one specified tribe of Indians.

It may be urged that the Executive Department is to be held responsible for the treatment of these wards of the nation. Indeed, this is the commonest Congressional disposition of the whole matter. Having meddled and muddled until the scheme of government of the Interior Department—if it has a scheme of government—is left in dire confusion, Congress calmly turns aside to its President-making and its contemptible party politics, and says: "Now take up this mangled matter at the best and see what you can make of it." The system of appointing humanitarian agents for the Indians originated during Grant's Administration. It was purely an Executive invention, but was taken up and indorsed by Congress. It was not long, however, before Congress worked over that policy and voted and legislated and manipulated the whole scheme in such a way that only a shadow of the original policy remained. Congressmen voted in favor of apportioning the responsibilities of the Indian service among Episcopalians, Methodists, Presbyterians, and so on, and then went to the Interior Department and lobbied for the benefit of red-nosed political bummers as agents.

It is unprofitable to multiply words upon this subject. Congress will assemble in a few weeks. There are few subjects of more immediate and commanding importance which it can consider than the general policy to be pursued toward those Indian tribes who are neither semi-civilized, like the Delawares and Pottawattamies, nor wild and predatory like the Ogallalla Sioux. The wrongs of the Poncas and the rebellion of the Utes are proper and cognate subjects for Congressional discussion. One of these tribes was dispossessed of its reservation and driven into active hostilities by what is alleged to be a mere blunder in a survey. The other was exasperated by a persistent attempt to make an agricultural people of a tribe of Indians who refused to have their lands plowed, and who sulkily held themselves aloof from the arts of peace sought to be introduced upon their reservation. Is it not possible and practicable for Congress to define some general principles, by the practice of which similar disasters may in future be avoided?

ᔐ In the Way

December 24, 1879

The oratory that followed the luxurious indulgence in creature comforts, wherewith the New-England Society celebrated the stern virtues and simple tastes of the Puritans, was somewhat varied from the rhetorical monotony of congratulation and self-admiration customary on such occasions, by the diversion of Gen. Sherman against the Indians. After reminding the company that we had a vast, unpeopled domain that would have to wait many years yet for the plowshare, he declared that the little surviving remnant of the original possessors of the continent would have to get out of the way for advancing civilization. We have millions of acres of fertile soil yet untilled, and vast wildernesses whose primal solitude is still undisturbed, save by the screeching wild-fowl, the howling beasts, and the roaring cataracts. We are urging the surplus population of other countries to come and take a share in this vast domain. We tell them there is room for them for generations to come, and yet we have no place to be allotted in peace and security to the few thousand aborigines who still linger about our borders.

They are "entitled to fair consideration," says Gen. Sherman, but they are continually getting in the way, and must move on whenever the superior white man takes a fancy to the particular spot they chance to occupy. We have always treated them with "fair consideration." We have a peculiar theory, which they obstinately refuse to understand, but which we find wonderfully convenient for making them get out of the way. All the territory within the boundaries of the United States is subject to the jurisdiction of its Government, which may be exerted whenever there is any object to be promoted by it. Every human creature within those limits must yield obedience to the behests of the Government, whenever it sees fit to put its authority in exercise over them. And yet we have always dealt with the Indians as if they were an independent people, and fostered the delusion that within such domain as they were permitted to occupy they were subject to no Government but their own. We have made treaties and agreements with them, such as no national authority ever before made with its own subjects. They have been led to believe that they were not subjects, and so they have entered into bargains with a perverse expectation that these would be respected. Having thus flattered them with the notion that they were independent within certain territorial limits, we have proceeded to establish agents, under the pretense of carrying out our agreements with them, and have insisted that they should be submissive to these representatives of national authority. This they cannot be made to understand; but they are perverse barbarians. We permit them to be robbed and exercise no jurisdiction for their protection; but when white men suffer from collision with them, we remember that these are subjects of the Government and must be protected and even revenged. Our theory has two entirely different faces, like the shield in the fable; one side is presented to the Indians, the other to the whites, and it is no wonder that they are continually quarreling as to what it is made of.

The National Indian Policy

When we negotiate and make treaties with Indians, and induce them to accept certain reservations of land, we deal with them as an independent people, and they so understand it. The land is theirs, and under the agreement the authority of the United States is withdrawn from a certain circumscription. That is the side of the theory presented to them, and yet the other side is kept in view, turned toward the advancing white man. The authority of the United States may still be exerted over the Indians at the will of the Government and against the will of the other party to the agreement. Settlers and miners may still go on their way into the plains and forests in any direction, for these are under the jurisdiction of the Government, according to this side of the theory, and the pioneers are its subjects and entitled to protection. When the Indian possessions are reached, the Indians are in the way. They must move on. Civilization and progress are coming, and cannot be impeded in their course. Indians are not independent peoples, and their lands are not their own. The jurisdiction of the Government is over them and their territory, in spite of treaties and agreements. They must move on. This is Gen. Sherman's view. It is the view on which our Indian policy has all along been based, and it has led to continued misunderstanding and a settled sense of wrong and injustice on the part of the Indians. It can have no consummation but the final extermination of all the aboriginal tribes. Civilization must ultimately overrun and surround them, and gradually extinguish their existence as completely as it has that of the Mohawks and Senecas. Can there not be enough humanity injected into our statesmanship to give us an Indian policy that shall look to the preservation and protection of this race, instead of its destruction? It can only be by adopting a theory consistent with itself and understood on both sides, and acting upon it.

⤺ A Profitable Policy

January 18, 1880

The English are, as is well known, a dull, stupid people. This is conspicuously shown by their treatment of the Indians in the British territory north of the United States. When an Indian commits a crime, such as the shooting of a white man or the robbing of a trapper, the English authorities simply send a policeman to arrest the culprit. After he is caught he is duly tried, and if found guilty is punished, just as though he were a white, black, or yellow criminal. The want of statesmanship shown in this sort of proceeding is obvious. It leads to no Indian wars, and results in no confiscation of lands. An Indian belonging to a tribe occupying valuable mineral lands may commit a crime and be punished for it, but the lands will remain in the possession of the tribe. In fact, we cannot find a single instance in which the British Government has made a tribe of North American Indians give up eligible mining property on the ground that a single individual of the tribe has committed a crime.

Our practice is directly opposite to this. If we find that an Indian tribe owns lands which is [sic] valuable, either for mining or agricultural purposes, we first exasperate the Indians until some one of them misconducts himself, and we then promptly send troops to drive the tribe away and open their territory to white immigration. We never waste time by sending a Police force to arrest the culprit. This would give the Indians the erroneous impression that law and justice are not the exclusive property of white people. Once in a great while we ask the head men of the tribe to induce the guilty man to surrender himself and submit to hanging, but as the Indian murderer is as averse to hanging as is the white murderer, he declines to be persuaded to surrender, and we then inform the head men that we must have their land. We have pursued precisely this course with the Utes. A handful of Utes killed the Agent Meeker, and instead of capturing the guilty men, we inform the Chief Ouray, who had always been a friendly and peaceable man, that he must induce the murderers to come and be hanged. As he has been unable to do this, he is now informed that he and his tribe must give up their land— which is supposed to be full of valuable mines. Thus, the crime of half a dozen vicious savages is punished by confiscating the property of their innocent neighbors, and a new area of freedom and silver mines is thrown open to the white men.

The superiority of this method over that pursued by the dull Englishmen across the border is obvious. It is by this method that we gained possession of the Black Hill country. It is by this method that we have rid ourselves time and time again of the treaty obligations which would otherwise have compelled us to permit Indians to retain the ownership of valuable property. There is not the least doubt that our system of dealing with the Indians is the finest system the world ever saw, and the most profitable, so far as the interests of white men of mining proclivities are concerned.

There are, of course, a few sentimentalists who oppose our Indian policy and pretend to believe that the English system is a better one. Instead of listening to them we ought to extend our Indian policy to white communities. If we were to do this, the Indian Bureau, with the aid of the Army, could do the whole work now done by our policemen and courts, and could provide thousands of destitute people with lands and other property.

There is the community of Leadville, for example. The mines are monopolized by a set of people who have owned them quite long enough, to the exclusion of other people who would gladly take possession of them. Two or three weeks ago a Leadville man committed a murder. If Mr. Schurz were to demand of the leading citizens of Leadville that they should induce the murderer to surrender himself, they would undoubtedly reply that he declined to hold an interview with them and discuss the subject. It would then be in order to send troops to shoot the Leadville people and drive them out of the country, so that deserving men who want the mines could take possession of them. In due time another murder would probably be committed, and a new opportunity thus given for redistributing the Leadville mines.

Then there is the charming community of Huntington, Long Island. Some years ago a man was murdered in Huntington in a peculiarly atrocious way, but under our judicial system the murderers have never been punished. The Huntington farms are valuable, the village is beautifully situated, and there are thousands of destitute people in this City who would gladly live in the Huntington houses and cultivate the Huntington farms. Let Mr. Schurz demand the immediate surrender of the murderers of Kelsey, and when the local leading citizens reply that the murderers decline to surrender, let him send a regiment and drive the Huntingtonians into the pine barrens of the east end of the island. The destitute population of New-York will then rush in and occupy Huntington. Justice will be done, Kelsey will be avenged, and hungry New-Yorkers will suddenly find themselves in possession of nice houses and profitable farms.

What is justice in the case of Indians ought to be justice in the case of white men. If an Indian tribe is to be shot and its property confiscated for the crime of one of its members, a white community can be similarly held responsible and punished for individual crimes. By all means let us substitute the simple and profitable practice of the Indian Department for the clumsy courts and expensive Police of our white communities. Suppose we begin with Denver City. A good many crimes have been committed there, and the property owned in the city is valuable. "The Denver people must go." Let them choose between removing voluntarily to Alaska and undergoing extermination. Surely they cannot object to the application to themselves of the policy which they insist should be applied to the Utes.

⌇ Twelve Indians Wanted

January 24, 1880

There are about nine hundred Utes, men, women, and children, now gathered at the White River Agency. Of these, 475 are women and girls, and 425 are men and boys. They have been educated of late years, to consider that the United States Government is their Providence. It has been a somewhat uncertain Providence to them. Nevertheless, as the pagan infant said of his ragged and tattered doll, it is the best Providence they have. In other words, it has been the policy of the Government to pauperize the Indians. Just now, the Indian paupers are in a woeful predicament. Their Providence has shut off their supplies. The Government of the United States is bound, by certain solemn treaties, to feed and clothe the Utes. Each year it has been the custom to send them supplies and clothing. This has been somewhat fitfully done, to be sure, as the contractors have often failed, and various causes have conspired to make things very uncomfortable for the Utes. Nevertheless, having educated the Indians to consider that the Government was their better angel, so far as food, drink, and raiment are concerned, it has been suddenly resolved that they shall starve until they give up the twelve Indians who are concerned in the troubles of last Summer. We are not in the habit of keeping our agreements with Indians. It is a historical fact that the United States never kept one treaty which it has made with Indians. From the foundation of the Government until now, the white man has been the first to break the treaties made with the aborigines of the soil. We do not in this sweeping declaration include the oft-quoted compact between William Penn and the Indians. But no treaty between the Government of the United States and the Indians has ever been kept by the Government. By all means let us keep the treaty with the Utes, or, at least, so much of it as shall starve 475 women and children and 425 men and boys until the 12 wicked Indians have been surrendered. It is late in the day to begin observing treaties. But let us draw the line somewhere.

The Utes are used to being starved. In a moment of weakness we agreed to give them $25,000 per annum for the lands which they relinquished. This tidy sum was to be paid, according to the solemn treaty of 1873, "annually forever." Why should the noble white man keep his word with a miserable Indian? We have not paid the Utes their $25,000 "annually forever," or any portion of it. The excellent Hayt, when asked by the Senate why this is thus, ingenuously replied that he thought we might, some day, want the remainder of the land belonging to the Utes, and then it would be handy to have their annuity to make them comfortable elsewhere. To be sure, the treaty said that the $25,000 per year arising from their trust funds should be "invested or expended" for their benefit, and it has been neither invested nor expended. But this was only in a treaty with Indians. Why bother about the provisions of an Indian treaty? Then again, in the Autumn of 1877, just after the excellent Hayt came into office, the contractor charged with delivering supplies to the Utes failed utterly, and the provisions were left at Rawlins. According to the best available official information, that was an exceptionally severe year. Meteorologically speaking, snow fell in mid-summer, and the mountain ranges were impassable in September, so that the supplies could not be forwarded to the Indians. At least, this is the official explanation, and, as it is characteristic of official utterances that they are always unanswerable, we must believe that there was no way of feeding the Utes in September, 1877, after the contractor had failed. Therefore, as we have already remarked, the Utes are familiar with starvation. When they crossed the mountain ranges, later in the Winter, perishing with famine, and fed by white settlers along the line of the railroad, in search of the food which they had been taught to expect, but which had not been sent them, they were merely being familiarized to the process of starvation which is now being applied to them. And it is entirely in consonance with the intelligent and statesmanlike policy which we have adopted toward the American Indians that we should resort to the not unusual device of starving them into surrender. The only difficulty about the case is, as before hinted, that starvation is no novelty.

Going back to the original proposition, however, we see that the Utes are not approached as ordinary criminals. If there should be a murder committed in the Fourth Ward of this City, as many murders are, the Police Department should stop the bakers and butchers on the boundaries of that unsavory precinct, until the offender was found by the inhabitants and given up. If Jersey City should be the refuge of a fugitive criminal, the State of

New-Jersey should declare that municipality in quarantine, or in a state of siege, until the guilty man should be hunted out of the slums and surrendered. The great and mighty Government of the United States, with its Army, Navy, detectives, and police, goes to the borders of the Ute reservation, and makes solemn proclamation that all treaties are suspended, all supplies withheld, and all communication is cut off, until the twelve offenders are produced. It does not seem to have occurred to anybody that a powerful Government like ours ought to catch its own criminals. Chief Ouray, pushed to desperation, has agreed that, if he has time given him, he will kill the guilty men and bring in their heads. This is the pagan way of looking at the matter. But it is not more pagan than the United States Governmental manner of approaching the business. It cannot be said that the 475 women and children, fairly reckoned as non-combatants, now peaceably starving at the White River Agency, are responsible for the doings of the twelve bad Indians who cannot be found. Nevertheless, since we have adopted the novel expedient of compelling a community of innocent people to be their own Police force, we may as well make thorough work of it. Indians have no rights except when we want something of them. And, having got what we wanted by a juggling treaty, it is quite legitimate that we should dismiss them to the limbo of irresponsible and reprobate savages. We demand twelve guilty Indians of the Utes who are not guilty. It is treaty law that they give up these twelve. We have not kept the treaty heretofore. Let us begin by starving the helpless relatives of the wicked twelve.

◁ The Indian Severalty Law

May 27, 1887

A few weeks hence the Interior Department will begin to enforce a law whose enactment marked the adoption of a new policy concerning the Indians and the reservations which they occupy. Probably the importance of the Severalty act is not fully comprehended by a majority of the people. The principle which it embodies had been set forth with more or less clearness in bills which two or three Congresses failed to pass, and when at last the Forty-ninth Congress accepted it the measure received less attention from the public than it deserved. There are now upon the reservations about 260,000 Indians, and they occupy 135,000,000 acres of land, a very small part of which they use. The purpose of the law is to place these Indians (the members of the five so-called civilized tribes in the Indian Territory excepted) upon farms of reasonable size; to secure these farms to them in fee simple in such a way that they shall be unable to sell or give away the land until the expiration of a period of 25 years; to open the surplus lands to white settlers under the homestead laws and for the pecuniary benefit of the Indians, and to make every Indian who takes a farm so allotted in severalty a citizen of the United States.

The reservations in which the department will begin its work are small ones—the Devil's Lake reservation in Northern Dakota, the Lake Traverse in Eastern Dakota, and the Siletz, on the Pacific coast in Northern Oregon. It is reported that in these, as well as in thirteen other reservations, a majority of the occupants not only approve the allotment plan but are also anxious that the allotments shall be made without delay.

The execution of the law in certain small reservations where surveys have already been made will be followed by its enforcement in the great reservations, where millions of acres are now of no value to those who hold them, except so far as the leases procured by cattlemen yield small sums to the tribes. It is of great importance that at the beginning, as well as throughout the entire work of making allotments, the law shall be enforced with a scrupulous regard for the interests of the Indians, and that the Government's agents shall be honest and capable men. It is fortunate, therefore, that these agents are to be appointed by the President, who will doubtless pay special attention to their qualifications. The Government will permit representatives of the Indian Rights Association to be present when the allotments are made. This association warmly supports the law.

The department will be opposed either openly or secretly by the corporations which hold very profitable leases of the Indians' surplus lands and by an organization called the National Indian Defense Association of Washington. The leaseholders naturally are unwilling to be deprived of the use of millions of acres of grazing land for which they pay an annual rent of two or three cents per acre. They exert considerable influence among the Indians who receive the money. But these leases were made without authority of law, and they will all be swept away. The loss of the annual rent for their surplus lands will tend to convert the tribes to the support of a policy that will make these lands again a source of income. The National Indian Defense Association holds that the tribal organizations should not be broken up, but that the Indians should continue to hold their vast estates in their present condition. Its attitude is fairly shown by the expressed wish of its Vice-President, the Rev. Dr. Byron Sunderland, of Washington, "that a wall of adamant high as the stars and permanent as heaven might be erected around the Sioux Reservation," thus making a quiet and secluded wilderness out of a tract of 32,000,000 acres in Dakota. These opposing forces will not prevail.

Fortunately, the surplus land to be released can be taken by settlers only under the homestead laws. If the same restrictions could be enforced with reference to the lands released to settlement by the opening of the railroad indemnity belts there would be insured a more equitable distribution of those lands than can be made under the other laws which have been so extensively used by land grabbers.

ᓚ Our Indian Policy

December 2, 1890

The total absence of any allusion to the widespread Messiah delusion is a marked feature of the annual documents that deal with the Indian question. We may assume that the reports of Commissioner Morgan and Secretary Noble were made up before the current excitement broke out, and that the President has ignored it because they did, yet the existence of the delusion as a matter of importance was pointed out both by Indian Agents and army officers as long ago as last April, during the troubles at Tongue River. But if the Interior Department fails to give any information on this important point, it at least throws a side light upon some current causes of dissatisfaction among the red men, in saying of the Tongue River troubles in Montana that "the appropriations made by Congress have not heretofore been sufficient to furnish food enough to prevent hunger among the Indians." Precisely the same lack is now reported at Pine Ridge, in South Dakota, by Gen. Brooke, who telegraphed on Sunday: "The Indians here are suffering for food; I have nothing to give them." It is not to be wondered at if, in such circumstances, there are occasional depredations upon the cattle of the ranchmen. We find the further statement in the current report of the Secretary that upon learning that the census of the Sioux showed the number at Rosebud Agency to have been greatly overestimated, "action was immediately taken by the Indian Office to reduce the quantity of food for the delivery of which arrangements had been made." Whether the census was as little satisfactory to the red men as it seems to have been to many whites we cannot say; but if, as is now alleged, the astonishing mistake of 2,000 in excess of the real number had been formerly made at Rosebud Agency, errors in the other direction may conceivably have been made elsewhere, so giving some bands less food than they were entitled to.

The great work of the year has been the purchase of surplus Indian lands. Here again we are reminded of possible causes of dissatisfaction, apart from the religious frenzy, on learning that while the Sioux have given up millions of acres to the Government, the promises made to them a year ago have not yet been fulfilled, and Congress is now urged to make appropriations to fulfill them. The extent to which this eagerness for acquiring Indian lands has been carried is shown by the fact that during a period of twelve months about 13,000,000 acres, according to Secretary Noble, and since March 4, 1889, about 14,726,000 acres, according to the President, have been obtained. Within the limits, therefore, of a single year, fully one-ninth of all the lands held by Indians outside of Alaska have been purchased from them, and no fewer than eight commissions, at the latest report, were engaged in bargaining in various quarters for further purchases. It is lamentable that with such anxiety to get possession of these lands the stipulations made at the time of their purchase should not be faithfully and promptly carried out; but the red man long ago became accustomed to such treatment.

Taking this reduction of the reservations to be the central feature of the year's Indian policy, there is much to be said in its favor, although it need not be put upon the high moral plane to which some official comment assigns it. The Sioux Reservation was a barrier in the path of direct communication between the civilized communities east and west of it, and it was expedient to throw down a part of that barrier, if the red men would consent. The extension of the boundaries of Oklahoma may be defended on like practical grounds. Besides, the Indians of most tribes have more land than they need, since there is no longer much, if any, game on it, and they cultivate only small areas. We shall probably see still further inroads made upon Indian land possessions until allotment in severalty, which is the declared policy of the Government, becomes almost a matter of necessity. The change of policy in this respect wrought even among the best friends of the Indian during the last few years, has been most remarkable. It is not so long ago that the rigid separation of the red men from the whites was the foundation of our Indian system; and even the proposal to run a railroad across a reservation, with full compensation for land taken, was indignantly repelled. Now the aim is rather to give the red men more advantages of civilization, and to try to substitute for the tribal relations those of American citizenship. It is this change of views which has made possible such a record as that of the past year, and which is likely to continue to turn Indian real estate into funded money, to be used for the support and advancement of the tribes. But in all such bargains absolute good faith in the fulfillment of the minutest stipulations made by the Government should be observed.

ᔕ Gen. Miles on the Indians

December 29, 1890

We were deploring the other day the lack of any authoritative report upon the Indian question, which would enable people to understand what the Indian question at present really is. It makes a great difference to us whether the hostile feelings and actions of the Indians of the plains have merely been worked up by malicious Indians, and have proceeded from the natural course of events and the "cussedness" of the Indians, or whether they have been provoked by the action of our Government or of its agents. In the former case there is nothing to be done but to punish the Indians by military power for any hostile demonstration they may make. In the latter it is our business to redress the grievances for which we are responsible at the earliest moment, so as to leave the mutinous Indians with no excuse.

Fortunately, the want of an authoritative opinion has been supplied by a paper of Gen. Miles's in the current number of the *North American Review*. The paper is, of course, unofficial, but it comes much nearer to giving satisfactory answer to the questions that intelligent and conscientious Americans wish to put upon the subject than all the official reports to and of the Indian Bureau put together. There is no man in the country who is better qualified than Gen. Miles to treat the question, both by long and intimate acquaintance with the subject and by disinterestedness, which is, at least, equally important. He represents the army, and the army has never been suspected of responsibility for the Indian troubles, being merely called in to get the country out of scrapes that civilians may have got it into. Moreover, the officers of the army are more interested than any other men in the country, except the privates, in preventing Indian wars. These are wars in which every danger and every hardship are to be encountered, including dangers and hardships that do not occur in civilized warfare, and in which there is no promotion and no reputation to be got, not even the cheap compliment of a brevet. To be anxious for an Indian war an American soldier must necessarily be an extraordinary fool.

For these reasons nobody is so well entitled to talk about the Indian question as an experienced officer, or to analyze the causes of any particular Indian trouble. What would satisfy the Indians is a sheer impossibility, for it is nothing less than that civilization shall stop short of the border of the Indian country, or at least shall enter there only for the purpose of providing the Indians with modern firearms. The Indian in his savage condition, it is to be noted, takes up a great deal of room. If the buffalo had not been exterminated, the whole region between the Missouri and the Rocky Mountains and the Canadian border and the Rio Grande, which Gen. Miles defines as the scene of the existing trouble, would not be too large to maintain the Indians who are left, living by hunting, whereas it is capable of supporting a hundred times as many whites following the pursuits of civilized life. We simply cannot leave to them such a reservation or any adequate reservation. If the Government were to attempt to secure to them a territory in which they could still live by the chase, it could not succeed if an army ten times as large as our own were employed for that purpose alone. The game is gone and the land is needed. That is the ultimate Indian grievance, and it is that which, as Gen. Miles explains, the "Messiah" is expected to redress, by driving out the white man and bringing back the buffalo.

This is the Indian dream, but the more intelligent Indians know that it is incapable of realization. They know that they must become "agency Indians," one of whom Sitting Bull emphatically declined to be. In return for their land, which we can put to better use than they, and for the game we have exterminated, we owe them a living, which they must take upon our conditions, but we owe them a living all the same. The question is whether we have given them a living, and to this question Gen. Miles returns an emphatic negative. The fact that the Cheyennes "have not received sufficient food is admitted by the agents and the officers of the Government who have had opportunities of knowing." The Sioux "claim that they have suffered for want of food, and the evidence of this is beyond question and sufficient to satisfy any unprejudiced, intelligent mind." Gen. Miles disclaims any intention of reflecting upon the integrity of anybody concerned, but that some of the tribes have been starved into revolt he holds to be perfectly clear. Of course somebody is to blame, and it is the business of Congress, since the Interior Department does nothing with regard to it, to find out who that somebody is. It is a still more urgent duty for Congress to make sure at once that the Indians whom we have undertaken to support are supported, and that we do not bring upon ourselves the national disgrace of starving our dependents into rebellion and then killing them for rebelling.

⌒ The Reservation System

October 19, 1891

The ground taken by Commissioner Morgan's annual report in favor of further reducing the Indian reservations, with a view to their ultimate disappearance and the absorption of the red men into the general body of American citizens, is not novel. His immediate predecessors looked forward to the same result as inevitable and desirable. It falls in, of course, with the eagerness of settlers to procure a share of the lands now set apart. But this policy furnishes a broad contrast with the earlier one of the Indian Bureau, which was directed to making the barriers around these "wards of the Nation" as high and strong as possible. It is not many years ago, for example, that even the crossing of an Indian reservation by a railroad track, which must otherwise, at great expense and loss of time to travelers take a circuitous route, was bitterly and successfully opposed. Now the Indian Bureau often approves such railway transits, when the tribe is satisfied and properly remunerated. Railway travel over such lands has proved as safe as elsewhere, and sometimes Indians have earned an honest living by hauling or otherwise laboring for the road. We find a like change in the views of societies and of individuals specially devoted to the welfare of the red men, some of whom demand the abolition of the reservation system as pernicious in principle and result.

Yet this system was established from the best motives, and in fact was an absolute necessity and still is so. It will gradually be superseded by a better system, whenever the Indians are fitted for it, but both for them and the white settlers it was at one time essential. Pioneers went to the West because the aborigines were restrained within fixed bounds under the guardianship of troops; while the Indians themselves could only be assured in that way of protection against greedy whites. Some of the latter may still hold that the red men have no rights which they are bound to respect, and are fair targets if found outside of their limits. Reservations have, in fact, sometimes been over-run by armed prospectors in search of gold, and the Indians driven from the homes pledged to them. Save for this system, enforced in the main, there would have been more Indian hostilities, if not almost an extermination of the race.

However, the Severalty Allotment act passed by Congress four years ago was the result of a growing conviction that tribal allegiance must be destroyed, tribal organizations broken up, and lands no longer held in common. What Commissioner Morgan advocates is outlined in that law, from the operation of which, nevertheless, the more advanced tribes of the Indian Territory and some others are expressly exempted. Still, the effort has been to secure the voluntary adhesion of the Indians to severalty allotment, so that it has naturally moved on slowly, and has thus far been applied to only a small fraction of them. But it is going on quite fast enough in proportion to the rest of our Indian work; and, in fact, it is well to avoid the notion that reducing the reservations is the panacea for all Indian troubles. Severalty allotment is premature until the band to which it is applied is fitted to profit by it. If tribal allegiance is taken away, a better substitute should be ready. During the last few years there must have been something like 20,000,000 acres acquired from the Indians by purchase. They probably still have five times that amount left, and could sell the larger part of it without being crowded for room. But education in the ways of civilized life becomes the more imperative with severalty allotments. The wise provision of the law prevents the alienation of these lands for twenty-five years, else greedy settlers might get a large part of them.

Most Indians who have come to middle life or old age can hardly be expected to change their habits so as to support themselves by farming their lands or to give up all tribal relations. Besides, as Secretary Lamar once pointed out, the Indian race is not altogether homogeneous, and the policy suited to one tribe may be premature and disastrous for another. Allotments suppose ability to farm them, and many Indians are unable to get a living by tilling the ground, although they might do better by the grazing of cattle and horses. Even whites, in many regions of the West, cannot farm to advantage without combining in costly schemes of irrigation, such as only the Government could arrange for the Indians. We could conceive, however, if tribal relations are broken up, of the substitution of small communities, each with its self-supporting appliances, its store for food and clothing, its shops for blacksmithing and carpentry, and its Government sub-agency for supplies. The Indians will long have to continue thus grouped, and be cared for by Government agents, although the abolition of reservations implies that they will be as free to come and go as whites. But, no doubt, the process of acquiring surplus Indian lands will be pursued from year to year, and wisely enough if they are paid for promptly and liberally, and if efforts are proportionally increased to make the Indians fit for citizenship whenever and wherever the reservation barriers are thrown down.

◄ Promoted Indian Pauperism

November 15, 1900

A revival of interest in the Indian problem is provoked by the report of William A. Jones, the United States Commissioner of Indian Affairs. It is altogether too common for occupants of that office to dwell upon the substantial advancement toward civilization of our Indian wards and to be fertile in suggestion of new and expensive methods of material relief. Commissioner Jones's annual report is therefore novel in presenting some discouraging features of our Indian policy, and in the recommendation that it shall be modified so as to cut off the supplies of rations that encourage a condition of pauperism, and the annuities that are largely helpful only to make the Indians who receive them more vicious and idle than they would be without them.

For many years there has been controversy as to whether the Indians are decreasing or increasing in number. As long ago as when Jefferson wrote his "Notes," and when the population of Indians was a mere matter of conjecture by a few explorers, there was an impression that in spite of war, pestilence, and famine the Indian population had increased since America was discovered by Columbus. In recent times the population has been ascertained or estimated at from 400,000 down to 230,000. The Indian population according to the census of 1890 was 248,000. It was 249,000 in 1893. Commissioner Jones now reports it to be 267,000.

None of these reports by persons authorized to ascertain the Indian population is set forth as accurate, and the presumption is that the population exceeds the highest reports. But whether they are in excess of 267,000 or less than so many in number, there is no doubt that the Government is daily issuing rations of food, and frequently giving supplies of clothing and blankets and other goods, to some 57,000 Indians. This has long appeared to some students of our policy as calculated inevitably to promote and perpetuate a condition of dependence that must defeat any attempt to make the Indian a self-respecting, because self-supporting, person. The tendency has been admitted in the effort to reduce the rations in variety and quantity, and Commissioner Jones gratifies our reason if not our sympathy when he urges the immediate stoppage of the indiscriminate issue of food. The old, the disabled, the helpless, may be supported gratuitously; all others should be required to work for what they receive, and those who have been educated in Indian schools should be required to depend entirely upon their own resources.

The annuities are another obstacle to Indian civilization. They were paid to the amount of $1,507,543 last year, in amounts varying from $255 to 50 cents per Indian. Commissioner Jones says that the larger the annuity the greater the resulting demoralization. Instead of helping the Indian up, as intended and expected, the annuities are degrading the Indians who receive them and corrupting the whites who help them to spend them. "They nullify the good effects of years of labor." They are the cause of increasing Indian pauperism, and they cause a condition described by Commissioner Jones as "a scandal and a disgrace."

With the Indian population increasing, and Indian pauperism thus promoted, the outlook is alarming enough to justify all true friends of the Indian and all patriots who have common sense, to expect early reformation of a policy that is manifestly wrong. To abolish the issue of rations to the able-bodied may surely be brought about without much delay. To get rid of the annuities will take time. It is suggested by the Commissioner that these annuities may be gradually extinguished by the maintenance of schools and at the end of twenty-one years, by a per capita distribution; or that the lands belonging to the tribes be distributed to the Indians per capita. Either plan will be distasteful to the Indian. The adoption of the last one would bring him suddenly to the alternative of work or starvation. As we are responsible for having brought the Indian to his present condition, any plan of reformation that is to be adopted ought to be tempered with mercy and persisted in with firmness and common sense.

4 The Chiefs

Now that Chinamen have become common and Japanese have lost the charm of novelty with our citizens, it is hardly to be expected that a company of red men should excite any unusual interest by their appearance in our streets. And yet the Indians who reached here a day or two since are powerful Chiefs, whose names until lately have been a terror to the borderers of the North-west. We may smile at such names as Red Cloud, Red Dog, Blue Horn and Slow Bull, but in the Northwest their names recall a long series of bloody massacres, and they are mentioned with hatred and dread.

—*New York Times*
June 6, 1872

AMONG ALL THE TOPICS covered in nearly a half-century's accumulation of *Times* editorials on the Indian problem, none stands out more boldly than that of Indian chiefs. *Times* editors never appeared to lose interest in the Native Americans; when it came to the Native American chiefs, they were unequivocally fascinated. Through their news and editorial columns, they made household words of the names of such Indian leaders as Red Cloud, Sitting Bull, Geronimo, Captain Jack, Satanta, and Joseph. The editorial-page treatment of the chiefs demonstrates as clearly as any other measure the difficulties the Indian problem presented for *Times* editorial writers. Variously, the chiefs received their most scathing and venomous condemnation and their most exalted acclaim.

While the *Times* denounced the government's policies of treating the Indian tribes as sovereignties and holding whole tribes culpable for the actions of individuals, it readily accepted the fact that Indians followed the lead of their respective chiefs. In other words, it held chiefs accountable. If a large tribe went to war, the *Times* was inclined to blame its chief. If a small band of Indians performed heroically, the *Times* was likely to bestow editorial praise upon the band's leader.

In retrospect, it seems probable that images of the chiefs portrayed through the editorial columns of the *Times* were very close to the images held by most people at the time—images that remain vivid today. Yet the images that emerge from the pages of the *Times* go well beyond mere stereotypes; each chief seems to have been perceived in his own right, according to his own behavior. If there is a destructive flaw in the editorial writers' perceptions and portrayals of the chiefs, it is in the fact that once a chief's character was cast, variation never again seemed to be an option. Once a Sitting Bull was ranked as evil, he was to be evil forever.

Easterners began to get their first look at the great chiefs of the Western plains in the early post-Civil War period. Peace initiatives toward the Indians in the administration of President Ulysses S. Grant brought various chiefs to Washington, where their views were heard and their positions duly reported by the *Times* and other Eastern papers. In part to impress upon them the size and might of the nation, the government helped arrange visits by the chiefs to New York and other cities as well as to the capital.

Certain chiefs already had impressed the *Times* editorial writers with their abilities as orators. As *Times* correspondents had duly reported on the successes and failures of various peace councils, the chiefs' rhetoric came in for serious attention. These reports appeared in the news columns and generated highly positive reviews in the editorial columns.

Yet the *Times* writers appear not to have been fully prepared for the impact Red Cloud had on residents of New York during a visit in June 1870. Despite their own prior acclaim for the speaking abilities of the chiefs, they must have been astonished by what they saw and heard that day. The *Times* editorial on the chief's extraordinary speech at the Cooper Institute, "The Last Appeal of Red Cloud," is one of those included in this chapter. It was to be expected that when the chiefs visited Washington and New York they would attract a great deal of notice. The visiting chief accepted impassively "the homage of the small boy who congregates in great force near his hotel doors, and accompanies him with noisy demonstrations whenever he appears in the streets," the *Times* reported in a June 1872 editorial. Further, he "conducts himself in public like a well-bred gentleman, and . . . the impression which he produces upon the general public is decidedly favorable." The celebrated impassivity of the chiefs was in some measure responsible for the misconceptions about Indian character, the *Times* said. This was not a compliment, for the character referred to was that of the murderous savage whose conduct in the wilds was precisely opposite that of his "quiet good-behavior in the drawing-room or in the street."

The *Times* liked to contrast its view of Indians with that portrayed in the popular novels of James Fenimore Cooper. Cooper, it contended, romanticized the Indians and had given the American public a distorted picture. The *Times* seemed determined to define Indians—and particularly their chiefs—in terms of actual rather than romanticized behavior. Actual behavior frequently was violent and destructive. Chiefs who led their tribes in bloody wars, unless the justness of their cause was remarkably clear, would gain little praise in the editorial columns of the *Times*. This was the light in which Sitting Bull and Geronimo would be permanently cast.

The demonizing of Sitting Bull went beyond the usual standards of the *Times*. At the same time, however, the celebrated Sioux chief generated some of the most colorful comment to grace the editorial columns of the *Times* during all the decades in which the Indian problem was a matter of consuming interest. When Sitting Bull returned to the United States after a period of self-imposed exile in Canada, the *Times* made clear its displeasure. It had been a great relief to most Americans that the chief had determined to stay north of the border, noted a January 1879 editorial. "The news that this prodigal son has returned will not only be unwelcome to his elder brother, but also to his Great Father in Washington," it said. This particular prodigal had killed the fatted calf before he went away, the editorial continued, and it was unlikely there would be any merrymaking on his return.

On many occasions, Sitting Bull's treatment by the *Times* was ugly and vicious. Following reports that he was converting to Catholicism, the *Times* commented that the chief's bigamy promised to upset the plan. "Unless he gets drunk and scalps one of them before the time of his baptism arrives," said a short editorial-page paragraph in late 1883, "the church will be compelled to doubt the reality of the sentiments he professes." But it said he still might "combine bigamy and free rations" by moving to Utah and offering himself to the Church of the Latter Day Saints as a Mormon missionary.

While the *Times* feared the influence of "bad" chiefs such as Sitting Bull, it put great stock in the abilities of "good" ones. An example of the latter was Ouray, an important Ute chief. In a brief editorial in the summer of 1880, the *Times* lamented Ouray's death—not as a matter of individual loss, but because of his role in negotiations for a peaceful transfer of the tribe from Colorado to another reservation. "Nothing but the great personal influence of Ouray with his people" could have secured the tribe's consent to the agreement, the *Times* believed.

Geronimo, while enjoying precious little positive press on the part of the *Times*, at least escaped much of the viciousness with which the editorial-page writers treated Sitting Bull. One reason may have been that the Apache chief was only in the news for a short time compared to the durable Sioux. In the spring of 1885, a long editorial on Geronimo and his band of Chiricahua Apaches stated that their return to the warpath seemed to have been caused by nothing more than restlessness and an inherent depravity. Although it had been two years since the ruthless band's last rampage, the editorial said, "This Spring found them weary of a peaceful life, and in a day they were transformed from farmers into bloodthirsty and pitiless assassins." In another editorial a few days later, the *Times* declared that "Geronimo and his bucks are no better than wild beasts." It said kindness was wasted on such "inhuman and bloodthirsty wretches" and added, "The blood of the murdered settler will cry from the ground, and the cry will be heard."

While the *Times* editorial writers reserved their strongest language for Sitting Bull and Geronimo, they were no less forceful in their comment about chiefs for whom they expressed respect and admiration. The *Times* was generous in its treatment of chiefs it considered to be honorable men devoted to the good of their tribes.

The editorials that follow include some of the most powerful statements the *Times* made on the Indian problem. Those critical of "bad Indians" are most prominent. At the same time, few individuals—Indian or white—were the subject of more respectful editorial comment than Chief Joseph. Examples of that also are included in this chapter.

↩ The Red Man Eloquent

November 9, 1867

Whatever may be the result of the councils and treaties just concluded between the big chiefs of the red and white races on the Western Plains, they have furnished some unsurpassed contributions to our small stock of original Indian eloquence.

During the progress of the negotiations with the various wild tribes of the prairies, our correspondents on the spot have kept our readers very fully apprized of what was going on, and have also reported for us the speeches of the warrior chiefs, as they fell from their lips or were translated through the mouth of the interpreter.

Those who have given themselves the pleasure of reading these accounts and reports have obtained a better idea of the wild life and feelings of the untutored savage as he now exists and roams upon the Great Plains, and of the modes of thought, forms of expression, and style of oratory that belong to such natives as the "simple great Man," that one of them claimed to be, than they could obtain in any other way except as participants or observers at the councils themselves.

On this occasion the Indian has done justice to his traditionary fame for eloquence. The characteristics of Indian oratory have been the subject of no little criticism. It has been frequently dissected by the most skillful critics, and even our greatest scholars and orators, like Jefferson and Webster, have not disdained to study and analyze its nature, and to point out and illustrate its features of force and beauty. The pathetic speech of Logan ("who mourns for Logan?") was for a long time our finest specimen of it, but since Logan's day we have had many other examples no less distinguished for natural beauty and simplicity of figure, for strength and terseness of statement, for delicacy, for pathos and sentimentality, for the concord of sweet sounds, and for effectiveness. Nothing could well differ more than these speeches in external form and architectural design from the oratorical masterpieces of the race to which we belong; and yet, in one as in the other, we discern certain broad laws of thought and effect which appear and work themselves out, consciously or unconsciously, as other laws of the universal humanity work themselves out, with approximate similarity, in other departments of intellect and action. The studied, logical and tremendous eloquence of Demosthenes—the vigor, ornateness, incisiveness and skill of inversion displayed in the orations of Cicero—the monumental orations of our familiar, though none the less great modern names, from Burke to Webster—do all, assuredly, differ as widely from any existing specimen of savage eloquence as the architectural piles of Athens, London or New-York differ from the groups of Indian tents in which the red man spends his life; and if, after these immortal memories, we mention the grotesque names of Big Mouth, Red Cloud, Poor Bear or Satanta, an irrepressible smile necessarily follows. And yet we need not explore the Infinite half as far as some of the German philosophers have done, to discover that intrinsically there are points of intellectual and rhetorical resemblance which can be traced much further than those may imagine who have never troubled themselves with a thought about the matter. But we neither propose to follow them out nor to make any extended analysis of the general, special, or distinctive characteristics of Indian eloquence, as recently displayed.

It must be remembered that the orators at the recent councils belonged to the real wild Indians of the Plains—not individuals of such tribes as have been brought under the influences of civilization and education, and whose mental habits and ideas have received their basis in the knowledge of the white man—but chiefs of the prairie and the tent, of the tomahawk and the scalp-lock, of the whoop and the charge, of the breech-clout and war-paint, of the buffalo and antelope, of nature and native power, of the Great Spirit and immemorial traditions. They assembled from far distances at appointed places on the Plains to hold council with the representatives of the white man as to his interests and theirs. Not a few of them were right from the war-path—from bloody fights with enemies of our color and of their own; and among the things to be discussed were some means of stopping the war which has been waged for three years, or rather for three centuries, and at the same time reconciling their natural rights with our imperative necessities. The purpose was a great one, and the stake was great, involving the possession of an empire and the destiny of two peoples; and the Indian approached the subject with a dignity and a majestic reserve becoming its importance and also natural to himself. Each of the speakers at all of the councils put forth the Indian claims in a way essentially similar to the others, generally basing them simply on nature and justice; but at the same time every one of them had arguments and illustrations of his own, which frequently showed remarkable powers of reason and imagination.

Probably the most striking of all the brief speeches delivered was that of the chief Big Mouth; but, on the whole, Satanta, the old warrior chief of the Kiowas, must get the palm for varied, frequent and graphic displays of oratory. Satanta, as our correspondent who reported his speeches has mentioned, has no equal on the Plains in cunning or native diplomacy, while in boldness, daring and merciless cruelty he is far beyond Red Cloud, who is his rival in influence. He first distinguished himself, to our knowledge, for eloquence, in May last, when he confronted Gen. Hancock and the other leaders of a hostile expedition at Fort Larned, and in a fiery speech, denounced those who were heaping wrongs upon his race. This speech was a striking effort, from its opening, in which he proclaimed, by the heavens and the earth, that he would "talk straight," till its close, in which, looking round upon the prairie, he pronounced it, as well as the heavens above, large and good, and declared he did not want the earth stained by the blood of war. Another speech of Satanta was delivered at the grand council which opened on the morning of the 19th of October, and at which 400 chiefs were assembled. He alluded feelingly to his desire for peace and freedom, and asked earnestly to be permitted to lead such a life as he had been accustomed to from his youth. "I don't want to settle. I love to roam over the prairies. I feel free and happy; but when we settle down we grow pale and die." The latest of his speeches was the farewell speech he delivered at the conclusion of the treaty of peace with our Commissioners on the 24th ult. On this occasion the old chief was accompanied by one hundred of the principal warriors of the Kiowa tribe; and immediately after its close, this tribe, as well as the Comanches, struck camp and left for the Cimmarone River in the South. He spoke with a gravity and earnestness that added force to his words. "If," said he, "the treaty bring prosperity to us, we of course will like it the better. If it bring prosperity or adversity, we will not abandon it." He alluded delicately to the fact that the white man often forgot to keep his treaties with the Indian; and then at the close, referring to the treaty just made, he rose to the heights of friendship, offering his heart and his hospitality, and adding: "For your sakes, the green grass shall not be stained with the blood of the whites. Your people shall again be our people, and peace shall be our mutual heritage. Good-bye! You may not see me again. But remember Satanta as the white man's friend." He is spoken of as having a very grave yet musical voice, and at times displays the deepest emotion. On the occasion of one of these speeches, our correspondent says that when he graphically pictured how he loved his land, his free life and his traditions, there was a world of feeling in his tones, betraying his knowledge of the vast difference between the power of the aggressive pale face and his wandering race. A certain dim foreboding of the Indians' fate swept across his mind, and in its passage lit his eyes up with a fierce light, and his voice rose to a pitch of frenzy as he exclaimed: "We don't want to settle—I love to roam over the prairie; there I am free and happy."

The Appeal of the Red Man

June 8, 1870

We might search in vain through a month's file of the Congressional *Globe* for a speech so interesting as that delivered by Red Cloud at the Indian Council yesterday. The Chief comes to the point without any periphrasis, and states his grievances without ambiguity. "Whose voice was first heard in this land?" is a question wrung from the depths of a nature more finely touched than we are apt to ascribe to the red man. "Our nation is melting away like the snow on the side of the hills when the sun is warm," bespeaks the mournful presage of coming doom. "Tell the Great Father to remove Fort Fetterman," is the Chief's mode of redressing what he believes to be a great wrong, and is as concisely stated as his demands to keep "Black Hill" and "Big Horn" free from the invasion of the railroads, and to remove the stakes that have already been driven into the ground. The Chief firmly rejects the proposed reservation on the Missouri, since he has learned by experience that his children and old men die there like sheep. With a certain quiet dignity he refers to the man—Gen. Mitchell—who, eighteen years ago, dealt truthfully with him, intimating at the same time his conviction that various subsequent transactions have scarcely deserved a similar compliment.

A plain and dispassionate statement of the Indian view of the standing problem between barbarism and civilization, is precisely what most people required, and it is what this oration of Red Cloud, endorsed as it was by his companions, affords. It is not a little startling to hear the bold reminder of the Chief, "You are the people who should keep peace," and one-sided as it is, there is in it much matter for reflection. The clear conception which this unlettered savage possesses of what he claims as his rights, and what he is disposed to resent in his wrongs, shows very plainly the necessity for treating with the leader of the aboriginal "nations" on some straightforward and intelligible principle. The attempt to cajole and bamboozle them, as if they were deficient in intelligence, ought to be abandoned, no less than the policy of hunting them down like wild beasts. Whatever may be the theories we hold about the ultimate future of a decaying race, we cannot fail to recognize the wisdom of meeting Red Cloud and his people in a spirit of frankness and firmness. In this respect we need not be above learning a lesson, even from the savage.

↫ The Last Appeal of Red Cloud

June 17, 1870

Yesterday the races immediately interested in the solution of the "Indian problem" were brought face to face. It was an occasion which will long be remembered by those who were spectators of it—an occasion invested with a strange, memorable, and even pathetic interest. The descendants of the first occupants of our soil came from their wildernesses into the very heart of our greatest City. Men who have been used to solitude and a life of wild adventure and excitement, suddenly appeared upon the platform of Cooper Institute—a most inappropriate looking place—to implore simple justice on behalf of a vanishing race. A few years more, and the great Chiefs who yesterday were before the New-York public will also have melted away, like "snow upon the hill-side." Their attempts to tell their own story to the white men, instead of allowing it to pass through all sorts of corrupt and adverse channels, will hereafter rank conspicuously among the historical events connected with the Indian race.

No one who listened to Red Cloud's remarkable speech yesterday can doubt that he is a man of very great talents. It is almost wonderful that he could make a speech at all under the circumstances. The hall—or huge cellar—was densely crowded, and the heat was almost intolerable. It was easy to fancy how the Indians must have sighed for a breath of fresh air from the prairies. It is always a trying thing for a man not given to much talking to be called upon to address an immense audience. It must have been doubly trying to Red Cloud, for everything relating to civilization—except lying and cheating—is new to him. He has spent his life in fighting the battles of his people, and one day he is transplanted to Cooper Institute and asked to put on a clean shirt, a new waistcoat, a high-crowned hat, and then make a speech. Among all the vicissitudes of his life this must be the most startling, and, perhaps, not the most agreeable.

Although the audience labored under the disadvantage of not knowing what Red Cloud said, until his words were filtered through an interpreter—and no doubt greatly weakened in the process—still his earnest manner, his impassioned gestures, the eloquence of his hands, and the magnetism which he evidently exercises over an audience, produced a vast effect on the dense throng which listened to him yesterday. His speech was like a poem. When we consider that education and civilization have done nothing for him, except to teach him, in the words of the Psalmist, that "all men are liars"—and that he was placed yesterday in a situation which must have been most embarrassing, and possibly distressing to him, it is impossible to refrain from being much moved by his appeals. "You have children, and so have we. We want to rear our children well, and ask you to help us in doing so." It seems to us that this is not an unreasonable request, even though it does come from a "savage."

The solemnity of Red Cloud's manner, an impressive way which he has of throwing both his arms upwards when referring to the "Great Spirit," and the intense pathos which he threw into his tones at many parts of his speech, thoroughly enlisted the sympathies of the audience in his favor. Everybody could understand the thrilling power which a speech from this man would carry with it when addressed to his own tribe, on a question in which they were all deeply interested. Less severe in his manner, but equally effective in another way, was Red Dog, the orator of the Sioux. He appears to be the wag of the tribe. Red Cloud is a man of war, and looks like it; but Red Dog has a fine intellectual face, and a somewhat portly figure. He said: "When the Great Father first sent out men to our people, I was poor and thin; now I am large and stout and fat. It is because so many liars have been sent out there, and I have been stuffed full with their lies." Many persons on the platform were astonished to find that an "illiterate barbarian" could handle the weapon of sarcasm. The truth is that the Indians spoke far better than ninety-nine out of a hundred members of Congress, and as for their "action," it would have satisfied Demosthenes himself.

And now what is to be the result of all this? People have stared at Red Cloud in his "stove-pipe" hat—and a more monstrous incongruity in costume we admit we never beheld; they have flocked in thousands to hear him speak, and most of them admit that there is a great deal of truth in all that he says. Is he, then, to secure the redress he asks for? Of course there are bad Indians—we have even heard of bad white men for that matter. But as Red Cloud truly said yesterday, the whole Indian race has to bear the punishment for the crimes committed by the Indians on the frontiers, who have been corrupted and demoralized by our whisky. All that Red Cloud asks for on behalf of his people is this—have just men sent out to them as agents, and let them be protected on their reservations. They only beg that they may not be deceived, plundered, and betrayed. Is that so preposterous a demand that we ought not to comply with it? We have broken faith with the Indians on many occasions, and then declared that a war of extermination was the only thing to bring them to their senses. When the people yesterday, at the invitation of Dr. Crosby, proclaimed their disapproval of this policy, and their opinion was translated to Red Cloud, the chief rose with much emotion, shook hands with Dr. Crosby, and bowed to the audience. He has, perhaps, not knowing our civilized ways, and consequently not being aware that our pledges sometimes mean nothing, overestimated the importance of the promises made to him yesterday. He is not aware that there are many men of the Spotted Tail order eastward of the prairies. But still we cannot help hoping that this visit of the Indians will achieve some good. It ought at least to set people inquiring whether or not we have been guided by a sense of justice in our treatment of the Indians—and the more they inquire (especially if they go into certain army reports relating to Indian massacres) the more foundation they will discover for the belief that poor Red Cloud's complaints and appeals have been provoked by long and bitter ill-usage. We have long been doing justice to the negro. Is it not almost time to see what we can do for the Indian?

A Sioux Hero

August 6, 1871

The American savage, it is to be feared, has wofully degenerated from the attractive ideal of aboriginal romance. If Uncas were suddenly brought back from the happy hunting grounds to the wigwams of his people on the Plains, the condition of things would scarcely edify or please him. He would find the noble red man rather dirty and degraded, much given to fire-water and petty pilfering, and altogether an adept in various vices that would move his deepest scorn. Perhaps Uncas himself, indeed, was very little better before he fell into the hands of the novelist. Yet every now and then, some descendant of this doomed and outcast race gives us a flash of such real nobleness of spirit as makes Cooper's myths seem almost possible. The death of the Santee-Sioux Chief, Standing Buffalo, as described by the Indian Agent at Milk River, smacks of antique heroism. He had made a treaty with the pale-faces that he would not go to war. A band of the Yancton Sioux, on the war path against the Assiniboines, besought the aid of his prowess. They begged him to be their leader, but Standing Buffalo felt bound by his pledge and refused. Then they reviled him and flung at him the cruelest taunt that can be given a savage. They called him a coward, and he yielded. He consented to join them in order to wipe out the insult, but avowed his intention to do it by his death. So having called the head men of his tribe together he gave them wise counsel to keep at peace with the pale faces, and then, like the Roman Consul, went forth to die for a principle. Meeting a much larger body of the rival tribe, he plunged at once into their midst singing his death song, and not deigning to fire a shot himself, fell almost instantly riddled with bullets.

There is something very touching in such devotion, whether it be exhibited by a savage or a civilized hero. Abstractly speaking, of course, Standing Buffalo did a rash and foolish thing in yielding his better judgment to a meaningless insult. But, according to his wide standard of right and wrong, he showed a degree of magnanimity and unselfishness which few white men, so placed, would have equalled. Uncas, himself, we may be sure, will not disdain to welcome him to the happy hunter's ground, where Sioux and Assiniboine hunt together in peace, and the meddling pale-face can never intrude. Let us hope that the worthy chieftain's countrymen will emulate his fidelity, without his suicidal courage.

A people capable of such individual acts of highmindedness cannot be wholly irredeemable. And, although we may not at once persuade them to turn their scalping-knives into pruning-hooks, and their tomahawks into ploughshares, judicious treatment may at least avert those weapons from ourselves.

⇆ [Untitled]

October 5, 1873

After a long delay the dreary Modoc story has come to a fitting close in the execution of Capt. Jack and three of his chiefs, who were most directly concerned in the murder of Gen. Canby. It was not the purpose of the tragedy enacted at Fort Klamath, on Friday, to avenge Gen. Canby, and harm instead of good will follow from the executions if this idea is allowed to become lodged in the minds of the Indians. They should be made to understand that the Government was not exacting retribution but vindicating the law. They will thus understand that Capt. Jack was an assassin not a warrior, and with this knowledge they will acquire a true idea of the relations they occupy to the Government. Permanent peace cannot be secured between the whites and Indians until both are shown that they cannot commit murder and call it war. The execution of Capt. Jack has put one side of the case beyond dispute, but we must not expect this deserved punishment to have its full effect until white outlaws are treated with equal severity. If the miscreants who murdered the Modoc prisoners had been caught and hung on the same gallows with Capt. Jack, the purpose of the Government would have been comprehended by both races, and there would have been less chance of outrages by either. In future dealings with both, care must be taken to punish all crimes of violence with equal severity.

⌑ The Apotheosis of Capt. Jack

October 23, 1874

One might suppose that Capt. Jack, the Modoc brave, being hanged, dead, and buried, would no more disturb the earth. But his apotheosis vexed a Boston audience last Sunday night. The occasion was a meeting for the discussion of ways and means for the improvement of the condition of the Indian. A clerical gentleman, locally known as Father Gleason, eulogized Capt. Jack, and defended his shooting of Gen. Canby and Commissioner Thomas. Col. Meacham, who was one of the Commissioners in that tragical affair, and was severely wounded, happened to be present when the reverend eulogist advanced this ultra humanitarian view of the doings of Capt. Jack. He stood up and said that he took no part in any such verdict, and declared that the assassination of Canby and Thomas was a dastardly outrage. To this Father Gleason replied that he had read in the papers that Col. Meacham was a political adventurer, and that if he had offered to Capt. Jack the terms the President had desired, Gen. Canby and Commissioner Thomas would not have been shot. To this curious argument Col. Meacham made no rejoinder. Probably he thought that the charge of being a "political adventurer" had no possible connection with the argument. Confusion reigned in the assembly, and the perturbed spirit of Capt. Jack, probably pleased with the disturbance which he had created in the white man's meeting, subsided once more.

The reappearance of this turbulent ragamuffin is, however, a good example of the persistence of what we call the Indian question. It will not down. In this case some well-meaning, but misguided people, of whom Father Gleason is a type, were anxious to testify to their belief in Capt. Jack as a martyr, and in the abstract Indian as a deeply-injured being. Indeed, we are not sure but that Col. Meacham, who entertains what may be considered advanced views upon this subject, was present at the Boston meeting for the purpose of giving countenance to the proceedings as a friend of humanity. The enthusiastic defense of Capt. Jack was too much for his sense of justice, however, and he bolted from the conclave. To the complexion of Father Gleason and his following, all sentimentalists who deal with the Indian question must come at last. They will not abide with Gen. Sherman's opinion that it is better to feed the red men than to fight them; they insist upon coddling him, and treating with him as if he had ten centuries of civilization behind him, instead of the meagre results of a very doubtful experiment in that direction. It is true that some appeal may be made to the Indian's reason and knowledge of right and wrong; but behind that appeal must always be kept in plain sight the military power of the United States Government. If the Modoc war taught us anything, it taught us this. Capt. Jack is in his grave; the Modoc war is done; let the woful blunders of that tragical chapter of history sleep with him. We are learning as the Indian melts away. Even Capt. Jack's apotheosis can teach us no more.

⌐ Satanta

November 5, 1874

There are Indians and Indians. Frontiersmen, as a rule, are too apt to have but one theory on the subject of the noble red man, and they sum it up in two phrases: "Injun is pizen," and "The proper reservation for the savage is six feet below the soil." But we fancy that most persons who do not come into either daily or occasional contact with the red-skin, and who are never shocked by the erratic impulses of his impetuous nature, are willing enough to separate the race into two categories, good and bad, just as the pale-faces are divided. We have recently been called upon for a tribute of admiration to "Osage Joe," who has taken pains to inform the Indian Commissioner that he henceforth proposes to cultivate the arts of peace, and to instruct his followers in them. The pacific expressions of this bronze-colored Joseph incline impartial observers to believe that he is a good Indian—such as we read of in the romances of our youth, and religiously accepted as the prevailing type until the progress of the railroad disclosed the tribes in their non-picturesque squalor and unpoetic thievery. "Osage Joe" will certainly be able to make his good conduct counterbalance many of the iniquities which the unrepentant of his race still perpetrate, and which they seem likely to cleave to until the whole Indian family is extinct. The amiable Osage needs, however, to be very good indeed to atone for the recent conduct of the Kiowas and their chief, Satanta, who has just been brought in chains to Fort Sill in the Indian Territory.

We suppose Satanta will pass for a pretty fair type of the "bad Indian." He has certainly consummated some atrocious villainies. Yet it is impossible not to admire the implacable hostility, the unbending scorn, and the almost Olympian majesty of this uncompromising savage, whose proud spirit has not been broken by the manacles and the degradation of a long captivity in a Texas penitentiary. Child of the mighty plains of the South-west, one of nature's noblest products; an accomplished chieftain, with a demeanor as polished as an ambassador's, and a form as symmetrical as a Grecian statue; with a pride as deep as his hate, and a hate as strong as his sinews of steel, there is a magnificence in his scorn and a rude poetry in his every action which render his career a fascinating study. There is no touch or hint of the decadence of the Indian in this Kiowa leader. He is of the old impressive school; his dignity and repose, his graceful courage, are worthy of the time when the Franciscans tried in vain to convert his ancestors, and when the friars themselves confessed that the savages were as superb as the demigods in their calm and impenetrable manner, their feats of arms, and their powers of endurance. But inasmuch as Satanta has been at his old vindictive tricks once more, and as he is a constant menace to the white man when at large, it is probable that he will be remanded to the jail from which he has not long been absent, and the world will henceforth lose sight of him.

When he was sent back to his people, it was hoped that he would teach them in future to live at peace with the white man; but he had no sooner left the jail than he began to plot fresh murder and strategy, and as soon as his foot was once more on his native heath he led his warriors against the palefaces. Wherefore a want of confidence in Satanta pervades the military headquarters, and there will probably be little sympathy expended on him.

Satanta belongs to that class of Indians who can never forgive the white man for his invasion of their soil. He looks upon the white as his natural enemy, and doubtless wonders at the clemency which induces the Government to spare his life, or why the braves of Gen. Davidson's command do not torture the noble captive now that he is once more within the scope of their vengeance. There is something pathetic in the unbounded confidence which this royal savage has in the justness of his cause; neither laws, nor chains, nor humiliation break his haughty spirit. In the prison where he was so long confined he sat quietly for days with arms folded across his massive breast, refusing to share in the labor which was compulsory for the other prisoners. Failure and misfortune did not bow him then, nor will they now. In his own mind he is the unfortunate monarch whose enemies, with violence, have stolen away his domain; and he counts it a high duty to break his plighted faith with them, to give them no rest whenever he can vex them, and to submit with fortitude to their punishment when he is caught. Nothing will ever convert him; he is deaf to expediency, dumb save to utter mockeries or to give promises which he intends to break, blind to reason and to the fallacy of a future hostile policy. If left at liberty he will be like a raging whirlwind of destruction; he will be content with nothing but war. Yet it seems pitiful to cage so fine a savage among a herd of vulgar criminals in a penitentiary.

The Surrender of Chief Joseph

August 11, 1877

After one of the most stubborn and gallant running fights known to Indian warfare, Chief Joseph and the remnant of his band, harassed and worn out, have surrendered. Gen. Miles makes known the fact in a quiet note, whose only symptom of exultation escapes in the subdued phrase, "our usual success." The point where Miles caught and held Joseph was, apparently, a short distance up Snake Creek, near Bear Paw Mountain, not far, therefore, from the border line beyond which Joseph would have been safe. The force which Miles took with him consisted of three companies of the Second Cavalry, three of the Seventh Cavalry, and eight companies of the Fifth Infantry, of which latter he is Colonel commanding. Two other companies of the Seventh Cavalry were on the way, and probably joined him during the three days' fight, as did possibly some other companies of Sturgis' regiment. All these companies, however, were slim in numbers.

While these troops are the immediate victors, some of the praise must be given to the commands of Howard, Gibbon, and Sturgis, who had successively struck Joseph during the long chase. Miles reaped what they had sown. Joseph had run the gantlet of our field forces from Oregon and Washington Territory across Idaho, and thence up to the extreme northerly part of Montana. The official date of the beginning of the expedition against him is June 15, thus making a campaign of nearly 120 days. After the first outbreak of the Indians came Norwood's fight at Cames Creek, followed by the fights of Whipple and Perry on the Cottonwood, from the 3d to the 5th of July. Howard collected a large force and gave battle on the Clearwater, July 13 and 14. Then followed the long chase on the Lo Lo trail across Idaho. There a mistake made by a detachment posted to meet him, allowed Joseph to escape; but Gibbon, by a forced march, overhauled him and fought the bloody affair of Big Hole, Aug. 9. With Howard still after him, Joseph pushed rapidly northward, and was struck by Sturgis, Sept. 13, near Yellowstone Mountain. Eluding Sturgis on Clark's Fork, Joseph reached Cow Island, and, on being driven off by the little garrison there, headed straight for the Canada line. At this juncture Miles, who fortunately had had the small force already spoken of in camp and watching Sitting Bull ever since the middle of June, moved it rapidly over toward Eagle Creek, and after a severe and prolonged fight, worried the brave chief to a surrender.

So ends the Nez Percé war—a war gallantly fought, but a costly and sanguinary blunder. A peaceful, non-treaty chief, who, after being wronged in other ways, had been peremptorily ordered to go upon a reservation where he did not belong, was thus goaded to the war-path. Our troops have pursued him and his allied chiefs with tireless energy, and have fought him most gallantly, being met by an energy as tireless, and a bravery even more desperate, than their own. The skill and courage with which Joseph, White Bird, Looking Glass, and their Nez Percé warriors have conducted this campaign are unsurpassed in our Indian annals.

As to the fate of Joseph, much must depend on the terms of surrender. But even supposing it to be unconditional, he and his men deserve the treatment of foes, not of felons. By refraining from scalping and mutilation, by their frequent release of women and children, and sometimes even of unarmed citizens, they have set an example in Indian warfare which should earn them consideration. If they have inflicted terrible losses on our troops, it was in a war for their homes and what they believed to be their rights. We rejoice that this slaughter is over; but the fate of Joseph and his Nez Percés should not be that of Capt. Jack and his Modocs.

ᐳ An Impudent Indian

September 4, 1877

The North American Indian is utterly and irredeemably bad. For the truth of this assertion we have the unanimous testimony of the gentle and cultured frontiersmen, besides the calm, judicial decision of an eminent Federal General that "the only good Indian is a dead Indian." While it is thus impossible that Chief Joseph, of the Nez Percés, should be really worse than other totally depraved red men, it is very certain that a more gratuitous and uncalled-for fiend never vexed a peaceful squatter or annoyed a well-meaning Federal commander.

The life of this man Joseph is one long record of uninterrupted infamy. From his earliest manhood he has been conspicuous for unparalleled impudence. Instead of murdering and robbing an occasional white man, as the consistant [*sic*] savage would have done he has until very recently been guilty of the effrontery of behaving himself like a peaceful and honest man. Not one of his band was permitted to perpetrate a single outrage upon a settler during the whole time that he was living at peace with the United States. Thus this miserable savage impudently aped the customs of civilized and Christian men and took away from his white neighbors every plausible pretext for exterminating him.

Not very long ago the Government, which must have become thoroughly tired of Joseph's impudent peacefulness, notified him that he must give up to white settlers the reservation upon which his tribe lived, and which had been solemnly guaranteed to the Nez Percés by a treaty. Instead of promptly obeying the order, Joseph, with a degree of impudence which was really startling, remonstrated with the Government, and actually hinted that it was under obligation to maintain its own treaties and to keep faith with him. Of course, the idea that a great and enlightened Government ought to keep faith with a feeble tribe was too absurd to merit notice, and Joseph was once more calmly requested to hasten his departure. In the meantime white men entered his reservation, in spite of his ridiculous claim that he had rights of property which anybody was bound to respect. Presently it so happened that one of his young men was killed by an energetic settler. Incredible as it may seem, Joseph went to the extreme length of asserting that this trifling incident was a murder, and sent to the nearest settlement and gravely requested the authorities to arrest and punish the so-called murderer. One can fancy the inextinguishable laughter with which this request was greeted. Had Joseph requested the punishment of a man who had shot a woodchuck or a prairie-dog his impudence would have been sufficiently amusing, but that he should expect a white man to be punished for killing a mere Indian was perhaps the most absurd idea that ever entered the aboriginal brain.

Upon the hollow pretext that to be turned out of the home which the Government had guaranteed to him, and to have his young men shot for the amusement of frontier riflemen, constituted a grievance, Joseph deliberately took up arms and made war against the United States. There was something heroic in the conduct of the patriots of the Revolution who preferred to fight the British Empire rather than to pay taxes without representation, but there is nothing to relieve the vulgar impudence of the chief of a small band of savages who prefers to fight forty millions of people rather than to give up his wretched little country. Of course, after he had thus displayed the full malignity of his nature there was nothing left to be done except to exterminate him, and troops were sent against him for that laudable purpose.

It shocks all our finer feeling to be compelled to say that so far Joseph has fiendishly refused to be exterminated. He has not only defended himself with a skill that is plainly the direct inspiration of the devil, but he has willfully refrained from perpetrating the outrages which we have a right to expect from a savage foe. When Gen. Gibbon's Army attacked one of his villages the women and children were heroically killed by the troops; but when Joseph the other day attacked a little band of white people he released the women without injuring them. This was clearly the act of a cold-blooded, calculating savage, who cunningly pretended to place his enemies in a false light by permitting them to monopolize the cruelties of which he ought, in accordance with his aboriginal nature, to have been the sole author. He wanted to be able to say, when people exclaimed against the blood-thirsty Indians who spare neither age nor sex, "Excuse me! there is a trifling mistake here. It is my women and children—not yours—who are shot and bayoneted." There can, moreover, be but little doubt that this subtle savage has secretly induced his enemies to scalp such of his tribe as have fallen into their power. If he had any sense of decency he would have done all the scalping himself, but he can now point to Nez Percé scalps in the hands of the white men and make them the text of impudent and sarcastic remarks.

The longer this unspeakable wretch postpones his extermination the more he deserves our indignation. There never was a holier cause than that for which our troops are fighting. We are sustaining the sacred right of our Government to repudiate its treaties and protesting against the wicked assumption that an Indian can ever have any rights whatever. In opposing this noble cause, Joseph is invoking the condemnation of all fair-minded men, while his wanton refusal to kill women and children, even after we have kindly set him the example, ought to create a whirlwind of indignation all over the land. At the same time we should humbly confess that we are not altogether blameless. If we had poisoned Joseph and his band years ago we should not now be forced to fight him. Since the only good Indian is a dead Indian, we have criminally neglected our duty in not long since making all our Indians thoroughly good ones. We are a Christian people, acquainted with strychnine and familiar with prussic acid. With either of these beneficent agents we might have quietly removed every Indian within our territory and thrown open all the reservations to those who are now suffering from want of room in the narrow confines of the Continent. Though we exterminate Joseph and his warriors, and though we shoot every woman and bayonet every baby of his tribe, we cannot fully atone for our neglect to poison them in the days when that good work could have been done cheaply, safely, and easily.

↬ The Indian View

November 15, 1877

It appears that Sitting Bull has been much misrepresented. Like other great men, Senator Conkling, for example, he is a much more elegant gentleman than he is popularly supposed to be. Indeed, if he had a seat in the United States Senate, which unhappily he has not, he would undoubtedly rise to a question of privilege, and, in the most sweeping manner, deny all the evil things which have been said about him, and which have been put in his mouth. Since reading the report of Col. Corbin, one of the committee sent to invite Sitting Bull to return to this bereaved country, we are confident that the chief never said that all Americans are liars. Col. Corbin says the great chief is agreeable and intelligent. It is hardly necessary to say that no agreeable and intelligent person, even though an Indian, would stigmatize all the citizens of this great Republic as liars. If he had compared them to grasshoppers in a fence-corner, or had referred to a Cabinet Minister as little in stature, we might have thought that he was really a bad Indian. But, since he has only criticized the nation in general terms, and has not indulged in any of the gross personalities which are peculiar to statesmen from the interior of New-York, we can believe the report of the Commissioner who says that Sitting Bull is very much of a gentleman.

This is all exactly in accordance with the course of human history. We are constantly finding out that the devil is not nearly so black as he is painted, and that the heroes of the past were very much over-rated. The Father of his Country, we are told, was penurious; the great Marlborough was a screw, and the eminent historian, William M. Tweed, informs us that Horace Greeley, while he preached total abstinence, liked to take his glass of wine behind the door. Dionysius the Tyrant, so called, was an estimable person who had a weakness for anatomical experiments; Caligula was the victim of misrepresentation, and Lucretia Borgia was a virtuous and tender-hearted woman, who would have been a City missionary among the poor and the lowly if she had lived in our times. Why, then, should it not turn out that Sitting Bull is an amiable gentleman, of agreeable manners, and only forced by painful circumstances to slay his enemies. The prejudices of the frontiersmen, who are notoriously hostile to the red race, are to be charged with the circulation of the stories of Sitting Bull's brutalities and savagery. He has been a much misrepresented Indian, and it is high time that he had justice done him.

Some eloquent philanthropist, possibly Mr. Wendell Phillips, has derided the often-repeated saying that Custer and his men were massacred. It is urged that the engagement thus stigmatized was a fair fight and that the overwhelming defeat of the attacking party naturally resulted in their being all killed. We need not be surprised, therefore, to learn that Sitting Bull "repudiates the idea that Custer and his men were massacred." He says that the desperation of the assailants of the Indians "made it necessary to kill them." The Indian General, of course, laments the stern necessity of war. The attacking party would have killed the Indians if the Indians had not killed them. The affair was a case of justifiable homicide on a large scale; and Sitting Bull expresses his regret that Custer's refusal to surrender made it necessary to put him to death. It is even said, in extenuation of that wholesale slaughter, that the troops charged into the Indian camps with such impetuosity as to create a temporary panic. When the attacked party recovered from their first dismay, and found that only a handful of white soldiers had ventured into the hostile camp, they were highly indignant. They outnumbered the troops ten to one; they revenged themselves by killing every white man on the field. Sitting Bull says that he admired Custer's bravery very much, but not enough to spare him.

It is evident that the Sioux Chief considers the armed contests between Indians and white men as warfare. This is contrary to the notion which obtains on our side of the line. White soldiers and officers declare that there is no more glory to be obtained in fighting Indians than in fighting wild beasts. Unhappily, the same idea is so common in all walks of life that it is very likely that a man could get more compliments and "press notices" for his skill and courage in chasing the fiery, untamed anise-seed bag in a Long Island "fox-chase" than in the most daring campaign against the Sioux. Such is the perversity of fashion. And so long as there is no Sioux brush, tips, or mask to show as trophies of the chase, it were better for an officer to win the smiles of beauty at polo, or in the imminent deadly breach of the anise-bag. This is not Sitting Bull's view of the case. He thinks that fighting is serious work and warfare, and demands high strategy and generalship. Retired upon his laurels, he can afford to criticise our false views of Indian fighting. He is evidently proud of his share in the miserable business which we persist in calling a massacre.

Perhaps we shall make more progress in our efforts to exterminate the Indians—if this be the aim of our fights—when we take the same view of Indian fighting that the Indians do. In this particular instance, the Sioux looked upon the little detachment sent against them as an invading army. They resolved to repel the enemy with slaughter, or to sell their own lives as dearly as possible. They were successful, and they were very much "set up" by the result. Superior numbers, which our rebel friends used so often to deplore in contests, were this time against us. The object of the Custer attack was to "punish" the Indians. Indeed, the whole campaign was apparently undertaken as a punitive measure. On the whole, lamentable as it may seem, the Indian notion of affairs seems to have been justified, rather than ours. The Commission to Sitting Bull's camp has brought back this lesson if nothing more. The Sioux chief may or may not be the agreeable gentleman which he is described. His view of the situation is worth consideration.

⌒ The Exile's Return

December 21, 1877

Sitting Bull has returned to the United States. This distinguished and particularly discontented exile, having left "the house of his Great Mother," as he calls Canada, has thus burned his bridges behind him. A deputation from the United States Government was sent to him, and he was entreated to return in peace. But he prefers to come in war; his first salutation to the despised Americans is in bloodshed. There was something quite noble about the eminent Sioux chief when he rose to his full height of savage defiance and informed the Commissioners that he would have nothing more to do with the people of the United States. One could not help thinking of the late Edwin Forrest in the character of *Metamora*, when he used to stalk upon the stage, (with that peculiar slap with the bottom of his feet,) and say, "You've sent for me and I have come. If you don't want me I'll go back again," &c. Sitting Bull was quite as melodramatic as the "Last of the Wampanoags" ever was on the Bowery stage. Addressing the Commissioners, he said, "Go back home where you came from. This country is mine, and I intend to stay here and raise this country full of grown people." If he had wildly "chewed soap," and had wound up his harangue with a snort and a guttural "Yah-ha!" the likeness to the dear old *Metamora* of our youth would have been complete.

Sitting Bull is a cheap and contemptible humbug. While he kept his warriors together and outnumbered the white soldiers twenty to one, he gave us infinite trouble. He fought as bravely as any Indian ever fights when he has a small force to contend with; and when he was pushed by a tolerably large detachment of troops, he fled over the border like any other horse-thief with the constables after him. A great deal of fustian sentiment was wasted on the gallantry with which he had engaged his white enemies, when a handful of them had driven him into a corner and had indiscreetly fallen upon his camps. And those who have formed their estimates of Indian character on the tales of Cooper and the play of "The Last of the Wampanoags," were delighted with the rude eloquence in which Sitting Bull denounced the people of the United States as liars, and declared his intention of staying in the house of his "Great Mother." It is said that Sitting Bull is an intelligent Indian, and is endowed with a statesmanlike mind. If he is, he knows perfectly well that he has never kept any agreement that he ever made with the white people, and that his thieving, murderous raids had no excuse in the treatment which he had formerly received in the United States. He knew perfectly well, too, that he was not wanted in Canada; that the Canadian authorities were anxious to get him out of the country; and that when he shook hands with the representatives of the British Government with great cordiality, and assured the American Commissioners that these were his friends, with whom he should stay forever, all this was the veriest humbug. It has turned out just as might have been expected. After all the high and mighty scorn of the redoubtable Sioux Chief, and after all his grandiloquent pretense of friendship for the Canadians, he is back again over the border, raiding the white settlements in the good old Indian fashion.

Nevertheless, we believe that Sitting Bull has been conciliated. He would not behave so obstreperously if he had not been. As long as he was in Canada, and was severely let alone by the United States Government, he was quiet, though sullen. In an evil hour, the British Government undertook the office of peace-maker, and invited us to send a deputation to the illustrious exile to coax him home. The Commissioners talked to the Indians in honeyed accents. They promised them lands, wagons, rations, garden-seeds, and, for all we know, public documents and offices. The Government of the United States was presented in the attitude of begging these thievish murderers to come back and all should be forgiven. Of course, all this was done with the best intentions, and nobody doubted the honesty of purpose which prompted so conciliatory a policy toward the sullen Sioux. They have been greatly wronged. Whenever they have rebelled against the authority of the Government, and have gone off with the identical arms and ammunition which that paternal Government had given them for their own defense, they have been pursued and killed, just as though they were not noble savages, but lying and treacherous rascals. But here was a deputation bearing an olive branch and entreating them to return and kill the fatted calf. The more they were conciliated the madder they grew, and when the Commissioners were fairly back to Washington they burst over the border. They show the extent to which they have been conciliated by killing, not the fatted calf, but the first white men they meet.

We have heard a great deal about the superior manner in which the British Government treats its Indian wards. Sitting Bull and his comrades evinced such a strong desire to be adopted into the family of their Great Mother that we had fondly hoped they were to stay permanently in Canada, and that the mild management of Great Britain would fit them for the society of the most fastidious. But there seems to be something in the Sioux blood which urges him to plunder and deviltry. The atmosphere of Canada was too moral for Sitting Bull. He finds congenial occupation among the "liars" of the United States. Unhappily, he cannot again return to "the house of his Great Mother."

⮌ The End of Victorio

October 29, 1880

There seems to be no room for further doubt as to the death of Chief Victorio, though the leader of the Rio Mimbres Apaches has been too often slain in dispatches to make any mere report of his taking off at all credible. Besides, as there is a standing reward for his head, the temptation is obviously strong enough for those in search of it to accept any dead Apache as a good enough Victorio until after its payment. But the commander of the Mexican forces co-operating with our own gives the details of the time and the place of his surrounding Victorio's camp, and he adds that the combat left "Victorio, 60 warriors, and 18 women and children dead; 68 women and children prisoners." He confesses that 30 Apaches are still loose, and these are enough to make a nest-egg of future troubles. But deprived of their leader, they are likely to disperse, and indeed, the lack of ammunition, which was the cause of Victorio's downfall, must also operate fatally on those of his band who survive him.

A war that lasts 20 months, calls into action the spare troops of two countries like the United States and Mexico, and costs the lives of perhaps 500 of the combatants and of settlers, besides the loss of thousands of cattle, is worthy of some retrospect when it comes to an end. There is no extra sympathy to be expended on Victorio and his band. They were a hard set of outlaws and horse-thieves. Like most of the Indians in the South-west, they were of a low type, having plenty of cunning and audacity, and naturally predatory and murderous. It is this Apache race, inhabiting the Rio Grande Valley, that has raided for generations into Texas, and that raided on white man before any such place as Texas was known. They have few or none of those traits of magnanimity, generosity, devotion to duty, and love of country that distinguished, for example, Chief Joseph, the Nez Percé, making his gallant running fight for liberty a chivalric affair, that put his white pursuers and their scalp-taking Bannock allies to the blush. Victorio reveled in a career of murder and rapine, and few bolder or more successful Indian raiders have been known to our history; yet ordinarily competent and honest management would have kept him from going on the warpath at all.

First or last, parts or the whole of the Fourth, Sixth, Eighth, Ninth, and Tenth Cavalry, and of the Thirteenth, Fifteenth, Sixteenth, and Nineteenth Infantry have been employed in trying to head off and destroy Victorio's band, which probably never in its prime numbered at any one time, in one body, more than eight score warriors. The Mexicans have been almost as busy on their side, particularly during Victorio's two invasions of their country, the last of which proved fatal to him. Victorio had an Indian's natural contempt for that impalpable and invisible thing called a boundary, and to him Mexico and the United States were one. He killed, it is estimated, 250 people, in Grant, Dona Ana, and Socorro Counties in New-Mexico, gained repeated victories over the troops, which were regularly reported the other way, ravaged Arizona, demoralized the whole border, surprised trains and butchered the passengers, slew prospectors, took possession of villages and shot the people if they came to the windows to look at the weather, cut off the Territory from its supplies of bacon and flour, which the freighters were afraid to bring, and, when he wanted fresh horses for his band, he coolly ran off, by night raids, the stock of the regular cavalry, leaving them involuntary infantry. A warrior able to accomplish so much, against odds so vast, and to sustain himself so long, is, making all allowances for the *terrain*, which is hostile to regular campaigning, no inconsiderable figure in history.

With all his natural predilection for plunder, Chief Victorio was really driven to the warpath. He and his band were well situated at the Warm Springs, where they were satisfied. But, for some mysterious reason, the Indian authorities in that region persisted in transferring them to San Carlos—since become notorious as the centre of frauds for contractors and Indian Agents. Once and again Victorio and his band escaped from this change; the third time they went not to come back. And yet, their last flight is thought to have been due to measures of arrest for former offenses, taken out against them in local courts, when the act of inviting them to return may fairly be said to have been an official condonation of old crimes. Unable to distinguish between local courts and the Interior Department, when a Sheriff appeared on the reservation, though, as it is claimed, not for the purpose of arrest, but only to avoid a roundabout course in his travels, they vanished between two days. The Indian Bureau agents seem to have stories, also, of alleged bad conduct of Army officers toward Victorio. It is not necessary, however, to go into these criminations and recriminations. It is enough to know that a strictly preventable war has been waged for years, at vast cost of life and property, and at last has been ended, it is hoped, by the combined action of two nations to crush one little band of pestilent Indians.

↝ Sitting Bull

November 25, 1880

In leaving Montana for Washington, Gen. Miles has declared the Indian question on the Canadian border to be practically settled by the coming in of nearly two thousand Indians hitherto classed as hostile. But while so much has been done, it would be a great mistake, apparently, to abandon further efforts to secure the submission of Sitting Bull. To say that the surrender of the great Sioux chief might save our troops a Winter's campaign in that high latitude only imperfectly expresses its importance. It would take away a standing menace to the settlement of the far North-west, and solve the chief remaining Indian problem of our day. Sitting Bull, with a force not a half as great as he has since commanded, annihilated Custer and all his command on the Little Big Horn, leaving not one man to tell the story. Victorio, with less than two hundred Apache warriors, ravaged Northern Mexico and Southern New-Mexico and Arizona for twenty months, killing hundreds of people and stealing or slaughtering thousands of horses and cattle. So long as Sitting Bull remains hostile his camp becomes the resort of all disaffected Indians from the Northern reservations, and it is this fact, rather than his present numbers of his present attitude, that is important.

Had Sitting Bull invaded the Yellowstone region at the time of the Nez Percé war or the Bannock war, he would have made havoc of life and property. He had pledged himself, however, to Major Walsh, of the North-western Mounted Police, not to wage war again, and loyally kept his word. Undoubtedly, also, he has been greatly weakened by the defection of his warriors during the past two years. When, after his defeat and massacre of Custer, in the Summer of 1876, the Sioux chief saw troops from all quarters assembling to take vengeance, he hastened northward, and in the Winter crossed to Canada. In the following Autumn, as will be remembered, Gen. Terry headed a commission empowered to seek him out and offer him terms of surrender. The negotiations were conducted with the help of Major Walsh, who had already established the Sioux camp at Bear Mountain, and resulted in the contemptuous rejection of Terry's terms. In due time, however, hunger did its work. The region in which Sitting Bull found himself was not so good for hunting purposes as that south of the border. The larger his band grew, from the disaffected refugees and hostile Indians of various tribes escaping from the reservations, the more difficult became the problem of supply. While the Dominion maintained what seemed to our troops a marvelous faith in the harmlessness of Sitting Bull, it gave him no rations. He was compelled to follow the buffalo on the American side of the boundary, and as often as he did Gen. Miles was ready and anxious to drive him out.

Winter before last was a hard one for Sitting Bull's band; last Winter saw it breaking up; he has now another Winter in prospect, and has sought to lay in supplies by a buffalo hunt. But the greater part of his band have, as Gen. Miles says, resolved to abandon this precarious livelihood, and to take Government rations. The first real tidings of their purpose came through Allison, a scout, who was discredited at Washington, where the many previous Sitting Bull rumors, now of invasion and anon of submission, had begotten a chronic incredulity. But Gen. Terry, who knew Allison, believed him. It had already been arranged that Miles was to go out Indian hunting the present Autumn; Terry sent him word to stop all expeditions, and to give Sitting Bull a chance to come in. But Miles, needless to say, was the first to see the opening ahead, and was far away and pushing on toward the border when Terry's messenger reached Keogh.

The result of the movement thus far has been to bring under Government control an almost unexpectedly large number of roving Indians. Still, Sitting Bull is not among them. It is reported from Winnipeg that he and his followers have had much success in hunting. This may dispose him to keep up his attitude of independence. Still, it is by no means clear that he could not be induced to accept the Government's terms—the surrender of arms and ponies, to be sold for the benefit of the Indians, and willingness to accept any reservation agreed upon. With Sitting Bull safely out of the way, and his band distributed, our military forces would be more free to move, as the necessity of watching him has always retained a strong body of troops on the northern frontier, no matter what the need of their services elsewhere.

ᑏ Geronimo's Band of Thugs

June 2, 1885

Now that Gen. Crook is in the heart of the district where so many horrible murders have been committed by Geronimo and his men, some progress will probably be made in the work which the troops have been trying to do. The General seems to have reached Fort Bayard on Saturday. On Sunday he telegraphed from that place that the outlook was "very bad," and that it would be very difficult to suppress the marauders. It may be that he is now ready to admit that satisfactory progress might have been made and that some valuable lives might have been saved if there had been more troops in the field; although one would say that in two weeks twelve hundred soldiers, cavalry for the most part, ought to have made some impression upon a band of only fifty Indians. His superior officers were directed on the 24th ult. to check the ravages of Geronimo's band "in the shortest time possible" and to call for all assistance that might be required, but on the 27th he declared that no more troops were needed.

In the light of what has happened in the last two weeks it is not strange that the people of Southwestern New-Mexico are complaining so bitterly. It was on the 17th of May that these Indians—whose number was said at the time to be fifty, and afterward to be only thirty-four—broke away from the reservation and began their bloody work. It should be remembered that these Indians were the worst offenders two years ago, and that for this reason they were isolated in the northern part of the San Carlos Reservation and placed under the supervision of the army. The officer in charge of them was Lieut. Britton Davis, of the Third Cavalry. The dispatch that announced their departure from the reservation also declared that the military authorities had been "expecting trouble" and were prepared for this movement. They certainly should have been prepared, for they had taken the responsibility of caring for these red-handed murderers, whose nature and impulses they well understood. Gen. Crook had saved them from punishment and had promised that they would give no further trouble. He had even insisted that they should be allowed to retain their arms. Very plainly the military authorities either were not prepared for Geronimo's flight, or, being prepared, were very unfortunate in an attempt to do their duty. It is true that the Apaches pass rapidly from point to point, and their escape into Mexico would not have been a remarkable feat if they had traveled in that direction with a fair start. But they did not do this. They remained for fourteen or fifteen days in Southwestern New-Mexico, north of the Southern Pacific Road, murdering settlers. They did not seem to be anxious to get beyond the border, nor did they seem to fear the troops. For fifteen days they carried on their bloody work almost without hindrance and their trail is marked by the mutilated bodies of scores of victims. They were only fifty, and the pursuers were more than twelve hundred, but the settlers could not be saved. Some of them might have been saved if additional troops had been brought from the posts in the two Territories and from those in Kansas and Colorado.

The raid is greatly to be deplored, not only because of the lives already lost, but also because it will serve to encourage and strengthen the Indian haters and to weaken the position of the Indian's friends. In view of its probable effect in that direction the Indian's friends must all the more keenly regret the well meant leniency that gave these Chiricahuas their liberty and their arms. These men who have escaped are the bad men of the reservation; there are thousands remaining peacefully within its limits who do not sympathize with Geronimo, and who know that Geronimo's deeds only deepen the settler's hate for every being that has a copper-colored skin. Since the depravity of these Chiricahuas was so well known they should have been guarded with the greatest care, for the sake of the other Indians of Arizona as well as to insure the safety of settlers.

The troops may not be able to catch these wretches, who are worse than wild beasts. If they do overtake them, and if any of the Indians shall escape the soldiers' rifles, we do not see why those who may survive should not be hanged. They should be punished for their horrible crimes, and their punishment should be either execution or imprisonment for life. Not one of them should ever be allowed to go again upon a reservation.

⌒ Disposing of Geronimo

October 15, 1886

The belief is said to prevail at the War Department that the Chiricahua captives now at San Antonio will soon be sent to join the remainder of their band at Fort Marion, Florida. Should this disposition be made of them its justice would hardly be called in question, and it seems to have been the plan which Gen. Miles contemplated, judging from the brief summary of his official report which has been made public. Indeed, we may suppose that the detention in San Antonio has been made in great part for the purpose of clearly ascertaining all the facts in the case before proceeding to the final disposition of Geronimo, Natchez, and the other leading chiefs.

It seems to be clear that the misunderstanding as to the surrender of Geronimo did not arise from anything in the dispatches of Gen. Miles, but from the restatement of them in their transmission through the division headquarters to Washington. Gen. Miles telegraphed to the division commander, Gen. Howard, that the hostiles had surrendered as prisoners of war, and that he would hurry them out of Arizona as soon as possible. It may be remembered that Gen. Miles had already been making arrangements for a similar disposition of all the other Chiricahuas who had not gone on the warpath. In sending the news of Gen. Miles's success to Washington, Gen. Howard after mentioning that Geronimo and others were held "all as prisoners of war," added the words "surrender unconditional." The latter phrase, however, was not in the dispatch of Gen. Miles, and hence the criticism made upon the latter in some quarters in regard to his supposed use of these words was entirely unfounded. We believe that Gen. Howard, on the receipt of subsequent inquiries in regard to it, stated that the phrase was his own, and was employed simply because he judged it to express briefly what he himself inferred.

Any supposed discrepancy in the matter must have been greatly exaggerated in view of the peculiar phrase which, if we do not mistake, was used by the War Department authorities themselves last Spring, when Gen. Crook was engaged in similar negotiations. At that time, it may be remembered, Geronimo had met Gen. Crook for the purpose of surrender, and a part of his band, chiefly women and children, did surrender unconditionally. Geronimo, however, proposed that he should be taken away from Arizona for a certain period and then returned to the reservation. Gen. Crook submitted this proposition by telegraph to Washington, and two days afterward received a reply, the substance of which was, we believe, that the surrender must be unconditional, "sparing only their lives." In the meantime, unfortunately, Geronimo had become alarmed and broke away with nearly all of his warriors. But the point to note is that here was a case in which the technical term of unconditional surrender was apparently held not to conflict with the giving of an assurance that the lives of Geronimo and his men should be safe. It is also evident that had the dispatch from Washington, just referred to, reached Gen. Crook before the flight of Geronimo, during the conferences at the end of March, and had the chief then been willing to accept it, a result would have been reached at that time, under the express sanction of the President and his Cabinet, no more favorable than the one achieved by Gen. Miles, and on which so much unjust criticism was recently passed.

In fact, it cannot be positively stated that, even if Geronimo had remained last March to hear the results of the telegraphing, he would at that time have accepted terms which did not include his ultimate restoration to Arizona. Now, however, it is practically certain that if he goes to Fort Marion he will never be taken back to his old reservation; and in addition Gen. Miles has procured the deportation of all the troublesome Chiricahuas and Warm Springs, nearly five hundred in number. It is probably this stroke which has caused the satisfaction of the people of the afflicted Territories with Gen. Miles's policy and results to be widespread and outspoken. Hitherto in this region cries for the trial and execution of Apache prisoners have been fervent and relentless, but to be rid at one swoop of such a collection of pests of the frontier must for them dwarf in importance the question of whether the chief hostiles shall be exiled or executed. Officers, too, who, like Crook and Miles, have had years of experience in Indian campaigning, are better judges of what can and what can not be accomplished in it than people without such experience, and they seem to agree that whenever the hostiles can be put where they can do no further harm not a single life of our gallant officers and men should be sacrificed in a needless prolongation of the campaign.

Exit Sitting Bull

December 16, 1890

There seems to be no doubt that one of the most mischievous and turbulent Indians in the United States has been killed, in the person of Sitting Bull. It is a good many years since Sitting Bull began to trouble the souls of Indian agents and officers of the United States Army. Like a bumptious and bombinating journalist of this city, whom he much resembled in his character and career, the late Bull was distinguished for the impracticality and apparent motivelessness of many of his most conspicuous performances. It is impossible to account for his public course upon any other hypothesis than that of "pure cussedness." Bull would undoubtedly have been a much more comfortable old savage if he had settled down under the aegis of the United States to draw his rations and to lament loudly whenever he found them deficient in quantity, for it is inconceivable that the red man should reject anything edible on the score of its quality. He has been, however, persistently of the opinion that

"One crowded hour of glorious life
Is worth an age without a name,"

and in his time he has had many crowded hours in setting traps for the United States troops, or in fighting them, or in running away from them.

Like a great many of our leading local statesmen and Napoleons of finance, he has had seasons when seclusion on the Canadian side of the border seemed much more wholesome for him than exposure to process of law on the American side. For some years after he had led his people to defeat and starvation he preferred Manitoba to the Territories of our own Northwest, and he there openly practiced polygamy, free trade, and other revolting vices at which we were aiming moral and patriotic legislation. It appears that he was at the bottom, more than anybody else, of the recent disturbances and rumors of disturbance. The old reprobate was himself unavailable as a Messiah, but he was as well aware as any copper-colored inhabitant of the country of the political value of a Messiah, and of the extent to which a belief in him might be worked. The announcement of his death is not calculated to arouse any other emotions than those excited the other day by the slaying of a "rogue" elephant in Cincinnati, though no quadruped ever did so much widely-extended and long-continued mischief as Sitting Bull.

⌇ Chief Joseph

April 24, 1897

Not the least picturesque figure in the Grant Day parade is likely to be that of Chief Joseph, the head of the remnant of the Nez Percés. Twenty years ago his name was very familiar throughout the country. He was driven into fighting the Government by what he sincerely regarded as its injustice toward his people. Those who served against him are prepared to testify that he fought it bravely and skillfully, and that before he was finally overpowered his rebellion had given the Government an amount of trouble out of all proportion to the number of those who took part in it.

When he was at last convinced of the utter futility of resistance to the power of the United States, he surrendered in good faith, and he has never, in the long interval, shown signs of a disposition to make further trouble. He has appealed, in behalf of his tribe, solely to the justice and magnanimity of the Government, and it is in the furtherance of such an appeal that he has now for the first time come East to be impressed anew with the irresistibleness of the power against which he ignorantly contended.

The American bison is scarcely more completely extinct than the savage, unspoiled by civilization, of which the chief of the Nez Percés is a very typical specimen. What he asks in behalf of his tribe seems to be moderate and reasonable, and it is to be hoped that the Interior Department may see its way to grant the application, on behalf of a people no longer at all dangerous, of the chief who was so determined and so fair a fighter, and who has so faithfully observed the pledge he gave at the time of his surrender. His participation in the Grant Day parade would be as striking a feature in the procession as in the triumphs of the Roman Empire were the Germanic or British chieftains who bore to that civilization about the same relation which Chief Joseph bears to our own.

5   The Indian Wars

Indians sometimes have a disagreeable way of not staying whipped, whereby more than once the report of "All quite [*sic*] on the Platte" has been the cue for a bold raid or savage butchery. But this time there is ground for putting faith in Gen. Sheridan's claim that he has "broken the backbone of the Indian rebellion"—broken it, we may trust, not in the sense in which the Confederate backbone was broken at regular intervals during the war, but in the Petersburg and Five Forks sense.

—*New York Times*
January 19, 1869

NOT SURPRISINGLY, it was the long and bloody warfare between Indians and whites that provided the *Times* with more grist for its eager editorial mill than any other element of the Indian problem. The Indian wars offered a demanding test of the newspaper's ability to report from the far frontiers, while interpreting the long-running conflict proved an immense challenge to the newspaper's sense of fairness—particularly given the we/they perspective of the *Times* editorial writers.

Before the Civil War, the *Times* expended a great deal of editorial energy on castigating the military for its failure to protect white settlers along the frontier and particularly those crossing the plains to the West Coast. After the war—having grown more familiar with the military commanders now in charge of the effort against the Indians—it generally was much less critical. By this time, also, the *Times* recognized the changing nature of the conflict. As growing numbers of white settlers cast wistful eyes on land occupied by the Indians, the ascendant national policy had at its core the isolation of the Native Americans on reservations. Forceful chiefs such as Black

Kettle of the Cheyenne and Satanta of the Kiowa led their tribes in resisting such confinement. Red Cloud and other strong chiefs, meanwhile, were determined to keep white settlers out of the Sioux country to the north.

In a September 1867 editorial on the work of a peace commission recently established by Congress, the *Times* applauded a council between the commissioners and a group of Sioux chiefs. It noted that the Indians' main complaint was the encroachment by whites on Indian territory. The chiefs told the commissioners "in most emphatic terms," the editorial reported, "that the whites are invading their territory, cutting roads wherever they please, running railroads without stint, and building forts and filling them with soldiers, thereby driving all game from the country and depriving the Indians of the means of living." They said when the roads were closed they and the whites could live at peace again. The *Times* said General William T. Sherman responded to the chiefs "with great plainness" and told them the roads would stay. Further, wagon roads would be replaced with railroads, and whites from the East and the West would be located along these routes as "thick as grasshoppers." The chiefs were given a choice, according to the *Times*, between a war that would end in their extermination "or a life of idleness at the expense of the government."

Just two months later, a follow-up editorial reported that the peace commission was on its way back to Washington, having failed to come to terms with the Indians. Among other reasons, the *Times* said, the tribes had been discouraged by "the hundreds of petty swindlers who make their fortunes by dealing with the Indians." This may not have been too difficult, the editorial suggested, since the "savage's experience with councils and the white men's promises has not been of a character to induce him to place much confidence in them."

While the potential for armed clashes always simmered somewhere beneath the surface of the Indian problem, during the decade of the 1870s it boiled to the top in an escalating series of brutal confrontations. Chief Sitting Bull and a band of Sioux, whose rights had been trampled in the rush for gold in the Black Hills, retaliated in the Battle of the Rosebud and the Battle of the Little Big Horn. The Red River War in the Southwest proved costly to both sides, while a small band of Modocs led by Captain Jack waged a determined fight in northern California and southern Oregon. The tragic Nez Percé War in the Northwest made the name of Chief Joseph familiar to readers in the East. And the Utes in Utah and Colorado struggled against white encroachment until nearly the end of the decade.

Ironically, the *Times* began that fierce decade with editorial expressions of confidence that long-term peace with the Indians was at hand. The army had no desire to provoke a fight, it said in a March 1871 editorial. The reservation system was working, it contended, and reports from both military and civilian sources indicated nothing to suggest an Indian outbreak. When the Modoc War proved the fallacy of that view within a matter of months, the *Times* saw ample blame to go around. The Modocs clearly had been the aggressors, it believed, but the conflict "does not appear to be a credit to anybody concerned; it may become a reproach to the entire nation."

The *Times* was persistent in its concern for adequate military strength to carry out operations against the Indians. In the summer of 1874, while still optimistic that there would be no general Indian war, it argued that President Ulysses S. Grant's peace policy needed to be backed by stronger military might. Any hostilities, it asserted, ought to be suppressed immediately. And it noted that the number of potential trouble spots was growing.

The army's defeats at the hands of the Sioux in the Montana Territory in June 1876 were interpreted by the *Times* as vindication of its position. A July 7 editorial on Custer's catastrophic defeat on the Little Big Horn, included in this chapter, blamed the losses in part on the retrenchment polices of Congress. But it also pointed out the "needless irritation" of Custer's earlier expedition into the Black Hills. The more the Indians were hemmed in, it suggested, the more determined they would be in combat. In a brief editorial two days later, the *Times* clearly fixed much of the liability for Custer's defeat on the general himself. Had Custer carried out the plan prescribed by his superior officers, it said, "in all probability, the sad issue of that days' fighting would have been reversed."

Although it resolutely supported the army in its Indian campaigns, the *Times* by the mid-1870s was beginning to show more consistent editorial sympathy for the Native Americans involved in combat against superior military odds. This position was expressed most forcefully during the Nez Percé War of 1877. "The present outbreak has its origin, like so many of its predecessors, in a sense of wrong felt (whether with or without reason) by the Indians," the *Times* said in a July editorial. And now, it continued, Chief Joseph and his followers were battling a military force equipped with Gatling guns and howitzers. "Of course," said the *Times*, "Joseph takes a desperate course in throwing down the gauntlet to our Army, but he has not more odds against him than had Capt. Jack, who yet made the Modoc war a bloody one." It said the Indian, when roused to fight, hardly took note of the odds or was deterred by the chances of failure.

A month later, in a brief editorial paragraph, the *Times* asserted that, "If the penalty fell on those who deserved it, there would be a certain degree of poetic justice in the spectacle of a great nation like our own baffled in its attempts to bring to peaceful terms a tribe of Indians whom it has for years cheated, persecuted, and plundered." The Nez Percés, it explained, historically had been friends with the whites. Their struggle was hopeless, it added, "and sooner or later they will be crushed out; but their cause is essentially a good one. It adds incalculable bitterness to the regret with which the country witnesses the misfortunes of its soldiers to know that they are suffering for the neglect or the treachery and greed of those who escape scott free."

The respect that *Times* editorial writers developed for Chief Joseph and his Nez Percé warriors is reflected vividly in two August 1877 editorials included in this chapter. Through all the years in which its editorial columns focused on the Indian problem, the *Times* never disparaged the Indians as fighters.

Most of the open warfare between Indians and white settlers shifted to the Southwest in the 1880s. The *Times*, in turn, directed its attention to Geronimo and the Apaches. But the *Times* continued to look warily at Sitting Bull and the Sioux, as well, and worried anew that the army was underfunded. When Red Cloud sought permission to take a band of Sioux from the Dakota Pine Ridge Agency to Wyoming to join other Indians in a "picnic excursion," the newspaper suggested in a brief August 1886 comment that a body of Indians so large, "bent on having a good time, may naturally arouse some trepidation."

The Ghost Dance disturbance of 1890, which led to the death of Sitting Bull, led the *Times* to agonize once again over prospects that serious Indian wars might yet lie ahead. And it still fretted that those most responsible for a violent conflict would not be the ones engaged in the fight. That latter concern in many ways epitomized the editorial position of the *Times* as it had labored for four decades to examine and explain the hostilities commonly called the Indian wars. While the battles and bloodshed were the visible manifestations of the Indian problem, the underlying causes often were more subtle and difficult to discern. The *Times* editorial writers worked diligently to draw together the threads of cause and effect. The success of their efforts is exhibited in the editorials that make up the rest of this chapter.

ᨒ Frontier Matters

July 3, 1861

Our Washington correspondence of this morning gives some items of a startling character, touching life in Arizona. It is now something more than ten years since our frontier line has been thrown from the western limit of the great valley of the Mississippi, to those regions known as the Rocky Mountain slopes, bounded by the British possessions on the north and by Mexico on the south. During the early period of the California emigration, when emigrants in large bodies rushed across the country, we heard little of Indian depredations. But later, when civilization attempted to make a stand in sections of the intermediate countries, and emigrants in small bodies wound their slow and weary way over a variety of routes, the wild Indian commenced his systematic course of plunder and butchery. Our correspondent states that he estimates the number of white settlers and emigrants killed by the Indians in our frontier regions, at one thousand per annum. This is a fearful estimate, and but for our confidence in the knowledge and accuracy of our information, we should be disposed to consider his calculation as highly extravagant.

It is undoubtedly a fact that our Indian difficulties have been augmenting since 1856. It has especially fallen to our lot to chronicle Indian depredations of the most frightful character in Arizona and New-Mexico, during the past three years, month by month—yes, almost week by week. We believe there is a department in Washington whose business it is to look after Indian affairs generally along the frontier; and yet reports come from that department and from the War Office as well, couched in the language of ease and content, and congratulating the country on the peculiarly happy manner in which the business in their particular charge is managed, but which, in fact, is so wofully mismanaged as to be a disgrace to a civilized nation, to which the dying shrieks and groans, and the bleaching bones of thousands and thousands of our murdered pioneers can testify.

The Indian Wars

ᴄ⁊ The Indians

August 12, 1865

There is one war in this country to which time brings no surcease—that of the white man against the red man. It has been waged for over two centuries—the Indian always defeated, yet never defeated. From all their vast hunting-grounds on the Atlantic seaboard, in the Valley of the Ohio, and in the Valley of the Mississippi, they have been driven, till now, in their last refuge on the great plains and under the shadow of the Rocky Mountains, they find themselves confronted and surrounded by the old white enemy, and no possibility of further retreat. The Indians are at bay. They are bewildered; they are helpless. It is not in their nature to adopt the habits and follow the pursuits of the white man; and it is not in the nature or destiny of the white man to permit the Indian to follow his hereditary habitudes. Feuds and fights, cruelties and hatreds, wretchedness and despair, exile and extermination, constitute the present, as the past, history of the poor Indian, in presence of the white settler.

It is very hard upon the Indian. And the worst of the matter is that we can see no good way in which his career is likely to close. There is to be a great convention of all the tribes, wild and civilized, held next month at Fort Smith; and our government is to be represented by an excellent delegation, among whom will be the distinguished descendant of Red Jacket, Col. Parker, of Gen. Grant's staff. But what is it possible for the convention to do? It can neither guarantee the Indians their lands, their rights, or their lives. They are scattered over an immense surface, and will everywhere be in enmity with the contiguous settlers, and we fear it is impossible to get them all to live together. If they would take it into their heads to move southward to *Mexico*, where the bulk of their race is now concentrated, it would be a happy thing for them and us.

ᴄ⁊ Cruelty to the Indians

October 11, 1865

Gen. Connor, the Indian fighter of the Rocky Mountains, has proclaimed war to the knife against all the red men of that section. We doubt very much whether the government will sustain him in any such policy. He has been fighting these people very hard and very steadily during the last four years;

and the latest reports of his operations had statements that could hardly be explained in any other way than that he had been guilty of massacres. There is among the papers of last Congress a terrible document containing the details of the Indian massacre in Colorado, by Col. Chivington, and we fear the fact that Chivington has thus far been allowed to go unpunished, has led other officers operating against these Indians to act with a ferocity that is disgraceful in a Christian people. We have heard all that can be said against the Indians, and we understand perfectly the anxiety of Western settlers to have the entire race exterminated. But a great government cannot, with impunity, permit injustice, even to the most helpless of its people.

New Indian Difficulties

September 2, 1866

We are having renewed reports of Indian difficulties in various parts of our far Western territories. It has just been proved that the Indian massacres which were reported as having occurred a few weeks ago in Arizona, California and Nevada, never took place, and that the reports were started by parties in the localities referred to, for sinister and selfish purposes. But on the very heels of these denials and revelations, we have reports of other Indian outrages in two or three other localities. It is unquestionably true that one at least of these newly reported Indian difficulties is genuine; but others of them we have the best of reasons for doubting entirely, or for attributing the blame to the side opposite from that blamed by the telegraph. We have so frequently stated—what is proved by all the records of the Indian Bureau, and by all the experience of residents in our newly settled regions—that in these Indian difficulties, bad white men are in nearly every instance the originators and aggressors, and that motives of selfishness and gain are at their base—that it is not necessary to ask our readers to be critical concerning the statements that are telegraphed to the country, from time to time, for the purpose of exciting public feeling, and inducing the desired action on the part of the Government. Had the recent Arizona fictions been credited, for example, there would by this time have been dispatched to that territory one or two additional regiments of infantry and a regiment of dragoons. This would involve the disbursement along the line of march, not merely of thousands and tens of thousands, but of *hundreds of thousands* of dollars, as the late experience in transporting a regiment to that locality has proven; and the stationing of such a force in the Territory would put money in the pockets of every white settler there, from the consumption of grain, fodder, and other supplies for man and beast. Here is a sufficient motive for getting up a small difficulty with the Indians, and sending a large report of it over the country. We have good reason for believing that most of the stories we have lately had of Indian difficulties on the Central route are prompted by this motive; and, indeed, it applies with a frequency quite incredible to those unfamiliar with such matters in the Far West. It is well that the disposition and locating of our troops is in the hands of such a man as Gen. Grant. He understands, we have no doubt, the whole matter, and will take good care, while protecting settlers and traders and travel upon the Plains, to avoid playing into the hands of the unscrupulous knaves who are at the root of most of our Indian troubles.

✍ Our Indian Policy—The Recommendations of Gen. Grant

December 9, 1866

Gen. Grant, in his recent report to the Secretary of War, suggests "for the consideration of Congress the propriety of transferring the Indian Bureau from the Interior to the War Department, and the abolition of Indian agencies with the exception of a limited number of inspectors." Formerly the Secretary of War controlled these matters, and as the officers of the army who were our Indian agents performed their duties honestly and disinterestedly, all things considered, there was comparatively little trouble. Now, however, the state of the case is quite different, so that we find the greater portion of the report of Lieut.-Gen. Sherman is devoted to the discussion of the proper method of treating the Indians.

There can be but little doubt that in many cases the "red man" has been deeply wronged by the whites who reside upon the borders of his reservations; but at the same time it must not be forgotten that the majority of the Indians who inhabit the plains are dirty, thieving fellows, who murder the weak and unprotected, and never attack an armed foe. In speaking of them Gen. Sherman says:

"The Indians who have heretofore been located on reservations, such as the Wyandotts, Shawnees, Pottawatomies, Pawnees, Cherokees, Choctaws, Creeks, &c., &c., have given little or no trouble the last year, and do not come within our supervision more than our own people. But the wandering

Sioux, who rove from Minnesota to Montana, and down as far as the Arkansas, have done acts of predatory hostility almost impossible to foresee or to prevent. In like manner the Arapahoes and Cheyennes, Kiowas, Comanches and Apaches, Navajoes and Utes, though supposed to be restricted to reservations, will not settle down, but they roam, according to their habits, over the vast plains; and they, too, have done acts of hostility, though the old men and chiefs of the tribes deny the acts altogether, or charge them on their young men, who, when absent on the hunt, are beyond their control."

While, then, peaceable tribes of Indians should not be molested, the testimony of the officers who have to deal with them and the reports which are constantly reaching us of their attacks upon emigrants, show that a change of our policy toward the hostile ones has become a matter of necessity. The country over which these hostile tribes hunt is being constantly crossed by trains of emigrants, miners and traders who have a right to be protected from such lawless marauders. Those who know them best report that treaties with these Indians are like treaties with the buffaloes and bears which inhabit the same country.

The plan of Gen. Sherman, which is that of every army officer who is conversant with Indian affairs, is to confine these tribes within a specified reservation, and to deal summarily with all those who are found outside of its limits without a written pass. Care also should be taken to prevent any arms or ammunition being sold or given to them, although, if necessary, food and clothing could be supplied. Again, in case they are to be fought, it should be in their own fashion, and chiefly by cavalry mounted on half-breed horses. For this purpose as many friendly Indians as possible should be employed, those already authorized being formed into one or two battalions, instead of being scattered about as now, a few at a post, where they can necessarily have but little effect. Such expeditions, armed with repeating rifles, and carrying their baggage on pack mules, have almost invariably succeeded in overcoming even the most active of these tribes. The Indians with whom we are now at war have never been thoroughly whipped, and it will only be necessary to do it once to finally subdue them.

The expeditions sent against these tribes should be commanded by officers who will not be easily discouraged, no matter how laborious their task, or insufficient their food; and who will fight on every occasion and attack at the instant.

In the Department of the Platte, on the road from Fort Laramie to Virginia City, the Indians have killed Lieut. Daniels, of the Eighteenth United States Infantry, 24 soldiers and 20 citizens connected with trains. Gen. Sherman says that these deaths must be avenged next year. The General further adds that

"It is our duty, and it shall be my study, to make the progress of construction of the great Pacific Railways that lie in this belt of country as safe as possible, as also to protect the stage and telegraph lines against any hostile bands, but they are so long that to guard them perfectly is an impossibility, unless we can restrict the Indians as herein stated."

At the first glance, the measures proposed may seem harsh and even cruel, but not when we consider the savages who are to be dealt with, and remember the unfavorable influence their depredations must have upon persons desirous of settling in the Far West. It is doubtless the fact that the Indians have been sadly sinned against; but we find that when they give up their roving habits and apply themselves to cultivating land and raising cattle and horses, they become wealthy and respectable, as is the case with many of the Choctaws, Chickasaws, Cherokees and Creeks. Gen. Pope, in his report, also speaks of the Sioux, Comanches, &c., and says that he has no doubt that hostilities will again break out on the Platte, the Smoky Hill and the Arkansas Rivers before the beginning of Winter.

Last year a committee was sent by Congress on a journey over the plains to investigate existing evils and suggest appropriate remedies; but their report has not been made public.

Now that Gen. Grant and Lieut.-Gen. Sherman have again, in such a marked manner, called public attention to the subject of our Indian policy, it is to be hoped that some further action will be taken in this matter before the close of the present session of Congress.

∽ Sheridan's Winter Campaign

December 4, 1868

Fighting Indians in the dead of Winter, in their own villages, and tracking them in snow twelve inches deep, is new business for our soldiery. But they have done both very well, and the first fruits of their campaign is a surprise and a victory after the hardest-fought and bloodiest Indian battle which has taken place on the continent during many a year.

It was a "salty dose," as Sheridan would say, that Custer administered to the Cheyennes, Arapahoes and Kiowas. Our loss was severe—nineteen men and two valuable officers, the gallant Major Elliot and Capt. Hamilton being killed, and eleven men and three officers wounded. But Black Kettle's loss was far more severe—he and 102 of his warriors were left dead on the field, (probably no quarter was given,) and his whole camp, with great quantities of ponies, buffalo skins, powder, lead, arrows, tobacco, rifles, pistols, bows, lariats, dried meats and other provisions, were captured. In brief, the whole village, with all its lodges, its Winter's stores of arms, ammunition, food and forage, and the wives and children of the dead warriors, fell into our hands at one stroke.

In a former article, we showed how the campaign would probably open upon the Canadian River—a stream which, rising in New-Mexico, flows due east across the northwest corner (or "pan-handle") of Texas, into and across the Indian Territory to where, near its eastern boundary, it empties into the Arkansas. The Winter home of the Kiowas is in this "pan-handle" corner of Texas, among and to the west and south of the Antelope Hills, and along the series of petty tributaries which there swell the Canadian and the Red. In directing Custer's command (eleven companies of the Seventh Cavalry) upon this point, Gen. Sheridan struck right at the heart of the hostile forces. The Wachita (a branch of the Red River) rises in the Antelope Hills; and striking its head waters, and following it down, Custer soon came upon the Cheyenne camp of Black Kettle. The Summer hunting-grounds of the Cheyennes and Arapahoes are much further north, namely, in Northern Colorado and Western Kansas and Nebraska, say along the South Fork of the Platte and the Republican Fork of the Kansas River. But the approach of Winter and the operations of Sheridan had combined to drive them southerly to the point just indicated. The battle took place in the Indian Territory, not far east of the Texas line.

"This," says Sherman, "gives Gen. Sheridan a good initiation." Probably, when the truth comes to be known, it will turn out to have been a pretty murderous affair. As we have intimated, it looks as if no quarter were given, for whereas mention is made of killing 102 warriors, nothing is said of a single one being captured—from which we may guess that all were dispatched. Moreover, in ordinary battles, the proportion of wounded is four or five to one; in this fight, the killed far outnumbered the wounded, even on our own side—a sufficient proof of the desperation of the battle. It is a consolation, however, to reflect that our troops fell on the right bands. Black Kettle's warriors were the men who first committed the outrages on Solomon and Saline Forks, last Summer, and opened the unprovoked war in Kansas. The Arapahoes, neighbors of the Cheyennes, had joined them in hostilities. As for Satanta, he is the splendid Kiowa chief who took part in the famous peace negotiations conducted by Gen. Hancock and others, and was imposing in his presence and eloquence.

The Indian agent is, as usual, "apprehensive that innocent Indians will suffer in the campaign." Indian agents are *always* apprehensive of something of this sort. We admit, too, that there is some danger of this; but the necessity of striking a hard blow has been long apparent. No Indians who have applied to go on reservations will suffer—that is very sure. Moreover, it is a consolation to know that, at any rate the *first* blow has struck the guilty parties. Gen. Sherman says he considers Sheridan's personal presence as a guarantee that "nothing will be done but what is right."

The fight on the Wachita is a proof of the theory that a Winter campaign, and that alone, can avail against the Indians. It is a hard and perilous affair, and "nature presents many difficulties," as Sheridan says. Troops are lost or frozen in the blinding snow; supplies are ice-bound in rivers; it is a kind of Moscow campaign on a small scale, with bloodier than Cossack foes, ready to take advantage of a mistake. But "stout hearts" will do much; and one or two repetitions of Custer's victory will give us peace on the Plains.

↶ The Indians

August 27, 1874

The news of the various hostile outbreaks by the Indians upon the frontier is hardly alarming enough as yet to warrant the conclusion that a general war is to ensue, but it is evident that the columns of the regular army, now on the march in the Indian Territory, Texas, New-Mexico, and among the Black Hills, are likely to encounter serious opposition. The latest dispatches from the Wichita Agency in the "Territory" show that the Kiowas, at least, manifest an inclination for battle. It appears that Gen. Davidson, with four companies of the Tenth Cavalry, had gone to the Wichita Agency to disarm certain inimical Comanches, who had left their reservations without permission and taken to the war-path. While the General was engaged in this work, which he was accomplishing peaceably, some Kiowas, who had also left their reservation without the knowledge of the agents, attacked the cavalry, and a general fight ensued, in which several soldiers and Indians were killed. Numerous unoffending citizens have also been murdered by the Comanches or the Kiowas, and further troubles are expected. In this case the Indians clearly seem to have been entirely to blame, while in the recently reported hostilities between the Osages and the Kansas Militia the whites appear to have been the aggressors. A reasonable explanation of the sudden malice of the Kiowas may possibly be found in the fact that the whole section of the Indian Territory in which they live is overrun by whisky peddlers and low white banditti, who spread drunkenness among the red-skins. The officers of the regular army would do well to turn their attention a little to these white men, as they have been compelled to do once or twice before, and to either clear them out of the Territory, or hang them.

But it is not from the Indian Territory alone that reports of warlike demonstrations reach us. It is asserted that Gen. Custer, who is now in camp at Cowpens, in the Black Hills, is in danger of attack, and that the chiefs who are organizing forces for the war-path boast that they can bring four thousand warriors against his little expedition. Our attention is also invited to the raids of the Apaches from California into Mexico, and to divers causes for apprehension along the whole frontier. Formidable and well-drilled bodies of savages here and there hover on the trail of soldiery, and amuse themselves, when not manoeuvring against the troops, by scalping defenseless bands of emigrants, cattle drovers and settlers remote from the protecting agencies. The marauding bands which rove up and down the vast plains between the Red and Wichita, and the Pecos and Rio Grande, and which have never received half the punishment they merit, although some of the most gallant officers of the regular army are constantly chasing them, have been unusually daring of late. They have gradually become convinced, by the immunity from effective punishment which they have enjoyed, that they are able to cope with the United States Government; and until they have had stern proof to the contrary, they will continue their thievery and murder. Their favorite field of operation is along the Rio Grande, in Texas. When they are followed, they take refuge on Mexican soil, where they can, of course, bid defiance to Texan settlers, and to the cavalrymen from the forts, who are naturally forbidden to cross the boundary line. The cavalry corps which Col. McKenzie is organizing at Fort Concho, in Western Texas, may do some effective service against these Indians, and will undoubtedly punish with severity such as are convicted of having left their reservations—if they can be caught.

But the army ought to be able to catch and punish every refractory Indian, or body of Indians. The savage would never leave his reservation if he were fully convinced that behind the "peace policy" there would always be sufficient force to punish any infringement of that policy on his part. It is by no means certain that it was wholly wise for Congress to push economy so far as to deprive the army of the means for properly patrolling the Indian country. The old proverb, "If you wish peace, prepare for war," should have been heeded in this case. It is to be expected that there will be outbreaks of a serious nature on the frontier from time to time, and if they are encouraged by non-resistance—if they are not, rather, immediately suppressed—they can cause incalculable mischief. A few evil-disposed Indians, incited to revolt by the liquor, and emboldened to fight with the weapons which mean whites sell them, can carry desolation through a wide tract of country before they can be stopped, because there are no troops near at hand to check them. Cavalry only is really effective in following up Indians. The ten cavalry regiments, averaging hardly six hundred men each, now on duty among the Indians constitute a force quite inadequate to the task it is invited to perform. How can these ten regiments thoroughly police the region between the Missouri and the Mexican frontier, the immense district in Kansas and the Indian Territory, as well as New-Mexico, Arizona, Oregon, Nevada, California, Nebraska, Dakota, Wyoming, Montana, and Utah? As it is, they accomplish things which seem like miracles; but it is preposterous to ask them to cover the whole ground. If there ever should be a general and concerted Indian outbreak, the scattered detachments of this tiny, though sturdy, and withal heroic force, would be of small avail. And it is quite possible that either Col. Miles, who is beating about the country between Fort Dodge, in Kansas, and Fort Sill, in the Indian Territory, with a handful of men, or Col. Davidson, who has been moving up from Texas to Fort Sill with a regiment, and, as we have seen, has already had a brush with the red men, or Gen. Custer, with his small but resolute band, pushing in among the jealous Sioux in the Black Hills, may meet with more vicious Indians than their diminutive forces can handle.

We believe in the continuance of a "peace policy" with regard to the Indians, so far as it is practicable. But we see no reason why the pursuance of that policy need imply such a reduction of the military force as will gradually induce the Indians to hold the Government in contempt. Give the Indian a peace policy and protection so long as he deserves it, but let the army have the power to inflict speedy punishment upon him the moment he willfully and wantonly does wrong.

∽ An Indian Victory

July 7, 1876

So few newspaper readers have followed the course of the Indian warfare in the North-west that the overwhelming defeat of Custer's command and the butchery of this gallant commander and his men, will produce both astonishment and alarm. We have latterly fallen into the habit of regarding the Indians yet remaining in a wild or semi-subdued state as practically of very little account. It is only now and then when some such outburst as that of the Modocs, which resulted in the slaying of Gen. Canby, Commissioner Thomas, and others, or that which we now record with so much sorrow, comes like a shock, that we realize the character of the Indian and the difficulties of the situation. Sitting Bull's band of Sioux left their reservation with hostile intent. They refused negotiations for peace. They defied the power and authority of the United States. They invited war. A force was sent against them. This force became divided, and Gen. Custer, with five companies, coming up to the main body of the Sioux, attacked them impetuously, without waiting for the support of the remainder of the column. The result was that the entire body of men, numbering between three and four hundred, and including Gen. Custer and several other commissioned officers, fell into a death-trap; they were overwhelmed by superior numbers, and were all slaughtered. The precise particulars of that horrible catastrophe will never be known. There are no survivors. The course of the detachment, after it began the attack, is traced only by the bodies of the slain. How gallantly these poor fellows fought can only be surmised. The Indians carried off some of their dead and wounded; others were concealed, or *cached*, with Indian cunning, in order that the white man should not know how much damage they had suffered.

The streams on which the late tragical events happened are branches of the Yellowstone, which in this region—Southern Montana—has a general course from west to east. Going up-stream one successively passes on the left, or southern bank of the Yellowstone, Powder River, Tongue River, Rosebud Creek, and the Big Horn. The last-named stream was supposed to be the extreme western limit of the operations of this expedition. Gen. Terry is the senior and ranking officer in the active force, Gen. Custer having been second in his immediate command. The Army, however, was divided into three columns, one being under Gen. Crook, and operating far to the south of the Yellowstone, and one under Gibbon, who was to the north in supporting distance of Terry. On the 17th of June, Crook's forces met the hostile Sioux, under Sitting Bull, on the headwaters of the Rosebud, about seventy miles from the junction of that stream with the Yellowstone. The Sioux were probably not in full force, but they outnumbered the whites and their allies, the Snakes and the Crows. Gen. Crook was repulsed and fell back in a southerly direction, with a loss of ten killed and thirteen wounded. About that time the commands of Gen. Terry and Gen. Gibbon were encamped on the Yellowstone, far to the northward, one at the mouth of the Powder, and the other at the mouth of the Tongue River.

We cannot tell when Terry learned of the defeat of Crook, if he did at all before his next movement, which was in the nature of a scout in search of Sitting Sull. That chieftain was supposed to have a large camp somewhere on Rosebud Creek. At last accounts, Custer, with nine companies, was to cross over to the Rosebud, passing west from Tongue River, feeling for the Sioux. Terry, with seven companies, was to follow within easy supporting distance. Gibbon, we must suppose, was to follow the general route westward, but was to keep to the northward, in order to be before the Sioux, in case they attempted to turn to the eastward. Not finding the Sioux on the Rosebud, Custer kept on and struck their main camp on the Little Horn, a branch of the Big Horn, and about fifty miles west of the point where Crook had been turned back, June 17. Custer's command was divided, Major Reno commanding part and Custer the remainder. Without once reckoning the disparity of numbers, (for the Indians are reported to have been four or five thousand strong,) Custer impetuously charged upon the foe. The result was appalling. No such catastrophe has happened in our Indian warfare since the Florida war.

It is useless to attempt to discover all the causes which have led to this disaster. The general management of the campaign may have been faulty. It is well known that military operations in the North-west have been crippled by the mistaken policy of retrenchment adopted by the present House of Representatives. Gen. Custer was a brave, dashing, but somewhat imprudent soldier, and his natural desire to save his superior officer (with whom he had not been in perfect accord) the responsibility of an attack, may have hastened his fatal descent upon the enemy. Then, behind this, we cannot help seeing the needless irritation caused by the expedition into the Black Hills country last Summer. Sitting Bull's band were alienated and enraged at that time; and nothing but the interposition of friendly Indians prevented a massacre of the Commissioners sent out to treat with the Sioux. The Indians who have just wrought this bloody revenge are nominally on reservations. They have refused to stay there, and the expedition intended to chastise them and compel them to return has met with frightful disaster. The victory of the savages will inflame the border, and restless tribes will be impatient to share in the glory suddenly achieved by Sitting Bull and his braves. Year after year, the wild Indians have been hemmed in; they fight with no less desperation for that; and, now that we have been defeated in a considerable engagement, defensive tactics must precede the operations necessary for the chastisement of so dangerous and determined a foe.

᧥ The Indian War

July 18, 1876

It is possible that the natural apprehensions of the border men have exaggerated the possibilities of a general Indian war. A great calamity like that of the massacre on the Little Big Horn is sure to cause a wide-spread panic along the frontier and among the non-combatants who subsist at the military posts through the so-called Indian country. Nevertheless, it is probable that the victory of Sitting Bull, dearly bought though it may have been, has aroused a dangerous desire of emulation. We need no signs of excitement among the bands which are nominally friendly to prove this. The roving Indians of the North-west, whether constructively on reservations or not, have made warfare their occupation. It is difficult for a white man to understand how they abhor any peaceful pursuit. Hunting the buffalo, destructive, bloody, and exciting as the Indian usually makes this sport, is tameness itself compared with the war-like pursuits in which the Indian has been bred, and of which the traditions of his tribe furnish such stirring memories. By thousands of camp-fires the story of the annihilation of Custer's command has been told before now, with due accompaniment of yells of savage applause and excitement. By some strange system of aboriginal telegraphy, the minutest particulars of any serious collision between the whites and the Indians are carried from tribe to tribe in an incredibly brief space of time. When Canby and Thomas were killed by the Modocs, half-friendly Indians on the head-waters of the Yellowstone and on the reservations of Arizona, far to the south, were early in possession of all the main facts of the disastrous affair. They chafed under their loose bonds when they heard in some way of the achievements of red men far away on the other side of the continent. It is reported that the Sioux have been reinforced by Cheyennes and Arapahoes; and a large body of Cheyennes, heretofore at the Red Cloud Agency, is moving northward. In the late attack on Sibley's scouting party, Cheyennes were observed in the Sioux ranks, and a famous Cheyenne chief, White Antelope, was thought to have been recognized. Of course, much of this is conjecture, but it would be impossible for eight hundred Indians to leave an agency and join another tribe, whose dress, manner of warfare, and general appearance are so much unlike their own, and long escape detection. If Cheyennes have joined the Sioux, we shall soon find it out, and, unhappily, we shall find it out to our cost. Though the Sioux are dashing, subtle, and fiendish in their cruelty, the bravery, endurance, cunning, and relentless barbarity of the other tribe have long since made the name of Cheyenne a synonym on the plains for all that is horrible and to be feared.

Gen. Crook has information of this movement on the part of the Cheyennes. He proposes to have them intercepted by the reinforcements now on the way to his command from Fort Laramie. This may detain the relief party some time, and it will also postpone the attack on the Sioux which has been planned to take place when the reinforcements come up. It is, of course, highly desirable that the punishment of the Sioux, when it falls, shall be most condign. In the present temper of the Indians, who are naturally boastful and inordinately vain, nothing short of a crushing blow will be an effectual corrective. Gen. Terry desires Gen. Crook to join forces with him before the final onslaught is made, and in deference to Crook's long experience as an Indian fighter, Terry, who is his senior in rank (reckoning by date of Brigadier's commission,) is willing to waive all questions of military etiquette and place the responsible command in the hands of his junior. The troops, under whomsoever they may be placed, will fight at disadvantages which they well understand. They are in a difficult country, but one with which the Indians are familiar. The motions of the troops cannot be long concealed from the alert and fleet-footed foe. Numbers and position are usually in favor of the Indians. The white man overpowers by weight of metal and superior tactics.

It is idle for volunteer critics, sitting in secure offices and scanning an unmeaning map of the Indian country, to attempt intelligent direction of a campaign like this. Gen. Crook, for example, has spent years fighting the Indians, both in the North-west and in Arizona, where he succeeded in whipping out the Apache, an aborigine who probably comes nearer to being an incarnate devil than any creature upon the earth. It is easy for a well-meaning but uninformed citizen to find fault with the movements of a soldier like this, and to give suggestions as to the management of his campaign. Even a peace-loving regimental commander, who prefers a quiet life in St. Louis to a charge against the Sioux on the Big Horn, may freely relieve his mind concerning Custer's manner of fighting. But all such criticism recoils upon its author. Candid people are willing to believe that the men who have taken their lives in their hands and have gone out against a wily and vindictive foe, are doing their best to win the fight. The least that the stay-at-homes, military or civilian, can do is to keep their mouths shut and silence the fault-finding fire in the rear. In the dispatches which daily come to hand, we learn of innumerable brave deeds performed by individual fighters, and by detached parties. The march of the three scouts through a hostile country, from Terry's command to Crook's, and the blood-stirring exploits of Sibley's little band, belong to this order of military adventure. These incidents show a heroism, daring, and power of endurance of which Americans may justly be proud.

ᔐ The War with the Nez Percés

August 14, 1877

Making all allowances, Gen. Gibbon's bloody fight in the Big Hole Pass cannot be reckoned a success. When we find an officer of Gibbon's record telegraphing that the affair has left him in need of everything, and begging that aid may be sent him, it is doubtful whether we can concede him even a drawn battle. The preceding fight with Joseph, at the mouth of Cottonwood Creek, which Howard claimed as a triumph, was at best but a Cadmean victory—a struggle in which the nominal victors suffered quite as much as the vanquished.

The remarkable feature of the war with the Nez Percés is the skill with which the Indians have fought. We do not now refer to simple feats of valor, but to the actual tactical conduct of battle; for they have in every respect proved themselves as thorough soldiers as any of our trained veterans. In the affairs on Camas Prairie their celerity and boldness were conspicuous. In Howard's battle on the Clearwater, there is little doubt that he outnumbered the hostiles, and he had the advantage of artillery; yet, despite his Gatling guns and his howitzers, the Nez Percés got on his line of supplies and for twenty-four hours threatened to destroy him. Their manoeuvres have in every way proved skillful. Whether the demand is for selection of the battleground, for skirmishing, for flanking, for threatening communications, for attack in mass, for intrenching with rifle-pits, for detaching sharp-shooters "to command a spring of water," as in Howard's fight, or for charging "a high, wooded bluff," which proves to be the strategic key of the position, as in Gibbon's fight, the Indians exhibit instincts and methods as strictly military as if they had been acquired at West Point.

Joseph and his band have been much underrated by the common reports. He is no vagabond putting on the war-paint from thirst of blood and greed of booty. He has a cause which, we regret to say, is too much founded in justice; he and his tribe have been wronged; and the costly war he is now waging could, with ordinary good sense and a sincere purpose to do him justice, have been prevented. His braves are by no means a gang of besotted brutes, with no instincts above drinking, thieving, and scalping. Who are the Nez Percés? They are a tribe who have, by long and friendly intercourse with the whites, acquired not a few arts of civilization. Well endowed by nature, some of them have shown, by their skill in agriculture on the reservation, considerable capacities for progress. From the time of Lewis and Clark's expedition to this day the Nez Percés have maintained a reputation decidedly superior to the average of Indians. They have been mostly peaceful, and some of them have picked up considerable education. Lawyer, the main chief of the tribe, is a man of character; his brother is a regularly-ordained Presbyterian preacher in Oregon. Joseph's band, as we have before explained, have never been in the Nez Percé reservation, which was set apart in 1855, but have been allowed during more than twenty years to have their liberty of roving and their own little patch of ground, with its grazing facilities, from which they were lately driven out by the desire of white men to possess it. It is probable that even this might not have led to war, had not steps been taken to force Joseph upon the Nez Percé reservation, although Joseph claims that his father was a non-treaty Indian. Coupled with this grievance were sundry others, in the redressing of which nobody took the slightest interest. Accordingly, Joseph declared war, and a bloody business it has proved. Of course, it must now be pushed on till Joseph is killed or captured; but hereafter our Richelieus who engage to manage a band like Joseph's will do well to try "all means to conciliate" before employing "all means to crush."

✑ Modern Indian Campaigning

August 16, 1877

Probably many readers have asked themselves the question, how it is that, with all the appliances of a large and costly military establishment at our command, a band of savages like Joseph's can repeatedly hold their own against our troops on comparatively even terms. A satisfactory answer to this question would show that since the breech-loading epoch the whole problem of Indian warfare has been changed. To begin with, Joseph's war should open the eyes of the country to a truth long known to the Army, namely, the matchless skill of the frontier Indians as mounted infantry soldiers. The cavalrymen of the Don and the Volga, of whom we nowadays hear much, cannot be compared, for efficiency as skirmishers, with the dusky horsemen of the Columbia and the Missouri. The dashing Uhlans, who rode far and wide through France in advance of the German columns, were inferior, both as riders and marksmen, to the red warriors who with fleet ponies scour the Plains on either flank of the Rocky Mountains. This superiority, in some respects, of its barbarian foes cannot well be insisted upon by the Army itself, lest the latter should expose itself to a satirical retort. But the fact is really not discreditable to the Army; indeed, the remarkable prowess of the modern Indian soldier ought to be more thoroughly taken into account by the people, not only in order to determine how much we can fairly expect of the Army, but how large a force we need at the North-west.

It was to meet the peculiar exigencies of Indian warfare on the Western Plains that the cavalry in our Army from an early day bore so large a ratio to the infantry—a ratio which the mere number of regiments does not fully show, because the cavalry regiment has twelve companies, (usually subdivided into three battalions of four companies each,) whereas the infantry regiment has but ten. When the troops were first sent out to protect the tide of emigration setting westward from the Mississippi and the Missouri, they found the Indian horse-soldier even then, except at long range, a fair match, with his bow, for the white soldier with his carbine or his musket. As to the sabre, it quickly lost its old prestige, and went out of fashion as useless. When Gen. Wayne defeated the Indians, in 1794, on the banks of the Miami, his official report of the action noted that "Lieut. Covington, upon whom the command of the cavalry then devolved, cut down two savages with his own hand, and Lieut. Webb one, in turning the enemy's left flank." We hear nothing of that sort now; and what the historic weapon of cavalrymen has since become is told by Col. Blackett, in his history of this arm of the service. "The sabre in Indian fighting," he writes, "is simply a nuisance. It jingles abominably, and is of no earthly use. If a soldier gets close enough on an Indian to use a sabre, it is about an even thing as to which goes under first." The sabre, in fact, nowadays has no place in Indian campaigning, save by the courtesy of imaginative artists. Clinging to and directing his fleet pony by his legs alone, the Indian was a dangerous enemy even when armed only with his bow, and was able, Parthian-like, to do great damage in a running fight. His first progressive step was to get a carbine; but the tricky traders did not always, at the outset, sell him the best, and besides, the time required for loading the weapon at the muzzle while riding was a clear objection. But when at last he obtained the breech-loader, the Indian mounted soldier became truly formidable. The introduction of that weapon, from which so much advantage was expected by our troops, turned the scale of advantage to the side of the Indian. While the aim of most of our cavalrymen from their saddles is uncertain, the mounted Indian preserves that traditional steadiness and accuracy which he had when his only missile was the arrow or the lance. He is aware of this advantage, and it gives him confidence. Hardy and tough, carrying no baggage of any sort, requiring very simple food, accustomed to endure hunger, thirst, toil, and privations as no white soldier can, a born horseman, the Indian obviously needed only a weapon that could be used on horseback with the rapidity of the bow, and at greater range, in order to become a perfect soldier in his way—and this weapon the repeating carbine furnished him. And when, as, of course, generally happens in pitched battle, the Indian dismounts, and acts as an infantry soldier, he has another skill, derived from his hunting habits, such as no skirmishing drill in the schools will give—a perfect skill in taking advantage of tree, rock, or inequality of the ground, to hide his stealthy approach, or his swift movement from point to point.

We might go on to another class of suggestions, based upon the advantages which the Indian derives from the nature and extent of the country he campaigns in, being ordinarily able to run until he prefers to stop and fight, and in fighting to pick out a ground that will either entrap pursuers or at least allow him to escape. But it is enough for our purpose at present to show that if Congress could figure to itself, in place of the various Indian tribes now so strangely underrated as efficient troops, the choicest soldiers of the world, equally hard to manage and equally liable to take the war-path, it might understand better than now what force should be kept at hand for protection in the North-west until the problem of Indian civilization is solved.

➥ The Indian Frontier Movements

April 29, 1878

The contemplated movements of troops in Dakota and Montana, which have excited some comment, are doubtless to be regarded as purely precautionary. There is no reason for supposing that any cavalry scouting that may be done this Spring will be done with hostile intent, or with the expectation of precipitating a general Indian war. With our past experiences on the border, the wisdom of taking the ounce of prevention cannot be doubted; and the uncertainty prevailing with regard to the intents, not only of the Indians on the other side of the line, but of those on this side, makes the need of precaution greater.

During the past five months—indeed, ever since the failure of the embassy sent to Sitting Bull—there have been constant and constantly contradictory rumors about the purposes and the movements of that chief. The officers of the North-west Mounted Police have steadily insisted, in the face of all reports, that Sitting Bull would remain at peace, through the Winter at least. It is plain that they were right; for, although Sioux from Sitting Bull's camp, and the chief himself, have been frequently reported by our scouts to be on this side of the boundary, yet either the scouts were wrong or the crossing was done while hunting buffalo, and with no hostile intent. Recent reconnoitring parties found a few hundred Indians, supposed to be Sioux, in camp on the Upper Beaver Creek, below Dry Fork, and also among the hills in the Big Bend of the Milk River, in Montana, north-west of Fort Benton. But this was an insignificant fraction of Sitting Bull's force—if they came from his camp, which is doubtful. The points here indicated are near the boundary line, and scores of miles away from settlements. The scouts admitted that the Indians said "as long as nobody hunts us we will hunt nobody." It is also admitted that no hostile demonstration has been made by them.

These are the omens of peace. But the Sioux warrior in Spring is a different man from the Sioux warrior in Winter. To suppose that, simply because the border Indians have been quiet while campaigning was out of the question, they will so remain all Summer is by no means safe. Sitting Bull's capacity for mischief is formidable. It has been represented that his escape from Miles, a year ago, was less a triumphal march to Canada than a disorderly flight and a rout; that he lost many of his warriors in crossing the treacherous ice of the Missouri, just then breaking up, and carried off little plunder. But he at least had the spoils of Custer's command, with all their arms, ammunition, and equipments; and it is further understood that traders have since made their way freely into the Sioux camps with the best rifles and cartridges. Our scouts report them to be liberally supplied in this respect, some of them carrying two or three filled cartridge boxes and belts instead of one. It is certain that they have all the arms and munitions of war that they need, and of the best sort. It was at one time said that both the Sioux and Nez Percé Indians were almost starving last Winter, subsisting chiefly on horse-flesh; but it is known that the Winter was comparatively mild, that buffalo and other game was plentiful, and that the Indians were in good health and condition.

As to numbers, Sitting Bull must have a good-sized army with him. The estimates of his force differ widely, even among those who are most likely to judge well. There is little doubt that he lost heavily at the fight with Custer on Rosebud Creek; and up to that time the most careful estimates did not give him more than 1,500 warriors, exclusive of the women and children. He has since been greatly reinforced by refugees, including not only Sioux, but Cheyennes and Nez Percés who escaped under White Bird from Miles' victory over Joseph. Some of the scouting parties that lately reported to Capt. Williams, of the Seventh Infantry, at Fort Belknap, claimed that Sitting Bull had 2,000 lodges with him, and upward of 5,000 fighting men. But this seems a great exaggeration, being based on reckoning an unusually large number of warriors to the lodges, and also on his getting all neighboring Indians to join him in hostilities. Among the Sixth Infantry, at Fort Buford, some officers estimate, from what are considered trustworthy reports, that there are about 1,500 lodges of Sioux and Nez Percés, with perhaps 3,000 or more warriors to be relied on. Gen. Crook has recently been reported as estimating Sitting Bull's fighting strength at about 3,000 or 4,000. Consul Taylor, of Winnipeg, has also formed a high estimate of the chief's strength, although Manitoba is apt to be alarmed on the subject.

Supposing that, at a moderate estimate, Sitting Bull has 2,000 well-armed warriors that he could lead to battle, this would be a formidable force. For, it must be remembered that, as was the case during the Nez Percé campaign, the larger part of the frontier troops must remain in garrison. Gen. Sheridan lately stated that there were upward of 13,000 Indians between the Missouri and the Canada line, exclusive of Sitting Bull's forces and the other roving Sioux and Cheyennes who either have joined their fortunes to his or are ready to do so. To watch the frontier lines against these Indians, as well as others further south, on reservations, would detain many troops from field service against Sitting Bull. If, in addition, Sitting Bull should effect a general hostile alliance of Indians on both sides of the border, one of the most serious Indian wars of the century would be waged. It might prove to be the last great Indian war, if eventually ending in the downfall of the coalition, but it would be very bloody and destructive while it lasted.

Thus far there are no indications of such an alliance, or even of any hostile purposes on Sitting Bull's part. He has not yet falsified his expressions of a desire for peace given to Major Walsh and Col. MacLeod; but it would be a total failure of duty, with such elements of possible danger—fuel ready to blaze into a conflagration on both sides of the border—for our Army to neglect precautions. Should a lack of reconnoissances or of suitable preparations lead to a surprise of some small outlying post, like Fort Peck, or to a raid on the settlements, the outcry would be general and thoroughly justified.

⌁ Indian Wars as Investments

August 20, 1878

If it be true, as tidings from Idaho assert, that the Bannock war is substantially over, we shall soon be entitled to an official reckoning of what it has cost and what it has come to. Happily, it has not proved nearly as bloody as most of its predecessors, comparatively few soldiers and settlers having perished; but its pecuniary cost, reckoning the expense of transportation, of volunteers, of extra supplies, of material used up or lost, and so on, is likely to approach or exceed a million dollars, exclusive of the property destroyed by Indians. Yet, on the high authority of Gen. Crook, it is declared that "hunger, nothing but hunger," drove the Bannocks and Shoshones to the war-path; and Commissioner Hayt says that these Indians had, through insufficient appropriations, long been on short rations, which was their cause of complaint, and that he had urged an increase of $15,000, which Congress refused to grant.

If this latest of our Indian wars stood alone in the negligence or recklessness that caused it, it would still point a moral. But it is only the last item in a disgraceful as well as costly catalogue. Not to go back more than a quarter of a century, the Sioux war of 1852 to 1854 [is] estimated to have cost upward of $20,000,000, besides hundreds of lives and much private property. At the close of that war there broke out an $8,000,000 war in Oregon, lasting two years; some accounts trace the original cause of trouble to an outrage by a white man on an Indian woman, although it was unquestioned offenses of the Rogue River Indians that our troops punished. The four Navajo campaigns, arising from trivial causes, cost, it is said, $28,000,000, though this seems an extravagant estimate.

The famous, or, rather, infamous Cheyenne war of 1864 is well remembered. A ranchman went to Camp Sanborn and accused the Cheyennes of stealing his stock. A detachment of troops went to find the stock in the Cheyenne camp, and failed. Coming upon some armed Indians, they undertook to disarm them. An encounter followed, and so began the war. However, during the following Winter some of the chiefs, with their bands, voluntarily surrendered at Fort Lyon. The officers guaranteed them protection, and caused them to camp on Sand Creek. While there encamped, a regiment of Colorado volunteers, under Col. Chivington, approached, and began an indiscriminate slaughter. The warriors, who were mainly absent consulting with the rest of the tribe or procuring food, were driven to fury by the butchery of their wives, old men, and babes. The Kiowas and Comanches joined them, and this Cheyenne war is said to have cost $35,000,000, though that is perhaps an overestimate. It certainly cost many lives, for the slain soldiers and settlers were numbered by hundreds. So much for firing upon peaceful Indians, to whom the national flag was no protection.

A treaty of peace with the Cheyennes, made without difficulty in the Autumn of 1865, was so well observed that, a year later, Sept. 30, 1866, Gen. Sherman wrote:

"The tribes are harmless and peaceable, and the Cheyennes and Arapahoes are off after the buffalo, God only knows where, and I do not see how we can make a decent excuse for an Indian war. I have traveled all the way from Laramie without a single soldier or escort. I met single men unarmed travelling along the road, as in Missouri. Cattle and horses graze loose far from their owners, and most tempting to a starving Indian; and though the Indians might easily make a descent on these scattered ranches, yet they have not done so, and I see no external signs of a fear of such an event."

In the following April Major-Gen. Hancock attacked a village of Cheyennes and Sioux, on the Pawnee Fork, burned down the homes of three hundred lodges, and all their provisions, clothing, utensils, and property of every description. The Secretary of the Interior reported to Congress, the next year, that this attack was "without any known provocation." It is not to be believed, however, that any officer of the regular Army would make such an attack without known provocation; but for our present purpose it is enough to note that the resulting war was estimated by the Secretary to have cost $40,000,000.

Just prior to that war, *i.e.*, in 1866, came a bloody and costly struggle with the Sioux, produced by the location of forts in the Powder River region, claimed by the Indians. It is said that this war cost the Government $10,000,000; it certainly cost hundreds of lives. At the close, peace was made by a mixed military and civil commission, on which four Generals of distinction served, who reported that "the treaty was broken, but not by the savage." They added that "the war was something more than useless and expensive—it was dishonorable to the nation."

In 1868, Gen. Harney, then in charge of the Sioux, reported that he could "unhesitatingly declare that, to secure perpetual peace with the Sioux Indians it is only necessary to fulfill the terms of the treaty made by the Peace Commission." In 1874, however, occurred Gen. Custer's expedition to the Black Hills, which discovered gold. A rush of miners broke down the Government guarantees under the treaty. While negotiations for buying the Black Hills were pending, some of the dissatisfied Sioux wandered off to visit Sitting Bull, a non-treaty and marauding Sioux. With the reinforcements thus acquired, he annihilated Custer's command in the Battle of Little Big Horn. The war was short, but cost the lives of 283 brave soldiers, besides the wounding of 125 men, and $2,312,530 cash.

We might also speak of the Modoc War, which had its origin in forcing the Modocs on the reservation of the Klamaths. It began with the treacherous murder of Gen. Canby and his associates, while under a flag of truce, and it cost 160 lives of white men and some millions of dollars to hunt down a few scores of Modoc warriors. The Nez Percé War of last year was produced by a like attempt to force Indians on a reservation where they did not want to go, in order to give their homes to white men who coveted them. Chief Joseph, with law on his side and Government promises, was driven to a war costing $931,329 and many gallant officers and men.

If to such an array of Indian wars, we add the present season's, it must be admitted, we think that the most expensive use the Government can put an Indian to is to fight him. Even as a question of economy, it is high time to change an Indian system so fruitful in fraud, mismanagement, broken faith, and violence, and leading to such costly wars.

⤳ Another Indian War

October 3, 1879

Patriotic practical men, who despise the sentimental philanthropy which pretends that the Indian is a human being, will be glad to know that we have a new Indian war on our hands. The Utes, who have hitherto been an unusually peaceful tribe, have at last taken up arms and given us an opportunity to exterminate them and seize their lands. The war has begun in a most hopeful manner, the Utes having defeated a detachment of troops, and thus opened the way for effective denunciations of their brutal barbarity. It may take some little time and trouble to kill the entire tribe, but there can be little doubt that in the course of one or two campaigns the Utes will be improved off the face of the earth, and the Ute reservation will be parceled out among the hardy miners of Colorado.

There is a good deal of similarity between the origin of the Ute war and that which led to the redemption and civilization of the Black Hills country a few years ago. It will be remembered that the Government had given the Black Hills region to the Indians as a reservation, and had solemnly promised by treaty that no white men should enter it. Gold having been suspected to exist on the reservation, miners flocked into it. The Indians complained of this as an infraction of the treaty, and after the failure of an effort to induce them to sell the reservation for a trifling sum, the Government sent troops to protect the miners and to drive the presumptive copper-colored wretches out. In like manner, the Ute reservation was guaranteed to the tribe, and has latterly been invaded by miners prospecting for gold. The Utes had the impudence to object to this, but obtained no satisfaction. Then Mr. Meeker, the local Indian Agent, undertook to cultivate for his own purposes, land belonging to the Utes. As those wicked savages made this a pretext for fresh remarks concerning their pretended rights, Mr. Meeker promptly sent for troops. The Utes, perceiving that their days on that particular reservation were numbered, decided to begin the fight at once, and thereupon fell upon the troops and beat them. The result will be extremely gratifying to all but the sentimental philanthropist. Fresh troops will be sent, the Utes will be killed to a wholesome extent, and the few survivors will be sent to some distant reservation. The miners will then occupy the present reservation, and, as in the case of the Black Hills, will reclaim it from barbarism and plant on its waste places cultured Christian communities like Deadwood and Leadville. The business has been managed much more easily than those who knew the peaceful reputation of the Utes thought it could have been, and if Mr. Meeker has fallen a victim to savage brutality, he will long be remembered as the able originator of a desirable Indian war.

It is humiliating that the sentimentalists of the Eastern States have hitherto had sufficient influence to compel the nation to conduct its Indian policy in a very disingenuous way. What that policy really is, every one knows. It is built upon the theory that the Indian is not a human being, and that hence the ordinary laws of morality and honor are not binding upon white men in their dealings with him. We hold that while it is right to keep faith with civilized and powerful nations, and to abstain from openly robbing them, we can treat the Indians in a totally different way. Hence, we are at perfect liberty to break any treaties that we may have made with them; to seize on their so-called property; and to kill them whenever they venture to show any dissatisfaction. It is a cowardly fear of the silly philanthropists that prevents us from frankly admitting that lying, treachery, cowardice, and cruelty are the cardinal principles of our Indian policy. No man thinks he is under obligation to keep promises made to a dog or to respect the animal's claim to property in specific bones. The strictest moralist feels at liberty to seize his dog's kennel for fire-wood, or even to shoot him, if his continued existence is deemed undesirable. The Indian, being a mere brute, is entitled to no better treatment than is the dog or any other professed animal, and hence we can lie to him, break faith with him, rob him, and shoot him, whenever we think that the interests of miners and squatters will be benefited thereby. If we made a treaty with Englishmen or Frenchmen, or in fact with any nation possessing a fleet that could harass our coast, we should feel bound as honorable men to keep it, but as the Indians naturally have no fleet, and are few and feeble, it is sentimental folly to claim that honesty or honor need have any place in our policy toward them.

While our Indian policy is a plain, practical, and profitable one, it is a pity that we do not openly acknowledge its character and boldly defend it, instead of making a feeble pretense that we regard Indians as human beings entitled to just and honorable treatment. It is time that Congress should pass a few frank, bold resolutions formulating the policy that we have hitherto shrunk from confessing. It should be solemnly declared that the United States, having an inalienable right to the lives and liberties of the Indians, and to the pursuit of their property, acknowledges no rule of morality or honor in dealing with them; that treaties made with Indians may at any time be violated at the pleasure of the United States or any of its citizens; that Indian reservations can be seized whenever it is judged desirable by anybody, and that inasmuch as, in the words of Gen. Sherman, "the only good Indian is a dead Indian," the public or private killing of Indians is to be recognized as a meritorious act. We have long acted upon these principles in our relations with the Indians, and it would be manly and straightforward were Congress to publicly recognize the fact. Why should we longer falsely profess to hold the principles of Indian policy which are acted upon by the effete British Government on the other side of the line? Let the mean-spirited Britons live in peace with their Indians if they choose. We are a more independent and high-spirited people, and we claim the right to cheat and kill our own Indians as one of the proud privileges of the Great Republic.

↰ [Untitled]

August 12, 1882

A dispatch from Tucson, Arizona, says that the Indian chief Eskiminzin is making preparations for war, and that the settlers of the region (the San Pedro country) are greatly alarmed. The same dispatch describes Eskiminzin as "one of the most treacherous and vindictive Indians in the Territory." This is merely a lying trick for ulterior purposes. The chieftain referred to was, at one time, actively engaged in hostilities against the whites. In 1871 he capitulated, and from that time to this he has been noted for his friendliness to the whites and for his peaceable disposition and behavior. Eskiminzin is a thrifty farmer, and his example and influence have been of great value in civilizing his Indian neighbors and associates. It is the custom in certain remote districts of the country to get up an "Indian war" by circulating just such reports as this above mentioned. The settlers want Quartermasters' contracts for hay, grain, and transportation. They accuse a peaceable chief, or band, of entertaining hostile purposes. An expedition is sent against the unsuspecting aborigines. Resistance follows, and a small war is begun in earnest. But the "alarmed settlers" get the contracts and the greenbacks, and prosperity returns for a season to the land of the cactus and the horned toad.

ᑐ Gen. Crook's Victory

June 14, 1883

Gen. Crook is back again over the border, bringing with him more than three hundred prisoners from the Apache stronghold which he has surprised and destroyed in the Sierra Madre. The story of the expedition and its success is an interesting one. It proves that audacity, courage, and intelligence, when rightly directed, will enable a regular force to overtake and defeat an Indian war party. Many frontiersmen have insisted that this was impossible. Wise heads were shaken when the expedition of Crook launched over the border and disappeared in the mountainous wilderness of Northern Mexico. The victorious return of Gen. Crook confounds his critics who were clamorous recently for reinforcements and rescue to be sent to him without delay. The General has accomplished what he set out to do, and he has done it without any flourish of trumpets. He left American soil on May 3, he returned June 11, his errand successfully executed.

The results of this unique campaign are highly important. For more than 20 years the border of New-Mexico and Arizona has been harassed by predatory Indian bands. Nothing short of a cordon of troops guarding a line of territory several hundred miles long could prevent the incursions of the Apaches from Mexico. Nothing short of an army could head off and destroy these raiders on their return from the American territories which they harried. There was no concert of action between the Mexican troops and those of the United States. The region just north of the line was made uninhabitable by the raiders. Some idea of the terror which the Apache band has been to the country on both sides of the line may be gained from the references made to the amount of booty recovered. The Indians had greenbacks, gold and silver coin, watches, ponies and mules, and other plunder in great quantities. These articles not only represent many robberies but many murders. The lost child of Judge McComas and wife, murdered by these miscreants, was found in the hands of the captors. The Mexican population, although more sparse than that on the American side of the border, has also suffered much from the Apaches; and Crook's victory relieves Northern Mexico from a long-endured terror.

Gen. Crook is said to be awaiting instructions as to the disposition to be made of his captives. He has brought back nearly all of the women and children of the renegades, as well as many redoubtable fighting men. The warriors who were absent from camp when the capture was made have escaped. Their families are in the hands of the troops. Most of these people, warriors and non-combatants, have been on ostensibly friendly terms with the United States. They are fugitives from our reservations. They cannot properly be returned to the reservations, except as prisoners of war. And, as prisoners even, they would cause a tumult among those already there. Certainly such notorious chiefs as Loco, Nana, Bonito, and Geronimo, who have been hunted unsuccessfully for years, must be kept in close confinement during the rest of their days. There will be a popular demand for their instant execution. The disposition of this knotty question, however, may be safely left to the Secretary of War, who has from the first reposed absolute confidence in Gen. Crook's ability, as well as in his wisdom in managing the difficulties arising from the Indian troubles of the border.

↶ The Restless Cheyennes

July 11, 1885

Although the farmers of Southwestern Kansas are recovering from their fright and Gov. Martin is now satisfied that the troops recently stationed along the southern boundary of the State will protect the settlers and prevent an invasion from the Territory, the attitude of the Indians on the Cheyenne and Arapahoe Reservation is still so threatening that Gen. Sheridan has left Washington for Fort Reno, and it is believed that an attempt will be made to deprive the Cheyennes of their arms. Gen. Miles, an Indian fighter of renown, will arrive at Fort Reno on Monday or Tuesday next. Orders have been sent westward, it is said, to the effect that the insurrection must be suppressed even if in the work of suppression the Cheyennes are wiped out of existence.

Not long ago it was said that these Indians were peacefully awaiting the arrival of Commissioners appointed to hear their complaints. Now it is reported that about 100 young men of the tribe have left the vicinity of the agency and gone to the head waters of the Cimarron because it was proposed that their arms should be taken from them. Notwithstanding the large crop of rumors that has already been harvested it does not appear that the Cheyennes have gone upon the warpath, but if the Government shall try to take their arms they will in all probability do a great deal of harm. The result of Gen. Crook's experiment with the Chiricahua Apaches at San Carlos has shaken popular confidence in his policy, but he knows something about Indian ways and Indian character, and what he has said about taking their weapons deserves consideration. His report concerning his campaign of 1883 in Mexico contained the following on this subject:

"It is not practicable to disarm Indians. Their arms can never be taken from them unless they are taken prisoners with their arms in their hands, while engaged in fighting, by sudden surprise or disabling wounds. . . . The disarming of Indians has, in almost every instance recorded, been a farcical failure. Let me cite the case of the Cheyennes who surrendered in 1878. They were searched with the greatest care when they were confined, and it was believed with the fullest success; yet when they broke out of prison at Fort Robinson, Neb., they appeared well armed with guns and knives and ammunition."

The Cheyennes already have learned from their agent and in other ways that the Government would like to disarm them, and if the troops undertake to deprive them of their rifles and ammunition a collection of almost worthless weapons may be turned in, but their best arms will be hidden for the use of the warriors who will not hesitate long about turning them against the whites.

But why have these Indians become uneasy and dangerous? This is an important question, and the Government should strive to discover whether or not they have just cause for complaint. We have been unable to find any excuse for the last revolt of the Chiricahua Apaches, but the Cheyennes are Indians who have been peaceful for many years. Reports submitted in 1877 by Gen. Pope and recently made public for the first time prove that he well knew then how badly the Cheyennes had been treated. They were starving to death, and the army was directed to prevent them from leaving the reservation in search of food. "It is inhuman," said he, "to compel Indians to remain at the agencies on their reservations slowly starving to death. If they do what any man would do under the circumstances—leave the localities where they are placed to procure food to prevent themselves and their families from starving—it is considered the duty of the army to pursue and force them back and to compel them to starve peaceably. In other words, the military forces are required to compel these Indians to starve to death quietly or be killed if the are not willing to do it." In the following year these Indians broke away and were not subdued until they had been guilty of pillage and murder. The Cheyennes are not starving now, but they have been disturbed by the encroachments of the cattlemen whom Secretary Teller allowed to get possession of their lands.

There are 4,297,771 acres in the Cheyenne and Arapahoe Reservation. The leases held by cattle men under the protection of the Interior Department cover 3,832,520 acres. A representative of the tribe who was recently in Washington declared that these leases left for the Indians not more than fifty acres each and less than four acres each of tillable land. Many of the Indians have opposed the leases from the beginning, and hundreds still refuse, he says, to take their pro rata share of the lease money lest they be accused of having sanctioned the leases. It is reported that the agent has continually favored the lessees at the expense of the Indians, and has been striving by threats and in other ways to draw the Indians from their homes to the neighborhood of the agency, where they are unwilling to live. Deprived of their hunting grounds by means of leases that many of them opposed, and deprived of their money by the settlement of claims for damages preferred by the cattlemen, they have become restless. There are many indications that the invasion of the reservation by the leaseholders under the protection of Secretary Teller has caused this trouble. If it be true that the Indians are really opposed to the leases, why should the cattlemen be allowed to remain in possession? There is no warrant in law for the existence of the leases. If the removal of the cattlemen would make these Indians peaceful, their expulsion would be a much more economical method of suppressing the threatened insurrection than any other that has been proposed.

∽ The Apache Campaign

November 13, 1886

One point in Gen. Miles's official report of his operations against the hostile Chiricahuas, which has only recently been given in full to the public, is specially worth notice. He says that in the pursuit of Geronimo infantry had to be employed sometimes in hard climbing, where the cavalry could not take their horses, and that their efficiency was greatly impaired by their poor shoes. His language on this point is very emphatic. He speaks of the Government shoes, which were made in Leavenworth Prison, as so wretched that they fell to pieces after a few days' marching. This criticism on an important matter did not appear in the first abstract made of the report for the press, but it seems that the War Department instituted an inquiry into the matter, and that the report of the investigating board has just been handed in. The shoes furnished from the Leavenworth Prison have sometimes been complained of by individual soldiers in ordinary service, but we do not remember of ever before hearing an official complaint made of them in actual field operations against the enemy. This disclosure by Gen. Miles, therefore, seems to be in several ways an important one. Of course the usage to which the shoes were subjected in that terribly rough country was exceptional, but it appears that they "fell to pieces" very quickly, which is a different matter from being worn out or cut up by the flinty rocks.

Gen. Miles seems to have "organized victory" at the outset of his campaign. The Lieutenant-General, who is too experienced a soldier not to know exactly what amount of liberty a subordinate requires, only instructed him to be careful that Indians on the reservations should not be made hostile, and that the regular troops should have a large and prominent share in the operations. In other respects Gen. Miles was left untrammeled. He carefully arranged his plan, in which the procuring of information bearing on the movements of the hostiles played a remarkable part. His report especially calls attention to the use of heliography in actual operations; and perhaps this will be eventually recognized as the most important addition made by this campaign to the general art of war.

The enormous labors and fatigues so courageously borne by the troops, the incessant calls upon the immediate pursuers of Geronimo for the most arduous exertions, the weary tramps over thousands of miles, up one side of a mountain range and down the other, and so on for range after range, are set forth for official record in Gen. Miles's report. Justice, also, is done to two remarkable cases of gallantry in rescuing and carrying off wounded comrades under a sharp Indian fire. As to the final surrender of the hostiles, it is perfectly clear that the temporary difficulty which arose in regard to the supposed terms conceded was due to a misunderstanding not fairly ascribable to Gen. Miles. He at no time in any of his dispatches said that the surrender of Geronimo was "unconditional." That word was an interpolation, or, more properly speaking, a comment which occurred during the transmission of the news to Washington. He said that the Indians had surrendered to him as prisoners of war, and in the present report he explains that while he assured them that he would not kill any of them, yet that for the subsequent disposition of them as prisoners of war they must trust entirely to the Government.

Under this arrangement it has become possible for the Government without breach of faith to send these Indians to Florida, and to keep them also as prisoners there. That Gen. Miles acted fully within his authority as a commander in the field in arranging the surrender as he did cannot be questioned. As for the wisdom of the arrangement the peace now prevailing on the frontier sufficiently attests that. Gen. Miles also sets forth most convincingly his reasons for insisting, against some opposition, on the transfer of all the Chiricahuas and Warm Spring Indians from Arizona to Florida. These Indians, numbering more than 400, were technically friendly, but it is believed that they had furnished information and aid to hostiles, and certainly their reservations were nests for future hostilities. Gen. Miles, therefore, wisely completed his job by packing all these people also off to Florida, where, it is to be hoped, they will permanently remain.

ᔕ The Ute Outbreak

August 24, 1887

Both the Government and the frontier settlers have strange relations with the red men. From the beginning of our dealings with Indian tribes the Government treated them like political bodies, each responsible as a whole, not only for any violation of its engagements as a tribe, according to our *ex parte* interpretation of those engagements, but for aggression committed on white men by any individual. This mode of dealing was long so universal that Government contracts with them took the form of treaties, and it is less than twenty years since future treaty making was prohibited by an act of Congress. A great part of our subsisting valid agreements with Indian tribes therefore resemble engagements between independent, sovereign, treaty-making powers.

But on the side of the Government no such responsibility of the whole for one white man of course was admitted. If the Government undertakes to punish an Indian thief by arrest, it is law; if the Indian tribe seeks justice by its own hands against a white assassin, it is war. Often the act of the tribe is treated as murder, as no doubt the law must regard it. Only within two or three years has Congress recognized the fact that Indian civilization is not to be secured by treating the reservations as almshouses, and that the assignment of lands in severalty and the substitution of American citizenship for tribal bonds are steps in true progress. If the Government has been thus tardy in discovering the proper methods of dealing with all but the least docile tribes, some of the frontiersmen on their part may well go astray. In the present instance Colorow's band has been long absent from the reservation and beyond the agent's jurisdiction, and hence has risked being roughly handled. The settlers cannot but feel uneasy in the knowledge that Indians are roaming among their ranches, threatening the safety, not only of their stock and crops, but of their families. This does not justify them in shooting at Indians like wild beasts on sight. Some of the frontier newspapers in times past have advised settlers to kill Indians found off their reservations. This is treating them worse than convicts, since nobody feels it to be his individual duty to shoot down an escaped jailbird. In point of fact, the reservations are not penitentiaries, but lands bought and owned by the Indians, the consideration being giving up all claim to other lands. They are of course bound to stay on the reservation, except when permitted by the agent to leave it, as a part of the contract which also keeps white settlers off. But absence itself, even without permission, is not a crime punishable by death. Some of the 150 cowboys now forming part of Sheriff Kendall's posse may have been in the employ of the syndicates who break the laws by fencing in public lands, but they would hardly consider that sort of lawlessness reason for their being shot down by the troops. Granting that Colorow's band consists of "renegades" from the reservation, it is noticeable that no outrages of any sort were charged against them, so far as appears by the accounts hitherto, prior to this alleged horse stealing, regarding which one story now current is that the Indians were those originally wronged.

A difficulty in reaching a settlement as peaceful and just as in the case of the Cheyennes and Arapahoes, of the Indian Territory, is the inability of the regular troops to interfere at this critical stage of the affair. Colorado is a State, and the laws of Congress are strict as to the use of the army in a case like the present. Even the State militia seems to have been held in the background, at least for a time, in order to give the cowboys a chance. The Indians indicted ought of course to be arrested, and the Sheriff evidently does not look for too tame a solution of the affair, as he has taken the precaution to carry a warrant for the apprehension of Colorow as well as of the two alleged horse thieves. The best outcome would be the peaceful surrender of these men on assurances of a fair trial, and the return of the rest of the band to the reservation with a pledge to remain there; but whether so sensible a result can be expected, with the unruly temper of Colorow's band and with the expressed desire of the authorities, military and judicial, as well as of the cowboys, to "clean out" the Indians, is very uncertain.

↩ The Indians and the Army

November 24, 1890

Whatever the outcome of the Indian troubles at the West, they have already raised the question whether it would not be good policy for Congress to authorize a moderate increase of the army. It has been suggested, indeed, that the present excitement may have been purposely exaggerated in the reports with a view to securing such an increase. That, however, is an assumption. No doubt some frontiersmen and traders find a profit in the presence of the soldiers, and would be very glad to see a larger number of them, for purposes of trade. Still, their alarm seems to be genuine enough now; and although it has been based in most cases on unsupported rumors, yet such protection is due to them as will relieve them and their families from constant apprehensions. As to the army itself, the conservative and, for the most part, reassuring tone of its officers during the present Indian troubles is evident.

The main point to consider just now is the ability of the troops to cope with the red men in case of a general uprising. And the question is not about mastering them finally, since there is no doubt on that score, but about doing so in season to prevent those atrocities which might be expected from a people whose savagery would be increased by the double stimulus of race hatred and religious delusions. The present troubles are mainly found in the Department of Dakota, while reinforcements have been sent to threatened points from the neighboring department on the Platte. The aggregate enlisted force of these two departments is probably about 7,500. But, as is well known, the number for field duty, after excluding the sick, those on detached service, and the large number that must be left to guard the numerous forts and the Government property, is a small part of the aggregate present and absent. It has been said that the number of troops available by rapid transportation within twenty-four hours of any point now likely to be threatened is about 3,000, while more distant garrisons could be mobilized and appear on the scene after a time. That would be a very fine force with which to take the field against a single tribe, as in ordinary Indian wars, but the case would be different with the concerted uprising of half a dozen or a dozen tribes, some starting the move and others joining in when they found the garrisons which guarded their own agencies marching elsewhere. State troops and volunteers could be called out, but the resort to them should only be made in a great emergency.

If we remember the size of the forces required to hunt down and reduce to submission—and that only after many lives of settlers and soldiers had been taken—the small bands of Geronimo and his Chiricahuas, of Joseph and his Nez Percés, of Captain Jack and his Modocs, and others, it may perhaps be imagined how many troops would be needed to take care of the Sioux, the Cheyennes, the Arapahoes, the Utes, the Shoshones, and the various other tribes now carried away with the Messiah delusion. That is to say, while the final result would not be doubtful, the question is as to the damage and slaughter that meanwhile might be wrought in so extensive a region, with lines of such length to guard, particularly with the advantages enjoyed by Indians in a rough country for eluding pursuit, lying in ambush, and prolonging a war. Gen. Miles, who has so remarkable a record of accomplished successes in Indian fighting, will know how to manage the present business, and has taken proper precautions; but we only call attention to what is possible.

And yet this sort of police duty, as it may be styled, is only one part of the calls made upon the army, and it is also a part gradually growing less and less urgent. For the last eight or ten years, indeed, the perils of Indian outbreaks have been constantly diminishing. It has been said, and with truth, that the railroads are solving the Indian problem, by their facilities of transportation, and that the gradual abandonment of the reservation policy and the move toward allotment in severalty will soon show good effects. The last two years have been, upon the whole, freer from Indian hostilities than any similar period for a very long time. Yet now we see almost unprecedentedly widespread disturbance, arising, too, for a cause—the supposed coming of an Indian Messiah—such as nobody could have foreseen. But while this lesson of the danger of assuming that the troops are no longer needed for the Indians is so impressive, it is also evident that more troops will soon be required for the seacoast and lakes. Congress has begun to provide a series of new batteries for guns and mortars, which are imperatively needed; and it is a mere matter of calculation to show how many men will be wanted for handling the new ordnance and guarding the new works. It is true that some reliance might be placed on the proposed militia heavy artillery, but there must also be regulars for constant duty. Only a slight increase of the enlisted force, perhaps a few thousand, would be needed for all purposes now apparent, but a nation of 63,000,000 or more must consider how long the 25,000 mark of many years ago should be allowed to remain. If even the supposed approach of millennial days makes such an outpouring of warlike forces necessary among the Indians, still more must be expected for the less blissful happenings of an age when the spear is not yet beaten into the pruning hook.

↫ The Coming Indian Fight

January 6, 1891

It is of a piece with everything that the Administration has done respecting Indian affairs that it should now be dispatching to Gen. Miles urgent telegrams exhorting him to avoid further bloodshed. There is a pathetic old song in which a girl is moved by the conscription of her lover to express the wish that "those who make the quarrel" should "be the only ones to fight." If this wholesome rule were now in force, the United States Army would be relieved of all responsibility for the Indian campaign. On one side would be the starved and plundered and enraged Indians. On the other all the people who have been concerned in starving and plundering and enraging them, from a pilfering agent's clerk up to the Secretary of the Interior and the President of the United States himself. If all these latter persons were assembled, armed with Winchester rifles as good as they have been directly or indirectly engaged in selling to the Indians, they would perhaps be out-numbered, but if the contest could be made equal in this respect the patriot and the philanthropist would contemplate it with more equanimity than they can command in regarding the actually impending conflict, in which the lives will be risked of brave officers and men who had nothing at all to do with fomenting the "Indian troubles."

There is no hope that such a spectacle will be afforded to the lovers of justice and of humor. There is good ground for fear that the greatest and bloodiest Indian battle is about to be fought that has been contested since white men landed upon this continent. Most of the Indian battles that have occurred since the United States became a nation have been obscure squabbles. The bloodiest of them would be classed in the language of civilized warfare as "affairs," and would scarcely rise to the dignity of "engagements." Once in a very long time the attention of the country is arrested by an Indian fight by reason of the conspicuousness of the leaders of it or of something especially striking and dramatic in the circumstances. Gen. Sheridan's charge upon a Piegan village and the slaughter of Custer and the Seventh Cavalry are incidents of this kind. But the battle that seems to be imminent in Dakota threatens to be far greater and more deadly than any of these. The force of white troops ready for it is estimated, loosely and probably with exaggeration, at 8,000. The strength of the hostile Indians who are watched by these troops is estimated, still more loosely, at 4,000, though a considerable deduction must be made from any estimate, seeing that by no means all of the gathered "hostiles" are fighting men. At any rate the contest is not rendered unequal by their mere inferiority in numbers. This is made up by their superiority in those points in which the savage is superior to the civilized man, in their greater ability to support hunger and cold, in their ability to eat with gusto what a starving white man would reject, and in their better knowledge of the country. That the "bucks" of a warlike tribe can fight white soldiers on equal terms if they be as well armed is a familiar fact, and, thanks to the Indian agents and the Indian trader, the savages are as well armed as the troops. But they are at one very conspicuous disadvantage, which arises from the scale of the campaign. They would be too numerous to be effectively directed by savage generalship, even if they were all of the same tribe. As a matter of fact, they are of many tribes that have little in common excepting their hatred of the whites. There can be no generalship in such an army and no discipline extending throughout the whole body, and so there can be no concerted plan of battle. This is where civilization has its advantage. The white troops will fight, if there must be a battle, under the direction of a single will. The Indians will be broken up into many bands, each fighting desperately under the direction of its own chief, but without reference to any other.

It is probable that most of the settlers in the region immediately affected earnestly wish that there may be a battle and that the Indians concerned may be exterminated and done with once for all. If it were possible to exclude human pity from the consideration of the fate of human beings, this desire would be justifiable. Assuredly the very existence of these Indians is a nuisance and a danger to the pioneer of civilization. A savage whose own pursuits are taken from him by the advance of civilization, and who will not or cannot conform himself to the pursuits of civilization, cannot be other than a curse to himself and to his civilized neighbors. Even if his civilized neighbors care for him, he is neither useful nor ornamental as he accepts their bounty. If they agree to care for him and break their agreement, it is not to be wondered at that his savage instincts should assert themselves, and that he should bite the hand that fails to feed him. For this failure in the present case the Administration is responsible, and when the dishonesty and incompetency of its agents have resulted in stirring up a revolt, which it has done nothing to quiet, it is adding insult to injury for it to warn the men who are engaged in putting down the revolt to "avoid bloodshed."

∽ [Untitled]

May 30, 1891

The verdict of "not guilty" which the Sioux Falls jury, under instructions from Judge Shiras, rendered in the trial of Plenty Horses, the slayer of Lieut. Casey, on the charge of murder, is in some respects a new departure in the way of treating Indian hostilities. The Judge held that "a state of war" existed when Lieut. Casey was shot, and, accordingly, that the act of killing him was not murder; and he intimated that if the slaughter of the Indians at Wounded Knee is to be justified, it must be on the ground that war existed. And yet we have seen the United States Senate for many years refusing to confirm brevet promotions for gallantry in Indian hostilities on the ground that such hostilities did not constitute war. The War Department's official list of promotions only a short time ago contained an announcement that an officer had been promoted to *vice* Lieut. Casey, "murdered by an Indian," which was a different judgment on the case from the one rendered at Sioux Falls. Experts in law may be left to discuss the merits of this particular ruling; but it is clear that should the view of Judge Shiras be established, officers and men who now lose even the credit of having died a soldier's death on the field of battle or in campaigning, and are put down as perishing by private assassination, will at least receive a record that is usually thought more covetable.

6 Encroaching Civilization

Frequent contact with the white race seems to have deprived the American Indian of that imperturbable stoicism which once characterized him. Indian visitors to our cities used formerly to assume the haughtiest indifference to the sights which were designed to impress them. Those now in Washington complain of their hotel accommodations because they do not command a good view of what is going on in the streets. Like most civilized folks, they want front rooms.

—*New York Times*
May 22, 1875

FOR FORTY YEARS, the men who set the editorial policies of the *Times* saw but two possible outcomes to the Indian problem. One was for the Indians to be exterminated—favored, the *Times* asserted, by a disturbing number of white citizens, particularly in the West. The other was for the Indians to be "civilized."

To become civilized, even in the eyes of the enlightened editorial writers of the *Times*, the Indians had to become more like the white men and women whose European-based culture was the standard for the new, fast-growing American nation. There is little evidence that those whose opinions filled the editorial columns of the *Times* understood, or had much interest in, the native cultures. Here, again, the divided we / they perspective of the *Times* editorials left very little room for middle ground.

It is apparent that it was the best-intentioned opinion leaders who were most concerned about civilizing the Native Americans by reshaping them in the image of white culture. The *Times* never varied from its belief that the Indians' true path to fulfillment lay in their adoption of the whites' way of life. To give up the roving life and the hunt for a sedentary existence based on agriculture, to be educated and trained in manual skills, to exchange their pagan religions for Christianity—these were the keys, in the view of the

Times editorial writers, not only to the Indians' immediate survival but also to eventual peaceful coexistence with the detested white race.

The religious zealots and missionaries who would go among the Indians and help teach them the ways of the whites were heroes to the *Times*—at least until they proved themselves corrupt. It applauded philanthropists who committed themselves to helping improve the savages. In a brief editorial-column report on a Quaker meeting in June 1871, the *Times* noted that Quaker agents had "awakened in the Indians a sense of the advantages and duties of civilized life."

The *Times* liked to point to the scattered remnants of tribes remaining in the East to show the positive effects of white culture on the Indians. When General Alfred Sully proposed relocating the plains Indians in the East, the *Times* noted that reservation Indians in New York were doing well. Still, the newspaper took no firm position on General Sully's plan, which is outlined briefly in the first of the editorials included in this chapter.

Having consistently supported the policy of confining the Native Americans to reservations, the *Times* saw in this scheme the best mechanism for teaching them a better way of life. In the summer of 1876, the *Times* praised the work of former Indian Commissioner E. P. Smith in introducing the "factory system" to the reservations. That was a system that combined industrial and manual training with a profit-sharing plan as one method of "civilizing or improving these wild tribes." Smith, the *Times* recalled, had entered the Indian service as a religious missionary and then served as an Indian agent in Minnesota before his appointment as commissioner by President Ulysses S. Grant.

One of Commissioner Smith's primary goals, the *Times* noted, "was to combine on each reservation industrial training with moral and mental education." It said there had been some notable successes. One of the examples cited was work with the Utes, to show that even so wild a tribe "can be induced to cultivate the ground." The change was introduced gradually: "Here, the first effort was to tempt the Indians to work little gardens; then they were aided to construct small homes, so as to break up the habit of wigwam life. A steam saw-mill was built which was soon worked and managed solely by Indians. Cattle were supplied them, that they might learn the milking and care of stock, they being allowed their own profit from these small enterprises." The Ute women were not neglected either. Mrs. Smith introduced various domestic arts, the *Times* editorial said, including mat weaving, basket making, "bread-making and civilized cookery."

The *Times* lauded the wisdom and humanity of Commissioner Smith's efforts. But it said there was a fatal weakness in the system. That weakness was the knowledge given to the Indians that they had a right to government aid, aggravated by "the great multitude of vagabonds, traders, interpreters, and the like, who had made a good profit out of the old Indian management" and encouraged the Indians to seek government support without working for it.

A few months later, in a lengthy editorial on the annual report of the Secretary of the Interior, the *Times* acknowledged that there were many people who saw "the final extinction or absorption" of the Native Americans as the only solution to the Indian problem. But it suggested there was universal agreement that the Indian "must be educated to take care of himself, as far as possible." The *Times* recognized, however, that many would argue "that the red man is by nature a wild man and utterly untamable." The *Times* had now begun to back away from its support for the reservation system. The American people, it said, would not consent to Indian reservations held sacred and inviolate for all time from the larger purposes of trade and commerce.

Ironically, some of the most important questions about Indians' rights involved situations that were not at issue so far as white citizens were concerned. When the *Times* noted in a May 1880 editorial that the courts faced a difficult decision regarding the Indians' status under the Fourteenth and Fifteenth Amendments, the case at point involved the sale of liquor to an Indian. That was illegal. But one of the most persistent problems of encroaching white civilization for decades had been the wide distribution of liquor to the Indians.

The unwillingness of white society to compromise on questions of Indian culture was illustrated dramatically in the furor created by reports that two graduates of the renowned Carlisle Indian School had been seen participating in an Osage tribal dance. The *Times*, in an editorial in June 1887, acknowledged that a Senate committee had been shocked that the Carlisle graduates had participated "in a heathen dance." But it took the more liberal position that civilized education and native propensities need not be in conflict—a position somewhat contradictory to its own usual leanings.

In contrast to the Carlisle graduates, the *Times* cited the work of a graduate of the Hampton Institute who had subsequently served as an army scout in the Apache campaign. His skill as a tracker proved invaluable to the army, the *Times* said, suggesting that "the education of this Indian evidently did not rob him of those fine physical traits and aptitudes which distinguish his race."

The *Times* continued to call for greater emphasis on Indian education as the best means to bring them into the mainstream of white civilization. That movement was too slow, it said in August 1883; substantial results could not be expected as long as only a small fraction of the Indian population was being schooled. Still, the *Times* was willing to wait another generation, if necessary, for educated Indians to become the predominant element in the various tribes. But it believed the price of not providing educational opportunity was too high. "Since the only alternative to the assimilation of the Indians is their extirpation," it pleaded, "a proper regard to the good name of the Nation requires that we should not too carefully count the dollars we spend in trying to bring about the more humane settlement."

But however lightly the *Times* editorial writers regarded the qualities of Indian culture, they were not reluctant to attack the ills of white society as they affected the Native Americans. Many of the most powerful editorials on the Indian problem related to just this topic. As much as they desired to see the Indians move toward the whites' way of life, they freely admitted and vigorously protested the brutal price exacted from the Indians through contact with white civilization. That theme emerges more clearly than any other in the editorials that make up the rest of this chapter.

In the final analysis, it is a sad irony that during all the years of editorial-page observation of the Indian problem, the *Times* itself manifested the deficiencies of the civilization it espoused countless times without ever appearing to question the validity of its own stance. When white culture failed the Indians, the *Times* merely treated such examples as exceptions, not as the commonplace habits of white civilization. Such shortcomings might be in the nature of the beast but, the editorials seemed to imply, the beast still was superior to the alternative native cultures.

ᕲ What Shall Be Done with the Indians?

April 23, 1867

There could be but one solution to a question of force between the United States and the troublesome tribes of Indians that hang upon the skirts of our frontier settlements and harrass [*sic*] the travelers across the plains. They would, of course, be subdued and badly punished. Whether this or a more peaceful mode of quieting the disturbances now so rife shall be adopted, was the proposition laid before the last Congress, and to which it gave a simple hearing. Between the belligerent army officers and the corrupt traders of the Bureau it has been difficult to obtain a clear insight into the actual situation of affairs. The recent wholesale massacres, however, the frequent attacks upon emigrant trains, and the rumors concerning a coalition of the larger tribes, indicate the necessity of immediately recognizing the difficulty.

The contact with white men has, we are obliged to admit, opened the doors of debauchery, intemperance and wretchedness to the Indians, giving them in homeopathic doses the veriest attenuations of morality and virtue. Whisky, guns, powder and shot have for years been our staples in trade with them, and under the influence of the first it has not been difficult to cheat them with the rest. Using the firearms for shooting game, the Indians had almost forgotten the bow and arrow and calculated on the fulfillment of the treaties with the white, which insured them a yearly supply. Suddenly, for reasons best known at headquarters, these essentials are denied the Indians, who are, nevertheless, drugged more than ever with the vilest whiskeys. Angered by the want of faith shown by the whites and maddened by the strong drink, they have indulged in a series of outrages whose frequency demands the serious attention and prompt interference of the Government. One party clamors for their annihilation; another begs for a continuance of trading facilities, hoping by strategy to secure all the Indians possess and by drink to debase them below the level of enemies whose anger need by feared. Is either of these courses justifiable? Can a Christian nation permit the wholesale murder of these men, women and children? Or can it answer to its conscience for consenting to their debasement as an indirect preliminary for their destruction?

It seems to us that a war with the remnants of these tribes would be disastrous, whatever its end. We might, undoubtedly, after a little, exterminate them, but meanwhile overland communication with the Pacific slope would be rendered extremely hazardous, if not destroyed; millions of dollars would be expended, many lives would be sacrificed, and after all our only gain would be the "renown" of a successful Indian war. As our frontier forts are managed at present, they seem to present at once a temptation and a prize to the roving bands who *must* live in some way, *must* obtain ammunition or starve, and knowing this, revenge themselves for broken treaties upon the nearest and weakest representatives of those who have cheated them. We have but little to point to with pride in this whole Indian matter. It has been a bargain and a dicker from its earliest history. Against the occasional missionary efforts made among them, stand in formidable array the persistent treachery, trickery, and bad example of the agents, traders, and speculators who have managed our affairs.

The plan suggested by Gen. Sully is that "so far from concentrating them and treating them as we do, as a foreign nation, it would be better, when people wished the land the Indians occupy, instead of pushing them into the wilderness, to even purchase a tract of land in some of our densely populated Eastern States, and place them there, for there, in a few years, they would be forced to adopt the habits of civilized life, or they would soon become extinct." Whether this plan can at any time be adopted we know not, but it will be remembered that in our own State the Indians on the Reserve are "in a prosperous condition, and increasing in numbers and wealth." The need of the present is an increase of the armed forces on the frontier; the need of the immediate future would seem to be fair treatment, the keeping of faith with leaders, equitable exchange of property, and possibly the adoption of some plan similar to that set forth by Gen. Sully. As at present situated, Gen. Hancock has quite enough to do in providing for the emergencies of the passing moment.

ᔕ Our Indian Troubles—How to Meet Them

July 19, 1867

The question of our Indian troubles has been brought up in Congress, and seems to be attracting from the members that cool consideration to which it is entitled. There is, of course, a wide difference of opinion as to the proper means to be employed to secure a cessation of hostilities, and a return of peace and good order to the border districts; but that some means must be adopted, and speedily, too, seems to be the settled conviction of all who have as yet participated in the discussions. A plan has been submitted which contemplates the complete and final settlement of all difficulties between the pioneers of the West and their red-skinned neighbors. A commission is proposed, to consist of several prominent General officers of the army, who are to enter into negotiations with all hostile tribes of Indians, and endeavor to persuade them to give up their nomadic habits, and to settle down upon certain designated tracts of land, and there to quietly remain, interfering with no one and being molested by none.

In the course of the debate which this proposition has elicited, it has been stated that the existing difficulties are costing the Government at the rate of $100,000 per day, and that a single express company has already lost during the present season upward of $1,000,000, while other enterprises have suffered in a like degree. The same speaker estimated that if the Indian depredations are continued for two months longer, they will have cost the Government not less than one hundred millions of dollars. The favorite Western idea of extermination is shown to be utterly absurd as a matter of policy, to say nothing of its inhumanity. The official records prove that in all Indian wars from three to five white men have been slain to one Indian, and that the pecuniary loss has been all on the side of the whites. While one or two of the members of Congress have favored the extermination policy, and others have declared that the settlers have provoked the present troubles, and are entirely to blame for them, there are others who take the more sensible view, that both have been in error, but that no matter with whom the provocation lies, the troubles must be a once put an end to, in the interest of humanity, civilization and good policy.

It is thought that the proposed plan will withdraw the Indians from their wild nomadic life, and wean them from their hostility. While nothing has yet been mentioned to that effect, we presume the scheme proposed embraces one of education for the rising generation of Indians. If the adult red-skinned population can be prevented from committing depredations in the future, it will be as much as we can reasonably expect from a race which has been so grossly abused as they have been. If, however, we adopt a different policy toward their children, treat them humanely, educate them, and show them that civilization means peace, good will and prosperity, rather than barbarous warfare, bad whisky and bloody scalps, we may hope soon to so absorb the Indian tribes that all traces of them will be lost.

But in placing them upon reservations there are several important points to be observed. So far as appears from the discussions in Congress, certain tracts of land are to be set aside for their use for all time, and upon these the Indians, who will thereby be deprived of their natural means of obtaining a livelihood, are to be supported at the Government's expense. The members of Congress may hope to make a "happy family" of the several Indian tribes, and induce them to occupy a cage in common; but if they do so they will have accomplished more than ever Barnum did with his cats and his mice, or his hawks and his chickens. Fire and water will assimilate quite as well as will the Sioux and the Chippewas, or the Blackfeet and the Assiniboines. There are hereditary feuds existing between these and other tribes, which can only be extinguished by the march of civilization and education. For this reason no one reservation will suffice for their accommodation. Not only many miles, but entire States must separate them.

Again, why should not some prominence be given to the idea that the present generation of Indians can be made self-supporting? A tribe possessing sufficient intelligence to fight for its rights possesses sufficient energy and enterprise to support itself. If we deprive the Indian of his natural means of support, and drive beyond the reach of his bullet or his arrow the buffalo and the antelope, we are in duty bound to teach him the use of the plow and the harrow, and to show him how to make the earth yield him that subsistence which heretofore has obtained from the wild beasts which roam it. When once he is located upon his reservations, he should be taught that if he "tickles the earth with his harrow," she will "laugh with a harvest." This has been done with several tribes, and the experiment—although only an experiment and badly conducted—has been comparatively satisfactory. Tribes so located and furnished with the necessary implements of agriculture, and the machinery requisite to supply the wants of a colony, have lived peacefully, contentedly and happily. They there learned that a good house over their heads and a plentiful supply of corn in the granaries was to be preferred to a wigwam on the prairies and an empty larder at meal time. Indians have ever manifested a willingness to learn the ways of civilized life whenever the opportunity has been presented to them.

It has been justly said in Congress by those who have investigated the matter, that the Western settlers are a constant source of irritation to the Indians, committing petty depredations upon them, driving them from their lands, and in a thousand little ways stirring up their ill-blood. If the Indians are to be kept quiet the white man must be kept from their midst, or at best only those admitted to them who are honestly interested in their welfare. The idea of placing them upon reservations—colonizing them in fact—is unquestionably the true one. In arranging the details of the scheme, much care will be required in providing for ample employment of the present generation, and the education of that which is to succeed. By such means, carefully and honestly executed, the wild, savage red man of the plains will soon be a thing of the past, and in his place we shall have a hardy, intelligent, industrious race of his dark-hued sons, who, instead of obtaining a precarious subsistence by means of the chase, will contribute of their agricultural products to the welfare of the nation.

The Quakers and the Indians

April 25, 1869

Narrowed down to its actual limits, the Indian question no longer remains a grave one, whether we look at it in the light of war or charity; but there is no doubt that it is cheaper to support them as paupers than to subdue them as enemies—always provided we can secure the honest disposition of the charity funds. We believe that the Quakers who have been appointed as Indian Agents will accomplish this, and that, consequently, we shall have a peaceful and cheap administration of Indian affairs in all the districts except those which lie upon the great thoroughfares of travel and emigration. Here we fear that Quaker honesty and influence will be powerless to avert conflict between the Indians and the white settlers as long as the Indians remain in these localities.

The observant student of the late Indian war just concluded in Kansas and Colorado will have observed that the seat of war was confined to the valleys of the Kansas and Platte Rivers, and that the belligerent Indians were composed of the Kiowas, Comanches, Cheyennes, Arapahoes and Apaches, numbering in all, according to the latest census, 18,800 souls. To the south of the tribes living on the line of emigration and the great routes of travel to the west are ten other tribes numbering 67,635 souls. To the north of them are twenty-nine other tribes, with a population of 54,126. These thirty-nine tribes, besides the other 175,000 of our Indian population, have been and are still peaceably inclined, and, secure in reservations apart from the routes of emigration and uncoveted by emigrants, they are content to draw their annuities and not their bows. The trouble has been wholly with the five tribes whose reservations are in Kansas and Colorado, and whose war-path runs parallel with the Pacific Railroads. These reservations the white men want and will have, and unless the Indians are moved further south the Quaker agents, with all their honesty and prayers, will be powerless to prevent conflict between the settlers and Indians.

If the reservations of the Colorado and Kansas tribes are changed, there is no good reason why the mild rule of the Quakers should not be successful and lead eventually—if a second Administration is wise enough to continue it—to the absorption and civilization of the tribes, as they now exist, in something of the same way that the Six Nations in this State were, and as the Cherokees are, rapidly being absorbed and civilized. The most enlightened and peaceful, as well as most numerous, tribe in this country at this time is the one with which the civilizing influences have been combined with the removal, as suggested, of the Indians from contact with their natural enemies, the settlers. The Cherokees now number 14,000 souls. Their educators were the Jesuits, not the Quakers; but the civilizing influence of the latter is not less than that of the former. The Jesuit missionaries appeared in Cherokee Georgia long before the settlers in East Tennessee and Southern Georgia had penetrated to the mountain district where they were located. It was the Jesuits who really formed their alphabet and framed their written laws. But, in 1836-7, the Georgia and East Tennessee settlers heard that there was gold in the mountains of Cherokee Georgia, and the tide of emigration set in that direction, as it now sets toward Colorado and Kansas. Conflicts between individual settlers became frequent; assassinations were numerous; at length the Georgia militia was ordered into the Cherokee reservation, and a serious conflict would have ensued had not a new missionary appeared on the scene in the person of Major-General Winfield Scott. He brought out the Cherokee nation, bundled them off to beyond the Mississippi River, and gave the new gold region up to the speculators, who disposed of it in a grand lottery scheme. The settlers have not yet envied the Cherokees their new possessions, and they have ever since been peaceful and loyal.

We have now the same problem to solve once more. We have the Cherokees repeated in the five tribes of Colorado and Kansas; the Jesuits exist again in the newly-appointed Quaker agents; the old settlers figure again as westward-bound emigrants; and as a consequence the old conflict in a severer form has ensued. Have we also not a Winfield Scott and Phil Sheridan; and are there not numerous reservations remote from our traveled routes to which the Indians can be sent?

✐ The Duty of the Churches to the Indians

May 30, 1870

The letter addressed by the Secretary of the Interior to the Indian Convention which recently adjourned in this City, contained some very frank statements which our religious bodies would do well to consider. Mr. Cox urged very justly that President Grant and the public expected, on the appointment of a commission of Friends and well-known philanthropic citizens upon Indian affairs, that the powerful religious bodies of the nation would co-operate with these Commissioners and the Government to educate and Christianize the Indians; but that thus far the churches had done almost nothing, being so much occupied with the foreign heathen that they have almost utterly neglected these wards of the nation. The Secretary and the President esteemed these private philanthropic and religious efforts so highly, that the former asserted the alternative before the public to be, a vigorous attempt by the Christianity of the country to educate the Indian, or to witness the consummation of extermination in a general plundering and massacre of the wild tribes. Those officials both attach the highest value to the combined efforts of the churches and humane bodies of the nation in rendering justice to our own barbarians.

We may have overlooked the report, but we cannot recall in any missionary convention or church synod for the year, any important action originating new missionary and Christianizing efforts in harmony with the new Commission for our heathen at home. Action enough there has been about the Zulus, the Sandwich Islanders, and the Hindoos; but the American Indians, for whose miseries and crimes we are so largely responsible, have been mainly forgotten.

And yet any ordinary mission operation, such as might be started in South Africa or India, is not what is wanted. A solitary missionary, with Bible and prayer-book, going among the Comanches or the Sioux, can accomplish little in solving this great problem. Sufficient means should be raised to enable a missionary or band of missionaries to purchase and convey to some reservation all the material necessary for simple agriculture. There the mission should commence—as the old Spanish Catholic missions did, which were so successful with the Indians of the Pacific Coast—with teaching the rudiments of civilization, without which even the truths of Christianity will be of little avail to save them in this world. Beginning thus with instructions in planting crops, using farming tools, and tilling the ground, accompanying those lessons with the teachings of morality and the Divine truths of the Christian faith, material advancement will go hand in hand with moral and spiritual conversion. The wild nomadic Indian will get the rudiments of the great lesson of civilization; he will learn to labor for a result beyond the immediate moment; he will acquire the art of providing for his wants when game has disappeared or is scarce; he will possess a settled home and become accustomed to a steady occupation. This wise plan has already been tried with eminent success by an experienced Indian superintendent, Mr. Dent, Gen. Grant's brother-in-law, among the wild tribes near the Lower Colorado. He has proved what an advance in civilization can be made among the most nomadic tribes by a system of reservations, and the teaching of agriculture.

But the Church missionary would have an advantage in these labors possessed by no agent of the Government. The heart of every wild people is especially open to the sentiment of religion. A missionary comes as if from above. He has no selfish aims. He teaches the truth for all men and all times. No doubt agriculture will be easier learnt from a religious teacher, and religion from one who has the physical means to raise the neophyte above starvation and barbarism. No other system will at all succeed with aborigines, except this combination. And our Indian Commission, with its members, so influential among the churches, is especially the one to recommend and carry out such a suggestion. As fast as the wandering tribes are placed in reservations, the religious bodies should establish agricultural missions, with chapels, schools, plows and seed, with farmer missionaries, and teachers of the Bible who know how to plant corn. We fear, however, that the routine of the churches is too much fixed in the old method to allow of this innovation. And we dread that the fatal apathy of our religious bodies, wherever the heathen at home are concerned, may disappoint all hopes of any widespread missionary work for the Indians.

⬭ An Aboriginal Convention

August 3, 1875

A neat pamphlet, printed at Lawrence, Kansas, contains the official report of the proceedings of the sixth annual session of the General Council of the Indian Territory. That assemblage was composed of delegates duly elected from the Indian tribes legally resident in said Territory. To a sentimental person, possibly to a Thoughtful Patriot, there may be something pathetic in the fact that these few delegates represent the forlorn remnants of once great tribes. Students of Schoolcraft, Catlin, and Fenimore Cooper will recognize the names, but not the natures, of famous tribal organizations in the scanty roll of the convention; for there were Choctaws, Seminoles, Cherokees, Creeks, Pawnees, Shawnees, Pottawatomies, and other titles of nomads no longer terrible, no longer possessing even the charm which they once possessed for the young reader of American romance. But in the list of representatives lingers an element of the picturesque. Along with the meaningless names which white men have imposed upon the children of the forest are others of true native strength. Albert Barnes is well enough for a Cherokee, but Six Killer is more genuine, and Bean has the true flavor of the soil. John Williams may be good Choctaw, and T. Cloud is possibly an abbreviation of the Thunder Cloud of the Seminoles; but Mish-a-ma-tubbee is more melifluous [*sic*] and Indian-like. As for the rest, we find John Tomahawk, Joseph White Crow, Plenty Horses, Feathered Wolf, and numerous other aboriginal gentlemen gravely set down on the roll of the convention, and as gravely participating in the debates. On the Committee on Agriculture we rejoice to see that Messrs. Rabbit Bunch, Big Mouth, and George Washington figured; while T. Cloud, Black Beaver, Sah-ke-me-na-ka-pa, and (very appropriately) Albert Barnes served on the Committee on Education. The proceedings were decorous and regular; there was no occasion to move the previous question. There was no Congressman Holman, from Indiana, to say "I object;" and, though everybody spoke at least once during the session, not a red man of them could be called long-winded.

We cannot tell how much of the English report of this polyglot debate is to be credited to the resident agents. It is not impossible that the aboriginal idea, filtered through the refining mind of interpreter and official reporter, may be newly clothed before it goes into type. Even so great a man as the Sultan of Zanzibar is suspected of using less pious and conventional language than the gentlemanly missionary who is his dragoman in England delivers as the speech of that mysterious potentate. But if the legal residents of the Indian Territory do half as well as they are represented, they are very admirable spokesmen indeed. There was Big Mouth, of the once dreaded Arapahoes, for example, who said he had been trying to "make corn," and who confessed to having acquired such a taste for white men's manners that he would sooner ride in a wagon than on horseback. There is progress. An Arapahoe who rides in a wagon has given up scalp-hunting. Then, our old friend Bogus Charley, of the Modocs, is set down as having made a sort of closing-the-bloody-chasm speech, in which he confessed to having been brought in irons, and very much against his will, to the Territory, where he and his were represented as doing well. The ex-chieftain does not yet use "superb English," as he said that his people "appoint to commence farming"—a phrase probably modeled on the Western provincialism, "allow to begin work." These little roughnesses crop out in the report, though why a Seneca gentleman should say, "We have quit hunting, and don't practice the red horse" is more than we can fathom. Why red horse? An honorable gentleman from Pawnee, Mr. Running Chief, also alluded to that noble animal, the horse, saying, "The horse I cannot eat," thereby meaning that too many horses were inconsistent with peaceful pursuits, and not conveying any idea of experiments in hippophagy. The same speaker, who has not studied the *Congressional Globe* for nothing, rose to a question of privilege, and desired to call attention to a misstatement in a St. Louis newspaper. He denied that the Pawnees had invaded Western Kansas, as there set forth, and he regretted this publication as "very damaging to the Pawnee nation." There might have been "applause" punctuated in here; but we know that the red men are taciturn, and there was not even "sensation in the galleries," as during a speech of Fernando Wood in the War Congress, or a tearful episode in Mr. Tracy's peroration in a Brooklyn courtroom.

This "long talk," for it extended over two weeks, was diversified by reports from the various constituencies represented, and resulted in the appointment of a committee to draft a Territorial Constitution. The debate was not wordy, though it sometimes ran unnecessarily into oral advice as to the way in which proceedings should be conducted. One address had this bit of practical wisdom: "There is no use for a man to get up and talk by guess-work; a man ought to know what he is talking about." That may have been a rap at some raw debater, we have heard such before now, but it is a sound statement. There were contested seats, however, which shows that the red men are faithfully copying American politics; and, as the Osage contestants were allowed their expenses while their case was undecided, we see how close an imitation of legislative proceedings are possible in the Indian Territory. No trace of ancient hostility to the conquering foes of the red men is visible through this report. Once, indeed, a speaker spoke of the Modocs as having been "generally victorious" in their wars with the white men; but if there was any applause, or grunts of approbation, after that observation, it is judiciously expurgated from the official report. A Pawnee orator also alluded, with possible unction, to the time when the only way for a Pawnee chief to make his mark was to kill a good many of his enemies; but he added that the times had changed, and now true greatness was to be a great farmer, a great mechanic, or a great lawyer, as he understood some of his brothers to be. Shade of Tecumseh! A great Indian lawyer! Well might this redoubtable ex-warrior of the Pawnees say that the times have changed and men have changed with them. It is not half a century since the wars against the powerful tribes represented by these men were the difficult problems of the Republic. The tribes have dwindled, but the survivors, of full blood and direct descent, are tilling the ground, building houses, chopping logic, and holding conventions.

✍ The Kidnapped Klamath

September 14, 1875

The wretches who kidnapped little Charley Ross were right in believing that almost any sum of money would be paid by the unhappy parents for the restoration of their child. In this matter they displayed a certain business sagacity which entitled them to rank with the skillful brigands of Italy rather than with the ordinary thieves and burglars of America. But what can be said of the stupid fellows who last April kidnapped a Klamath Indian, and were recently glad to let him go again without a particle of ransom? Undoubtedly they fancied that the mere fact of kidnapping gives a commercial value to the kidnapped. Herein they showed a degree of folly worthy of the advocates of an inflated paper currency. The child of loving parents has for them a real and inestimable value, but the stray Klamath is totally devoid of any intrinsic value whatever. To impress the stamp of kidnapping upon a Klamath cannot make him valuable, or create the slightest demand for him. There is probably not an intelligent criminal outside of the Ohio and Pennsylvania Democracy who does not at once perceive the supreme folly of an attempt to inflate the kidnapping market with ragged, red-backed Indians.

The particular Klamath who was the subject of this kidnapping stupidity was one of a band of Modocs and Klamaths brought East for purposes of exhibition by ex-Peace Commissioner Meacham. The latter was one of the few companions of Gen. Canby who escaped the rifles of Capt. Jack and his treacherous followers, and he seems to have supposed that an exhibition of real Modocs, and of a real Peace Commissioner with real scalp wounds, would furnish a rational and moral amusement to which all the curiosity hunters would promptly rally. On the 26th of April last he had his Indians, as he imagined, safely boxed up in a New-York hotel, but, on counting them, was dismayed to find that one David Hill, called "for short," Walaika Skidat, was missing. As it was certain that Mr. Skidat had not been mislaid by any baggage-master, nor left on the seat of an omnibus by Mr. Meacham himself, the latter naturally supposed that he was merely temporarily absent, either with a view to whisky, or for the purpose of inspecting the fine stock of scalps which adorn the windows of local hair-dressers. Days and weeks went by, however, and Mr. Skidat did not appear. The Police were applied to by Mr. Meacham, who, having passed his life on the frontier, naturally knew nothing of the New-York Police, but they failed to find the missing Klamath. Somewhat later Mr. Meacham was mysteriously notified that certain persons were ready to return Mr. Skidat for the small reward of a thousand dollars. These mysterious dealers in cheap aborigines, however, failed to make good their offer, and all hope of finding the unfortunate Klamath was abandoned. Mr. Meacham and this friends probably hired a private parlor, and danced a funeral-dance in honor of the departed. At all events they never expected to see him again, and the conviction that Mr. Meacham was a careless person, liable to mislay and lose Indians at any time, seems to have seized upon his Modoc and Klamath friends, and led them to abandon their exhibiting tour, and return hastily to their native wilds.

The experience of the kidnappers was at least as unpleasant as was that of the kidnapped. They had caught their Klamath, but they found no one anxious to buy that sort of wild game. He had to be watched with the utmost care lest he should scalp his kidnappers, and the expense of supplying him with whisky and war paint, in order to keep him in a marketable condition, must have been very great. To get rid of him by killing him was not an easy task, since the Sportsman's Club would have been pretty sure to proceed against men who killed an Indian out of season. Finally they decided that the only thing to be done was to let the Klamath loose again. Accordingly they took him to the far West—probably in a bag—and opening the bag on a lonely prairie requested him to "scat." It is needless to say that he promptly obeyed, and a few weeks since he turned up on the Klamath very footsore and thirsty, and extremely dissatisfied with New-York and civilization generally.

If those kidnappers have any self-respect whatever they must feel heartily ashamed to look in a looking-glass. They went to the trouble of kidnapping an Indian, and their only reward was unlimited anxiety, and the expense of feeding him for four months. They have undoubtedly come to the conclusion that they were mistaken in supposing that their earthly mission is kidnapping. Something in the pocket-picking or sneak-thief line is only the business for which they are evidently fitted. Unless, indeed, they can obtain engagements to make Democratic speeches in Ohio—an occupation in which their lack of honesty and their experience of practical inflation, would make them peculiarly at home.

↜ The White Man's Secret

October 3, 1877

When the late James W. Nye, of genial memory, was appointed Governor of the Territory of Wushoo, he was, by virtue of his office, Superintendent of the Indians within his territorial jurisdiction. More familiar with New-York politics than with Indian affairs, Nye selected his propitiatory presents for the Piutes with a view to their advancement in civilization. But when the Piute squaws used his hoop-skirts for rabbit-traps, the Governor despaired of civilizing the Indians by means and appliances beyond their comprehension. Nevertheless, all barbaric races domesticated on our soil imitate the vices, weaknesses, and manners of the white man. A Chinaman does not consider himself Americanized until he can "swear like Melican man;" and the highest ambition of the Indian is to wear a high hat and affect the swagger of the whisky-drinking frontiersman, who represents to him the highest type of the all-conquering race. The Indians who come East are purposely shown the most striking evidences of the white man's power. The great ships, the steam-engines, the railroads, and the vast piles of buildings which he sees, all fill him with a surprise which he conceals with difficulty. Is it any wonder that this simple child of nature, awakened rudely to a sense of his own fatal inferiority, desires to secure for himself the secret of the white man's strength? It is natural that the dazzled aborigine should study the habits and manners of his strange oppressor, and eagerly hope, by imitation, to carry back to his wigwam the magic of the master race. He has seen his own people melt away before the white-skinned invader, like the snow before the climbing sun. He has seen how ineffectual were the struggles of the Indian tribes against the persistent, never-receding encroachments of the pale-face. If he would postpone the day of final extinction, and hold his own against the subtlety of his traditional foe, he must secure the secret of his mysterious superiority. He must be like the white man.

With a certain serio-comic earnestness, which makes us laugh while we pity, the Sioux who lately visited the President demanded things which, as they thought, should make them the equal of the white man. "We want," said Spotted Tail, "the kind of cattle which the white men have. We don't want cattle with long horns, but short ones." Who shall say that the red men have made no advancement in civilization, when they already know that short-horned cattle are better than long-horned? Then, again, they wanted a saw-mill and a grist-mill. Moreover, they asked for "agricultural implements and seeds." This was to steal the hidden secret of the white man's power. A Sioux chief, emulating the craft of his pale-faced enemies, once planted "a farm." He asked Prof. Marsh to come and see it. The white man—"the great bone chief"—saw a slight cottonwood rail-fence open at each end, parallel with the Platte, but inclosing nothing; and nothing more. The red chieftain sadly explained: "Plant um heap corn; bime by heap-dam sojer-mule, heap-dam hoppergrass eat um all up; no crop." Nevertheless, unwearied by continual defeat, the Sioux want short-horned cattle and "agricultural implements."

Nor have they studied the cities in vain. "I look around," said their orator, "and see that you have many stores. We have but one store, and when we pay our money there we have nothing to show for it. We want five or six stores, for then we could buy cheaper at one than we could at another." This is shrewdness itself. Spotted Tail has learned that competition makes prices lower. Monopoly in trade is odious to the savage as to the white man. With fine dramatic effect, these warriors of the plains came into the presence of the "Great Father," dressed in civilized apparel. The day before, they were representatives of untamed and savage tribes, pleading for their hunting-grounds, and they were decked in the barbaric finery of paint, feathers, and quill-embroidered skins. To-day, humbly pleading for the gift of the equipment of the master race, they appear in the prosaic and clumsy toggery of civilization. "Look at us!" cried the orator, contrasting with a gesture the awkward, ill-dressed Sioux and the comfortable group of officials, "we are well dressed, but we want $40 apiece to buy things for the women and children at home. You have overcoats, some of you. We want overcoats. We want trunks to put our clothing into." This was an advance into civilization. Another orator not only wanted an overcoat, but Catholic priests, "those who wear black dresses," and—think of it, ye who consider the Sioux a savage—"nuns to live among us and teach us." The petitioners were crafty, too, for they wanted it all in writing, "so that there may be no mistake." And one wanted forty boxes of money, a request whose vagueness suggests only the childishness mingled with cunning of the untutored savage. "Forty boxes of money" might mean as much or as little as the white man chose to make it. To the Indian it was untold wealth. But he wanted it all the same. Particularly, however, all were united in asking for short-horned cattle, agricultural implements, overcoats, trunks, and forty dollars a piece [*sic*]. This, at least, was civilization.

To the average citizen, unfamiliar with the wild life of the Sioux and Arrapahoes, it may seem a small thing that these savages should ask for school-houses, mills, priests, nuns, overcoats, and trunks. But it means that the Indians are anxiously reaching out for means of defense against the pale-faced invader. Fighting is no longer of any avail. If they are to meet the white man they must be equipped as well as he is. Anxiously looking around on the semi-circle of officials in the East Room at the White House, they saw overcoats. Perhaps overcoats, like Samson's locks, may be a source of strength. Why did not they ask for watch-chains like that of Secretary Evarts? or for Secretary Schurz's auburn whiskers? or his historic eye-glasses? or the pensive smile of Assistant Secretary McCormick? None of these did the Indian ever have. How should he know but any one of them was the talisman of power? It may be that when the Sioux go back to their country, they will, after brief experiment, tire of imitating the white man. Like Nye's Piutes, they may desperately give over their appliances of civilization to barbaric uses. The plowshares may be beaten into spears, the overcoats turned into breech-clouts, and the hoop-skirts into rabbit-snares. No matter, let the red men go home to practice the magic of the white man with overcoats, trunks, and forty boxes of money.

⟳ The Indians of the North-West

July 12, 1878

Though the specific origin of the Bannock outbreak has been fully made known, and is not disputed, there are yet elements in the pending war for which this assignment of causes does not account. Joined with the Bannocks are fragments of other tribes in no way concerned with the short-comings and complaints at Fort Hall and Lemha, and the fears expressed of a general uprising of the Indian tribes, both of the Great Salt Lake Basin and the Columbia River Valley, cannot be based on the supposition of mere sympathy with the grievances sustained by the bands of Buffalo Horn and Ten Day.

It is safe, no doubt, on general principles, to presume that every one of the restless and dissatisfied bands has had an experience of unfulfilled treaties, broken promises, agency frauds, or threatened coercion. Were these, however, the only sources of trouble, there would still remain the possibility of avoiding a general war by the familiar device of renewed promises, or of postponing the demand that non-treaty bands shall give up their lands and go upon appointed reservations. But there is, unhappily, reason to surmise that the real origin of the wide-spread discontent throughout Idaho, Eastern Oregon, and Western Montana lies deeper than the neglect or fraud of agents, traders, and Government bureaus.

The Indians of the far North-west have been nearly driven to the wall by the advancing tide of white civilization, and their attitude is that of a race at bay. The "irrepressible conflict" between their roving mode of life and the demands for strictly prescribed bounds made by civilization is leading to a final struggle in that region, before the red race, hopelessly worsted, sinks beneath the power of the white. A year ago that acute military observer, Gen. Sherman, passed through the region near the scene of hostilities on a tour of post inspection, and recorded his impressions in a series of letters to the War Department that are almost prophetic of the struggle now begun, and are suggestive of the extreme difficulty of avoiding it. His route brought him in contact with the Spokanes, Flatheads, Coeur d'Alenes, and Snake River Indians, all agitated by the then pending Nez Percé outbreak, being of a common type and class with the Nez Percés, intermarried with them, and having common grievances. He writes:

"All these see that the whites are rapidly occupying the best farming lands, and that they are in danger of starvation. These Indians vary from our plains Indians, for they seem willing to work; many have little patches of corn, melons, and vegetables. All depend on the salmon, which are gradually being extinguished by the netting and canning in the Lower Columbia. All these Indians want in the Spring to gather the camas-root, a kind of wild onion that grows on the moist and fertile spots, and all want reserved for their special use a large mountain region in which to get furs and skins for trade. Their habits were molded by intercourse with the old Hudson Bay Company, which furnished them guns, ammunition, flour, sugar, &c., in exchange for their peltries. Now, the Americans are here, slowly but surely creeping up from the south, who fence the land, make farms, erect saw-mills, and make impossible their former modes of life."

In this statement we find condensed the desires, the possibilities, and also the impossibilities with which the red men of this whole region are occupied. It is at once clear how strongly the Indians must be convinced of the justness of their cause, and why they are willing to fight for it. With the white race coming as interlopers, and occupying by force, or by treaties extorted through force, a large share of the lands once belonging to the red men, it seems to them but a slender favor to give them freedom to fish in the rivers, to dig their roots on Camas Prairie, and to hunt at will in the hunting season.

Some of the Army officers, sympathizing in these desires, have proposed to secure to all the tribes a great tract in the North-west, like the Indian Territory, where they could always pursue their roving mode of life. Were this possible, it might remove much of the difficulty in the Indian problem. It is, however, to be feared that the spread of civilization already would prevent this plan from being carried into effect, and that the future growth of the country might soon revoke it, even if temporarily accomplished. People in the East can, indeed, form no adequate conception of the rapidity with which new settlements spring up, as fast as new Army posts give protection, and even in advance of such protection. Gen. Sherman plainly takes the ground that the red man must submit to a disagreeable fate. All these tribes, he says, must "be made to understand that their former nomadic life is impossible, and that all must choose, individually or by tribes, a locality, and like the Coeur d'Alenes, *go to work*, make homes for themselves, and be content with fishing and hunting as auxiliary." In another letter touching the same theme, he says: "There is no help for it; the Indians must conform or be driven, like the Nez Percés, far away to the buffalo region or, if they prefer it, to their happy hunting ground. I have seen," he adds, "some Indians willing and able to take farms, build houses, and join in the white man's ways; and I honestly believe the Army could induce hundreds, if not thousands, of others to do the same, but if left as now, wandering about, hoping to restore the old order of things, an Indian will be a curiosity here in twenty years."

These are hard sayings, but they are probably wholesome; they bring up the practical question how the transition of the red race from a roving life to a settled life can best be effected. Thus far the efforts made in this direction have been of the feeblest description—not wholly fruitless, indeed, but pitiable in proportion to what they should have been. Our main civilizing process has been the rude and cruel one of war—the gradual crushing out of the weaker race by the stronger. Nor can we expect anything better than this, probably, until the Indians are placed under the sole charge of an undivided authority, the same in peace as in war, having an unshared responsibility, and uniting moderation and justice with energy and force. To constitute such an authority, civilian enough to teach the Indians the arts of peace, military enough to subjugate them, has as yet proved too hard a task for our statecraft.

ᗦ The Indian Lobby

January 17, 1879

A striking evidence of the rapid progress made in civilization by the Indians is found in the fact that several tribes maintain in Washington a lobby, the expenses of which are paid out of the income derived from trust funds held by the United States Government. The Indian has taken a leaf from the white man's book, and proposes to learn all of his little arts. The Cherokees, for example, annually receive the interest of $2,519,000, held in trust by the United States Government. Of this revenue, 35 per cent. should be dedicated to educating Cherokee children, under tribal direction. Prof. J. A. Seelye, in his report to the House, Forty-fifth Congress, charged that this income was misappropriated, that it was "borrowed" from the school fund and never returned, and that, notwithstanding the amplitude of the income of the tribe, which is increased by local taxes, the nation has incurred a debt of several hundred thousand dollars, and that its obligations are sold at very low figures. What becomes of this money?

In the report from which we have just quoted, Prof. Seelye says that "an expenditure, which sometimes reaches $25,000 a year, is made in the support of delegates in Washington." In his examination before the House Committee on Indian Affairs, last Winter, Col. Boudinot, of the Cherokee Nation, said: "For the first session of the Forty-fourth Congress, the delegates cost our people $30,000; for the second session of the Forty-fourth Congress, $29,000; for the called session of the Forty-fifth Congress, for only one month and half, they cost us $7,464, making an aggregate in two years for the Cherokee Nation alone, of $66,464." Subsequently, it was proposed in the Cherokee Council to give the delegates $10,000 additional, which they demanded, whereupon a member of the Council said: "As for me, I shall never vote another dollar to these delegates; they do not represent the people, and they are squandering our money." It was alleged at that time that this money was used in Washington by the Cherokee lobby to prevent passage of the bill to allot the lands of the Indian Territory in severalty. Who are the pensioners of that lobby?

These facts become especially significant when we perceive that certain Washington correspondents send forth inflammatory dispatches whenever the subject of disturbing the tribal relations of the Five Nations is alluded to. One of these sends to a New-York paper a warning that we may arouse another Indian war if the Indian lands are allotted to individual Indians. And we are threateningly reminded that one of the Five Nations—Creeks—has many warlike traditions, and that the Five Nations could call in as allies the Arapahoes, Cheyennes, Comanches, and other blood-thirsty tribes who have their grudges to gratify. This monstrous threat against the Government of the United States originates in the Indian lobby at Washington.

It is clear that if the surrender of tribal organizations, and an allotment of lands in severalty were made in the Indian Territory, the lobbyists and their agents would be out of business. At present, the custody and disbursement of the income derived from the trust funds held by the United States are in the hands of a ring. In the Cherokee Nation, as Prof. Seelye declares, they "borrow" the school money and do not put it back. They lump under one head of "expenses in Washington" such sums as Col. Boudinot refers to as being paid out for alleged lobby expenses. These men are fighting desperately to keep their places and their plunder. Including "adopted" white men and negroes, the Cherokees number 19,000, all told. They draw more than $160,000 per annum from the United States Government, and they collect over $10,000 in local taxes. Yet, with this net income of $170,000 a year, and without local improvements of any cost or value, the Cherokee Nation is to-day in debt to the amount of $189,000. Is it surprising that a well-fed lobby in Washington cries out against investigating the affairs of the Territory or disturbing the existing conditions of things?

The Indian lobby has invented a bugaboo. Railroads and railroad projects are in bad odor, and the Indian lobby industriously circulates the statement that the agitation of the Indian Territory question is in the railroad interests. But, just now, the question is not so much the allotment of the lands, as the crying scandals of this misgoverned Territory. The head men of the Five Nations arrogantly claim that theirs is a foreign country, and that the United

States Government, though it is the depository of the Indian trust funds, has no right to inquire into their domestic concerns. There is no law in the Territory. It is the refuge of outlaws and fugitives from justice. Last year there were 85 murders committed in the Territory for which no man was punished. To a large degree, the policy of the so-called nations is shaped by unprincipled white men and half-breeds. The so-called Legislatures are merely the registers of the men who pull the wires and spend the money. One meets in the Territory with very few real Indians who know or care what is going on in their national affairs. The so-called Principal Chief of the Choctaws is a red-headed Irishman who cannot speak or write a word of Choctaw. And, so long as the Indian Territory is fenced in by a wall of customs, laws, and habits separating them from all outside influences, so long will crafty managers enrich themselves and maintain a corruption fund from the bountiful revenue derived from the United States Government.

⌒ Improving the Utes

October 9, 1879

There is never any glory achieved in an Indian war. In the end the red-skinned combatants are defeated, and if they, like defeated white men, "accept the situation," they do not chant paeans of triumph over their foes. For obvious reasons, they send no Brigadiers to Congress after the fight is over. It is an ignoble contest at best. Brave officers from the Military Academy lead their troops against a savage foe. Nevertheless, the besieged band of soldiers which has just been relieved by Gen. Merritt kept up a brave and determined defense; and he must be dull who is not moved by sympathy when he reads the unaffected story of the battle and the siege detailed in dispatches from Capt. Payne's command. The attack on the expedition, in which Major Thornburgh was killed, was made on Sept. 29. Relief came on Oct. 5, and during the time which intervened, the survivors of the company were penned into a narrow gorge, their camp open to cross-fires from perpendicular cliffs opposite, and only five or six hundred yards distant. Here the men intrenched themselves, seeing nothing before them but a siege which must last until relief came. In the meantime, a company of soldiers from Bear River, under the command of Capt. Dodge, had reinforced the besieged party. But this did not give the camp sufficient strength to warrant an attempt to withdraw. When Gen. Merritt finally came up, the siege was raised. He must have come upon the Indians on their flank, and he killed thirty-seven of them in his attack.

The defiant attitude of the Utes was maintained to the last. Seeing inevitable defeat and capture before them, they offered to surrender their fighting material on condition that Gen. Merritt's column should not go on the agency. This was interpreted as being an effort to delay as long as possible the discovery of the havoc wrought at the agency by the Indians. It had already been conceded that there was no chance that the lives of the white people had been spared. But, whatever may have been the motive of the Ute chiefs in making such a condition, it is evident that they do not comprehend the gravity of the proceedings in which they have been engaged. Nor will the Utes realize, until they are broken up and scattered, their reservation taken from them, and their chiefs put to death, what consequences wait upon their outbreak. Their short-lived war is over. Their gradual extermination now begins.

It is not practicable, just now, to put the responsibility for this bloody conflict where it belongs. The cause of the outbreak is well understood. It was the policy of the Government, so far as that policy was represented by Agent Meeker, to bring the Utes under civilization, teach them farming, and assist them to maintain themselves by means of labor and husbandry. The Indians did not want to be "civilized." They refused to be taught by the white man, and they were angry when it was proposed to replace their hunting-grounds with grain-fields. The last straw on the back of this sulking tribe was the plowing of a field. Agent Meeker, firm in his conviction of duty to the untutored savage, declined to be warned by bullets fired at the plowmen. He persisted in his determination to teach agriculture by example. Nobody appears to have known how deep in the Indian breast was the hostility to the so-called improvements of the white man. In the nature of things, an outbreak must occur. The agent was bent on "civilization"; the Utes were bent on avoiding these burdens; when the collision came at last, the Utes had the advantage of preparation and position. But theirs was a futile struggle. Whether they fought with the madness of desperation or in dense ignorance of the power of the Government of the United States, it does not matter. Nothing but certain overthrow and extinction awaited them.

This is a clear case of extermination, brought on by efforts to improve the condition of the Indians. The Indians had been granted a reservation on which they were content to live in their own way. It was useless to tell them that they must learn to read and write, that they must plow and sow and eat their bread in the sweat of their brow. The gospel of labor they utterly rejected. Paganism and savagery were their choice. They hated the white man's clothes, and would not wear shoes while their wives were able to make moccasins for them. It was determined that these people, who really "did not know when they were well off," should be compelled to better themselves. In some such spirit of Christian enterprise, European nations have bombarded trade and commerce into China. In the same lofty temper, the English Army has been hunting Zulus as wild boars are hunted in Germany. We have had no general battle in the Ute country, as the English philanthropists have had in South Africa, each valiant soldier counting the heads of his slain as a mighty Nimrod might sum up his day's sport. Our soldiers did their whole duty manfully, and because somebody else had provoked a fight which must be checked. But the end is pretty much the same as is the case of the followers of Cetywayo. The Ute reservation will be rubbed out of the map of Colorado. The tribe will be broken up and dispersed. Some of the leaders will be put to death. Others will be imprisoned for life, and the remainder of the once-powerful nation will be scattered in separate groups throughout the extreme Western and South-western States and Territories. The name of the tribe will be speedily forgotten, and nobody will notice when the last of the race dies somewhere in captivity or exile. Perhaps this is destiny, as hurried on by the American people. But it is impossible not to feel at least a passing pang of commiseration for a tribe thus systematically improved off the face of the earth.

↶ A Triumph of Civilization

November 26, 1882

There is a story told of a party of distressed mariners, who, shipwrecked on an unknown coast, journeyed inland with many fears and much trepidation until they beheld a gibbet crowning an eminence, when they thanked God and took courage. They were sure that they were in a civilized country. The world has moved since then, but the gallows is still one of the indices of our advanced civilization. To be hanged according to law is to prove to the world that the culprit is the offering of a law-abiding people upon the altar of human justice. The ceremony is devoid of all passion and prejudice. The Judge, the Sheriff, and the executioner may each be the personal friend of the victim. They may be willing (although this is a violent supposition) to resign office rather than be in any way a party to the death of a man who is justly condemned, but whose extinction by legal process may, nevertheless, wring the hearts of his friends. Capital punishment is intended not so much to punish the sinner as to deter others from sinning. Imprisonment is theoretically, at least, at once reformatory and penal. Hanging is purely exemplary. This is supposed to be the highest manifestation of criminal law. Nobody pretends that the hanged man is made better by being put to death according to law.

Among savage nations, immediate and violent death is the penalty of invading the existence of others, always providing, of course, that the invader is caught. Usually, the survivor of a person murdered without due notice and opportunity for defense seeks out the homicide and slays him at sight. This is the practice of all semi-civilized and savage countries, as well as in a large portion of our own Republic. But in our missionary efforts with the Indians we have insisted that to take the law into one's own hands was barbarous. We have taught them that no man's life should be taken without due process of law, and that the custom of chasing an alleged murderer and killing him wherever found was simply a relic of a savage age. The North American Indian has always believed that one death should be avenged by another, and that any man who had the means, daring, and the opportunity to avenge the ghost of his murdered friend should go and kill the killer. But we have begun to civilize the Indian. His darkened understanding is to be illuminated with the fundamental principles of human justice. He is taught that a criminal should be strangled by law, not merely brained by the casual tomahawk of the passing stranger or of the family avenger of blood.

At last, after a few experiments in this direction, one Indian has not only been hanged, but he has acknowledged the regularity (if not the justice) of his execution, and has requested on the scaffold that the usual pagan ceremonies and revenges of his tribe be omitted in his behalf. Brave Bear, a Sioux Indian, was the first aborigine hanged in Dakota. Usually, when a Sioux had murdered one or more persons (and the number was generally plural) the people of the vicinage have collected and hunted down the murderer, killing incidentally as many as might be found. Brave Bear, having killed Joseph Johnson as long ago as 1879, was duly convicted by law. His learned counsel fought the case under civil rights and under the Criminal Code from court to court. Finally, legal means of delay having been exhausted, Brave Bear was hanged at Yankton, Nov. 15, 1882. Indian-like, he made neither confession nor denial of his guilt. He omitted the usual death-song, which, as in the case of the murderers of Canby, has been the savage defiance of the laws of the white man. More than this, calling for an interpreter, he did not ask that his grave be kept green, as did a Missouri bandit, hanged for numerous crimes, but he sent his dying requests to his brother Sioux. He told them not to attempt to avenge his death, to kill no horses whose brute shades were to accompany him to the happy hunting-grounds, and to omit all customary howlings, knife-gashings, sprinkling of ashes, face-painting, and other signs of lamentation and mourning. This done, Brave Bear was pinioned, and, a noose being provided, was judicially strangled. When life had been pronounced to be extinct, his body was cut down and buried in a Roman Catholic cemetery, from which we conclude that Brave Bear died in the order of sanctity and in the bosom of the Holy Catholic Church. He was interred in consecrated ground; and there is no report of his skeleton being wired for a medical museum, or of his skull and skin becoming objects of litigation among surviving friends. This is a triumph of civilization.

A Modern Indian

August 19, 1886

Day by day new and touching illustrations of the progress of civilization are made known, and each succeeding edition of the census shows a wider spread of sweetness and light among the people. Western theorists have declared that the only good Indian is a dead Indian, but they must sink into silence before the overwhelming evidences that the untutored savage is adopting the habits of his wiser white brother. Already he is the rival of civilized man in his capacity for firewater, and his noble devotion to aged and decrepit silk hats. Recently he has shown still further insight into the excellence of human excellence by entering with spirit and enterprise into the amusement business, and digging up the hatchet and gliding through the giddy mazes of the war dance for a reasonable share of the gross receipts at the box office.

Individuals, however, are always in advance of their race in the march of improvement, and it was therefore reserved for a single member of the happy band at Staten Island to clothe a prominent feature of primeval savagery with the habit of modern humanity. This young brave went alone to the wigwam of a Newark white chief, sang his song under the window, won the heart of the daughter of the house, and eloped with her after the manner of his good white brothers. How different is this from the old-time custom as set down by trustworthy authors in graphic tales designed to illustrate the relations existing between frontiersmen and the red men of the woods. Then the savage would have stolen forth at night, accompanied by thirty braves, the flower of his tribe, all painted in a manner to strike terror to any heart. They would have placed their ears to the earth and satisfied themselves that no heavy white foot was tramping anywhere within a hundred miles. Then they would have set out in single file, each moccasin falling noiselessly in the track of the one before it, and would have marched tirelessly through sixty miles of forest impenetrable to any other beings save bumble bees. Arriving within half a mile of the white man's house, they would have fallen at full length upon the ground and crawled like snakes in the grass up to the doors. Then they would have arisen with ear-splitting yells, stormed the house, tomahawked the unhappy father, dragged forth the screaming maiden by her golden hair, placed her on a pony, and set off for their village.

And the next morning Col. John Smith, the white lover of the lady, accompanied by Cross-eyed Pete, the lightning scout, who "never guv a durn fur enny Injun livin' or drunk," would set out in their pursuit. These two gentlemen would have read the signs of the forest like an open book, and have followed the tribe over mountain and through river even unto the bitter end. And just as the great chief was about to press his ruthless lips upon the fair cheek of the struggling maiden, a single shot would have pealed upon the silence, the brave would have uttered a yell, leaped six feet into the air, and fallen dead upon the sward. The next moment the two white men would have burst from the thicket, slaughtered and scalped the entire band, and carried the maiden home again to receive the blessing of her weeping mother.

That is the way it would have been done. But civilization has laid its softening hand upon the savage. It may be that in a few short months this latter-day Indian, who has simply eloped with a girl, may further fit himself for the age and country in which he lives by deserting her and running away with some other gentleman's wife.

Encoaching Civilization

⟲ [Untitled]

March 14, 1891

Secretary Noble's recent issue of a permit to Gen. W. F. Cody, better known as Buffalo Bill, to engage one hundred reservation Sioux for his Wild West Show is the more remarkable since only about seven months ago the Secretary expressly prohibited the issue of any more such permits. Indeed, still later, in his annual report, he had elaborately demonstrated that reservation Indians ought not to be used for show purposes. He had dwelt upon the bad effects of having them enact "the wildest and most savage scenes of Indian warfare" for the delectation of whites, who applaud the performances in proportion to their realistic merits. Commissioner Morgan, who had urged these ideas upon the Secretary, was delighted, of course; yet now we find the Secretary already taking back his own words and leaving the Commissioner in the lurch. It appears that Buffalo Bill collected testimonials from army officers as to the expediency of having him give as many as possible of the Sioux a chance to see the world and earn money instead of staying home to brood over the millennium. But Mr. Noble's change of view, which he can explain in his next annual report, does not help Commissioner Morgan, who is overruled in his special branch of the service and is made to take a back seat by the enterprising showman.

⟲ [Untitled]

March 16, 1891

The project of enlisting Indians for the regular army is one of the most striking of the many novelties which have recently been introduced into the military establishment that have made the last two years perhaps unprecedented in this respect by any like period of our army administration in time of peace. The present experiment naturally seems less of an innovation from the familiar employment of Indian scouts, but those are peculiar and separate organizations, whereas now the red men are to be regular soldiers, organized, trained, governed, and employed like whites. While even the colored men are never enlisted save in regiments of their own, the Indians are to form one troop in each white cavalry regiment and one company in each of the white infantry regiments, except the four of the latter now serving east of the Mississippi. This, therefore, will give eight troops and nineteen companies, so that at the prescribed enlisted strength of 55 we should have nearly 1,500 Indians in the army, besides the Indian scouts, who are to be reduced to 150. The commissioned officers will be whites, but it may not be very many years before young men of Indian blood will pass through the course at West Point to Lieutenancies in companies of their own race. That the Indians have plenty not only of the war spirit but of aptitude even for the methodical soldiership required in the regular service can hardly be doubted, although the actual working of the new experiment, especially in the routine of garrison life, will be followed with much curiosity as to the results.

∽ [Untitled]

February 6, 1892

The question whether "Lo" shall have his lager is one of those that the Indian Bureau is said to be proposing to Congress. The law forbidding the introduction of ardent spirits on Indian reservations is an old one, and its value, both to the red men and their white neighbors, is beyond doubt, in spite of its many violations, principally through the unscrupulousness of liquor sellers among the latter. But the statute, either through accident or design, did not specifically mention malt liquors, and defined "spirituous liquors or wine" as the beverages prohibited under its more general terms of "ardent spirits." For this reason, after some disputing as to whether sending ale or beer into the Indian Territory, among the five civilized tribes, came within the statute prohibition, a United States District Judge decided, a few months ago, that it did not. The Interior Department declined to accept that decision as binding, and, relying upon another law which gives the Commissioner of Indian Affairs general authority to make regulations for trade with the tribes, continued to destroy beer as well as whisky found in the Territory, and to break up the saloons that sold lager. It is now suggested that Congress would do well to avoid trouble by adding malt liquors to the list of forbidden drinks, since that would only be keeping out by specific law what has already been kept out by administrative authority and bureau regulations. The chances are, however, that Congress will not do this, perhaps holding that if the Interior Department possessed authority enough to do what it has done about lager it must have authority enough to keep on doing it.

ᗊ Indian Education

September 20, 1892

A dispatch from Kingman, in Arizona, announces that a few days ago representatives from five tribes or bands of Indians met at Pine Springs to protest against having their children taken away and sent to Government schools in the East. It is said that some of them were for resorting to arms, and that a great many families had gone to the mountains to prevent their boys and girls from being carried off. It is quite possible that the parents have exaggerated the risks they run, but their feeling that it is a hardship to have their children carried a long distance away is natural. The Fifty-first Congress at its second session passed a law authorizing and directing the Commissioner of Indian Affairs "to make and enforce by proper means such rules and regulations as will secure the attendance of Indian children of suitable age and health at schools established and maintained for their benefit." This compulsory attendance law furnishes the basis for the action of which the Arizona bands complain. But whether Congress foresaw that the authority thus given would be used to take children against the will of their parents hundreds or thousands of miles from their homes may not be so clear. To civilized people such a removal will, of course, seem a great opportunity for the youngsters. They are cared for, fed, clothed, and instructed without cost, and are made much fitter for citizenship and for success in life than their companions who receive no such advantages. But while we understand all this, to the Indian fathers and mothers the forcible wresting away of their children must look very much like kidnaping.

The Indian Bureau itself has recognized this difficulty in its rules and regulations, which prescribe that, "so far as practicable, the preferences of Indian parents or guardians, or of Indian youth of sufficient maturity and judgment, will be regarded as to whether the attendance shall be at Government, public, or private schools." But it is further provided that, if schools on the reservations are lacking or already filled, "or if for other reasons the good of the children shall clearly require that they be sent away from home to school, they will be placed in non-reservation schools." In this latter case, "the consent of parents shall ordinarily first be secured, if practicable"—which seems to mean that unless the parents part with them willingly, they may be taken away by force. But a law which is perfectly sound and wise, if administered by people of discretion, for procuring attendance at the reservation schools, might cause some distress if enforced to the extent of separating children from their parents for years together. Nor is it usually understood that the Eastern training schools are unable to get their quota of pupils without such a process. There are Indians, presumably, who allow their children to go to these schools. But, however that may be, it is particularly desirable, in neighborhoods where objection is made, if the Government schools are full and private or contract schools can take them, that they should do so where the provisions made by Congress will permit.

There is no doubt that the main hope of civilizing the red men and of bringing them into line with American citizens lies in the training of their children. It would be unwise to allow the prejudices of ignorant parents to deprive the rising generation of the provisions made by the Government for their benefit. Yet it is quite evident that in this matter sound judgment and careful consideration of the peculiar circumstances of the red men are needed. Commissioner Morgan has noted that the Indians "are loath to have their children taken from them, even for a short time. They are devotedly attached to them, miss their companionship, and are accustomed to rely upon their assistance in the performance of such simple duties as they are capable of." Perhaps in this statement may be found an explanation of the feeling of bitterness against the Government which is now reported to exist among some of the Arizona bands. It would hardly be fair to charge them with prejudice against education if what they are really prejudiced against should turn out to be simply the sending of their offspring far away. It does not appear from the dispatch that they would object to having them instructed in schools where the parents could still have a share in their companionship. The problem, no doubt, is a difficult one, but it is evident that, while an admirable work is done by the Eastern training schools—one of whose great advantages is in taking the children at an impressionable age away from their savage home surroundings—yet the ultimate reliance for the great body of the Indians must be in schools on and near the reservations. Commissioner Morgan in his last report made a strong appeal to Congress for the multiplication of day schools, fully supplied with all means to make up for the lack of home instruction. It would require no very extravagant amount to furnish sufficient schools and instruction for such of the Indian children of school age as cannot now be accommodated somewhere, and it might be a wise expenditure to do this within the next few years. With more reservation schools the compulsory attendance law would be enforced with a better grace and without embittering the lives of Indian parents in seeking the benefit of their offspring.

ᑫ [Untitled]

December 10, 1892

The judicious intervention of Gen. McCook has averted for the present what had threatened to be serious trouble on the Navajo Reservation. The act of March 3, 1891, authorizes and directs the Commissioner of Indian Affairs, under the direction of the Secretary of the Interior, to "make and enforce, by proper means, such rules and regulations as will secure the attendance of Indian children of suitable age and health at schools established and maintained for their benefit." Such rules were drawn up, and Agent Shipley, acting under them, sought to gather into the Navajo school the children of Black Horse's band. That chief, however, with his armed followers, met and drove back the agent's party, and roughly handled one them [sic]. Then the agent, as the report ran, wanted troops to go to Round Rock and take the children to the schools by force. This would certainly have been compulsory education in the fullest extent of the term. How it could have been inferred that the use of the army for procuring school attendance was what Congress meant by "proper means" does not appear. However, a few army officers had a little talk with Black Horse, and the trouble disappeared. As the Navajos are a tribe of over 16,000 souls with plenty of arms and resources, this seems a sensible way of dealing with the matter for more reasons than one.

ᑫ Indians and Civilization

September 5, 1899

There were two incidents reported in yesterday's paper which to a superficial observer might seem to illustrate, one with a suggestion of tragedy, the other in pure farce, the imperviousness to civilization of the North American Indian. One was the announcement that some Mexican Indians are endeavoring to procure ammunition in Belize for the purpose of resisting the payment of taxes on their favorite beverage of aguardiente. The other relates how a number of Osage Indians in Oklahoma, each of whom owns 900 acres of land and receives $50 in cash from the Government every three months, are solemnly going through the bankruptcy court with the amiable and undisguised purpose of cheating their creditors out of honest debts.

But objections to paying taxes are by no means confined to "Indians not taxed." The Caucasian millionaire, it is true, does not resort to the harsh methods of the Mexican Indian, but swears off the obnoxious levies. Still there have been whites engaged in the manufacture, sale, or consumption of "moonshine," who were so far below the level of civilization attained by the millionaire that the only way of escaping taxation that occurred to them was the crude one of killing an Inspector of Internal Revenue. It is true, however, that they seem to have found a way more in accordance with the dictates of civilization, since it is a long time ago that the latest killing of an Inspector was reported.

As to this Oklahoma business, it is really a proof of the spread of the ameliorating influences of civilization. That a whole tribe of solvent debtors should determine to go through bankruptcy and come out without a stain upon their characters and with a neat and becoming coat of whitewash in place alike of their native copper and of the war paint with which they would formerly have covered it upon being summoned to pay debts it was not convenient to pay denotes a high and novel appreciation of the "white man's way." Evidently nobody can take advantage of a bankruptcy law until he knows there is such a thing; and that is a great advance in knowledge on the part of the Osages. It is so great an advance as to suggest that the discovery was made for them by some paleface. The indignant Caucasian creditors may be commended to look for some Caucasian jurist as the real author of their woes.

7 Massacres and Lesser Injustices

It is reported from New-Mexico that various counties in that territory have offered, or are about to offer, rewards of from $250 to $500 each for the scalps of "buck" Indians, and that the ranchmen and cowboys are organizing armed bodies to go on an old-fashioned Indian hunt. The simplicity of this scheme, which assumes that all Indians are alike and none good except the dead, is only equaled by its shocking brutality.

—*New York Times*
October 12, 1885

IN THE YEARS FROM 1860 to the turn of the century, there rarely was a significant interval during which the *Times* editorial pages lacked comment about some new atrocity in the enduring conflict it referred to as the Indian problem. In the early years, the victims commonly were white. But over time, and particularly as more white settlers moved westward after the Civil War, that tide turned. White aggressors preyed on the Native Americans in one depredation after another.

One of the worst of these was the senseless raid on a Cheyenne village in Colorado in 1864 that came to be known as the Sand Creek massacre. The *Times* had little information on it at the time but would refer back to it in later years as an example of indefensible military action against the Indians. Nearly a year after Sand Creek, it called attention editorially to "a terrible document" in Congress that contained the details of that atrocity. The *Times* worried that because Colonel John M. Chivington, who led his Colorado volunteers in that ferocious attack on innocent Indians, went unpunished, others felt free to emulate his action. A "great government," it said, could not permit such injustices.

By late 1865, the *Times* was led to complain that cruelty and hatred had become the Indians' common lot in the presence of white settlers. The

Native Americans had been driven from the Atlantic seaboard to a final refuge in the West, it lamented. It found little reason for optimism in the existing circumstances. Accounts of attacks on the Indians drew expressions of outrage, sympathy, and a general sense of hopelessness in the *Times* opinion columns. And although one atrocity came to sound much like another, the newspaper mounted new fury over every report.

The *Times* recognized also that injustice was not limited to physical attack. In the search for an acceptable policy toward the Indians, it said in an April 1867 editorial, there were two important factions—and both were wrong. While one faction "clamors for their annihilation," it said, the other hoped to gain "all the Indians possess and by drink to debase them below the level of enemies whose anger need be feared." It questioned whether a "Christian nation" could permit the wholesale murder of Native American men, women, and children. And it wondered whether white Americans could face their collective conscience for allowing the Indians to be debased "as an indirect preliminary for their destruction."

The *Times* expressed little sympathy for those who rationalized brutality toward the Indians as being justified by the enmity of the tribes. As the first of the editorials included in this chapter demonstrates, *Times* editorial writers condemned such brutality in vigorous terms. Typically, they offered evidence that it was the whites, not the Indians, who started the trouble. The *Times* editorials, however, generally were more reserved in their criticism of military action. The newspaper contended that quick and decisive victory in battles with the Indians was more merciful than prolonged combat. But when a sizable army force attacked a Piegan village in Montana in early 1870, the *Times* reckoned that action a sickening slaughter with no redeeming merit. The ruthless killing of 173 Indians, including 90 women and 50 children, it said, was nothing but butchery. It called for an investigation by Congress. Another editorial on the Piegan massacre, included in this chapter, acknowledged that the attack may have been warranted. But under no circumstances could the *Times* condone the killing, when there was clear evidence that the tribespeople offered little resistance and easily could have been taken captive.

The *Times* frequently used its editorial columns to recount the details of events leading up to bloody encounters between the Indians and white settlers. These were of a common pattern. In almost every instance, the *Times* argued, the Indians were harassed by whites until some form of armed encounter was virtually inevitable. It blamed most of the problem on frontiersmen who, in many instances, actually were looking for an excuse to kill Indians. This pattern was particularly unfortunate, the *Times* noted, because without the white assaults the open clashes with Indians along much of the frontier could be ended. It believed there were enough friendly tribes to insulate white settlers against attacks from the remaining enemy bands.

The *Times* made every effort to demonstrate that whites committing depredations on Indians were just as vicious as Indians who attacked whites. White ferocity had been "disgracefully frequent" all along the frontier, the newspaper said, and news of every such incident inevitably spread among all the tribes. It hoped there might be balancing reports of justice that could give the Native Americans at least some promise of fairness over time. But since the white criminals rarely were brought to trial, it admitted, such prospects were limited.

The *Times* also pointed out that many of the bloodiest Indian wars had commenced with isolated crimes against the native tribes that went unpunished. It suggested that simple justice in such situations might do more to prevent further troubles than the application of military force. The editorial writers strengthened their calls for appropriate punishment of white perpetrators by quoting the reports of military commanders who took the same position. But unfortunately, the *Times* recognized, a nation that had been quick to apply civil law against the Indians was slow to apply it on their behalf. To the credit of the editorial writers, they were able to keep a balanced perspective. Indian atrocities against white settlers continued to draw forceful condemnation; the *Times* would express no sympathy for the murderous Geronimo, just as it had none for cowardly cowboys. Over time, however, it found fewer occasions to condemn Native Americans for attacking whites.

In its editorial columns, the *Times* continually reported on less dramatic injustices to the Indians as well as violent aggression. In a short editorial in October 1875, it pointed out the plight of the Temeculas in California. This small band had occupied its present land in San Diego County "for unnumbered centuries," the *Times* said, only to be told by the white government that the land belonged to others. Peaceful and self-supporting, the Indians now found themselves treated as trespassers on land inherited from ancient generations. Now, said the *Times*, they were wards of the nation. "The whole history of Indian relations to the General Government," it concluded, "may be summarized in the story of this hapless tribe."

The *Times* mistrusted government representatives who blamed the Indians when there were outbreaks of violence. Noting that an Indian agent had accused a tribal medicine man of stirring up trouble on the San Carlos Reservation in the Southwest in 1882, the *Times* questioned whether the real reason might not be the fact that the reservation had been reduced in size five times in six years. The anonymous editorial writer suggested that the land had been taken away from the Indians because of the discovery of valuable mineral deposits. "By this time, we should suppose, the Indians have learned that a mining discovery in their vicinity is simply a notice for them to quit," the editorial said. "Being merely untutored savages and unacquainted with law, they begin operations by fighting."

In the following year the *Times* called attention to proposed Congressional action to break up the Nez Percé reservation in Oregon. The white settlers would never rest until the tract "honestly and fairly belonging to the Nez Percés" was parceled out among them, it said. "Then, should a new war begin, there would be a frantic shriek for protection from the 'bloodthirsty savages' of the Northwest." The *Times* would find no shortage of land-grabs engineered by white settlers on which to vent its editorial frustrations. Like armed attack, these were a common element of white behavior toward the Indians.

Through the latter 1880s, some of the most vigorous *Times* editorials were written in defense of the Ute tribe in Colorado. Its editorial columns portrayed that tribe as one that had been starved into submission by the government and made vulnerable to the worst of frontier injustices. Then, as the nation moved into the final decade of the century, the *Times* was moved to offer one of its most poignant editorials analyzing events on a tragic day at Wounded Knee, South Dakota. That editorial, "An Indian Massacre," is included in this chapter.

Indian Outrage, and Indian Wrongs

April 28, 1867

We published an account a few days since of an interview which Gen. Hancock had with a number of Indian chiefs. The General addressed them at considerable length, dwelling particularly upon the statement that he was prepared to punish them for any depredations they might commit. He said very little, however, about the impositions practiced upon them by the whites, and made no promises regarding the swindling transactions of Indian agents and irresponsible traders. The Indians did not appear to heed the threats made to them, and received the Gener's [*sic*] speech in sullen silence. One of them, "Tall Bull," closed the interview with a few remarks, the tenor of which was that while the Indians did not want to war with the whites, the soldiers and white traders were constantly shooting them whenever they appeared in the neighborhood of the trading posts and forts.

The chiefs evidently attached little importance to this council; indeed, so few attended it as to excite the surprise of Gen. Hancock, who had summoned them. Notwithstanding the fact that the "pipe of peace" was smoked at this council by all interested, when the troops next day marched toward the Cheyenne village they were met by several hundred Indians in battle array. A consultation ensued, the troops went into camp, and the Indians hastily broke up their village, and departed at night with bag and baggage. Gen. Custer was sent in pursuit with a cavalry force, and the latest reports from him are to the effect that these Indians, who had so recently declared for peace, had burned three stations on the Smoky Hill route, and had killed and scalped several men.

It is very evident from these late reports from the frontier that several numerous bands of Indians have combined to war upon the whites, and that they have no confidence in the statements made by the agents sent to make peace with them. This is hardly to be wondered at. Our treatment of the Indians, wherever they have been found, has been characterized by systematic swindling and contemptible trickery. We have made treaties which read well on paper—and sounded satisfactory when read to the Indians, but which were simply the means whereby a few thieving agents and traders filled their purses. From first to last the ignorant savages have been robbed by those who should have been their protectors. Goods of an inferior quality have been sent to them to supply such clothing as they must have, but the money and valuable presents contracted for seldom got beyond the frontier post. At these posts, when the time for paying the annuities arrived, the Indians were assembled and forthwith made drunk, that they might be the more easily robbed by Government agents and irresponsible traders. These payments have always been characterized by scenes of drunkenness, debauchery, gambling and robbery. While the Indians were thus despoiled of their money, goods and senses, their wives and daughters fell victims to the lusts of the white man. Is it to be wondered at that the uneducated savage, with whom revenge is an instinct, should retaliate upon the whites for all the injuries done his race? Not content with degrading and robbing the Indian, the rough white settler on the frontier looks upon him in the light of "varmint," and does not hesitate to kill him on the slightest provocation. Could the facts be ascertained, we believe it would be found that for the past ten years for every isolated murder committed upon the whites by Indians, there have been two Indians killed by whites. We do not include here those unfortunates who have suffered by the wholesale massacres which the Indians have perpetrated. But even for these there is an offset. How much worse was the Fort Phil Kearny massacre than the slaughter perpetrated by Col. Chivington and his command when, without just cause, he shot down in cold blood men, women and children, simply because they were redskins? Within the present month a dispatch was telegraphed throughout the country to the effect that, in consequence of some Indians having stolen some Government horses, a Lieutenant had pursued the thieves with cavalry, "and twenty-seven Indians were killed." Not another word is said except in glorification of the "gallant" young officer; and these twenty-seven human beings were sent out of the world with six words. While the atrocities committed by the Indians are terrible in the extreme and greatly to be lamented, there are outrages on our side which cannot be overlooked and to which may be attributed the present hostility of so many tribes with whom we have been so long at peace.

From present appearances it seems impossible to avoid an extensive Indian war—a war which will cost the lives of many brave soldiers and still more Indians. The numerous tribes of the southern and middle plains are uniting with those further north, and appear in bands whose strength is not to be despised. They have captured one if not two forts, killing whoever was found within; have destroyed the mail stations on the overland route, killing all persons found therein, and appropriating all the stock they could find. Forts Mitchell and Benton are now surrounded by them, and there is reason to believe that these garrisons will soon be called upon to fight against double their numbers. The only possible way apparently to prevent a terrible Indian war is to throw a sufficient number of troops on to the frontier to protect the inhabitants and intimidate the Indians. To do this will require a larger force than is at present available for field service.

Suppose the Indians reduced to quietness once more, either by hard fighting or by new treaties, what will then be done with them? The management of the Indian Bureau has brought about the present uprising, and that Bureau clearly is not fit to deal with them in future. The military power, with the memory of recent massacres and hard fighting crowding upon it, certainly will not be in a humor to deal kindly by them. It has been suggested by those who have been most successful in dealing with the different tribes, that they should be withdrawn from the frontier and placed on reservations in some of the Western States, where they may be brought in contact with civilization. These agents represent that the Indian takes to agricultural pursuits almost naturally, and that any tribe properly located and fitted out would immediately become self-supporting. The experiment is at least worth trying. It certainly is possible to find honest and capable men to deal with them, and when that is done the battle is half won. But never will it be possible to civilize the Indians, or prevent acts of atrocity on their part, while they are surrounded by an army of thieves in the shape of agents and traders, whose profits are increased as the Indian becomes more degraded and debased.

ᴄ A Premium for Scalps

June 23, 1867

The white settlers on the frontier seem determined to drag the country into an Indian war, and are adopting every means in their power to foment a war spirit on both sides. The Indians have been tormented and assailed in every conceivable way, until in retaliation they have taken to pillage and murder. We have the authority not only of correspondents on the frontier, but of a Committee of Investigation, for stating that the present Indian troubles have been brought about by the whites. Gen. Sherman himself says that the Cheyennes, formerly friendly, whose village was destroyed by Gen. Hancock, are now numbered among our most implacable foes, and are seeking revenge for their wrongs wherever they come in contact with the whites.

With all their inhumanity and barbarity they have not yet equaled the white settlers of Colorado in bloodthirstiness. At a mass meeting held in one of the little towns in that Territory recently, a fund of $5,000 was subscribed for the purpose of *buying Indian scalps*, and $25 each is to be paid for scalps *with the ears on*. From this it would seem that the citizens of that delectable Territory cannot trust each other in a matter which they represent to be of such vital importance to themselves, and so require the ears to be produced with each scalp lest some dishonest cut-throat should make two out of one, and so obtain more than his share of blood money. One enterprising individual, who is enrolling a company of Indian scouts under the authority of Gov. Hunt, publicly boasts of his exploits as a guerrilla during the war, and proudly parades his infamous record as a reason why he should be employed upon a hunt for red-skins. Gov. Hunt himself sanctions all this fiendishness, and in his orders authorizing the enrollment of cut-throats, he promises that each shall be allowed to retain whatever plunder he may secure. The war-cry of "booty and beauty" has brought to his standard several hundred adventurers who are "eager for the fray," but, fortunately, the supply of horses and equipments is not sufficient to set them in the field. To remedy this a call is made for the loan of horses for thirty days, with the assurance that by the end of that time the troops will have stolen a sufficient number for their future use.

Gen. Sherman at first refused to permit this unauthorized warfare—if warfare it can possibly be called—but so great has been the pressure brought upon him, that he has finally consented to the equipment of volunteers to act under his orders. How subservient such troops will be to his will is evinced in their first orders calling for volunteers, wherein it is stated that the several companies will recognize no officers but their own, but will act as guerrillas, killing Indians wherever they may be found, and securing their scalps with the ears on. In this count of scalps it is the ears only that are available, and whether they belonged to the valiant warrior, slain in fair fight, or were cut from the head of some terrified, fleeing woman or child, is immaterial. A pair of ears are worth $25, and the market is not affected by age or sex.

While all this is most revolting to read, and a disgrace to our people and to the age in which we live, the blame should not fall entirely upon the frontier settlers. The responsibility rests with the Government, which has for years sanctioned such treatment of the Indians. Year after year the authorities have been warned by men familiar with Indian affairs, that unless the agents, traders and settlers were restrained from swindling and killing the unfortunate red men, the latter would combine for the purpose of retaliation. No longer ago than last Fall, the matter was brought before Congress, and the outrages which the Indians had sustained were freely detailed. No steps, however, were taken to remedy the evils. On the contrary, by sending a military force to the border, the commanders of which had no power to make treaties or to assume responsibilities, matters were rendered still worse. When the Chief Satanta told Gen. Hancock how his people had been swindled and plundered by the whites, and how the soldiers shot his young men whenever they saw them, the General replied, substantially, "I cannot redress your grievances—I cannot protect you in future—but, if you don't keep quiet, and submit to the white man, I can and shall punish you."

This is just what the settlers, without a shadow of authority, propose to do in the future on their own responsibility. Because the Indians, outraged beyond the power of endurance, have commenced making reprisals, they are to be slaughtered indiscriminately and their ears sold for $25 per pair. And this, too, when experience has demonstrated that Indians can, by proper treatment, be rendered quiet, orderly, self-supporting citizens. Indeed, so well-behaved, so intelligent and trustworthy have the Indians of this State become, that the propriety of giving them the right of suffrage is now being discussed in the Constitutional Convention. What has been done with the Indians of this State, and with other tribes West and South, can be done with every tribe that roams the prairies.

A Committee of Investigation, consisting of Gens. Sulley, Parker, Buford and Sandborn, and Messrs. Kenney and Blauvaies, have been visiting numerous tribes of the West this Spring and Summer, and have recently submitted, through Gen. Buford, their report. These gentlemen are unanimous in declaring that the present Indian troubles are brought about by the machinations of white men. They say "it is nothing but a raid upon the Treasury of the United States by the frontiersmen and army contractors. These men band together and make false reports of alleged massacres by Indians, and then call upon the Government to send troops to protect them, when in fact they only ask for them that they may grow rich from the supplies furnished them." They recommend that the Indians be located upon reservations in the Indian Territory, and that only such white men as are absolutely necessary to transact their business be permitted to go near them. Instead of thieving traders and bad whisky send them missionaries and teachers. Thus located they would raise stock, corn, wheat and all crops necessary for their subsistence. This policy which they recommend is unquestionably the true one to pursue in the future. For the present, a large number of troops should be hurried to the border for the purpose of protecting the whites and also of saving to the Indians their "scalps with the ears on."

✑ The Piegan Slaughter and Its Apologists

March 10, 1870

We can well understand how a friendly fraternal feeling, and a certain professional pride, quite proper in its place, should lead some of the army officers in Washington to uphold and approve the late massacre in Montana. They feel, and we all feel, that the Indians are a cruel and relentless foe who must be struck hard if struck at all, and that their brutalities are as exasperating as they are hideous. For all that, the Piegan slaughter, as actually conducted, seems to us to be wholly indefensible.

It is indefensible on two grounds, first, by reason of its needless barbarity and brutality, and second, in its retroactive influence on our new Indian policy—it was, in that, both a crime and a blunder. As to the first point, we need add little to what has already been said, and little to the emotions which the recital of facts arouses. We need not accept entirely Mr. Vincent Collyer's version of the affair, especially as Gen. Sheridan has vehemently protested against its being regarded as the true story. But how much better is the official statement made to Gen. Sully? The latter tells us that, of the 173 killed only thirty-three were men, "and of these fifteen only were such as are called by them young or fighting men," *i.e.*, between the ages of twelve and thirty-seven. Out of the rest, no less than ninety were women, and fifty were children all under twelve years of age, "and many in their mother's arms." Does this account help matters at all? Gen. Sheridan replies by showing how "at least 800" whites, men, women and children, have been murdered, more or less brutally, by Indians, since 1862. Does the accumulation of all the Indian slaughters for eight years, throughout all the Indian command, offset this wholesale slaughter of 140 women and children in a single camp of a single tribe? Or is it pretended that the Indian murders are commendable?—for surely we are not to regard that as virtuous in us which we shudder at in savages. Had the women and children been spared, and the braves been slaughtered—even though the affair was so one-sided that we lost but a single man—everybody would have applauded, as in the raids of Custer and Carr. But it is yet to be shown how, granting that the expedition was needful, non-combatants could not have been captured instead of killed.

It is, however, chiefly because of its injury to our new Indian policy that we now review this affair. The new policy has been distinctively announced as one of peace, protection and civilization. This policy could not and cannot furnish a cloak for Indian maraudings; misdeeds of that nature must still be punished by the sword. But it is of the highest importance that in our hostile, as in our pacific dealings with the Indians, we have right on our side. The Blackfeet had committed many crimes in Montana, and Winter was the season for striking them; but by striking them as Red Horn's camp was struck the old anti-military spirit is roused, and the resolute efforts of the Administration to keep peace on the Plains through army intervention may very likely be foiled. It would be hardly possible, for example, to transfer at this moment the Indian Bureau to the War Department; and the sincerity of the desire expressed by officers for peace on the Plains becomes widely, though we think unjustly, distrusted.

The only plan finally possible for the Administration or the army is one of peace and protection. Mr. Wilson's bill for promoting the civilization of the Indians and preparing them for the rights of citizenship, strikes the key-note of the true policy. Of course this is only possible with peaceful Indians, and the wild tribes must be treated otherwise. But we must not forget that those we now call "peaceful" were once "wild," and it is all but a question of degree and of time. The policy we cannot listen to, even for the wild Indians, is extermination; and any movement looking toward the latter should be promptly discountenanced and disavowed.

ᔕ Another Border Atrocity

June 10, 1873

Indian treachery has been surpassed by white brutality, and Capt. Jack can hold up his head to look the world in the face again. Under the circumstances and from the Modoc stand-point there might be some palliation for the murder of Gen. Canby, but it is impossible for any casuist, savage or civilized, to find an excuse for the massacre on Saturday of the Modoc prisoners who were being taken to Boyle's camp. As yet this horrible story is far from complete, but enough is told to show that white ferocity is more than equal to Indian savagery. Seventeen Modocs, some of them being women and children, crowded into a wagon, unarmed themselves, and without an armed escort, were set upon by white miscreants said to be Oregon volunteers, armed with needle-guns. The prayers of the women and escort for mercy were unheeded, and shots were poured into the wagon until a number of the prisoners were slain; all would have been inhumanely murdered had not the approach of a squad of soldiers put the assassins to flight. Such in brief is the terrible story told in our dispatches, but to it must be added the additional enormity that the murderers knew that no Modoc charged with any heinous crime was among these prisoners.

This event is a repetition, even an aggravation, of incidents which have been disgracefully frequent in our border history, and it will bear the same fruit as all the others. The story of this massacre of helpless prisoners will penetrate all the Western solitudes, and will be told around every Indian camp-fire. Everywhere it must have the effect of increasing savage hatred and distrust of the paleface. Every warrior will nurse his wrath and bide his time for retaliation. No one of them will be able to understand that a Government which can crush them could not have prevented this wanton butchery. Brooding over this new wrong, the Indians will sullenly submit when they must, but in time another Capt. Jack will arise to startle the country with a still more signal proof of what will be called the innate ferocity and treachery of the Indian character.

There is one way in which this bitter result may be avoided, and the peace policy shown even to the savages to be something better than a new devise for crushing them. It is settled now that Capt. Jack must pay the penalty of his crimes. The Government has wisely determined to show the Indians that murder by them is a crime to be rigorously punished, and care should be taken at the same time, to prove that the murder *of* them is an offense of equal atrocity. Extraordinary exertion should be made to secure the men who shot the Modoc prisoners, and if the facts are judicially established as related by Fairchild and the other witnesses, these cold murderers should be hanged on the same gallows with Capt. Jack. This would be a spectacle that both Indians and white borderers could understand. Both would see that the constituted authorities have the will and the power to punish and protect all according to their deserts. If, on the other hand, Capt. Jack is hanged and these white murderers are permitted to go unharmed, both parties to a contest that has so long disgraced the nation, are incited to new outrages.

This massacre can hardly fall within the reasoning of Attorney General Williams, and these murderers must be apprehended and punished by the civil authorities of the State where the crime was committed. If the perpetrators were Oregon volunteers Gov. Glover should spare no pains to bring them to justice. He was very anxious the other day to have the indicted Modocs turned over to him for trial, and his demand was logical. If he desires to serve the peace and prosperity of his State now let him show equal anxiety to bring to justice these white assassins. And while the hunt is out for these outlaws Gen. Davis might profitably employ some of his leisure moments in reflecting whether in the present state of feeling it is entirely safe to allow parties of Indian prisoners to be transported about the country without an armed escort. It is plain that if the party which was attacked had been provided with even four or five soldiers, it would not have been molested. The nation cannot afford to have this disgrace repeated, and we trust Gen. Davis will take proper precautions in the future to guard his prisoners from the fury of the white savages.

↫ Umatilla Troubles

October 25, 1878

It would seem a supply quite in excess of the demand were a third Indian war to be provided for the country this year, with the Bannock and Cheyenne campaigns scarcely over. Yet there is much reason to fear a Umatilla outbreak, caused, as usual, by the outrages of white men. Gen. Howard has notified the War Department that recently an unarmed Umatilla Indian, while engaged in herding his horses a few miles from the agency, was, without provocation, murdered in cold blood by two whites—"driven into a cañon and shot down like a dog," says Gen. Howard. Lieut. Farrow, of the Twenty-first Infantry, examined the case, and reported that there were white men enough who knew of the outrage to convict the murderers, but nothing was done to catch them. Gen. Howard accordingly asks if the United States District Attorney cannot be instructed to "attend to this and other cold-blooded murders of Indians by white men." A few punishments of these murders would, he says, "do more for peace than a whole Summer's campaign."

It is worth recalling than [sic] an atrocious murder exactly like the one just recorded preceded the Nez Percé war; and that then as now the murderers were suffered to escape. The bitterness and the hopelessness of justice engendered in Chief Joseph's mind, after that atrocious shooting of a peaceful member of his tribe by Finley and McNall helped to drive him to war. But the Umatillas have more to complain of. Gen. Howard asserts that within four weeks they have had over five hundred horses stolen from them by white thieves, and yet they hardly dare to resort to harsh measures, lest they shall be accused of "rising" and going upon the war-path.

What makes this conduct specially atrocious and perilous is that the Umatillas have remained the faithful allies of the Government during the past year, and to them was largely due the suppression of the Bannock revolt. Their aid, given at a critical moment, may have saved hundreds of lives and vast amounts of property to the settlers and to the Government. When the Bannock war broke out the hostiles made overtures for them to join in. Constant encroachments on their lands by the whites inclined a part of their warriors to do so. But before this intention had been carried out, they returned to their reservation, impelled by the same fidelity which had prevented them last year from joining the revolted Nez Percés, with whom they were closely united by friendship and intermarriage. To attest their friendship, and to show their repentance for having thought of aiding the hostiles, they then, without asking any remuneration, offered fully a fourth of their warriors, selecting the bravest, to help the Government. One war party encountered the Snakes, early in July, forty miles south of their agency, and inflicted on them a heavy loss. Others joined Gen. Howard as scouts, rendering inestimable services. The remaining Umatillas agreed to fight the hostiles if they entered their reservation. It was a force of Umatilla Indians with which Col. Forsythe struck the Bannocks, about the middle of July, killing a large number of them, and capturing many women and children and horses. It was the Umatillas who attacked the famous chief, Egan, routed him and his party, and bringing back Egan's head in token of their triumph.

Despite these services and many others, making it within bounds to say that, save for the Umatilla and Nez Percé scouts, the war might be going on to this day, these allies have since been shamefully treated, as, indeed, they were before. Though numbering but 849 souls, the Umatillas are said to have 17,000 horses, 5,000 cattle, and a large number of sheep, which are the objects of the greed of white men. Their lands, also, to which they are much attached, are among the most fertile in Oregon, and accordingly are the subject of constant encroachment. Whether to aid or avoid this encroachment, a bill was introduced last Winter by Senator Mitchell, of Oregon, designed to remove them to another reservation, on the ground that their present land was in the line of contemplated railroads extremely valuable to the business interests of the State. This bill was "reluctantly approved" by the Indian Office. The upshot of the matter seems to be that those who want the valuable lands have determined that, as Kearney would phrase it, "the Umatillas must go"; and meanwhile, if they are not driven into some act of desperation, which will be seized upon as an excuse for plundering and massacring them, this will not be the fault of the horse-thieves and murderers who, if we are to believe Gen. Howard, ply their vocation with impunity.

To show the animosity of some of the settlers against these Umatillas, their Agent, Mr. Connover, reported, three months since, that, in spite of the fact that Umatilla Indians had led in almost every successful encounter with the hostiles, in that region, and had killed Chief Egan and twenty-five of his warriors, the people of Pendleton threatened to kill every Umatilla found near their town, and actually carried an Indian off the reservation to prison. To protect them from violence, the Agent applied to Gen. Wheaton for a guard, which was furnished. In addition, many of these Indians lost their crops either by the hostiles or by stampeded stock breaking into their fields. It is, therefore, possible that hunger may play its part this Winter in producing disaffection among this tribe.

It is evidently time that the protection of the civil law should be extended to the Indian, as well as its vengeance. The numerous thefts and murders committed by white men at the expense of the Indians are quite as worthy of punishment as the less frequent crimes committed by red men at the expense of the settlers. The testimony of officers like Gens. Crook and Pope is that only by a rare exception are outrages upon the Indians punished, whereas Indian retaliation in kind is dealt with as war.

⌐ The Wronged Poncas

December 19, 1879

In the history of blunders and wrongs characterizing the so-called Indian policy of the United States, (which is no policy,) we find no darker page than that on which are recorded the wrongs of the Ponca Indians. This tribe was permanently situated on a reservation in Southern Dakota. They were there by virtue of a treaty between the tribe and the United States. The land was absolutely theirs, although they could not alienate it without first obtaining the permission of Congress. These Indians were semi-civilized, although, in a strict sense of that elastic word, they may be said to compare favorably with people who make more pretensions. They cultivated the soil, supported themselves, maintained public worship, and sent their children to school. There was no apparent reason why these people should not live where they were, thriving, comfortable, and happy. But the evil genius which is forever stirring up the never-settled question of the relation of the red man to the Government of the United States, was working for the ruin and dispersion of the tribe.

During the administration of Gen. Grant, under what malign influence we cannot say, Congress passed a bill to remove the Poncas from their reservation to the Indian Territory. This removal, however, was conditioned on the consent of the Poncas being first obtained thereto. That consent never was obtained. In the Autumn of 1876, the Poncas for the first time learned that they were to be sent away; and it is a striking illustration of their civilized condition that the information came to them from the preacher to whose discourse they were listening at their little church on the last peaceful day of their lives. Several of the head men, Standing Bear being the leader, refused to leave the reservation. They had gathered their crops, and were engaged in preparing the ground for Winter. They had earned and held the right to own many articles used on their farms, and they had a fair supply of household stuff which they had bought and paid for from the avails of their own industry. These were all taken from them, and, whatever may have been done with them, the rightful owners have never seen them since. In spite of their entreaties and expostulations, the Poncas were finally removed. Their lands, it was said, had been ceded to the Sioux, and they must go to the south. But, before they could be induced to go, it was necessary to send troops to awe them into submission.

Torn up by the roots from the soil on which they had so long lived and prospered, the tribe were driven upon a tract of unimproved wild land in the Indian Territory. The climate was unsuited to them, being almost tropical, as compared with the bracing atmosphere in which they had been born. They sickened and died like pestilence-stricken sheep. Instead of being at work, and kept cheerful by activity, they were given nothing to do but such odd jobs as they might pick up about the sparsely-settled region. Their only real employment was to maintain the agency which the Government kindly established among them. In desperation, one or two of the chiefs made a pilgrimage to Washington, where they laid the story of their wrongs before the President. Nothing came of this, and they were told that they must stay in the Indian Territory where they were sent. Weary and sick at heart, they went back, and, during the following Winter, they made up their minds to work their way to their old homes in Dakota. The rest of the story is fresh in the minds of most of our readers, though the hurry of constantly recurring events may have dimmed the vividness of the narrative. Arrested in Dakota by Gen. Crook as vagabonds and escaped prisoners, Standing Bear and his comrades had no alternative, apparently, but to submit to military rule. But friends were providentially raised up for them, and an appeal was made to the United States Court to determine whether these Indians, who had never been in arms against the United States, were lawfully restrained of their liberty. The presiding Judge decided that an Indian is "a person," and has a standing in the courts of the Republic. Furthermore, he decided that Gen. Crook, acting under a color of authority of the United States, had no lawful right to restrain these persons of their liberty, and that there was no lawful authority by which the tribe could be forcibly removed to the Indian Territory. This was a great gain. It gave peaceable and law-abiding Indians some color of right which they had never before maintained.

But the Poncas have not yet got back their lands, and by what hocus-pocus those lands have been treated as a part of the unoccupied domain of the United States, it will be necessary to inquire hereafter. We know that the rightful owners of the soil, in direct and willful violation of the rights guaranteed to them by a solemn treaty, have been driven forth as vagabonds and wanderers. They have been forced from a soil on which they were living contentedly and prosperously, and, without complaint from any of their white neighbors, they have been transplanted to a strange and uncongenial land, where they have wasted in sickness and despair. There has been no explanation or attempt at justification of this great wrong, except the semi-official statement that it was all the result of a misunderstanding and a mistake. Nobody can explain why these poor people have been torn from their homes and consigned to vagrancy. But, after enduring incredible hardships—wandering and hunted like savage fugitives—their case is before Congress. If the American people can afford to be committed to further wrong, the petition of the Poncas will not be heeded. But, if we are disposed to be as honest and as just toward the Indian as we ask our fellow-men to be to us, these hapless people will have their rights. They ought to have their lands again at any cost to the Government under whose authority they have been so tyrannically despoiled.

⌁ The Southern Utes

August 27, 1885

In calling the attention of the authorities at Washington to the starving condition of the Southern Utes Gen. Miles only reiterates the warning of his predecessor in command of the Department of the Missouri. Eight weeks ago Gen. Augur telegraphed that information had reached him through Col. L. P. Bradley, commanding the Department of New-Mexico, and Col. P. T. Swaine, commanding at Fort Lewis, in Colorado, that the Southern Utes were in great distress for the want of food. "Rations," said Col. Swaine at that time, "should be issued immediately to these Indians to prevent their leaving their reservation to hunt. I invite attention to the *immediate* necessity for feeding these Indians, so as to prevent their leaving their reservation." At the garrisoned posts there is always a surplus of commissary stores in order to provide against an emergency, and authority was promptly given to succor the starving red men by a temporary issue of food to them.

Now, however, after the lapse of two months in which to make permanent provision for the Utes, we find a second appeal from the military authorities, as urgent as the preceding and put upon the same ground, that unless food is given to the Indians they will go upon the war-path. The troubles in the Dolores and Mancos Valleys at the end of last June were plainly traced to this cause. Some Indians, it is believed, in search of food, came to the edge of their reservation, or perhaps beyond it. Cowboys who were taking care of the vast herds of foreign capitalists in that region, pasturing their cattle upon public domains without paying for the privilege and in defiance of the laws, started the story of an Indian outbreak. According to some accounts received at the Indian Office the cowboys brutally fired upon one family of Indians and killed half a dozen of them. Retaliation was feared and perhaps taken. At all events the whole region was quickly the scene of panic, and Southwestern Colorado called loudly for protection. People abandoned the settlements near the reservation and fled in terror. But when the military authorities investigated the matter they found the real difficulty to be that the Indians had nothing to eat. If it was then a fit subject for indignation that an outbreak from such a cause had been barely avoided, it is doubly so that now, after that warning, the danger should be renewed.

Few Indian tribes perhaps have more reason to complain of Government neglect and shortcomings than the Utes. Evidence was given to Congress after the outbreak of the White River Utes, some years ago, that the Indian Office at that time had failed to send the supplies pledged to them. It was shown that some of them were compelled to travel with their families 175 miles to Rawlins Station, on the Union Pacific Railroad, in order to escape starvation, and that their supplies had been left there undistributed until partly spoiled. During a period of three months in the Summer of 1877 these Indians had no flour except a single issue of fifteen pounds to a family. When the hostilities were over they were turned to account by the compulsory acquisition of twelve millions of acres of valuable lands from the Utes, that this land might be thrown open to settlement or to the pasturing of the cattle of the great syndicates.

The Southern Utes during those hostilities remained quiet and peaceable. But they, like the Northern Utes, had large sums of money due them in the Treasury from which they had received no benefit. Indeed, the most remarkable feature in all the Government's dealings with the Utes is that this tribe, even at the times of its keenest sufferings from want of food, has had scores of thousands of dollars to its credit at Washington above its regular annuities. Even now the tardy purchase of supplies at the urgent demand of the military authorities is apparently to be made with these people's funds. No wonder that the Utes are discontented, especially when some of the newspapers published in their neighborhood advise that any Indian found off the reservation shall be shot at sight.

✒ The Ute Indemnity

January 14, 1888

The Colorado cowboys had their fun last Summer with Colorow's band of Utes, and now Congress is called upon to pay the bills. The Commissioner of Indian Affairs, who considers the Colorado performance a great outrage, had indeed recommended that the claims of the Utes for indemnity should be presented to that State for settlement; but the Secretary of the Interior holds that the circumstances demand a speedier redress than such a resort would be likely to secure, so that Congress has been applied to for it, under the form of a deficiency estimate, with suggestions of steps for ultimate reimbursement from Colorado.

Whether the treasury, if it once pays out the amount so demanded, will ever be reimbursed by Colorado, we leave to others to surmise; but that some compensation might wisely be made to the Indians for the loss of their property seems to be indicated by concurrent testimony from high official sources. This testimony shows that, while Colorow last August was represented in the news from Western Colorado as breathing fire and slaughter, he was really trying to escape with his people and his herds. He was at that time away from the reservation where he belonged; but this offense the Indian Office seems rather disposed to extenuate on the ground of erroneous impressions both as to the reservation limits and as to rights of hunting and fishing granted under former treaties. Still, there is no doubt that Colorow had no right to be on the old lands ceded by his tribe in 1882, and now forming a part of Garfield County.

The original trouble, as it appears from the report of Secretary Endicott, arose from an attempt to arrest two of this band on an indictment for stealing two horses. Commissioner Atkins apparently intimates that these horses, which had been previously "bought or gambled" from the Indians by two whites named Tate and Woods, were restored to the latter when found and claimed, and that nevertheless the indictments were pressed and others for "violating the game laws" added. Secretary Endicott recounts that the Game Warden of the county, with his posse, entered the Ute camp and without any notice of his purpose seized several of the Indians, who, while running for cover, were fired on. The Sheriff had been equally busy, and a party sent out by him burned the tents of an Indian camp occupied by squaws and children, who ran away. Colorow then secured an interview with sundry prominent citizens, and it seems to have been agreed that matters should remain *in statu quo* till the arrival of the Big White Chief. Colorow interpreted this agreement as allowing him to continue his march unmolested to the reservation, which he had agreed to accomplish in fifteen days; but his pursuers, consisting by that time both of State militia and the posses of cowboys and citizens, regarded his move as a breach of faith and surprised his camp. In the resulting skirmish several persons were killed or wounded on both sides. Then Lieut. Burnett, Ninth Cavalry, arrived and interfered successfully for peace. But about 2,500 sheep and goats belonging to the band had disappeared, besides nearly 400 horses, of which latter about a third have been returned.

Gen. Terry, reporting on this affair, says he does not think that "the burning of the unoccupied habitations of persons for whose arrest warrants have been issued or the opening of rifle fire without warning upon an unsuspecting body of men, women, and little children, are usual steps in the service of process." Gen. Crooks's report declares that "in every case the whites were the aggressors and fired first. Colorow had no desire whatever to fight, and made use of his weapons in self-defense only." Secretary Endicott concludes that "some effort should certainly be made for the restitution to the Indians of their property." A fair judgment seems to be that while the original offense was committed by these Indians in being where they had no right to be, the violent attack on them under the plea of serving civil process renders it hardly more than just and certainly good policy to make good their flocks and herds, which were seized and retained by the frontiersmen.

↪ The Indian Massacre

December 31, 1890

It would be an abuse of language to describe as a battle the encounter that took place on Monday between United States troops and hostile Indians. The Indians were captives and were surrounded by four times their number of armed white soldiers. They themselves were armed and it was the order to give up their arms that brought on the conflict. Nobody imagined that they would venture to attack their captors, or even to refuse to disarm themselves, nor can anybody be blamed for not entertaining such an imagination. An Indian can die or suffer torture very resolutely when there is no escape, but he is no more disposed to undergo death or torture than a civilized man if he sees any way of escape. He can fight also very bravely, but in order to stimulate him to combat he commonly needs to see "a fighting chance." The worst that could have happened to these captive Indians against whom no atrocities were charged, was to undergo a short confinement, where they would have been better fed and lodged than they were before they were captured. Afterward they would have been returned to a reservation and cared for at the cost of the Government, probably better than they had been cared for or than they would have been cared for before what is called an Indian rising, but would be more intelligibly described as a general Indian strike.

It is a proof of a high degree either of desperation or of fanaticism that the captives should have preferred to trust the chance of resisting an irresistibly superior force of whites. They must have known when they emptied the rifles they were required to surrender into the ranks of armed soldiers that surrounded them that they were sealing their own doom. They had no refuge, no way of fleeing without being pursued and overtaken, and no hope of mercy when they were overtaken. Their revolt was an act not of calculation, but of impulsive hatred and rage, that is to say, an act of insanity. The officer in command cannot be blamed for not foreseeing such an act, however much or little knowledge he may have had of the Indian character, for it is an act which the widest knowledge of human nature could scarcely have enabled him to foresee. Before making his demand for the surrender of the arms he surrounded the armed captives with troops ready to fire, and thus showed them that the penalty of resistance and refusal would be instant death. Even if he had foreseen the resistance he could have taken no more precautions against it than he did, short of shooting down the Indians before collecting their arms. The mad and reckless resistance of the captives is such an act of war as would have been celebrated if it had occurred in civilized warfare, all the more by reason of its madness and recklessness. If a party of French soldiers twenty years ago had forced their captors to massacre them in order to get possession of their weapons, we can imagine how an act which in that case would have been one of heroism would have been besung and bepainted.

It is different with the wretched, copper-colored starvelings who have just thrown away their lives, even from their own point of view, for they took very much less than their own number of white men's lives in exchange. There is nothing in this that civilized men feel moved to discuss otherwise than in prose. Civilized men will deplore, not that a gang of red cut-throats has been exterminated, but that their extermination has cost the lives of several gallant officers and brave soldiers. But the ultimate responsibility for the Indian war is the responsibility for the killing both of the whites and of the Indians, and that is not very far to seek. All the authoritative accounts agree that these Indians were starved into revolt, although nobody disputes that we pay enough to have them abundantly fed. Either the money or the food is stolen in transit by rascally agents or else the food is bought and distributed by incompetent agents so that the Indians do not get it. In either case the fault lies immediately with the Interior Department, and ultimately with the President of the United States. The points made by Gen. Miles in his paper on the Indian question on which we commented a day or two ago appear very conspicuously in the reports of this massacre. In the first place we starve those whom we pretend to feed. In the second place we allow to be furnished with arms creatures whom we know to be capable of committing ruthless murder on the slightest provocation. How came Big Foot's band to be in possession of the rifles they were ordered to surrender? An Indian does not need a Winchester rifle to shoot Government rations. It is desirable to him only in order to kill men and by preference white men. It is plain that we must feed the Indians and disarm them. It is at once shameful and silly to withhold their food and to permit them to bear arms.

A Lesson in "Civilization"

June 29, 1897

The Indian Rights Association, through its Washington agent, Mr. Francis E. Leupp, has issued a statement of an outrage on the Navajo Indians, in January last, which is not pleasant reading for the citizens of a Republic whose professed policy is to "civilize" the remnants of the Indian tribes. The reputation of the association and its extensive sources of information, as well as the character of Mr. Leupp as a careful, skillful, and honorable journalist, are such that the accuracy of the statement cannot be doubted.

Briefly, it is this:

Sixteen families of Navajo Indians, by Government permission, herded their flocks of sheep on United States land in Northwestern Arizona. On the 18th of January the Supervisors of Coconino County, in which the land lies, ordered the Sheriff to "assess" the Indians. On the 19th the Sheriff, with twenty deputies, armed, proceeded to the Indian settlement and ordered the heads of the families to pay $5 per 100 head of sheep, cash down, or move out of the county. The Indians had no money and were refused time to raise any, or to consult their agent. They were driven northward toward the Little Colorado River, in bitter cold, over deep snow, and in a storm. The river was swollen too deep for the sheep to ford, but they were driven in. The lambs and most of the ewes about to lamb were drowned or chilled to death. The one source of support of the Indians, the lamb crop of the year, was destroyed. Then the Sheriff and his posse returned and burned many of the Indian houses and corrals.

These Navajos are notably peaceful and industrious. They had committed no offense against law or society. They were driven out with this cruelty, not for refusing to pay, but because they could not pay an extravagant tax arbitrarily and unlawfully demanded with the plain purpose of making payment impossible. The whole business was in the whites an outbreak of savage envy and hatred.

These facts have been in the possession of the Government at Washington for several weeks. As yet nothing has been done about them. Surely something will be done. It is incredible that an outrage so cruel and contemptible should be utterly ignored. It may not be possible to bring the guilty to justice, but at least their victims could be compensated, and the United States Government could replace them on its own lands and protect them by all necessary force.

↶ The Indian Rising

October 7, 1898

It is not likely that we shall know for several days precisely what has happened in Minnesota. But the later reports seem to make it clear that there was no "massacre" of the troops. The soldiers were apparently acting as a "posse" to enforce a civil process against an Indian chief. He and his tribe resisted his arrest, and several soldiers and at least one officer were killed in the attempt to get possession of him.

Of course, there can be but one end to this. Civilization will have its way, the white man's law will be enforced, and the white man's power will be vindicated. The fact that the white man is irresistible had seemed to make its way into the minds of the red men. There can scarcely be a chief within the borders of the United States who is not aware of it, who does not know that it is better for him and for his tribe to yield to the inevitable than to be crushed in a futile attempt to resist it. That is what makes the rising so striking. It is "a bolt out of the blue." We had all come to consider that the extermination of the Indian, as a human being who will not work and hence is out of place in an industrial age and country, had advanced so far that there was no danger of an Indian war anywhere within our borders. Upon this comfortable notion descends with a great shock the announcement that a tribe is actually on the warpath within our borders and that not in one of what are still our Territories, but in one of the United States, a State furnished "with all the modern improvements," with clubs and trolley cars innumerable, and steel-framed sky-scrapers. It is very disconcerting.

We repeat that the ultimate issue of the rising cannot be at all doubtful. Civilization will prevail, soon and finally. Fitz James Stephen says of modern society that in it a criminal may occasionally overpower an isolated policeman, just as a dwarf might for a time and under favorable circumstances "hold down the little finger of a giant's left hand." That is all there is, or can be, in an Indian rising at this day.

The present case is the more pitiable because it seems clear that these Indians have a real grievance. Congress has refused to compensate them, to the extent of $35,000, for the improvements they have made upon the lands to which they cling, while ordering them to quit those lands. Accordingly, and animated by a real resentment of real injustice, they have risen in revolt, and have already done far more mischief than $35,000 would pay for. Now that they have risen they must be put down. But when they have been put down, common justice and decency demand that Congress should make them compensation for their improvements. Possibly the rising was needed to call attention to the injustice with which they have been treated.

8 Treaties and Other Broken Promises

Representatives of the Utes are in Washington, complaining
that they have been cheated in the agreement by which they
gave up nearly all of their Colorado lands. This is precisely what
might have been expected. They were cheated. It has been the
practice of our Government, from time immemorial, to cheat
the Indians whenever any treaty has been made with them.

—*New York Times*
March 11, 1881

WHILE ITS OWN editorial positions on the Indian problem tended to
shift from time to time with changing circumstances, the *Times* was
unbending in one opinion: The government of the United States had
amassed an unenviable record of deceit in its dealings with the Native Americans. Through the decades from 1860 to 1900, an extensive amount of space
on the *Times* editorial pages was devoted to what it saw as a shameful national record.

Although the *Times* consistently argued against formal treaties with the
Indians in the first place—because treaties implied tribal sovereignty—it was
firm in its conviction that once treaties had been agreed to, the government
had a moral obligation to keep them. But it complained that, sooner or later,
virtually every promise the whites ever made to the Indians was broken. In
instances of serious Indian uprisings, the *Times* made it a habit to look for
an agreement broken by the government that might be an underlying cause.
Sometimes it found repercussions from the whites' duplicity to be immediate; there were other instances in which months or years had passed before
results were obvious. It was not unusual for the roots of a conflict to lie
not merely in a single broken promise but in a whole series of them. A favorite *Times* approach was to offer a comprehensive editorial, or series of

editorials, tracing the causes of Indian difficulties through repeated deceptions, one building on another.

In addition to its concern over the issue of tribal sovereignty, the *Times* worried about another complication relating to treaties: the necessity for formal ratification by Congress. An agreement reached by government commissioners with tribesmen in a council in the West, for example, was likely to be revised extensively before it gained Congressional approval, or it might not be approved at all, even though the Indians thought they had a firm treaty. This was a process hard for the Indians to understand, complained the *Times*. And yet another problem, from the Indians' perspective, was the fact that policies tended to change from one administration to another. It was confusing to the Indians that agreements reached one year could be so readily superseded the next.

At the same time, policies were carried out by local Indian agents who had broad authority. The agent with whom a tribe had to deal on a regular basis tended to be much more important in terms of their needs than the "Great Father" in Washington. Given the fact that many tribes also were under military control—in some instances their agents were army officers— it should not have been surprising that the Indians often were perplexed about the way the government's pledges were carried out. Although the *Times* editorial writers obviously understood these circumstances, they rarely expressed much sympathy for the government in cases of violated agreements. They placed much of the blame on corrupt agents, for whom they held the Indian Bureau in the Department of the Interior accountable. They also faulted Congress for its general failure to make and defend sound policies and to act promptly on treaties with the Indians.

In the summer of 1868, the *Times* expressed its editorial opinion that Congress, through inaction, was to blame for much of the ongoing problem with Indians on the frontier. "The Indians, discouraged and disgusted at the non-fulfillment of the treaties which they entered into a year ago," it said, "are repeating their operations of last season, and roving bands are carrying terror to the hearts of hundreds of settlers." Statements such as these notwithstanding, the *Times* at this early period was less likely to excuse Indian violence on the grounds of abandoned government commitments. The newspaper went through an interesting evolution in its editorial-page treatment of what it saw as the results of the government's duplicity toward the Indians. During the 1860s, it was more inclined to emphasize the depredations committed by the Indians and secondarily to blame the government for providing them with an excuse. But through succeeding decades, it came virtually full circle; although it could not condone atrocities by the Indians, it was more likely to place the blame squarely on the government and its broken promises—implying, in effect, that the Indians were justified in their behavior.

In an early 1876 editorial on treaty obligations, the *Times* responded to a politician's statement that Indians "are the greatest liars and vagabonds on the face of the earth." It admitted that Indians might be great liars. "But if the red man had any representation on the floor of the Senate," it added, "he might have justly replied that if his people were not always given to telling the truth, their experience with the superior race had shown them that fibbing was not a practice exclusively monopolized by aboriginal peoples." There was no need to look beyond the Black Hills story for an example, the *Times* asserted. It said the government had assured the Sioux that whites would not be admitted to the territory, under an agreement ratified by the Senate. But that agreement was quickly jeopardized, the editorial continued, because "no sooner does it appear that there is some little gold in the gulches there than a prominent member of that body [the Senate] rises in his seat, says that treaty obligations mean nothing, and that white men ought to take the country if they want it." That might be termed a wise and enlightened policy by white people who had enjoyed the blessings of civilization, the *Times* suggested, but the untutored savage probably would call it "heap lie."

In October 1879, following an outbreak of hostilities by Colorado Utes, the newspaper blasted Congress for its failure to pay the tribe for the rich San Juan mining region purchased six years earlier under the Brunot Treaty. To begin with, the *Times* asserted, the government got an exceptional bargain, "about what a man would have who should purchase a block bounded by Fifth and Madison avenues for $100." Even so, Congress refused to appropriate the money. Chief Ouray, considered by the *Times* "one of the wisest and most sagacious of the red men," had warned repeatedly that the tribe was getting so irritable at the bad faith on the part of the government that he feared there would be violence. But Congress had been in a mood not to pay anything it did not have to, the *Times* said, and "the unfortunate Indians were the first sufferers, as usual." But Congress was guilty of false economy, it warned, "which the country will now have to pay for in a very different way."

In all the years during which the Indian problem was a major concern of the *Times*, there never came a period during which broken promises could be ignored as an issue. Whether the deception involved single tribes such as the Utes or Poncas, all the tribes with an interest in the Indian Territory, or merely a few individual Indians such as the Apache scouts imprisoned in Florida, the government's record, in the view of the *Times*, was disgraceful and inexcusable. The editorials that follow are diverse primarily in terms of the varied situations in which the *Times* perceived broken promises to be a serious matter. They demonstrate editorial expressions of the newspaper over a period of years. But their thrust is consistent. For every editorial in this chapter concerning some specific instance of broken faith with the Native Americans, there were a number of others applying to different situations that stated the same thesis. Broken promises to the Indians, according to the *Times*, was the government's common way of doing business.

⤺ The New War on the Frontier—How It May Be Prevented

July 1, 1868

Late reports from the frontier indicate that the labors of the Indian Peace Commissioners have not been attended with the good results that were at one time promised. Instead of peace reigning all along the border, various bands from hostile tribes, ranging from the British possessions to New-Mexico, have been committing depredations innumerable. Soldiers and citizens have been murdered in cold blood, ranches burned, stock stolen, and a reign of terror inaugurated. This result may be charged directly upon the failure of Congress to adopt a fixed policy regarding Indian affairs.

The Peace Commission, of which Gen. Sherman is the head, entered upon its duties last Summer with an energy which promised to overcome the obstacles thrown in their way by traders, speculators and others who are opposed to peace on the frontier. With great labor, and at a cost of much time and money, the Commissioners succeeded in reaching nearly all the hostile tribes, and making treaties which were alike satisfactory to them and to the country at large. These treaties, while they were calculated to secure the white settlers from depredations in the future, looked also to the welfare of the red men, guaranteeing them their rights and proposing for them a civilization which should fit them to become citizens. So far as the Commissioners were concerned, this work was well and thoroughly done, and the country began to congratulate itself upon at last seeing its way out of those Indian troubles which have hung over the Great West like a cloud, and delayed its settlement for many years. But the treaties were mere waste paper, without the ratification of Congress, and as yet they have not received the slightest attention from that body. There has been some general debate on Indian affairs in both Houses, but no approach to a ratification of the acts of its agents.

Meantime, the Indians are becoming discontented once more, and finding that the fair promises made them are not kept, that Congress is simply playing with them, are commencing again their work of murder and pillage. The very bands with whom the Commissioners made peace treaties are now reported as being the worst depredators and the most profuse in their threats of vengeance. While last year they expressed their willingness to occupy the lands designated for their future homes, and to live at peace with their white neighbors, this season they have grown more suspicious of the white men than ever, and evidently believe that the Peace Commissioners were sent out merely to make them promises which were never to be fulfilled. The Commissioners have lost much of their influence with the tribes with which they treated, because Congress has not kept faith with them.

The dissatisfaction on the part of the Indians seems to be even more generally diffused than it was before the Commission entered upon its duties. Bands that were previously friendly, or, at least, not actively hostile, finding that the treaties they signed were but "a delusion and a snare," have joined other bands, and seem determined to keep the frontier in a disturbed and dangerous state until the Government shall provide for them. This state of things will doubtless continue until Congress decides upon some plan of action regarding the Indians, and places its execution in the hands of honest, energetic men, who will see it carried out to the letter, impartially and fearlessly.

∽ The Kansas Indians

August 30, 1868

The Cheyenne and Arapahoe Indians, who committed so many murders in Kansas recently, having been driven beyond the borders of that State by the military forces, are now committing depredations in Colorado. Dispatches from Denver City, received last night, chronicle the killing of men, women and children, attacks upon emigrants and stages, the stealing of horses, and other atrocities. The settlers are in a terrible state of fear and excitement, and Gov. Hall is calling for volunteers to pursue the savages. Gen. Sheridan has authorized the troops at Fort Reynolds to cooperate with Gov. Hall, and a war of extermination against these particular bands seems to have been authorized and inaugurated.

Meantime Gov. Crawford and the citizens of Kansas have succeeded in obtaining from the Government, orders for the forcible expulsion of all Indians from that State, and Gen. Sheridan has directed their enforcement. Against this summary and sweeping procedure Indian Agent Wynkoop protests, and his protest is indorsed by Superintendent Murphy. The former says very emphatically that there are certain bands of Indians located in Kansas who have faithfully lived up to their treaties, have committed no depredations whatever, but have persistently refused to join the raiders in their murderous schemes. To drive these from the homes which have been secured to them by treaty with the Government, and by confining them upon tracts of land unknown to them, deprive them of their means of living, is manifestly unjust. It would speedily convert them into open enemies, thereby strengthening the force of the depredators who are now giving us so much trouble. Mr. Wynkoop suggests what seems to be an easy and fair solution of the difficulty. He proposes to summon all friendly Indians to rendezvous at Fort Larned, where they can be protected from the indignation of the outraged settlers, and where they will be in no danger of starving until some permanent arrangement is made with them. Such Indians as refuse to obey this summons he thinks should be proscribed, declared to be at war and properly punished.

The citizens of Kansas have been striving for several years to deprive these Indians of their lands, and there are those who believe that the recent raid was incited by white men for the purpose of forcing the Government to take precisely the course that has been taken. The previous action of the State officials and the violent denunciations of the Kansas Press, certainly warrant such a belief. But however that may be, the Indians who have been guilty of committing outrages should be punished as they deserve, but robbing the innocent ones will certainly never accomplish the purpose. Those Indians who have held aloof and observed their treaty stipulations are entitled to the protection of the Government, whatever Kansas may say to the contrary. We have more hostile Indians now on the border than our troops are able to take care of, and it is needless to add to their number by driving to desperation those who are now friendly.

⌐ The Brunot Treaty

February 22, 1876

Indian questions are not inviting subjects of discussion, and the public is pretty thoroughly tired of them; but the recent memorial from the Colorado Assembly to Congress is something to which attention ought to be directed. The question is frequently asked, Why do the Indian tribes make war? The usual answer is, that they are exasperated by the peculations of the agents and contractors; but the memorial shows, what is familiar to every one who has had personal acquaintance with the Indians, that a more potent cause of their dissatisfaction is the bad faith of the Government agents, and their disregard of the commonest principles of honesty in their dealings with them. The special case to which the Colorado Assembly refer is the non-fulfillment of the "Brunot treaty" with the Ute tribe, who occupy the south-western portion of Colorado. By this treaty, the United States acquired a large tract of country watered by the San Juan River. It is beyond question the most beautiful and picturesque portion of the Territory, and is rich in precious metals, which are now being got out by placer mining. The consideration agreed upon was an annual payment by the Government of $25,000, to be expended for the benefit of the tribe in such way as they might desire. This was certainly not an extortionate price. The country is fully worth every cent of the money; indeed, the Indians claim that they were cheated in the running of the boundary lines, which were made to include a large area of agricultural lands they never intended to sell. This, however, they probably would have thought little about, if they could have got any money at all; but though the treaty was signed more than two years ago, and the San Juan country is swarming with miners, the Indians have not to this day received a dollar of the purchase money in any way or shape. There is no reason for this, except the very simple one that Congress has refused to make the necessary appropriation.

The consequences are pointed out in the memorial referred to. The San Juan country is a long way from Washington, or probably the money would have been very punctually paid; but it is very near to some flourishing frontier towns and mining villages of Colorado, and the people there are somewhat naturally disinclined to have their houses burned, their crops destroyed, and lives threatened by the exasperated Utes, because the Government will not keep its own solemn pledges. The Territorial Assembly urge upon Congress the necessity for observing good faith with this tribe, and declare that, unless this is done, a frontier war will be the consequence. The life of every miner now in the San Juan country would not be worth ten hours purchase, if an outbreak should occur. It is impossible to hold the chiefs responsible for the now threatening aspect of the tribe. There are only two who have any influence, and they have always been consistent friends of the whites. Chief Douglass, at the White River Agency, and Chief Uhelay, at Los Pinos, are both intelligent, well-educated, and sagacious men. They have their houses at the two agencies, keep their buggies and spans of horses, are quite wealthy for Indians, and are universally liked by their white neighbors. But neither of them will be able to restrain the more restless spirits of the tribe much longer. Indeed, Uhelay, who had most to do with the making of the Brunot treaty, informed the Government surveyors who visited him last Summer, that the Southern Indians accused him of having kept the Government money for his own use, and were so exasperated that he did not dare to go into their country. Even at Los Pinos, he never moved far from his house without being fully armed; and in the opinion of those who knew him and the tribe best, the chief owed his life only to his reputation for daring courage, which deterred attempts at assassination. If he should be killed, and this would probably be the first result of an outbreak, the whites of the Colorado frontier would lose the most steadfast and wisest of their Indian friends, a man who has won the respect of all who have come in contact with him. Of course, if a war broke out in the Spring, as seems to be feared, it could have only one termination—at immense cost of life and property the Utes would be beaten and starved into subjection; but before this was done, half the whites now in the San Juan country would be murdered, and settlements which now give promise of future wealth and prosperity would be swept away in the flames of Indian warfare.

⌒ A Lesson from the Nez Percés

October 15, 1877

Now that the Nez Percé war has ended in victory, thanks to the energy and courage of our much-enduring Army, it is worth while, before it passes out of mind, to ask why it was fought. We freely express the opinion that the Nez Percé war was, on the part of our Government, an unpardonable and frightful blunder—a crime, whose victims are alike the hundreds of our gallant officers and men who fell a prey to Nez Percé bullets and the peaceful bands who were goaded by injustice and wrong to the war-path. It is greatly to be regretted that the immediate responsibility for its occurrence is so obscurely distributed that it is difficult to bring anybody to account for it at the bar of public opinion.

The Nez Percé comes into history as the white man's friend. The famous exploring party sent out by President Jefferson said of this tribe: "The Pierced-Nose nation are among the most amiable men we have seen—stout, well-formed, well-looking, active, their character placid and gentle, rarely moved into passion, yet not often enlivened by gayety." From their first warm welcome of our explorers in 1805, up to the present war, no full-blooded Nez Percé is known to have murdered a white man—an extraordinary fact which is on record in the Government archives at Washington. With the Nez Percés we have always been at peace; and when we have had wars with other neighboring tribes, the Nez Percés have invariably been the allies of our Army. While other tribes have been roving and hard to control, a large part of the Nez Percés have taken to grazing and farming. Most of them live in houses like white men, and build fences around their lands. The brother of Chief Lawyer is a Presbyterian minister in Oregon. These harmless and peaceful neighbors, these faithful allies in every war, were the nation that we drove to desperation and deeds of blood.

When white men first found them, the Nez Percés had bands, but no general chief—a system often, if not always, found among Indians west of the Rocky Mountains. Thirty-five years ago the United States Indian Agent for that region undertook to remedy this, which in his wisdom he conceived to be a defect, by giving them a grand chief named Ellis, whose main recommendation was that he had learned English at a mission-school, and so could talk to the agent. Less peaceful Indians than the Nez Percés might have gone to war rather than agree to the agent's labor-saving contrivance. The Nez Percés protested, but waited patiently for Ellis' death, when, however, they were pressed to choose a new general chief. The rivalry lay between Joseph, a scion of the most illustrious Nez Percés, the father of the present Joseph, and an Indian named Lawyer. As Lawyer, like Ellis, knew English, he received the powerful support of the Government agents, who gave him an enormous advantage by conducting all their business with the Nez Percés through him. Joseph's father at length withdrew in disgust from the councils of his tribe, still claiming the headship, if there were to be any.

The dwelling-place of the Nez Percés, as far back as their tradition goes, has been the Wallowa Valley, prized by them for its roots and its fishing, and now for its grazing. The whites at length began to increase in numbers, and, of course, took measures to dispossess the Indians of the valley. For this purpose they framed the successive treaties of 1855, 1863, and 1868, providing the Nez Percé Reservation and annuities instead of their lands. Old Chief Joseph, however, refused to go upon the reservation, and remained, with his band and the other non-treaty Nez Percés, so called, in the Wallowa Valley, rightly claiming that the rest of the tribe had no right to give it up to the United States and white settlers as against the non-treaty Indians, because it was held in common. It should be said here that the present Chief Joseph insists that his father never signed any of these treaties; that this was his father's instruction to him, and that the fact that their band remained away from the reservation shows it. But the Government is said to be able to show that Joseph reluctantly signed the treaty of 1855. Admitting this latter statement to be correct, as we have no doubt that it is, yet the treaty which definitely undertook to give up the Wallowa Valley was that of 1863, and this most unquestionably old Joseph did not sign, as he also did not sign the treaty of 1868. He died in 1871.

The claim of Joseph to his ancestral homestead was, therefore, good, *prima facie*—so good, at any rate, that there was no case for driving him out with the bayonet. Even the treaty Indians could almost have claimed to have the Wallowa Valley restored to them, for it is proved beyond any doubt that the Government never carried out its stipulations for land partition, which formed an essential part of the treaties. The Government, however, holds with reason that the continued acceptance of the benefits of the treaties partly meets that objection as regards them; and for the non-treaty bands, off the reservation, another means has been found—coercion, violence, and a bloody war.

Now, these are not fancy sketches or rumors; they are officially-ascertained facts, well known to the Government, and they are to be found in two admirably clear reports, drawn up and presented to the Government more than a year ago, by no less an authority than Col. H. Clay Wood, a staff officer of Gen. Howard himself. They are the result of most careful investigations, and one of Col. Wood's conclusions in a later report was that the present Joseph and his band have in law an undivided and individual interest in *all* lands ceded to the United States by the treaty of 1863, though he only claimed the Wallowa Valley, or rather the tract of land set apart by President Grant's order of 1873.

A brief reference to this last order must close the story. Settlers having begun to encroach on the non-treaty Indian lands, in June, 1873, President Grant ordered that these possessions should be "withheld from entry and settlement as public lands, and that the same be set apart as a reservation for the roaming Nez Percé Indians, as recommended by the Secretary of the Interior and the Commissioner of Indian Affairs." The decision took the form of an order, because no treaties are allowed since the act of 1871. Joseph continued, therefore, with his band to peacefully occupy his ancestral home in the Wallowa Valley under an order which warned off others from interfering with his rights. Two years ago President Grant issued another order summarily revoking the former, and saying that "the said described tract of country is hereby restored to the public domain." The settlers at once encroached; the Government ordered the non-treaty Nez Percés to go upon the reservation; to their pleadings against the injustice, the menacing reply was the gathering of troops which the Indian Department called for, in order, if necessary, to put them on by force. Just before the time set for executing this scheme, Joseph, who had held back for months, and to the last moment, from a resort to which the peaceful Nez Percés were repugnant, at length, counseling with his brother non-treaty chiefs, and seeing soldiers assembled to drive him from his home, desperately plunged into war—a war which, on our part, was in its origin and motive nothing short of a gigantic blunder and a crime.

⤴ The Cheyenne Tragedy

January 13, 1879

The bloody affair at Fort Robinson is, let us hope, the final scene in an Indian drama which, from beginning to end, has been a disgrace to the Government and the people. The Cheyenne bands of Dull Knife and Old Crow are not, it is true, the sort of Indians to excite sentimental sympathy. They do not compare favorably with the peaceful, friendly, and humane Nez Percés of Chief Joseph and White Bird, who were driven to revolt in the Spring of 1877 by preparations to force them from lands that belonged to them by treaty. They committed many outrages, on their road through Kansas, that contrast with the chivalric sparing, not only of women and children, but of unarmed settlers, by the Nez Percé warriors. It may be admitted, too, that they were mischievous and restless, and that there was no absolute necessity for their escapade from the Fort Reno reservation on the night of Sept. 9. Nevertheless, it is a demonstrable fact that the Government had been shamefully remiss in its treatment of these Indians, and thus tempted them to the revolt which has had so bloody a course and ending.

These Cheyennes had taken part with Sitting Bull, on account of the military incursions of Custer, followed by those of the gold-hunters, into the Black Hills—a region pledged to Indian occupation by solemn treaty. But when Sitting Bull went to Canada, they left him and surrendered voluntarily, in the Spring of 1877, to Gen. Crook at the old Red Cloud Agency. They were told that they must remove to the Indian Territory. A part of them acquiesced; others, including Dull Knife's band, barely consented, as an experiment; others, like Little Robe's band, held back, and were only on their way eighteen months later, when Dull Knife escaped; and still others are far north, and have not gone yet. But when they went, it was on a specific agreement. We need hardly say that the military annals for the past eighteen months have been full of complaints that the conditions were not fulfilled, and that the Indians were dissatisfied. "All the Cheyennes are dissatisfied," reports one officer, "and complain that they are not receiving what was promised them; that they would be satisfied if they received what the treaty allows." But the matter is settled when we also find Agent John D. Miles, under date of Sept. 30, making an official report to Commissioner Hayt on the cause of the Cheyenne revolt, in which he says, after enumerating other troubles:

"In addition to these general grievances, and others relative to things which they claim were *promised them as part of the consideration in obtaining their consent to come to this country,* I will say that *the full list of rations named in their treaty of 1876 has not been furnished them.*"

Agent Miles very properly goes on to show that he had done the best he could, and that he always gave the Indians plenty of beef, and also "such other rations as were in store," and that they were by no means starving. This, however, does not contradict his previous acknowledgment that the rations and other things promised on peaceful removal from their ancestral lands to a strange land and a strange climate had never been supplied. Can it be said that fifteen months was not long enough to wait for the fulfillment of the bargain? In addition, they were forced to do agricultural or other work, and when the warriors refused, their rations of coffee and sugar were stopped for weeks together, as Agent Miles' report shows. The Agent quotes department circulars of March and April, 1878, to justify him; but he does not quote any such justification from the treaty of 1876. The Indians made and acted up to the treaty, but they did not make or agree to subsequent department circulars or to acts of Congress.

Cheated under the contract for removal; forced, by cutting off their food supplies, to adopt at once occupations which, however foolishly, their customs had held degrading; prevented from going to hunt where game abounded, though other Indians, including some of their kindred who were still left north, could do so; and contrasting the malarial region in which they were with the healthy air of their old homes, they set out for the latter. They left their tents and everything in them; they did not strike a blow; it was only when they were pursued and attacked that they fought; and it was weeks after their battles, and only when soldiers and citizens closed in upon them, that they attacked the ranches on their route. After great exertions, the troops succeeded in capturing the fugitives, half-starved and half-frozen, in the Nebraska sand-hills, and took them to Camp Robinson.

That the dead of winter should be chosen for their return to the Indian Territory was quite worthy of a Governmental policy which has repeatedly picked out this season for such purposes; that their refusal to go should be followed by disciplining them with starvation was perhaps not unexpected, because the Government first agrees to give Indians specific annual rations as a consideration for going to the Indian Territory, and then, when they have gone, cuts down the rations unless they will work. It had been intended to give up a good part of these Indian warriors in Kansas, on the way back, so that they might be tried and hanged; and it should not be surprising that they preferred to die in battle rather than at the end of a rope. These dead Indians have been officially abused with consolatory vigor as lazy, trouble-making, hoe-hating red rascals, who would rather hunt buffalo than draw rations, and who would rather die than obey department circulars; but is there, after all, in this whole miserable business anything but a shameful record for the country and the white race?

⌒ The Ute Agreement

August 6, 1880

Assuming that the remainder of the Ute chiefs will follow the example of the Uncompahgres in reluctantly signing the agreement which takes from them eleven million acres of land, we may probably conclude that one of the most serious Indian troubles of the year has been safely passed over or postponed. Yet the best that can be said of this vaunted settlement of the Ute problem is that it has cunningly used the outbreak of a single band of Indians to despoil the whole tribe of their ancestral homes, in the alleged interests of peace for the future. No man can pretend that the Utes have not as good a legal title to their entire reservation as any house-owner has to his dwelling-place in New-York. Nor can it be questioned that they are now going through the process of surrendering this title against their protest, and by compulsion. Yet so desperately unjust is the Nation's treatment of Indians that the anxiety of many persons last Winter was lest Congress should not ratify Mr. Schurz's plan of land purchase, in which case it appeared probable that the surrounding settlers would rush upon the reservation and occupy it by force. It is precisely such compulsory arrangements with Indians as the present, in which greed masquerades in the garments of generosity, that have been fruitful of costly and cruel wars. We bewail the selfishness and cupidity of past generations of office-holders and frontiersmen who combined in such wrongs, and then we imitate them in our own day, and under the same plea of necessity.

The Ute tribe was until lately one of the most peaceful and prosperous on the continent—rich in lands confirmed to them by treaty "forever," and rich in horses, as well as in their comfortable and sufficient annuities. The yearly reports of their agents showed that some members of the tribe were making progress in farming, that their lands were admirably adapted for an Indian reservation, being healthy and abounding in game, and that the only cloud upon their prospects was the greed of mining prospectors and land speculators, who prowled upon their reservation in violation of law. A few years ago this greed began to take an organized form. Exaggerated stories were told of the mineral richness of the reservation; falsehoods were invented regarding alleged misdeeds of Ute Indians, and newspapers bordering on the coveted territory advised settlers to take their lands, if necessary, by force. When Colorado became a State, it seemed a good thing to acquire all this territory of the Utes at the expense of the general Government. Commissioner E. A. Hayt approved this scheme, but he prefaced his official proposal of it with repeated assurances of the "absolutely indefeasible" title of the Utes, and of the necessity of allowing them entire freedom of choice in treating for the sale. To such lengths of officially authorized seizure has the country since gone that this early proposition of Mr. Hayt seems benevolent by comparison.

The Utes, however, loved their homes more than any money the sale could bring; they loved hunting, fishing, and the Indian's roving life; and they found their existing annuities, derived from former sales of land, to be enough. But already the peculiar persuasions of Indian management had been applied. Half-rations were substituted for whole rations; sometimes there was no flour to be had, or else nothing but flour; and, instead of hauling the rations to the agency, they were left at a distant station, where the Indians, with squaws and children, must tramp for miles after them, in the dead of Winter, in the snow. A part of the money due the tribe was kept back in a lump; and when asked why, the Indian Bureau replied that the fund would be useful for removing these Utes some day, and the people of Colorado were determined the Utes should go. At last came the outbreak at White River. Savage as was the massacre at the agency, there is little doubt that the unfortunate Meeker sacrificed his life and that of his employes through his indiscretion. He tried to run his agency plow on lands claimed by an Indian as grazing ground for his horses. Even if the Indian was wrong, the matter was trivial. There was enough other land not so claimed; but the agent momentarily forgot that the reservation belonged to the Indians instead of to him, and called in the troops to iron or shoot those wards whom he was supposed to be specially fitted, as an Indian Agent, to deal with peacefully. When he saw the troops coming, he begged them to halt, but they refused. Then the Indians fought, and fought in traditional fashion.

The business-like skill with which this by no means causeless outbreak of a few Indians has been utilized to force the whole tribe out of eleven-twelfths or nineteen-twentieths of their land is a matter of history. Colorado called for extermination, and compromised on confiscation. A selected body of chiefs was called to Washington, and, after being cowed by the sight of mobs at the stations in Colorado, yelling for their blood, were lionized and feasted at Washington as people who were going to sell their lands. Then troops were moved into the territory, to begin hostile operations in the Spring, as the chiefs were told, unless the contract to sell was made. They were also assured that the settlers would rush in as soon as the grass grew, and that then the Utes would lose both the land and the money offered for it. They were promised that the agreement should not be binding unless freely ratified by the tribe; and, to make matters easier, a provision was inserted for large special presents to deserving chiefs, (and who more deserving than they?) and $1,000 a year was settled on their leader, Ouray. Thus bullied and bribed, they yielded and signed. Congress went to work, as soon as they were gone from the city, and, without consulting them, altered the agreement to its fancy. When the Commissioners took the agreement to Los Pinos, it was rejected unanimously—the Indians protested against being driven upon small severalty farms, with no hunting grounds in common, and they objected, also, to the character of the lands picked out for them. The United States Commissioners, in reply, offered them these terms or none, and notified them that that protection from trespass to which they were entitled by solemn treaty could not henceforth be relied on. The chiefs then signed, rather than be robbed and ruined. Now the Commissioners have gone to give the same "free choice" to the Southern Utes. And yet, such is our dealing with Indians that this Ute agreement is claimed as a triumph of humanity and justice, and many good friends of the red men are anxious for its success lest the alternative should be Ute extermination.

⤷ The President and the Indians

February 3, 1881

President Hayes has sent to Congress a manly and sensible Message on Indian affairs, the special occasion being the report of the commission appointed by him to inquire into the present condition, grievances, and desires of the Ponca Indians. It must be confessed that the public is somewhat weary of the woes and complaints of the Poncas. Perhaps, like the unjust Judge in the Scriptures, the average citizen may say that he is ready to give the Poncas whatever they ask, "lest, by their continual coming, they weary me." Nevertheless, since the outrage that has been committed upon this people is so thoroughly a typical one, it is worth consideration. It is not a unique case, although it has attracted especial attention. The efforts of the Interior Department to misrepresent the facts, and to besmirch the character of all who have been interested in proclaiming the woes of the Ponca Indians, has not served to mislead many honest people. And the President, when he says that he is deeply sensible that some of the responsibility for this wrong committed upon an unoffending tribe rests with him, and that he desires to make due reparation, is entitled to respect for his candor and magnanimity.

There are now about five hundred Ponca Indians in the Indian Territory. These are the survivors of the band forcibly removed thither during the first year of Mr. Schurz's official term from the Ponca reservation in Dakota Territory. There are about one hundred and fifty of the tribe still remaining on the old reservation. These are they who broke away from the Agent who was taking them southward, or who afterward decamped and found their way back to their former homes. The President recommends that the Indians should be prepared for the rights and responsibilities of citizenship by education, by being taught to support themselves. Next, lands should be allotted to Indians in severalty, and that these lands should be made inalienable for a certain period. He also recommends that these particular Indians should have fair compensation for their lands not required for their individual use, and that the rest of their lands should be sold and the avails invested for their individual benefit. When these things are done, the Indians should be charged and invested with the duties of citizenship. Finally, the Poncas should be left free to choose whether they will remain where they are in the Indian Territory, or in Dakota, and that they shall have their lands allotted to them in severalty wherever they elect to stay.

It is not necessary to say that the steps recommended by the President, by way of compensation and reparation to the Poncas, and to Indians irrespective of all antecedent circumstances, are quite unprecedented in our history. The policy of the Government has been to encourage the Indians in a belief that the lands ceded, reserved, or allotted to them were "permanently" their own, and to require them to move on whenever their lands were required for settlement by the whites. This was the promise made to the Delawares and the Winnebagoes nearly a century ago. This was the promise made to them so often, and so often broken, that we are amazed that they ever believed the United States Government at all. For, no sooner were the Indians fairly successful with their work, (and the records show that they were good farmers and prudent house-holders,) than the Government bade them abandon their homes and move further westward. While constantly recommending that the Indians be taught to earn their own living, they were uprooted from their farms and plantations by order of the Interior Department, and were taught, by the granting of annuities and indemnities, that they were merely Governmental wards and paupers, the creatures of capricious circumstances.

It is fortunate for the President that the obstinacy of Secretary Schurz has given him the opportunity to show how honorable are his own motives in this matter. The President says that as the wrong committed upon the Poncas was inflicted during the time when he was chief executive, he is anxious that reparation shall be made during his term of office. This tribe of Indians were in peaceable possession of their lands, which had been as solemnly "ceded" to them as other lands had been set apart for the "permanent" occupancy of other tribes. They were farmers, drovers, and mechanics, in a fair way to become entitled to deserve all the rights of white citizens, when they were ruthlessly driven from their peaceable homes, in order that selfish schemers should reap the benefit of their removal. It is creditable alike to the humanity and the candor of President Hayes that, when he is convinced of the injustice that has been done by his officers and agents, he manfully asks that Congress shall aid him in his efforts to right a much-injured people. It is too late to divide the responsibility for the wrong done. It is a good time to right that wrong and to begin a new policy in solving the long-vexed Indian problem.

✍ The Public Faith

April 21, 1882

Gov. Hoyt, of Pennsylvania, has the reputation of a clear-headed and practical public official. Although of philanthropic views, the Governor is by no means a sentimentalist. Nevertheless, Gov. Hoyt has proposed a new form of policy in the treatment of the Indians which is not only contrary to the practice of the Government in respect of those people, but is contrary to the usages of the United States Government ever since its foundation. Gov. Hoyt has prepared a platform of principles which he has caused to be sent to the Governors of all the States, asking them to procure from their several Legislatures an indorsement of the proposition and a memorial asking Congress to accept and act upon it. The fundamental statement in Gov. Hoyt's platform is that the Government shall never break faith with the Indians. It is not necessary to go any further into the matter than this. It is expected of us, as a nation, that, after more than one hundred years of systematic and persistent breaking of faith and disregard of treaties, we shall deliberately reverse our action, fly in the face of precedent, and travel in a new direction.

About a year ago, several hundred thousand people addressed to Congress a memorial asking that body to keep faith with the Indians. It was like saying: "Will Congress please be good, virtuous, and honest." Congress received the memorial, and then calmly went on breaking faith and upsetting treaties just as though nothing had ever intervened to change the current of its action. Treaties with Indians are made to be broken. It is possible that there has been a treaty made with the Indians by the Government of the United States which has been faithfully kept. But this is not probable. Every agreement of any importance has been broken so many times that one may well wonder why the farce of renewing a covenant is ever enacted. We hear a great deal in sermons and orations about "the national conscience." But the national conscience is so diffused throughout the body politic that it is nowhere manifest. The Government of the United States, so far as that is represented in Congress, has no conscience whatever. There are no obligations, covenants, agreements, or treaties that have on the body of Congress any more restraint than a spider's web has on the plodding ox that pursues his tranquil way through a thicket.

The theory on which our Government is conducted is this: The Indian is an objectionable straggler, to be hustled out of the way, to be got rid of as soon as possible, and to be amused, meantime, by empty promises. Successive Congresses, for a hundred years, have faithfully adhered to this general idea. Each tribe has been (after struggles more or less violent) put down upon a tract of land called a reservation, and told that this was to be their home "forever." Of course, there are other things which usually enter into the agreement made under such circumstances, such as the promise to pay the Indians annuities, furnish them with rations, &c. These minor promises are sometimes kept, and sometimes no attempt is made to keep them. But the main part of the treaty—that which relates to the permanent location of the Indians—is never kept. It has never been kept since the foundation of the Republic. It is contrary to our principles to keep any such promise. We may as well be candid in this matter. The man who persistently argues that a treaty or an agreement between the United States Government and the Indian is as binding as a similar contract betwixt man and man is no better than a sickly sentimentalist.

But we should take credit to ourselves for not breaking Indian treaties without a pretense of respecting them. For example, a tribe is fixed "forever" on a tract of land by solemn treaty. White settlers crowd around the exterior boundaries of the reservation, longing to break in. Murmurs of discontent are heard. Congress is told that the Indians must be removed. A commission is sent to "negotiate" for a formal abrogation of the alleged treaty. Sometimes a show of military force is necessary to hasten the so-called negotiations. There can be but one conclusion to this dismal and oft-repeated comedy. The Indians are sent away with a new treaty, which, in its turn, is certain to be torn into pieces like all its predecessors. He was a philosopher who told the irascible Frederick the Great that it was unsafe to disagree with a monarch who had such strong convictions and wore such heavy boots as his Majesty of Prussia. Sometimes during the farcical negotiation of a treaty of relinquishment there are reports that "the Indians are sullen and rebellious." This never lasts long. The North American Indian, after a century or two of experience, has learned how painful, even dangerous, it is to have mind and will of his own.

And yet, after we have settled into the policy of breaking treaties, and then substituting "agreements" for treaties, as less immorally to be broken, a philanthropic statesman asks that we shall take a new and radical departure. That impersonal and irresponsible body which we call the Government never keeps agreements that can possibly be evaded. It made a treaty with France, during the time of the Consulate, agreeing to assume the claims of American citizens against France; and it has never paid those claims. It made a treaty with Great Britain, by which it received a great sum of money with which to indemnify its own citizens for losses from Anglo-rebel cruisers; and it has never paid those losses. It received another large sum of money from Japan, playing the part of a highwayman's accomplice, and, although often entreated and often rated, it has never indemnified its own naval officers, nor has it paid back the extorted money. Is it any wonder that some of our fellow citizens, whose ideas of public morals are hazy, declare that "it is no sin to cheat the Government?" If they know anything about the Government, they know that nobody but a dreamer would propose, at this late day, that we should, as a Nation, respect any obligations from which we can safely escape.

⌒ The Indian Territory

December 5, 1884

"The time has passed," said Secretary Teller in his last annual report, recently published, "when large and valuable tracts of land fit for agriculture can be held by Indians for either hunting or grazing to the exclusion of actual settlers." This is the opinion of the head of the Interior Department, expressed at the conclusion of a paragraph relating to the leasing of lands which the Indians hold by treaty in the Indian Territory. It was also the opinion of the late Capt. Payne, chief of the Oklahoma raiders, although he did not attempt to make settlement upon lands which the Indians hold or lease, but only upon lands ceded by the Indians to the Government to be occupied by tribes transferred from other reservations.

The views of the Secretary, the bills introduced by Senators and Representatives from Kansas, the raids of Payne's followers, the leasing of Indian lands, and the recent passage of bills granting rights of way in the Indian Territory to two railroad companies, indicate that the demand for an "opening" of the Territory to settlement will soon be made more boldly than it has been made heretofore, and with a better prospect of success. The people of Kansas, Missouri, Arkansas, and Texas—four States that bound the Territory on three sides—have for some years looked over the border with longing eyes upon the fair domain from which they have been debarred.

The rights of the Indians have been attacked in three ways—by inducing them to lease millions of acres to which their title is clear, by entering upon the ceded lands of the Government in violation of law and without regard to Executive proclamations, and by granting rights of way to railroad lines in addition to those already built or located with consent of the tribes. Secretary Teller not only has allowed the leases to be made at two cents an acre, but he also suggests that the cattlemen would pay more if they could have some assurance that they would "not be disturbed at the whim or caprice of the Indians." He even directs attention to the act that "other tribes also have good grazing lands that might be leased at profitable rates." Senator Dawes, who knows something about the Indians, admits that the existing leases are unlawful, and that the tribes are in danger of losing all of their land by means of them. His view concerning the legality of the leases appears to be supported by the statute that says that "no lease or other conveyance of lands from any Indian nation or tribe shall be of any validity in law or equity, unless the same be made by treaty or convention entered into pursuant to the Constitution." The inquiry authorized by Senator Vest's resolution will bring before congress all the facts relating to these unlawful leases, which are said to have been secured by bribery and corruption.

The Territory contains 44,000,000 acres of land, about 14,000,000 acres of which were purchased by the United States from the four nations. Upon part of this purchased or ceded tract other tribes have been placed. Upon the remainder Payne and his followers undertook to make settlement and were expelled by United States troops. The Government has shown again and again that these unoccupied lands are not open to settlement, but are held by the United States subject to trusts specified in the treaties of 1866. The lands were reacquired by the Government under an agreement that they should be used only for the settlement of other friendly and civilized Indians or of those persons who had once been the slaves of Indian tribes. In response to resolutions of inquiry Secretary Teller's predecessors have told Congress that there are no lands in the Territory open to settlement or entry by any person under the public land laws.

The land grabbers who have barred out the settlers from millions of acres of the public domain should be forced to obey the laws. Not until the vast areas held by them unlawfully have been opened to the settler should an alleged scarcity of public land be allowed to have any weight as an argument in favor of an "opening" of the Indian Territory and a violation of the solemn treaties made by the Government with the civilized nations that hold three-fourths of the Territory. In years to come, when lapsed and unearned land grants and great areas now held by force or fraud shall have been reclaimed and exhausted by lawful settlement, the Government may be able to induce the tribes to relinquish for a fair consideration land which they may not then need, and in this way avoid a deliberate repudiation of its obligations.

9   Public Opinion and the Role of the Press

> The stubborn fight which Chief Joseph made last week, near the mouth of the Cottonwood, against a superior force of our troops, has roused the country to an appreciation of the fact that we have a war within our domains quite worthy of public attention. Its scene, to be sure, is far distant from our Atlantic sea-board; the operations, too, are on a small scale; but it is a war that has spread anxiety and alarm through hundreds of miles of the sparsely-settled North-west.
>
> —*New York Times*
> July 17, 1877

THE *TIMES*, in dealing with what it called the Indian problem, constantly faced two challenges that will sound familiar to present-day readers. First, it found a great deal of public apathy and ignorance on the topic. Second, it often found the prevailing public opinion—particularly in the West—to be at variance with its own views.

The *Times* took its role as an opinion leader seriously. It devoted generous space in both its news columns and its editorial columns to the Indian problem. But it knew that its influence was limited; its readers, for the most part, lived in New York. It knew, also, that many readers had only limited interest in events or situations involving the Native Americans. At a time when its attention to the Indian problem, on both news and editorial pages, was extensive, the newspaper acknowledged that readers were bored with the subject and generally skipped "any discussion as to the present or future of the fast-perishing red man." *Times* editorial writers could be hopeful, however, that their influence might extend at least as far as Washington. Since policy affecting the Indians typically was national policy, that was important. Overwhelmingly, their most ambitious editorial slings and arrows were aimed at the national capital.

Insofar as public opinion was concerned, the *Times* reserved its most vigorous dissent for Westerners—the frontier citizens and politicians alike. Neither governor nor common cowboy was likely to escape for long the ire of the *Times*. "The rabid manner in which the Governors of Colorado and Montana have set about their preparations for an Indian campaign, and the zest with which the settlers of those Territories come forward to embark in such warfare, have called from Gen. Sherman a restraining order," the *Times* noted in a biting editorial in June 1867. It said that citizens in those Western territories were clamoring for a war of extermination, even offering premiums for Indian scalps and forming companies of mounted men to hunt Indians.

The *Times* put some faith in the ability of General William T. Sherman, whose Civil War reputation had accompanied him to the frontier, to control the situation. Sherman demanded that Indian treaties be respected by both sides, the editorial noted, "and it is hardly probable that those who know his career will care to run counter to his mandate." But the *Times* worried that even the fearsome Sherman would have problems with the frontiersmen. While rigid enforcement of his rules would bring some order to the frontier chaos, it said, it was concerned that the general "will find quite as much difficulty in repressing the whites as in keeping the Indians quiet."

The *Times* soon learned that much of the information on the Indian problem it received from the West was not reliable. Except for military reports, it said in a brief editorial comment in August 1877, most of that information came through "sinister channels" and often was mere conjecture. Rival newspapers in New York, some with political leanings quite different from those of the *Times*, also were suspect. Just as the *Times* made political points in many of its editorials on the Indian problem, so did publications such as the competing *World*. That newspaper was among those readily classed as the "besotted partisan press" by editorial writers for the *Times*. The outrage, perhaps genuine or perhaps somewhat exaggerated, that the *Times* expressed toward the *World* for trying to make a political issue out of the annihilation of General George Custer and his troops on the Little Big Horn in the summer of 1876 is demonstrated in an editorial, "Politics Run Mad," included in this chapter.

The *Times* had its own share of political run-ins. One of these began with a lengthy series of editorials critical of Commissioner E. A. Hayt, who ran the Indian Bureau in the late 1870s. Hayt eventually faced an internal investigation and was fired by Interior Secretary Carl Schurz. Commissioner Hayt complained that publication of charges against him was a great injustice and blamed the *Times*. While the newspaper was not responsible for the premature release of the charges—that was done by a member of the investigating board—it nonetheless took obvious satisfaction in Hayt's eventual dismissal and considered the action to be a vindication of its editorial complaints. But the *Times* pointed out in an editorial column in January 1880 that, once the charges were made public, it had specifically called for a suspension of public opinion regarding Hayt until the investigation was complete.

As vigorous as it was in laying primary responsibility for the Indian problem squarely on the doorstep of government, the *Times* never underestimated the power of public opinion. It not only censured the overbearing anti-Indian sentiments of many white citizens—and particularly that expressed in the Western press—but it also attempted to make a case for the Native American point of view. As much as it despised Sitting Bull, the *Times* accepted the fact that it was irrational not to recognize that he viewed the world from a vastly different perspective.

Where the *Times* might not be able to influence public opinion directly, it encouraged the work of organizations it considered friendly to the Indians' cause. One of these was the Woman's National Indian Association. A major purpose of that organization, the *Times* reported in late 1886, was "to scrutinize all bills introduced into Congress bearing upon the Indians, and to use every influence to secure such legislation as will tend to their benefit." One reason the *Times* supported the work of the organization, clearly, was the extent to which the women's group agreed with the editorial philosophy of the newspaper. The *Times* quoted a statement by the organization's president assailing national policy that, she said, maintained Indian pauperism. But it took a cynical view of the association's support of missionary work among the Indians. "As for missionaries," the *Times* said, "as long as white agents are permitted to swindle the Indians out of their daily bread, it will be futile for white evangelists to preach to them." The *Times* suggested that one of the most important things the women's organization could do was to study and publicize the many wrongs done in the name of Indian policy. "Public opinion being enlightened," it said, "reformatory legislation is compelled to follow." Another organization that enjoyed strong support from the *Times* was the Indian Rights Association. Members of that group included a number of nationally prominent citizens.

However critical the *Times* may have been of the government, the military, or ordinary citizens in regard to the Indian problem, however, it would not countenance similar criticism from the foreign press. Following the tragic bloodshed at Wounded Knee in 1890, the *Times* expressed outrage over the treatment of that incident by the British newspapers. The English papers were generally ignorant about American affairs, it charged in a January 1891 editorial, and such ignorance was "most noteworthy just now in connection with the recent Indian troubles." In the British papers, it said, Wounded Knee was "almost uniformly treated as a bloodthirsty and wanton massacre." The *Times* made no reference to its own editorial on Wounded Knee, published December 31, 1890, titled "The Indian Massacre" (see chapter 7). But it worried that for the next decade, the British would believe "that Americans neither can nor will do anything but 'kill out' the Indians."

Between 1860 and 1900, the *Times* expended enormous editorial energy defining—and usually denouncing—public opinion on the Indian problem. It was confident that the press played a critical role in the formation of that opinion and took its own role seriously. In this regard, it commonly took issue with articles and editorials in other publications it disagreed with, and it called attention to and openly promoted material that supported its own point of view. All this filled countless columns on the editorial pages of the *Times*. The editorials that follow represent a diverse cross-section of the views to which *Times* readers were exposed, and at the same time shed a great deal of light on American public opinion relative to the Native Americans during the latter half of the nineteenth century.

✑ The Policy of Extermination as Applied to the Indians

May 16, 1866

A gentleman somewhat known in connection with adventure and speculation in our Southwestern Territories, has written a letter to Gen. Grant, proposing to take command of a regiment of cavalry, for the purpose of punishing the Apaches of Arizona. He says:

"I desire neither rank nor pay, only the absolute handling of this force without restrictions. I will then undertake to clear Arizona of Apaches in twelve months."

We do not suppose that Gen. Grant would ever entertain the least thought of acceding to any such proposition, any more than we doubt that, if he did, it would lead to the extermination of the wildest of all the wild tribes of the Western plains.

It is now unquestionably in the power of our Government to exterminate not only one obnoxious tribe of Indians, but the whole Indian race, from the savage Sioux of the far North to the untamable Apaches of the far South, from the wild Arapajos and Cheyennes of the central regions to the wretched tribes of the Pacific coast. And such a policy of extermination would receive almost universal support from the white settlers on the Western plains. At all events, those living within range of the Sioux would like *that* tribe extirpated, those living within range of the Apaches would like *that* tribe extirpated, those living within range of the Cheyennes would like *their* extermination, and so on. The white settlements that are now planted here and there all over the Plains, and on both sides of the Rocky Mountains, would eagerly cooperate with the military forces in the work of extermination; and these settlements are so numerous, so widely scattered, and so advantageously located, that they could operate to most sanguinary purpose. They would not be rendered the more averse to do so, in that they would acquire the coveted lands and the "plunder" of the Indians, and would secure the expenditure among themselves of vast sums of Government money. Under this policy, the red man, once so powerful and populous on this continent, now so lean and circumscribed in numbers and domain, would quickly be relegated forever to those shadowy "hunting grounds" where the "pale face" will never dispute his possession.

We think, however, that even those most covetous of the Indian's heritage might be satisfied at the rate with which he is exchanging the soil for the sod. Looking at the restricted and disconnected territorial allotments now left him, at the tenure of his possession and the conditions of his toleration— looking at the rapidity and the steadiness with which his range is ever being limited, and the swiftness with which he himself is fading away, one might think that such furious desires of extermination as are expressed in the afore- mentioned letter to Gen. Grant, and which, as we have said, are so widely entertained in the far West, might well be somewhat modified.

As for the Indian "outrages" of which we are continually hearing, and of which the Apaches in Arizona furnish the latest illustration, it must be said that we only hear one side. The Apaches print no newspapers, and have no means of communicating to the world a knowledge of the outrages com- mitted upon *them*. But it is on record, as the experience of all those most familiar with Indian affairs, that the aggressors in nearly all quarrels, and the beginners of nearly all outrages, are the whites—rarely indeed the Indians.

Our permanent policy toward the Indians should be, in brief and comprehensive terms, to exercise a steady pressure and influence toward securing the *aggregation* of the entire race and all the scattered tribes as far as possible; and secondly, to appoint military officers to the various Western posts who have a deep appreciation of justice, and who will be more anxious to avoid a quarrel than secure a fight; in the meantime spurning with proper contempt, as inhuman and unchristian, any and all propositions for exterminating any tribe in twelve months "with a regiment of cavalry."

∽ Our Indian Troubles—Feeling of the Western People

June 8, 1867

A dispatch from Gov. Hunt, of Colorado, to the Secretary of War, states that Indian depredations are of almost daily occurrence within that Territory, that the military force there is wholly inadequate for the protection of settlers, and asks that he be permitted to organize a mounted force for a campaign against the savages. Hon. A. K. McClure also writes to Secretary Stanton, urging the Governor's application upon his immediate attention, and adds that passengers and emigrants are wholly at the mercy of the Indians.

While there is unquestionably much truth in these statements regarding Indian depredations, it is equally certain that the remedy proposed would be quite as bad as the disease. To arm and equip a horde of border settlers, whose intense hatred of the Indian—whether he be hostile or friendly—is only appeased by his slaughter, and to send them out fully authorized to make war upon the savages, could only result in scenes of bloodshed at which the country would stand aghast. There would be no limit to killing so long as a red skin, man, woman or child, could be found. Frontier-men do not, as a general thing, look upon Indians as human beings, but rather as beasts of prey, that are to be destroyed in the interests of civilization. The extermination of the race would be highly conducive to the pecuniary interests of these rampant frontier-men. The Indians own millions of acres of fertile land, which these borderers covet, and which they, by inciting a war against them, might become possessed of. At any rate, the killing off or driving out of the Indians would deprive *them* of it, and in the scramble for plunder which would follow, the settlers would stand a chance of getting something.

But while there is much truth in the stories of these outrages, we are slow to believe them all. Too many of them have proved to be false, and in many cases where murder and pillage have been committed by Indians, investigation has shown that the original offence was with the white man, and that the savages were but returning murder for murder, and theft for theft. If a white man is killed or a pair of mules stolen by Indians, forthwith the "Indian outrage" is telegraphed to every paper in the country, and is read by everybody. But who hears of the Indians killed, of the Indian women ravished, or of the Indian ponies "accumulated" by white men? There are two sides to these stories of Indian outrages, and judging from investigations which have been made and the history of the past, the red man's record is by far the whitest, and the cry of retaliation comes with an ill grace from the white man.

That there is a war of races existing on the border, and that each race is reveling in bloodshed and pillage, and striving to exterminate the other, is a fact to which the Government cannot shut its eyes. That this is so is the fault of the Government. Its blundering, vacillating, thieving Indian policy for the past fifty years has brought its necessary result. Broken treaties and party fights for Indian spoils have not only destroyed the savage's confidence in the Government, but have tended to make him look upon every white man as his enemy, and even now, while all these "outrages" are being committed, and while "emigrants and passengers are at the mercy of the Indians," a strife is going on between the civil and military officers of the Government, as to which shall direct Indian affairs, and control the issues of beads and wampum.

It is time some active steps were taken by the Government to put an end to this state of affairs. The responsibility of reducing the belligerent settlers and the depredating savages to a state of peace and quiet should be placed upon the shoulders of some man possessed of firmness, decision, a moderate degree of common sense, and an ordinary amount of humanity. Neither Gov. Hunt, of Colorado, nor Gov. Meagher, of Montana, both of whom desire to enter forthwith upon the war path, is qualified for the position. Troops are required in large force upon the frontier, to give security not only to the settlers, but to the Indian. Scalping savages must be checked in their murderous careers, and bellicose Governors must be held in restraint. A single practical head is wanted to guide the troops—one that can see the beam in the white man's eye as clearly as he can the mote in the savage's. The troops that are sent must be available; infantry is worse than useless, for it can do no good, but only embarrasses the commissariat. Cavalry is required, active young men mounted upon hardy, enduring horses, who can travel as fast as Indians and fight as well, and they should be officered by men who have sufficient force of character to prevent their soldiers from committing unauthorized outrages upon the Indians. Heretofore the soldiers have had a demoralizing effect upon redskins, male and female.

The Government owes it to the country to at once adopt vigorous measures to secure peace upon the Indian frontier, and this is a duty which it cannot delegate to either Gov. Hunt or to Gov. Meagher. Government alone is responsible for the existing state of affairs, and Government alone can apply the remedy. Individual States may make raids and commit murders, but if they do the authorities at Washington will be held to account for it. The Indian question is national, not sectional, and the stigma of unnecessary slaughter will rest upon the whole people, not upon Colorado or Montana alone. It is a question which fillibusters are incompetent to handle, and the Government should emphatically assure them of that fact.

↪ Our Indian Policy

July 5, 1867

An article which was printed in the *Times* on Monday last, entitled "The Massacre of the Cheyennes," has called forth in reply a letter from Mr. O. J. Hollister, a resident of Colorado, temporarily sojourning in this City. His letter will be found on another page. While Mr. Hollister agrees with us in denouncing the Chivington massacre as entirely uncalled for, he regrets that that slayer of women and children, having once undertaken the work, did not do it more completely, and leave neither man, woman nor child of the tribe to tell the tale. He also claims that, because the few Indians who were left at that time have banded with other tribes and sought revenge from the whites for the murder of their helpless wives and babes, another massacre is now necessary. He takes the broad ground that all Indians are barbarous, savage beasts, incapable of being civilized, whom it is a mercy to slaughter. He claims that the broad prairies are wanted for the use of the white man, and because he is stronger than the Indian, the rights of the latter are to be ignored, and he crowded away from his hunting grounds. If he protests against such treatment, he is to be killed in the most summary manner, and his scalp sold in the nearest Colorado town, where premiums are offered for such commodities. In short, Mr. Hollister is an open and avowed advocate of the policy of Indian extermination. The causes which have led to the present hostilities are not to be taken into consideration at all. No matter whether or not the Indians have good reasons for committing depredations upon the whites, the fact that they have entered upon "the war path" is to be considered a sufficient excuse for slaughtering men, women and children in the future as has been done in the past. The opinion of Mr. Hollister would not be worth the space it occupies were it simply that of an individual; but unfortunately there is a very large class of men on the border who will indorse every barbarous sentiment contained in his letter. He claims that the pioneers of the Eastern States set the example, and that the Western idea of extermination originated in the East. This may be true, but two wrongs never made one right, and our forefathers did many things which will forever be a reproach to their memories.

It is true that the border States have much to complain of, but their complaints should be directed rather against the Government than the Indians. Baseness, cupidity, treachery and pillage have characterized our treatment of the Indians since the days of the Pilgrim Fathers, but never has it been so reckless as within the past few years. The policy of the Government has been to send thieves and swindlers among them to defraud them of their dues, while irresponsible traders debauched them with bad whisky and white settlers occupied their lands. That the Indians have been guilty of shocking barbarities is undoubtedly true, but it is also certain that whenever a tribe has dug up the hatchet and resorted to hostilities, it has been incited thereto by the bad faith of the whites. This is no idle statement, but is borne out by the reports of investigating committees who have at various times looked into the matter.

The Indians have never been treated as we treat foreign nations. As a government, we recognize that the Indians have certain rights, own large tracts of land, and are entitled to remuneration for that of which we have robbed them, and forthwith set about to invade their rights, occupy their lands, and cheat them out of their just dues. Until the Government adopts some fair and equitable policy toward the Indians, there will be murders and pillaging by them, and the border settlers will continue to clamor for extermination. But with all their barbarity, the Indians have failed as yet to equal the "Chivington massacre," or to reach the point of making scalps a merchantable commodity. And these are outrages against humanity for which the Government is responsible. The Indians and the settlers can never agree—their interests are at variance and can not be reconciled. The Government should mediate between them, protecting the one as fully as it does the other. Indians commit murders upon the whites, and whites upon Indians, without let or hindrance from the government, and to-day there are organized bands of white men hunting the savages simply to gratify their thirst for blood and plunder. There is no more necessity for exterminating the Indians than there is for annihilating the settlers. Both can be controlled by the Government if the proper effort be made.

In refreshing contrast to the extermination plan of Mr. Hollister and the citizens of Colorado, is the interesting letter written by Gen. Hazen, which we also print elsewhere. This letter is addressed to and written at the request of Senator Henderson, Chairman of the Senate Committee on Indian Affairs. Gen. Hazen has had a large experience among Indians, and his views are entitled to great weight. After alluding to the annual farce of treaty-making, the General submits a plan for our future treatment of Indians, which is substantially the same as the one recently set forth in the *Times*—colonization. He would assign to each tribe a certain trct [*sic*] of land, compel it to occupy it, and prevent all intercourse with white men, except such as are sent among them as teachers. He would place the control of Indian affairs in the hands of the Freedmen's Bureau, thereby securing an honest administration, and would then supply to the various tribes religious and other instructors, agricultural implements, domestic animals, and such rations and clothing as might be necessary. For two or three years the cost would be considerable, but after the lapse of that time the tribes would have gained sufficient knowledge of agriculture to make them self-supporting. The only care of the Government would then be in keeping the Indians at home. This could be done by promptly punishing such as should prove refractory, and a sufficient number of troops could be recruited from those who are peaceably disposed to form a vigilant and effective police.

This is undoubtedly the proper course to pursue regarding the Indians, and we earnestly call the attention of Congress to it. The subject will probably come up at the present session, and justice to the pioneers of the West, as well as to the Indians, calls for immediate action. Gen. Hazen is of opinion that this scheme can be put into practice effectually in three years; but we do not believe that so much time would be required, provided active, energetic, honest men be intrusted with its administration. Meantime the war of retaliation between the white and red men—for Indian hostilities now are nothing more than retaliation by one party for outrages committed by the other—will continue unless more troops are sent to the border to preserve order. Let Gen. Sherman be at once supplied with a force which shall enable him to overawe both the Indians and the whites, and while thus preventing violations of existing treaties, leave the way open for the introduction of the new system. Unless some definite plan is adopted for the treatment of Indians, and some scheme put in force which shall secure justice to all, the present destructive and horrible system of predatory warfare will continue, and will each year cost the Government millions of dollars. Troops for the frontier is the present want, and for the future a humane, comprehensive and equitable policy.

⥀ The Indian Question

September 22, 1867

The Commissioners authorized by the last Congress to proceed to the Indian country and enter into negotiations with the various hostile tribes with a view to locating them upon reservations away from the contaminating influence of white men, and of putting an end to Indian depredations, are meeting with violent opposition from the frontier settlers and traders. Many of the agents of the Government join in the hue and cry against the Commission. Gen. Sherman, especially—he being the Department commander as well as Commissioner—is the object of much vituperation in the local Press, and a fair share of this abuse is telegraphed to the East and reproduced in all parts of the country. The persons who thus violently oppose Congressional interference in Indian affairs are doubtless fearful that the Peace Commissioners will be successful in putting an end to hostilities, and that consequently their occupation will be gone. Should there be no war, there will be no fat contracts for beef, for transportation, for mules, rations, forage &c. With the cessation of Indian hostilities would come the withdrawal of troops from the frontier and the loss of the entire Indian trade. This would effectually destroy the exceedingly lucrative business of the Indian agents, traders, speculators, contractors, and many settlers. By a persistent system of swindling soldiers and Indians, hundreds of these sharpers have made fortunes on the frontier, and their successors are unwilling to yield so fruitful a field without a struggle. Hence the opposition to and abuse of the new Indian Commission, which, so far as we can learn, is quietly following the instructions of Congress, and striving to secure a permanent place with those Indians to whom we are indebted for recent depredations.

Many of the telegraph agents and border correspondents of Eastern journals are evidently engaged in the opposition interest, and from them come the daily accounts of "more Indian depredations." As an instance of how these numerous atrocities are manufactured we will refer to the last account of depredations committed. One night last week we received a special dispatch from a correspondent on the frontier, giving the details of an attack made on two trains, whereby the Indians captured a few mules, some stores, and killed a teamster. This outrage has been served up daily ever since its occurrence by the various correspondents and telegraphers, and each account has made the outrage a fresh one, so that the uninformed reader would be led to believe that the Indians for the past week had been devastating the entire country. These dispatches are framed in the interests of those who are desirous of an Indian war, who expect to make money by an influx of troops on the border, and who care nothing for the expenditure of blood and treasure the nation is put to. Such dispatches and correspondence are intended to weaken confidence in the Commissioners, and to destroy the effect in Congress of their reports.

The truth is, the Indians for the past few months have been, as a general thing, too busily engaged in hunting and attending to their own affairs to look for white men's scalps. They had also accepted the idea that the Peace Commissioners were coming to right the wrongs they had sustained at the hands of swindling agents, and were consequently on their good behavior. A few of the "roughs" of various tribes have made raids occasionally on wagon trains, and in a running fight may have killed a man or two, but their depredations for the past two months amount to no more than occur in the Sixth Ward of New-York weekly. In short, the Indians are looking with great anxiety for the Peace Commissioners, and hope through them to secure peace and justice from the white man.

The abuse which the Border settlers and the Border Press heap upon the Commissioners should have no weight with those who desire a speedy solution of our Indian troubles. That body of gentlemen—composed of trustworthy men, especially selected for their knowledge of Indian affairs—have scarcely entered upon the arduous duties assigned them. They have but just arrived in the Indian country, and as yet have met very few of the prominent hostile chiefs, owing to the fact that the principal bands were absent on hunting expeditions. Such councils as have been held, while in no sense conclusive, show an evident desire on the part of the Indians to form peace treaties, and from the tenor of the speeches made, it is highly probable that the Commissioners will be successful in carrying out the views of Congress, and that the Indians will be placed upon reservations at a safe distance from the great lines of travel and the contamination of agents, traders and settlers.

⟿ The Dying Race

May 21, 1875

Any question relating to the Indian is now popularly regarded as a bore. Readers of newspapers generally "skip" any discussion as to the present or future of the fast-perishing red man. Third-rate editorial writers—and most of them scarcely deserve to be ranked so high as third-rate—think it funny to put the word "Lo!" at the head of their dreary rubbish on the Indian. What they have to say is generally characterized by the same sort of felicity. To call the Indian "Lo," and to recommend his immediate suppression, is regarded as a treatment of the subject quite adequate to its gravity or importance. The recommendation in question is at least superfluous, for the melancholy figure of the North American Indian is steadily vanishing from the continent. Rum, robbery, and "civilization" are rapidly doing all that his bitterest enemies can desire. Occasionally these soothing forces are aided by a general massacre, like that which was carried out for the benefit of the Piegan Indians a few years ago, when women and children were cut to pieces in their tents as they slept. Then there was the awful slaughter at Sand Creek, under Col. Chivington, which probably few of our readers now remember, but which will forever leave a dark stain on the history of the country. Whenever the story of the Indians on this continent comes to be fairly written, it will be found that we have little reason to be proud of it.

There was a very large class of persons who believed, and who still believe, that the sufferings which fell upon the South between 1861 and 1865 were a sort of special punishment for the cruelties which they had inflicted on the negro. They saw the hand of an avenging Providence at work. It would be interesting to know whether the persons who held this view imagine that Providence only "avenges" cruelty and injustice when they are committed by the Southern people, and that Providence will never presume to interfere against ourselves. There can be no doubt that the Indians have been the objects of quite as much ill-treatment as ever the negroes were, and if such sins are inevitably followed by retribution—as many events in the history of the world seem to prove—why should we escape more than others? The advocates of the special interposition doctrine would do well to think over the point. Has ever any race on the face of the earth been treated worse than the Red Indian? Read the Chivington story—that is an illustration of one kind of "government" to which he is subjected. Read the long narrative of the treaties made with him—that is an illustration of another kind. He is placed upon a reservation under "guarantees," and the first thing he knows is that all the game has been driven off, and he himself is bound to follow. White men go to him with a religious tract in one hand and a bottle of alcohol in the other, debauch his wife and murder his children, and thus show him how to cease to be a savage and become a good Christian. If a bargain is made with him, it is always broken. If the Government sends money to him, it is stolen on the way. If he offers to trade with the superior race, he is invariably cheated. No doubt he strikes back when he can. Even a savage will do that. The crime and the wrong-doing have not always been on one side. But, then, the Indian does not profess to be better than we are; does not boast of his "cultivation" or "progress;" does not perjure himself on the Bible, and makes no attempt to convert us and save our souls. He leaves us to carry on that sort of talk. He says that he lived here long before we came; that his forefathers once owned these lands, and that he has a right still to find a home somewhere in the vast prairies of the West. We treat him merely as *fera natura*, and take care to dwell much meanwhile on the wickedness of the Southern people toward the black race.

When the President referred the Sioux Chiefs who are now in Washington to the Secretary of the Interior and the Commissioner of Indian Affairs, the Chief named Spotted Tail said: "He had been here before and talked with these chiefs. They had made promises to him which had not been fulfilled. They had lied to him, and he did not want to have more talks with them." No doubt that is not, strictly speaking, the language of the diplomatic circle, but it is true. And savages often speak out plainly what they mean, which is much too low a vice to be tolerated under our unrivaled civilization. The Indian Department has allowed its "wards" to be robbed by all sorts of scoundrels, and we cannot wonder that Spotted Tail and his fellow chiefs are weary of this treatment. The simplicity of mind which life in the open air often produces is shown once more in the fact that these chiefs think to do some good for their tribes by appealing for justice and mercy at Washington. Who cares for their appeals? Who pays any heed to their sorrows? The President has, indeed, taken a very great interest in the fortunes of the red men, and does all that lies in his power to get something like justice for them. There never has been a President who has done half as much before. But what has the Indian Department accomplished? Has it been better managed the last two years than at any previous period? We all know that it has not. The national faith has been pledged and broken over and over again. And so it will be to the end. Every treaty will be violated, and newspaper scribblers will continue to make merry over organized barbarity and roguery, carried out by civilized men at the expense of savages who are simple enough to trust them. If Spotted Tail and Red Cloud could read *The Times* they would find out by and by that we, at least, have not told them lies, and that they might as well have saved themselves the trouble of coming here. Let them go back to their distant wilds and find a grave, for generous treatment they need not hope to find.

ᑌ Enlightened Savages

October 24, 1875

The Creek Nation, inhabiting a part of the Indian Territory, has just given a proof of its advancement in civilization, and its regard for morality. Its Council has refused by a unanimous vote to permit a newspaper to be established within the limits of its jurisdiction. Newspapers and whisky are placed on the same plane in the estimation of these reclaimed savages, and they insist upon cultivating their land and conducting their legislative business without the aid of either stimulant.

Of course, those who look with awful reverence upon "the press," and include in that classification both the London *Times* and the *Arkansas Weekly Bowie-knife*, will be inclined to regard the hostility of the Creeks to newspapers as an evidence of their ignorant dislike of Progress and other nice things beginning with capital letters. But the Creeks, inhabiting a south-western region, judge of newspapers by the specimens which the South-western States furnish. To news, in the abstract, they probably have no objection, but news is a very small part of a South-western newspaper. If newspapers are established in the Creek Nation one half of the Creeks will be held up to the other half as the most depraved and ignorant of mankind. The newspaper will no longer permit the Creek voters to choose their chief in a decent and quiet way, but will demonstrate that the candidates for that position are drunkards, horse-thieves, and persons in the pay of white land speculators. Then, too, newspapers involve editors, and editors, according to the belief of the Creeks, are men who write libels in the evening and shoot each other in the morning. At present the Creeks are peaceful and law-abiding, and they have no desire to have editors shooting one another all over the territory. Having struggled out of barbarism themselves, they do not want to have a worse barbarism flourished in their faces by imported "journalists."

They do not understand in what way progress would be promoted by an announcement in the *Creek Tomahawk* that the editor of the *Creek Scalping-Knife* has eight squaws, or by the reply of the *Scalping-Knife* man that his rival has committed three murders of unusual atrocity, and is continually suffering from delirium tremens. Especially do they dread the appearance of the humorist who now so generally infests the newspapers of the Western and South-western States. If a Creek newspaper is established, it will have its comic man who will write funny Police reports, setting forth the imbecility of the local Judge, and the idiocy of imaginary Creeks, who will be alleged to have been brought before him. These will be quoted in other papers, and in time the writer will publish them in a book, and the innocent Creeks will be involved in the universal execration with which persons of ordinary common sense will receive the book. The Creeks are entirely right in their refusal to permit newspapers to exist in their Territory. If they really want to read the news, they can subscribe for St. Louis, or Chicago, or New-York newspapers. If they are judicious in their selection, they can read these without injury. For them to bring editors into their own towns and permit them to write daily libels and indulge in daily "difficulties," is as unnecessary as it would be foolish and unpardonable.

ᗗ Politics Run Mad

July 8, 1876

The grief which all true-hearted men must feel at the death of the gallant Custer and his band is mixed with indignation at the use made of this tragic affair by a besotted partisan press. As soon as the dreadful news is received in the *World* office that sheet goes into hysterical convulsions. The instant question with it is, how can this be made to help in the election? The frantic editor executes a war-dance, and shaking the gory scalps of the dead soldiers at the Republican Party, shrieks "Vote for Tilden and Reform!" We venture to say that no such monstrous violation of public decency was ever before witnessed in American politics. The Sioux, bloody and vindictive though they are, have never yet touched the depth sounded by the *World*, which parades the streets beating a tattoo on the coffins of the dead, and calling on all men to vote the Democratic ticket. With dishonorable perversion of the truth, the *World* says that if Custer "had retained his command of the Big Horn expedition, taken from him to punish him for his testimony before Clymer's committee," he would be yet alive and victorious. It is time that this falsehood concerning the command of the expedition, now many times repeated, was set at rest. Gen. Custer was never in command of the Big Horn expedition. There was never any intention, so far as can be ascertained, that he should have been; and there were abundant excellent military reasons why he could not have been at the head of the army thus employed. Two military departments co-operated in the organization of the Big Horn expedition and the execution of its work. These departments were that of Dakota, Gen. Terry commanding, and that of the Platte, Gen. Crook in command. There were, then, two regular Brigadier Generals in the field, of whom Terry outranked the other. Third in rank came Gibbon, who is Colonel of the Seventh Infantry. Custer, fourth in rank, was Lieutenant Colonel of the Seventh Cavalry, which he commanded at the time, his

Colonel, Sturgis, being absent. In their haste to make a point against the Administration, Democratic papers charge that Custer was killed because he was not in command of the expedition, and that he would have been in command if he had not incurred the displeasure of the President by testifying against Belknap. The malignant absurdity of this charge breaks it down. It is a pure invention and if it were not, it would force the conclusion that Terry, Crook, and Gibbon were parties to a conspiracy which brought the three hundred to their doom.

Mr. S. S. Cox, who might be supposed to have a modicum of common sense, arises in the House and childishly shrieks, "Where are your twenty-five thousand men?" And he wants to know why some of them are not "released from the throat of the South" and sent to join "the two thousand who are fighting the Sioux." This is bald nonsense. Mr. Cox has, or ought to have, in his desk the reports of Gen. Sherman and Adjutant General Townsend, which show where those twenty-five thousand men are. He knows, or ought to know, that there are less than eighteen thousand men, including the medical staff, musicians, and officers of every rank, in the entire Military Division of the South. This is less than the force now occupying similar posts in the Division of the Atlantic, commanded by Gen. Hancock, and embracing the North Atlantic coast and the Lakes. In the Division of the Missouri, Gen. Sheridan commanding, are about fifteen thousand of the twenty-five thousand men. The rest are scattered over the enormous territory west of the Rocky Mountains, from Alaska to Arizona. More than three-fifths of our little Army are west of the Mississippi; and more than one-fourth of the whole force (or exactly 6,284) is in the Departments of Dakota and the Platte. Gen. Sheridan, in his late report, says: "The Military Division of the Missouri embraces within its limits ninety-nine Indian tribes, numbering about 192,000 persons scattered over more than one million square miles of frontier territory." The commanding Generals in the several departments do the best they can with their small force—small, compared with the extent of the territory to be kept in order. But the persistent policy of the present Democratic House of Representatives has been to cripple the Army by cheese-paring frugality. They have struck at everything, from the forts in the Indian Territory to the rations of the lads at West Point. Then, when some terrible disaster, like the Montana massacre, falls upon the nation, they bawl, "Where are your twenty-five thousand men?" We have just shown where they are; and it is an insult to common intelligence for Mr. Cox, or anybody else, to prate about their being "at the throat of the South."

It is an ungracious duty to recall any personal qualities of Gen. Custer that may have precipitated the disaster which has ended his career. But it should be observed that "the sneaking innuendoes concerning his supposed rashness," which the *World* charges to the account of "leaders of Republican opinion," come from his brother officers. No military man ever charged Custer with conservatism, hesitation, excessive deference to the opinion of others, or unwillingness to "go in and win." Probably the *Sun*, which may be most fully acquitted of being a leader of Republican opinion, puts the case fairly when it says: "He meant to fight before Terry came up; to fight alone, and alone win a great battle and harvest the glory of a victory which should put an end to Sioux warfare. It was a great stake, gallantly but madly played for, and ruinously lost. The dashing cavalryman, charming gentleman, and accomplished scholar paid his life and the lives of his male relatives, and the lives of over three hundred of the best soldiers in the Army, as the penalty of his rash ambition." It is too late now to curiously inquire into the motives which led the gallant cavalryman to rush into the imminent deadly breach. Long will he be remembered as a brave soldier, a courteous gentleman, and a sterling patriot. Over his grave let the voices of criticism and partisan malice alike be hushed. Let the dead rest. The duty of the living is to strengthen those who remain. The problem of the government of wild and lawless tribes is not yet solved. A tragical experience has once more showed that the military arm cannot be weakened, nor the armed posts on the frontier be abandoned, while a single tribe remains nomadic and uncivilized. Least of all, will the nation endure with patience the partisans who seize upon such a calamity as this to wrest this melancholy lesson to their own petty and selfish purposes?

Extermination

July 12, 1876

The repulse of Crook, the defeat of Reno, and the slaughter of Custer and his men have profoundly stirred the nation. It is natural that we should smart under the victories of a foe whom we had despised. It is right that we should mourn with the sincerest sorrow the gallant men who died with the dauntless Custer. It is even desirable that our defeats should impel us to wage war in the sharp, vigorous manner which is the truest mercy to friend and foe. But it is neither just nor decent that a Christian nation should yield itself to homicidal frenzy, and clamor for the instant extermination of the savages by whose unexpected bravery we have been so sadly baffled.

All through the West there is manifested a wild desire for vengeance against the so-called murderers of our soldiers. The press echoes with more or less shamelessness the frontier theory that the only use to which an Indian can be put is to kill him. From all sides come denunciations of what is called in terms of ascending sarcasm, "the peace policy," "the Quaker policy," and "the Sunday-school policy." Volunteers are eagerly offering their services "to avenge Custer and exterminate the Sioux," and public opinion, not only in the West, but to some extent in the East, has apparently decided that the Indians have exhausted the forbearance of heaven and earth, and must now be exterminated as though they were so many mad dogs.

What is meant by "the Quaker policy" which is thus bitterly assailed? If it means anything, it means the policy of justice and humanity. Whatever may have been the faults of the present Administration, history will credit it with having at least made the attempt to treat the Indians fairly. Where we have become involved in war with the Modocs or the Sioux, the cause is to be found not in the maligned "Quaker policy," but in occasional acts of willful or ignorant injustice, which were so many deviations from the very policy to which the present Indian war is falsely imputed. We ordered the Modocs to remove to a barren reservation in Oregon, where they were in absolute danger of starvation. They left the reservation, preferring, as they expressed it, to die in battle in their own country rather than to starve in a strange and sterile land. The facts in the case have been fully set forth by Mr. Meacham, a man who bears the scars of Modoc rifle-bullets, but who still advocates the "Quaker policy," and who maintains that the Modoc war was in no possible sense the result of that policy. Neither was the Sioux war brought about by peace men, or Quakers, or Sunday-school sentimentalists. We bound ourselves by treaty with the Sioux to prevent white men from entering the Black Hills country, which we had ceded to them forever. We then sent Custer to explore the country at the head of a column of troops, and his report of the discovery of gold mines was followed by a rush of reckless gold-hunters. These acts, which were in direct violation of our solemn treaty obligations, were surely not the outgrowth of a peace policy. Custer's troopers were not Quakers, nor were the Black Hills miners Sunday-school superintendents. The one bright feature in this miserable business was the long forbearance of the savages to attack either the exploring expedition or the miners, and the loyal bearing of Young Man Afraid of His Horses, who at the council where the Sioux declined to sell a territory as large as the State of Michigan for fifty thousand dollars, saved the Commissioners from the massacre meditated by the wilder tribes. It was not until after we had failed to cajole the Sioux into a sale, and had openly abandoned all pretense of observing our treaty obligations, that the Indians attacked the miners, and with the aid of outlying clans like the band of Sitting Bull, renewed the fight of centuries against white aggression. This is the true and shameful origin of the Sioux war; and had the Quaker policy of justice been faithfully and intelligently carried out, neither the Modocs nor the Sioux would have been provoked into hostility.

If it is unreasonable to lay at the door of the peace policy results due strictly to deviations from it, there is a like lack of reason in the anger which styles Sitting Bull's recent victory a "fiendish massacre." Custer went out to beat the Sioux. Had he succeeded, would he have been guilty of a "fiendish massacre"? The soldier has blows to take as well as to give, and there is no justice in styling the defeat of an attacking force "a fiendish massacre," when its success would been called a glorious victory. We did not fancy that the Southern people deserved extermination because we were beaten at Bull Run, nor did the rebels call the defeat at Gettysburg a "fiendish massacre."

Over the border the Indians and the colonists live in peace. The peace policy which we have tried as a new thing—dropping it now and then through weariness or inadvertence—has there proved so complete a success that its wisdom is conclusively demonstrated. Is there a strange and baleful magic in the invisible boundary line, whereby the Indians who on the other side of it are peaceable and trustworthy, become on this side utterly treacherous and bloodthirsty? If not, there must be some mistake in the theory that extermination is the only policy which should be pursued toward the Indians of the United States.

We are now at war, and there is nothing left but to prosecute the struggle with the utmost rigor. Peace can be obtained only by the thorough defeat of the enemy, and for the moment any peace policy must necessarily be suspended. But we can wage war without displaying an unnecessary ferocity, more worthy of savages than of civilized men. We must beat the Sioux, but we need not exterminate them. And when the war is over it will be the duty of every humane man to demand that the peace policy which has made border warfare unknown in the vast Hudson Bay territory shall be made successful on our side of the line, in spite of the men who believe that the laws of God should be suspended in our relations with the Indians, and the dictates of humanity trampled under foot.

↶ Gentle Woman

October 14, 1879

The gentleness of woman is confessedly one of her greatest charms. Men are often rough, unfeeling and brutal, but women are full of tenderness and compassion. They cannot bear to witness, or even to hear, of acts of cruelty or oppression, and they are always ready to pardon and excuse the faults of the wicked and ignorant. If any one doubts the unvarying gentleness of women, he has only to read a letter written by Miss Rose Meeker, the daughter of the Indian Agent who was recently killed by the Utes.

The causes of the Ute war were chiefly these: In 1873 the Government bought a part of the Ute reservation, but until this day not a dollar of the purchase-money has ever been paid. Latterly, white men—miners and squatters—have overrun the reservation, greatly to the disgust of the Indians, who foresaw in this violation of the treaty stipulation the near approach of the day when they would be forcibly driven out of the reservation, as the Sioux were driven out of the Black Hills. In addition to these grievances, Mr. Meeker, the Agent, insisted upon plowing up the land of the Indians, because he was determined that they should abandon hunting for agriculture. When he finally sent for troops to assist him in thus forcibly civilizing the Utes, they began the war that was plainly inevitable by striking the first blow.

No one doubts that Mr. Meeker meant well, but his conduct was nevertheless the immediate cause which precipitated the outbreak. He was a professional philanthropist. He had been trained in early traditions of the *Tribune* office, and was one of the earliest and most prominent of the American Fourierites. It is the peculiarity of men of this type that they are prone to insist upon reforming other men by force. They are honestly anxious to do good, but they are determined to do good in their own way and in spite of the objections of those whom they propose to benefit. Mr. Meeker decided that it would be good for the Utes to become farmers, and having come to this decision, it was perfectly immaterial to him that the Utes preferred to live by hunting. Farmers they ought to be, in his opinion, and farmers they should be; so he plowed up their land with determined and aggressive benevolence, and called for troops to protect him in his violent philanthropy. Without desire to speak ill of a dead man, it must be said that Mr. Meeker's unlawful meddling cost him his life and plunged us into a war which might otherwise have been delayed for some time, and might even have been wholly averted, provided the Government should have suddenly resolved to pay its just debt and to respect its treaty obligations.

The gentle and truly womanly spirit in which Miss Meeker writes of the unhappy results of the way in which the Utes have been treated, is a conspicuous illustration of the noble qualities of her sex. She laments that "the cow-boys of Colorado" were not called upon instead of the slow-moving Government troops. Those gallant "cow-boys," she remarks, "would have made so clean a work of the red devils that it would have been hard to find one alive to-day." This, it is obvious, would have rendered a war with the Utes quite out of the question, since an enemy that has been exterminated by cow-boys is rarely in a position to subsequently fight regular troops. "The life of one common white man is worth more," continues Miss Meeker, "than all the Indians from the beginning of their creation until the present time." Of course it is. This is the reason why the "common white man," in the shape of a miner or a squatter, who has seized the land of an Indian, has a right to kill him and all the members of his tribe if the miserable red devils try to protect their property. They are, Miss Meeker assures us, "a savage foe, whose life or soul is not worthy of a dog." If this is true—and it would be rude to doubt the confident assertion of a gentle and Christian woman—it does seem as if our Lord must have made a mistake in dying for copper-colored souls "not worthy of a dog," and as if the Christian Church is wasting its efforts in trying to save so worthless a variety of soul. That the Government has done very wrong in not exterminating the red devils Miss Meeker is firmly convinced. She exclaims with gentle sarcasm, "What a magnanimous Government we have, to pamper a set of creatures whose existence should have been a thing of the past long ago." Perhaps the Government will do better hereafter, for Miss Meeker reminds it that "the blood of the martyred ones cries out for vengeance," and when vengeance can be executed in such a way as to result in escaping the payment of debts and securing a tract of desirable land, it has its manifest advantages.

The gentle, compassionate spirit of Miss Meeker is shared by many of her sex in the great free West. They overflow with pity for the white man who robs an Indian and is subsequently shot. Their eyes fill with sympathetic tears when they see a white man suffering from a knowledge of the fact that somewhere an Indian owns a valuable piece of land, and that, nevertheless, the Government has delayed to exterminate him. Of course, if these gentle women fancied for a moment that the Indian is a man, that God made him, that Christ died for him, and that at our hands will be required the blood of our red brother, they would transfer a little of their sympathy to him. They have lived, however, too long in the gallant West not to know that all this sort of talk is sickening cant. The Indian is not a man. He has only an apology for a soul—a sort of canine substitute therefor—and his only right is the right to be exterminated. He is a red devil, and the life of one drunken white scoundrel, who robs and murders red devils without compunction, "is worth more than all the Indians from the beginning of their creation until the present time." It is a fact beyond contradiction that the vast majority of men and women in the Western States hold these theories concerning the Indians, and so far as they can put them in practice, do so gladly.

Is there any God; any truth in the Christian religion; any future where injustice and brutality are punished? If there is, will not the ignorant Ute plead at the final bar with more success than the Christian advocate of Indian extermination?

✍ The Indian Bureau Troubles

January 16, 1880

If the Secretary of the Interior and the Commissioner of Indian Affairs would read carefully the comments of *The Times* on the troubles of the Indian Bureau, they would find that their criticism of those comments is based upon misrepresentation. The Secretary of the Interior, especially, makes objection to statements which have never appeared in these columns. For example, he assumes that "it was said that Mr. Hayt instigated the investigation into the administration of his predecessor for the purpose of securing his place." No such statement, or anything like it, was ever made in *The Times*. What we did say was that "Mr. Hayt went into the place made vacant in consequence of the investigation which he demanded." This is a very different thing from "instigating" an investigation, and it is difficult to see how a reference to the undeniable fact that Mr. Hayt succeeded a man who had been investigated out of place can be construed to mean that that investigation was the weapon by which Mr. Hayt drove Mr. Smith out of office. Neither has anybody, so far as we know, even intimated that Mr. Hayt was a candidate for the place when the investigation took place. The Secretary's denial of this candidacy is, therefore, superfluous. Nor is there any apparent reason why the Secretary should say that the statement that Mr. Hayt was a member of the Board of Indian Commissioners when the investigation took place is "erroneous." What *The Times* said was that Mr. Hayt, "as a member of that board, was active in pressing charges against Commissioner Smith." And this is exactly true. Mr. Hayt, while a member of the board, as the newspaper files of that day will show, did press charges against Commissioner Smith. It does not matter whether the investigation which took place, subsequently, when Mr. Hayt had left the board, was the result of the charges being thus pressed, or of the sanitary measures which the Secretary now says he adopted of his own motion. The fact was that Mr. Hayt was in the board when the charges against the Commissioner originated, that he left it before the investigation began, and that he was appointed to the place made vacant by the Commissioner's displacement.

As for the fairness of the tribunal before which the allegations brought by Gen. Fisk are to be maintained or dismissed, it is hardly necessary to multiply words. One of the members of the committee appointed to examine those charges has publicly denied that the Board of Indian Commissioners have any right or duty in the premises. And this, too, in the face of the fact that the law explicitly declares that they shall supervise all expenditures for the benefit of the Indians in the United States. And this Commissioner, having reluctantly consented to have this duty thrust upon him, adds that he will proceed to examine one charge—that of the Arizona mining business. That is to say, having been forced into the work of investigation, the board will take up only one of the numerous allegations made against Mr. Hayt, and that one the least important of all that have been named. After such an exhibition of partiality, is it surprising that men should say that the investigation, if made at all, would be a farce? In another place the Secretary says "that the statement that one of the members of the board was appointed through the influence of Mr. Hayt is incorrect." In *The Times* it was said that this gentleman "owes his place on the board to the recommendation of the Secretary of the Interior (otherwise Hayt.)" Since the Secretary disclaims being influenced by Commissioner Hayt in this matter, it would be desirable to know how it happens that an appointment which, according to law, is to be made "by the President, solely," was inspired from the interior of the Interior Department.

Commissioner Hayt must settle with Gen. Fisk in his own way. The publication of Gen. Fisk's charges was an unfair piece of business, so far as the Commissioner is concerned. But it should also be borne in mind that these charges are not new, nor do they originate with Gen. Fisk. They have appeared, from time to time, in a variety of ways, and from quarters of varying responsibility. For the first time they are gathered up and presented in an official form. Their publication, especially in their diffuse shape, is open to criticism. But it should be said that Gen. Fisk's reputation for those special qualities which the statute exacts of the members of the Board of Indian Commissioners is somewhat higher than Commissioner Hayt's reputation for official fitness. As for the complaint of the Secretary, in the Commissioner's behalf, that Mr. Hayt is made responsible for the failure to supply the Utes in 1877, it may be said that no adequate explanation of that unhappy business has ever been made. The Secretary says that this failure was chargeable to a contractor, and that after the contractor had failed, Mr. Hayt, who had just come into office, was not able to send forward the supplies, owing to the heavy snows which then covered the range. Mr. Hayt, it seems, went into office on Sept. 29 or 30. The failure of the contractor had already detained the supplies. But, as every man familiar with the character of the country of the Utes very well knows, there was no snowfall to make the roads impassable until long after that date. The Indians were able to come over for their provisions, which were not given them, as they were then under lock and key in a storehouse, impossible to be got at, although the Indians to whom they belonged were starving. The Secretary asks if it is likely that the starvation of the Winter of 1877–8 had anything to do with the outbreak of the Summer of 1879. Perhaps not. It is possible that an Indian's memory will not retain his sense of suffering and wrong from one year to another; but it is not likely. However, this is only one of numerous wrongs of which the Utes have "just cause of complaint." No satisfactory explanation of the failure to pay them the annuity due them has ever been made. Although the law says that this annuity shall be paid "annually forever," the yearly income from the trust funds has not been paid; and when the Senate asked, the other day, for an accounting of this money, it came out that it was an unproductive balance due, and this, too, in the face of the law, which says that the income of the funds shall be "expended or invested." When the Indian Bureau has explained matters of such grave importance as this, it will be time to dispute about non-essentials.

ᴄᴐ Missouri Missionaries

February 17, 1880

There is an easily recognizable flavor of the "manifest destiny" doctrine in all that the Western newspapers have to say about the proposed invasion of the Indian Territory. Congress is busy with various bills to open the Territory to settlement, it being expressly agreed that the Indians must first consent to any distribution of the lands. The President solemnly warns trespassers against entering the Territory. But the so-called invaders are very much in earnest. A Memphis paper, for example, says that, after waiting for many years for Congress to do something, "the people have resolved to settle this question for themselves." If the civilized Indians who own the lands object, the visitors will settle them, also. And these exceedingly energetic patriots declare that they are "determined to know whether a Chinese wall can anywhere exist on this continent to bar or stay American progress." Certainly not; if there is anything in the history of the United States which proves that a free-born American citizen does not take whatever he wants (when an Indian has it) we have not yet found it. Another organ of the children of manifest destiny, printed in Kansas City, makes liberal use of the English language in this fashion: "Nine months ago there was awakened in the restless bosom of those hardy pioneers who have peopled the four great States which embrace the Indian Territory a fitful fever of desire, which almost led to the permanent occupation of the fair land which is theirs by birthright." The writer goes on to say that "menacing soldiery and pompous proclamations" deterred the hardy pioneers, but now a new fever of unrest has seized the hardy pioneers, and that ten thousand men are ready to grasp the afore-said birthright, "by right if they can, and by might if they must." But they will grasp it, anyhow.

All this is so thoroughly in consonance with the spirit of the American people, in regard to the treatment of the Indians, that no reader can fail to recognize the sentiment embodied in the rhetoric. Hitherto "menacing sol-diery and pompous proclamations" have circumscribed the area of Freedom, and men who desire, as one of the Kansas papers declares, to dot the hill-sides of the Indian Territory with churches and school-houses, have not had half a chance in their missionary work. With an obstinacy which is galling to the child of destiny, the Government of the United States has, up to the present time, respected the right of the Cherokees, Choctaws, Chickasaws, Creeks, and Seminoles to the land which the Government sold them. There is really no excuse for this. To be sure, the fee simple of the lands was conveyed to these five tribes, and the bargain was confirmed by a solemn treaty or contract. But has not the Government of the Republic re-peatedly torn up treaties, as so much waste paper, whenever these have stood in the way of getting possession of the Indians' land? The invading patriots very properly say that the lands of the Indian Territory are theirs by birthright. All the land within the limits of the United States is theirs by the same token. Why don't they move into Iowa, where a few thousand farm-ers have managed to get possession of large tracts of "birthright" lands, which they hold under a ridiculous law of the United States which gives every man of them a homestead of 160 acres, if he will live on it. Is the area of freedom to be barred from the fertile fields of Iowa by an absurd statute which makes no provision for dotting hill-sides with churches and school-houses in the manner proposed for the Indian Territory by the church-going and scholarly Missourians? Let us hope not. And, when manifest destiny has begun to make itself felt in this pervasive and invasive manner, why should it stop inside of the limits of our own happy and free Republic? One of the able journals from which we have quoted expressly says that the boundless continent is ours. That "fitful fever of desire," which is reckoned such a com-mendable inspiration when it leads to the grabbing of another man's land, ought to take a portion of our fellow-citizens into Mexico, where there is a notorious scarcity of good government, churches, and school-houses. And another portion may as well try a similar invasion of Canada. The Canadi-ans might be surprised by the visit. But they should be taught what manifest destiny really is.

The records of prisons and the courts show to what "a fitful fever of desire" will sometimes lead one. A noble gentleman, who had a fitful fever of desire for Mr. Rufus W. Simpson's silver spoons, is now cruelly incarcerated in the Auburn Penitentiary; and an honest young woman who was actuated by a similar fitful fever of desire for Joseph Large's savings, $77 in all, has just been sent to the Penitentiary for a year. These sufferers do not seem to have pleaded that they were in pursuit of their "birthright," or that they had a bad spell of the fitful fever of desire, such as that which now agitates the honest yeomanry of Missouri and Kansas. It is urged that the civilized tribes of the Indian Territory do not use all the land which they own; and that if they will not sell their superfluous acres, they must be invaded. This is the true American spirit. If a man does not employ his wealth, let him be compelled to give up a part of it. We could point out several rich men in this City who have more money than they really need—more than they can use. Let the Missouri patriots move on them. Manifest destiny should require an equal division of all kinds of property, if we concede the distribution of land. The Government should heed this demand for the extension of the area of freedom, churches, and school-houses. We have become thoroughly accustomed to the robbing of Indians. This is no time to forswear theft and live honestly.

⮌ Indians and Skunks

February 18, 1881

The Legislature of Colorado has under consideration a bill "for the destruction of Indians and skunks." This bill was introduced in the House a few weeks since by Representative Coulter, of Clear Creek, and was reported to a special committee, of which Mr. Coulter was made Chairman. Subsequently, it was reported back to the House with a recommendation that it should pass. An official copy of the bill, duly stamped with all the marks employed to give authenticity to the document, would have been needed to show that the law-makers of Colorado have actually considered this extraordinary proposition. As legislators, even in the free and untrammeled West, are not so confirmed practical jokers as to print and refer bills which are introduced only "for fun," we must believe that the proposition of the gentle Coulter was made in good faith, and that it has been favorably considered by the Legislature of Colorado. To class Indians and skunks together is the habit of the free and boundless West. Only the sickly sentimentalists of the East demur at such a classification. It is in Colorado that people offer bounties for Indian scalps, meeting the savages on their own ground, as it were. A policy which presupposes that the Indian is a human being is stigmatized as "Boston philanthropy."

Senator Teller represents in Congress the Colorado idea. He is a believer in the truth of the saying that all the good Indians are dead. His colleague, Senator Hill, is troubled with weak human sympathies. He is not in favor of an extermination of the Indians. And a Colorado paper lately complained of him that he represents New-England, and has been, in consequence, "a fraud upon Colorado." And it was added: "He is a nice man, but he don't boldly take high Colorado ground." We are glad to know what high Colorado ground really is. It is a ground on which the Indian and the skunk meet on a common level. The genial Coulter, who represents the true Colorado sentiment, says in the preamble to his bill that the Utes have made several unjust discriminations in their predatory incursions and murders, and that Secretary Schurz is a monument of the friendly consideration of the red man. In the same preamble it is provided that "prosperity may follow in the wake of the pioneers, until every nook in the far West is settled by happy and thriving communities, and that every representative of the Ute family and the red man at large may become good Indians." That is to say, as the Indians have only killed those who have attempted to exterminate them, they should themselves be exterminated, in order that there should be peace and prosperity in the land.

The Colorado idea, according to Mr. Coulter, is that a bounty of $25 should be offered for Indian and skunk scalps, which bounty shall be paid out of the State Treasury on the presentation "of such scalp, or scalps, with the ears entire," together with an affidavit setting forth the needful facts in the case. The sentimentalists of the East, we apprehend, will regard this bill (which has been favorably reported upon in the Colorado Legislature) as cowardly and inhuman. There is a prejudice among our effete and sentimental people in favor of bravery, humanity, and justice. This, of course, is a weakness which characterizes only highly conservative and unprogressive communities. In the free and boundless West where the people are not fettered by traditions, nor swayed by considerations of sickly sentimentality, it is the custom of the country to class Indians with vermin, both of which are to be exterminated. And an enlightened Legislature, in order that the far

West may be settled by happy and thriving communities, is asked to authorize the State of Colorado to pay a bounty of $25 for each scalp of Indian or
skunk, "with ears attached," which may be offered by any lover of civilization, humanity, and progress.

It is barely possible that the Colorado Legislature, forgetting for a moment that dignity and decorum which usually characterizes the law-mak-
ing power of the State, has lent itself to a practical joke. Possibly, Coulter,
whoever he may be, has been permitted to air his own personal notions at
the public expense. And it may be that when Senator Hill is rated because he
does not occupy "high Colorado ground," but New-England sentimental-
ism, he is the subject of a playful jest. But, since Senator Teller, and other
representatives of Colorado opinion, do insist that the good Indians are dead
Indians, we are forbidden to entertain the belief that Coulter is a joker, and
that the Colorado Legislature is accessory to the joke. The Centennial State,
as it proudly calls itself, has the exclusive honor of proposing to offer a
bounty on the scalps of skunks and Indians. But it should be borne in mind
by these complacent legislators, who have just driven from their own lands
the aborigines whom they have goaded into reprisals, that two can play at
the game of scalp-hunting. Providence, in its inscrutable wisdom, has invented Indians, skunks, and Coulter. These seem to be at war with each
other. An impartial public, in favor of nothing but fair play, waits to see which
of the three natural antagonists shall first lose his scalp.

↫ A Difficult Question

September 20, 1881

The renowned chief Sitting Bull has lately sent a message to a civilized
Dakota Indian employed by the Government to assist in taking a census of
the outlying tribes. The sum and substance of his defense—for he defends
himself—is that he and his people were brought up to hunt and to live a wandering and roving life, and that, while hunting for game, he was constantly
interfered with and made to feel the sharpness of the white man's steel. Sitting Bull says that he never made war against white men, or, at least, he never
initiated war. He pleads thus: "While I was looking for buffalo they would
attack and shoot at me, and, of course, I had to defend myself, or else I
should die. But all the blame is put on me." We do not pretend to say how

much of this is sophistry, dishonesty, or special pleading. But it is the Indian's way of looking at the case. We cannot believe that there is only one side to the dispute. It is not possible that Sitting Bull should regard what we call "the Indian problem" from the same point which we do.

The Utes have recently been removed from the reservation in Colorado, the pressure of public opinion being too great to permit their being longer continued on their old lands. The country to which they have been taken is to them a foreign and inhospitable region. Whatever may have been the motives excited in the minds of their leaders, whatever the arguments brought to bear upon the men who signed the treaty, it cannot be denied that the main body of the Utes knew nothing of what was being done, and that their consent to the transfer was never intelligently given. No matter, in one way or another, the legal point was secured, and, although there was manifested a desire on the part of the Utes to recall the treaty, and a passionate declaration that the tribe had been "sold out," the bargain could not be re-opened. A newspaper called the *Solid Muldoon*, published at Ouray, Col., lately announced that a Vigilance Committee had been formed for the purpose of hastening the flight of the Utes. This admirable exponent of border civilization said: "The Vigilantes are determined that the Utes, both white and red, must go." The *Solid Muldoon* considers men who have a feeling of commiseration for the Indians as no better than a Ute, barring the color of his skin. And the same journal reports that an agent of the United States Government was lately scared out of Ouray by the Vigilance Committee for his "damnable and persistent lying on behalf of the Utes." It is not safe, in Colorado, for a man to set up the ridiculous pretense that Indians have any rights.

We have heard how, when these expatriated people were finally deported from their lands, they passed the last night of their sojourn in their homes with lamentations and weeping. The women kissed the ground in an agony of grief, and they wept over the graves of their parents and children just as though they were human beings gifted with the common feelings of humanity. Even in the night, while these scenes were witnessed in the old homes of the Indians, crowds of white settlers were hungrily hanging about the boundaries of the reservation, kept back by the muskets of the military guard detailed to escort the Utes to their new habitations. As the exiled red men moved off their reservation the avaricious settlers crowded in after them, and, as the last Indian disappeared westward, the valley behind him bristled with the stakes driven by quarreling white men. What will become of these nomadic and semi-barbarous people, thus forcibly deported to a country which yields them no supplies, it is impossible to say.

Something like this was once the lot of the Apaches, a warlike tribe, many years ago. The sub-divisions of this once powerful people were driven asunder, and the different bands were settled on reservations. They were, to all intents and purposes, a captive race, imprisoned on carefully guarded tracts of land. They had fought like Sitting Bull's people, and they had finally been driven into a corner, as the Utes have since been, from time to time. The Apaches are like wild beasts. They chafe under restraint, and they break loose and ravage whenever they find opportunity. Some of the Apaches at the Mescaleros Agency were concerned in the killing and robbery of a company of railway engineers and of a party of travelers by stage just over the Mexican boundary line. They were reported to be "out on leave" from the agent. Other Apaches, from the San Carlos Agency, in Arizona, are known to have participated in the attack on Gen. Carr's command. Against this hostile band three separate companies of military are now moving. The white settlers have armed themselves, and they have sent word to the San Carlos agent that Indians from his reservation will be killed at sight, no matter what warrant from the agent they may bear. The agent is reported to be in distress because some of the absentees are peaceable Indians to whom leave of absence has been given as a deserved favor. It is difficult to see where this indiscriminate warfare will end. But the facts here hastily reviewed indicate two things: The Indian problem is a difficult one; the only solution in the sight of the average American citizen is the extermination of the aboriginal race.

ᔐ Secretary Teller's Indian Policy

April 29, 1882

It would be a matter for regret if Mr. Teller, who has lately been installed Secretary of the Interior, should prove to be an exponent of the extreme Western idea in relation to the treatment of the Indians. There should be no essential difference betwixt Eastern and Western notions concerning this subject. As a matter of fact, however, many Eastern publicists, notably those of New-England, hold to original and somewhat impracticable theories relative to the course which the Government should pursue toward the aborigines. And, on the other hand, the Western men cherish views which are not only antagonistic to the philanthropic notions of Massachusetts, but are colored by hostility to the Indians themselves. The Eastern theorists seem to think that the Indian is never wrong; they of the West believe that the Indian is never right, and that he has no rights. Doubtless, we shall find truth and justice somewhere betwixt these extremes. But any compromise of views is impossible so long as Secretary Teller believes, as he is reported as saying he does believe, that the Eastern people "are utterly incapable of presenting any practicable plan for the civilization of the Indian." With equal propriety it might be said that ex-Senator Teller's constituents are incapable of presenting any plan for the civilization of the Indian that does not practically involve his extermination.

The interview from which we have just quoted was between Secretary Teller and the editor of the *Council Fire*, a journal especially devoted to the interests of the Indians. Being asked to define his policy, Mr. Teller replied that that could be summed up in the single phrase, "absolute justice, both to the Indian and the white man." This is, to be sure, a vague generality, but if the Indians should receive absolute justice they would have what has never been given them since the foundation of the Government of this Republic. What constitutes justice to the red man, according to the opinion of a citizen of Colorado, for example, is so very different from the opinion formed in the mind of a New-Englander that we should despair of ever reconciling the two. Descending to particulars, Secretary Teller is opposed to allotting lands in severalty to the Indians until they are "ready" for this radical change. He would have them hold their lands in common until they are taught some of the rudiments of agriculture, and are themselves desirous of owning their lands in severalty. Mr. Teller says that he does not think much of the plan of bringing Indian youths to the Hampton and Carlisle schools to be educated. He would have schools established at the agencies, and have the common branches of education there maintained. The instruction at Hampton and Carlisle, evidently, the Secretary considers too high for the Indians. "Practical industry is a great civilizer," says the Secretary with much force and aptness.

It is admitted on all sides, we may assume, that the Indian must be civilized before "the problem" of which he is the chief factor can be solved. The Western notion is unalterably determined against any allotment of lands to Indians in severalty. Secretary Teller's honest conviction in this matter fairly represents Western opinion in this respect. Other Western men, not so honest as the Secretary of the Interior, oppose the allotment plan because it makes impossible any further removal of the Indians. When the red man has secured his homestead he has acquired a stake in the land from which he cannot be driven. When he holds a tract of land in his own name, no man can lawfully demand that he shall move on further West. While the Indians are situated on reservations there is no treaty, no agreement, however solemnly executed, under which he can demand and secure any right to stay. This is the marrow of the whole matter. The Indians never will be civilized until they are secure in their landed rights. They never will be secure in those rights as long as they hold their lands in common, under treaties liable to be revised or abrogated by the Government of the United States. The history of the Indians in this country is a wearisome repetition of removals of tribes from point to point, each remove taking them further toward the sunset. The names of the tribes in the far West are identified with the early history of the Atlantic States. These tribes have been dragged, against their will, from one reservation to another, until their original nomadic habits may be said to have been confirmed and approved by the action of the Government. How can habits of industry be expected of a people who are taught that they are paupers to be fed and clothed by the Government? How can any people that are liable to be removed to-morrow from the lands they occupy to-day be expected to build houses, plant fields, and improve the lands they hold by a feeble tenure? If the Indian is not ready now to own his land, by himself and for himself, when will he be? Will he ever be, as long as he knows that he may be evicted at any time?

These are practical questions. We should be glad to see them answered by some competent authority. It may be said that the roving, lawless, lazy, and shiftless Indians of the present day would starve, or would ridiculously fail, if left to take care of themselves on their homesteads. To Secretary Teller's mind, probably, there is no middle ground betwixt an Indian penned into a reservation, where he is fed and clothed by the Government and encouraged to learn the arts of peace, and the Indian ignorantly perishing on a homestead that he cannot make available for his needs. There is, however, a situation between these and better than either. When the Indian is placed upon a reservation in which he is secure from molestation and secure from expulsion, he will be ready for civilization, and not until then. If the new Secretary of the Interior can invent some plan that will accomplish this, he will do what has not been done since the foundation of the Republic. Until this is possible the allotment of lands in severalty, the practical education of Indian youths, and judicious assistance from the Government seem to be the only hopeful means for accomplishment of the desired end. We confess that Interior Department views and Interior Department practices toward "the wards of the Nation" have usually been chaotic and irreconcilable. Let us hope that Secretary Teller has a practicable and consistent policy to unfold.

⌐ Mr. Welsh on the Indian Outbreak

March 29, 1891

Mr. Herbert Welsh contributes to the April number of *Scribner's Magazine* an article on "The Meaning of the Dakota Outbreak," which may be read with interest and profit by every American who wishes to know the truth regarding the present condition of the Indian question. The reputation of Mr. Welsh for candor and care in statement, the unusual opportunities he has had for informing himself in detail as to the recent facts in the history of the Indians, the unselfish devotion he has shown in the work of improving their condition, and the impartiality that he manifests in his comments, must give weight to this well-considered and very temperate paper. It is now about nine years since he entered earnestly on the study of the Indian problem, during which time he says: "While conducting the work of the Indian Rights Association I have three times visited the Sioux of Dakota, traveling on horseback or by wagon through all parts of the reservation, camping out at night, or receiving the hospitality of army officers, civil agents, missionaries—both white and native—and of Indians. I have also paid three visits to the Navajos and Pueblos of New-Mexico and Arizona, and one to the Apaches of the latter Territory." This indicates in brief the scope of his observations and the means he has possessed of getting at the truth.

The most important and significant fact brought out by Mr. Welsh, and one, we take it, that will be new to most of his readers, is the existence of a very considerable party among the Sioux, and in other tribes as well, who earnestly desire the civilization of their race, and who are doing all that they can to bring it about. Mr. Welsh terms them "a new progressive and what may properly be termed Christian party, whose life was begotten, nourished, and trained by missionary enterprise and devotion. As an example of the Indians of this class Mr. Welsh cites the Santee Sioux, a tribe of some 700, who, less than thirty years ago, "took a prominent part in the Minnesota massacre, but having passed through many vicissitudes and sufferings for their share in the uprising, are to-day among the most peaceable and industrious Indians to be found in the country," having "become citizens of the United States," owning "their own land in severalty, while their unused lands have been opened up to white settlement." Mr. Welsh does not give any complete estimate of the strength of the "new" party among the Indians, though he states that "from 7,000 to 8,000 (out of 28,000 in all) are counted as attendants upon the Episcopal Church," having been brought under the influence of the great work conducted by Bishop Hare of that denomination. He points out that there are necessarily great differences among the Indians who have been turned toward civilization from "the man from whose face the paint has just been washed . . . whose hair is still plaited, and into whose darkened mind have fallen the first faint gleams of desire for the 'new way'" to the "ripest fruit of Indian civilization," the native minister or physician, the graduate of an Eastern college, whose wife, perhaps, is a white woman, whose habits of thought and whose manners are those of a gentleman, and who stands on equal terms with the rest of the world." "And yet," he concludes, "in all this diversity to be found in the progressive party among the Sioux is clearly shown one controlling principle—an awakened moral purpose, new-born or well developed, the stirring of an enlightened conscience and of a long-dormant intellect."

This fact, as we have said, is important and significant. Here is a force ready to the hands of the Government that has the wisdom and strength to use it, sufficient gradually but surely to overcome the barbarism of the rest of the Indians. The recent outbreak gives ample support to this statement. It was caused in part by an access [sic] of religious fanaticism among the savage party of the Sioux under the lead chiefly of Sitting Bull, and partly by the mismanagement of the Indian agents, and of these causes the latter is perfectly easy to remove. At Standing Rock Agency, where the agent, Major McLaughlin, was a man of experience, capacity, and character, the "storm was faced with firmness and success." At Pine Ridge, where the agent had been changed for political reasons by Mr. Harrison, as had also been done before by Mr. Cleveland, the Indians were literally starved into fighting, and there was nothing for it but to subdue them by force. Here, then, is the key to the situation. If the Government will take the Indian service out of politics, if it will appoint agents only for carefully-tested fitness and retain them so long as they perform their duty well, there will be no insuperable difficulty in not only preventing Indian outbreaks, but in gradually extending the number and influence of the progressive party until the "Indian problem" is solved. We do not say that this will be a rapid or an easy process. We do say that it will be entirely practicable to perform it. For, with a body of intelligent and capable agents in charge of the immediate dealings with the Indians, Congress can be brought to a sense of its duty and induced to live up to the spirit of the engagements the Nation has assumed. Above all, that force in the Indian race itself, which has been shown to exist and to be capable of steady growth, will every year make the task easier.

10 Corruption

> It is strange that the Interior Department knows nothing
> about a lease of three million acres of the Crow Indian Reser-
> vation in Montana by "a syndicate of Colorado capitalists" for
> one cent an acre, especially when it is remembered that Mr.
> Teller has a large acquaintance in Colorado, and when it is
> said that the negotiators of the lease were Indian agents.
>
> —*New York Times*
> December 18, 1884

C HARGE IT TO THE INDIANS," according to the *Times*, was a motto among
people on the frontier. It meant that claims for settlers' losses, if
charged to the Indians, would be paid by the government with funds withheld from the Indians' annuities. This was one simple example of the way
government policies worked to reward virtually everyone else at the expense
of the Native Americans.

No other single facet of the Indian problem received as much notice on
the editorial pages of the *Times* as did corruption. The newspaper unearthed
and exposed corruption in the Indian service at every level of government,
from the president down. It scorned crooked agents and lashed out at dishonest traders and contractors. It disclosed to public scrutiny the unscrupulous practices of land speculators and developers and the scandalous
devices settlers used—often through government policies—to take advantage of uninformed Indians.

In a May 1867 editorial that became a litany of injustices claimed by Chief
Satanta of the Kiowas, the *Times* noted that it was the government's practice to withhold money from annuities due a tribe to pay for offenses committed by individuals of the tribe. And settlers, it added, might trump up all
kinds of charges against the Indians, to be paid by the government. Live-

stock killed by wolves, barns struck by lightning, or rail fences consumed by prairie fires might be charged to the government as Indian depredations. "Were such trickery practiced upon us," the *Times* concluded, "would we not be apt to retaliate?" But day in and day out, it was the government that the *Times* targeted for most of its wrath. Individuals who cheated the Indians under cover of government sanction would get no mercy from the editorial writers of the *Times*.

In the view of the *Times*, government agencies, from the top down, made corruption easy. It waged a permanent battle for reform. One reason the newspaper generally approved the performance of the army in regard to the Indian problem was that it seldom saw instances of corruption within the military establishment. When General Phil Sheridan suggested that the army should be given full charge of Indian affairs, the *Times* agreed. The idea was not new, it said in a November 1875 editorial, and it was in many regards a good one. It argued that the army officers were the best administrators of Indian policy the government had, because they were not corrupt. But the *Times* expressed doubt that politicians ever would approve an extensive transfer of "the Indian business" to the army. They had not been willing to reform the civil service system, it noted, and "they will not abandon patronage by employing the good military servants we already have."

The *Times* applauded President Ulysses S. Grant's policy of drawing Indian agents from religious bodies such as the Quakers. At the same time, it challenged the efforts of a clique of Western senators to gain control over agents' nominations. "Since our Indian Agents are so wretchedly underpaid, we may well inquire what there is in these offices which makes Western Senators so anxious to have them at their disposal," it teased in a March 1876 editorial. Then it went on to speculate that the appeal of Indian agent posts stemmed principally from the opportunities they offered for unscrupulous agents to profit at the Indians' expense. The editorial writers knew, of course, that the agency ranks were filled with unprincipled persons who had made substantial amounts of money by cheating the Indians and the government alike. The agents were receiving and disbursing officers who handled large sums of money and immense quantities of supplies, as well as awarding contracts; the system encouraged fraud.

Another action of the Grant Administration for which the *Times* held high hopes was the creation of a Board of Indian Commissioners, appointed by the president. The board was intended as an oversight body that would observe the work of the Commissioner of Indian Affairs and scrutinize the expenditure of money appropriated for the Indians. But in practice, the *Times* claimed in a shrewd editorial in January 1880, the board had become "a Greek chorus, which comes to the front of the stage, explaining and commending all that has been done." The *Times* found plenty in the work of the Indian commissioner that needed oversight. When Interior Secretary Carl Schurz called on the board to conduct a thorough investigation of the management of Indian affairs, beginning with the Indian Bureau in Washington and working through every agency in the nation, the *Times* predicted the undertaking would bring to light "another Indian scandal." It was right. The investigation revealed serious corruption and resulted in the dismissal of the Commissioner of Indian Affairs.

The *Times* campaigned for years against the brazen invasion of Indian lands by speculators. In most instances, however, it found little inclination on the part of government authorities to take action against such abuses. Still, the newspaper took issue with one marauder who ventured an opinion that the government had neither the will nor the legal grounds to keep him and his followers from taking up squatting rights in the Indian Territory. Since Congress had welcomed the railroads into the territory, the land raider speculated, private settlers would not be kept out. This, declared the *Times* in early 1883, was "a palpable fallacy, inasmuch as powerful corporations are allowed liberties which the individual citizen is not."

Two years later, the *Times* complained that members of Congress supported land speculators who violated the Indian Territory in direct opposition to the president. But the same senators and representatives, "who talk so eloquently about the rights of 'boomers' and the landless people of the West, do not get excited about the millions of acres in unearned and lapsed grants held by railroad companies that have no title to them," the *Times* argued.

It was no secret that patronage, nepotism, and cronyism were responsible for many of the worst abuses within the Indian Service bureaucracy. The *Times* uncovered new instances every few months. It reported one of these in a brief July 1889 editorial. The charge concerned Thomas J. Morgan, Commissioner of Indian Affairs, whose wife "has been appointed to be his private secretary at a comfortable salary." Not to be outdone, the editorial continued, the superintendent of Indian schools had asked that his wife be appointed a special agent in the Indian Service so that she could accompany him in his travels. That appointment also was approved. It was difficult to blame the Secretary of the Interior for sanctioning the appointments, the *Times* held. After all, President Benjamin Harrison had set the example, "and the Secretary must know that under this Administration 'public office is a family perquisite.'"

But many of the abuses were more serious, at least in terms of potential damage. The *Times* felt compelled to voice its emphatic condemnation of the system that led to the replacement of experienced Indian agents at the Pine Ridge and Cheyenne River agencies in 1890. At a time when an Indian uprising already was a danger, the *Times* said in a December editorial column, agents who knew the Indians and how to deal with them had been displaced by others completely lacking in experience. The reason? Political patronage. "We denounced this sort of thing when it was done under the last Administration as monstrous; it is monstrous now, and the consequences are likely to be even more serious," said the *Times*. "If there shall be bloodshed and lives lost, a good part will be the price paid for our servitude to the vulgar, sordid, cruel, wicked spoils system, which its advocates like to call 'American.'" Less than two weeks later, Sitting Bull would be shot to death as he was being arrested on orders of the army. Two weeks after that occurred the Sioux massacre at Wounded Knee.

With the extent of the Indian uprising still uncertain, the *Times* expressed its outrage in an editorial early in the new year, January 3, 1891. "If there is any question whatever that is just now a national question, calling for the immediate attention and action of Congress," the editorial charged, "it is this Indian question." Those in a position to know best, it said, "make no scruple of declaring that the Indian rising is due to a breach of the national faith through thievish or incompetent agents." If the *Times* editorial writers took satisfaction in their own vindication, they gave no hint of it. Instead, they went on to attack a do-nothing Congress that appeared out of touch with the "real needs and the real sentiments" of the country.

Eventually, the *Times* was able to take some satisfaction in reforms brought to the Indian Bureau. But for the rest of the century, the newspaper would continue to cast a wary eye, on guard against the kind of corruption that for decades had been so much a part of the Indian problem.

From 1860 through 1900, the *Times* devoted an immense number of editorials to the subject of corruption that related, in some way, to the Native Americans. The editorials that follow demonstrate the fervor with which it tackled that topic.

↜ The Sacs and Foxes and Their Wileys and Whistlers

December 20, 1868

Everybody knows something of the Sacs and Foxes, and of Black Hawk, Keokuk I, and Keokuk II—that the first great Chief, six-and thirty years ago, having withstood the whole military power of the Republic in the bloody Black Hawk war (of which Mr. Lincoln has preserved anecdotes) surrendered, and, like a modern Jugurtha, was led captive through the chief cities of his conquerors, to see and be seen; and that the last named Chief has for a score of years kept peace and firm faith with the whites, and brought up the torn and doomed remnant of his people in ways of agriculture and civilization.

Everybody does not know as much, apparently, of the leeching and plucking to which this tribe of red men has for years been subject, thanks to the Indian Bureau, Indian agents and Indian traders. A correspondent told a part of the story the other day, and, as unearthing Indian transactions is now in order, the exposure comes in good time. To make a long story short, it appears that an "Indian Ring" has fastened upon the confederate Sacs and Foxes, and is immersed in the praiseworthy study of finding our "how much it can secure, and how little the Indians shall receive, of their money?"

The main bait for these land-sharks is the annual income of the invested proceeds of Sac and Fox lands. Originally driven just beyond the Mississippi, these tribes have been incessantly compelled to "move on" by the policeman of civilization; and so, selling out their lands, they have gone westward until they are now permanently settled in Kansas. The annual income from these land sales is something over $50,000—not a great fortune, to be sure, but since, in our process of civilizing the Sacs and Foxes, they have been civilized down from 10,000 to 700 people, quite a tidbit to each soul, and an irresistible prize, as a whole, to Indian cormorants.

The mode of operating against this $50,000 is, it appears, *first*, to create a monopoly in all the goods—necessaries and luxuries—furnished them by the Government; and, *second*, to sell these goods at treble the market price. One Wiley (not a bad name for the purpose) is the agent, and one Whistler is the trader. The way this pair work the Wiley-Whistler see-saw appears to be this. Wiley gives (against repeated remonstrances) an *exclusive* right to Whistler to trade on the Sac and Fox reservation; and Whistler, in turn, charges, as Keokuk represents to the President, twice or three times as much as the same articles are sold for outside of the reservation, *e.g.*: "coffee, (poor quality,) two pounds for $1; sugar, (lowest grades,) four pounds for $1; calico, three yards for $1; blankets, (which can be bought for $6 off the reservation,) $12." Not content with that, the wily Wiley and accomplished Whistler are represented as having tricked the tribe out of about nine square miles of valuable land. The poor Sacs and Foxes pay dear for that Whistler.

Tired of these extortions, and hearing that Indian abuses were being talked of, Keokuk and some faithful chiefs, (such as Quah-quah-lup-pe-quah,) set out for Washington, to seek redress. Wiley, getting wind of it, threatened to depose the Chief, who had reigned for twenty years, and to arrest the whole party; and arrested they were and thrown into prison at Lawrence, as the telegraph lately told us. Released by that good fairy, (as the allegorical Oakey would say,) *habeas corpus*, they journeyed on to Washington and there had audience of the "Great Father," who remarked very pointedly and truly that "the agent of the Government should have been put in jail instead of the chiefs."

It is a small story, perhaps—one of only $50,000 a year—but it represents a great deal to the Sacs and Foxes, and it represents a great deal more to the people of the United States, as a specimen of the practices customary in the Indian Department. "The Indian Office and the Department of the Interior," says our correspondent, "both approve the action of the agent," and a rearrest of the Chiefs in Washington was ordered, while threats were made against them in case they should not return to the Reservation, and forward their complaints through that very agent of whose acts they complain! A fine system, of a truth, and exceedingly just toward our "poor red brethren."

All that we have said, or nearly all, appears in the petition made by Keokuk to President Johnson. Keokuk is a fine chief, who has governed twenty years, and whose name is familiar to our people—it was given (the Assistant Secretary of War at the time happened to be a Fox) to one of our war vessels. It is a shame to have his peaceful and Christianized tribe plucked and plundered right and left. This is the statement,—and now for the brief argument—is it possible that this is the only case of wrongful treatment of Indians under our Indian Bureau?

⌐ A Question of "Spoils"

March 20, 1876

Under the present system Indian Agents are appointed by the President, on the recommendation of religious bodies. Theoretically, at least, these various organizations present their candidates to the President and he appoints them, having due regard to a proper distribution of the places among all of the religions denominations who desire to be represented in the general work of civilizing and Christianizing the Indians. Practically, the names of the different candidates or applicants are submitted to the President by Senators and Representatives after they have consulted with the persons recommending them. This method of procedure is about all there is in the so-called "peace policy" as pursued toward the Indians. It is taken for granted that the appointees, though not strictly missionaries, will adopt a pacific policy in their dealings with the Indians, and that they will not call upon the military until they have exhausted more gentle measures in any case of difference with their wards.

This is simple enough. There does not appear to be any good reason why there should be a conflict of jurisdiction, so far as the appointments are concerned, as long as the religious bodies are themselves satisfied. But there is a claim on the part of Western Senators and Representatives that these appointments are peculiarly their own, because the agents are to serve on the Western frontier. We do not understand that the Delegates from the Territories make this demand, although the agencies, as a rule, are more largely confined to the Territories than to the Western States. Nebraska, perhaps, has a larger number of the Indian agencies within its borders than any other State, but the bulk of these posts are scattered over the Territories of Dakota, Wyoming, New-Mexico, Colorado, Utah, Idaho, Montana, Washington, and Arizona. When Colorado comes in as a State this list will be reduced in number, but it is not likely that New-Mexico will soon add two to the knot of

Western Senators who demand that the nomination of Indian Agents shall be considered as a special local privilege.

It is now complained that Senators and Congressmen from the Eastern and Middle States have an undue share of patronage. Because, it is argued, the head-quarters of religious associations are mostly in these States, it does not follow that the appointment of Indian Agents should be controlled by Senators and Representatives from that section of the Republic. The Atlantic sea-board and the great lakes, it is urged, have their Custom-houses, some of which maintain a great many officials, and these are appointed on the recommendation of men who represent such localities in Congress. Why should not the posts among the Indian tribes on the Western frontier be filled by men from the West, recommended by Western Congressmen? If these agents are to be Christian men, have we not just as good Methodists, Presbyterians, or Episcopalians in Kansas or Minnesota as they have in New-York or Massachusetts? It is not a fair division of the spoils which gives a large part of the Indian appointments, in addition to those of the Customs service, to the Atlantic and Middle States.

The complaint is probably made thoughtlessly, but it is a fair illustration of the way in which the average Congressman looks at such subjects. To him an appointment to a place of trust, if it has any honor or profit in it, is only a perquisite of his own office. Nominations falling in his district, Senatorial or Representative, are described as being "in his gift," and this contemptible little dispute about the right to nominate Indian Agents is merely a squabble over perquisites. We do not suppose that either of the disputants considers for a moment the good of the service or the welfare of the Indians. It is a mere vulgar question of spoils, and the real purpose for which the offices were created is the very last thing thought of. This is most discouraging to those who hope to see the civil service lifted out of the region of party or personal considerations. Just now, when the demoralization of official life has been so painfully illustrated in all parties, one might expect that public men would recognize and try to avoid one of the worst evils of our present system. Instead of that, we find Senators and Representatives taking up the question of Executive appointments in the same old sordid and selfish spirit with which they have all along considered it. Whatever may be said as to the policy of taking Indian Agents from the East or from the West, it is depressing to find that the whole matter is treated purely as a division of spoils. All just-minded citizens, anxious for the purity and elevation of the civil service, must protest against such a base use of the responsibilities of office. It is a lamentable commentary on the condition of public affairs that Senators and Representatives are more intent on securing patronage for themselves than they are on promoting the best interests of the service. They may delude themselves with the notion that their appointments will be the best that can be made. But still they cannot help regarding these appointments as so much merchandise, of which they may dispose to the highest bidder.

↪ A Standing Grievance

September 29, 1877

Simultaneously with the appearance, in Washington of a band of Indian petitioners comes the complaint from a far-off agency that some of the "wards of the nation" are on the verge of starvation. The Indians now besieging the White House only ask that they shall be sent to a region where they can exist. The report from the Cheyenne Agency is to the effect that the Indians at that point have absolutely nothing to eat, and that they are "being robbed by thieving agents." In the case of the Sioux and Arapahoes there is a protest against being removed to a reservation which they have had no voice in selecting. It was arbitrarily decided to place them on the Upper Missouri, and Congress went on with the legislation necessary to carry out that plan. The money for the support of the bands was appropriated, with the specified proviso that the Indians were to be located in the region named. Contracts for furnishing and delivering supplies were concluded under that law. And now, if the Indians are not sent there, there is no provision for feeding them anywhere else. Nobody engaged in managing Indians has a right to take it for granted that any particular tribe or company of them will be satisfied with a location which somebody else has picked out for them. It is complained of the Indians that they are "cranky" and over-particular; perhaps they are, but it is cheaper to defer a little to their notions than to fight with them when their discontent has broken out into rebellion.

The trouble with the Cheyennes is of a more exasperating character. According to the military authorities in that country the Indians have been cheated in the quality and quantity of their goods, even when they have had any, leaving the impression that they have been deprived of supplies at times. In this instance, the agents who act as the dispensers of the bounty of the Government are in default. They have robbed and cheated the Indians, who have been sent to their particular reservation with the explicit promise that they should be fed. No wonder they complain that they have been lied to and entrapped into doing what was distasteful to them. If an Indian outbreak should follow, as Gen. Pope says is possible, we should be obliged to sacrifice the lives of soldiers, as well as much money, in its suppression. We observe that the agent at Cheyenne explains that the trouble with the Indians there arises from the fact that they are "great beef-eaters," and want a larger ration of that viand than they now receive. This does not agree with the report which comes through the military authorities. But even if the agent's explanations be valid, the general accusation of mismanagement must still hold good against the agency. The Government pays liberally for the maintenance of Indians. The Cheyennes, once among the most formidable enemies of the white man, have kept faith with us. They are entitled to fair treatment in return.

It is an old story, so old that there is a popular notion, apparently, that we shall hear it annually repeated until the last red man fades away. For nearly a century the United States Government has tried experiments with the aborigines of the country, with varying sincerity, but with unvarying lack of success. Here and there, to be sure, we can be shown instances in which certain bands have, after years of trial, been well treated, restrained from war and violence, and assured in a certain degree of prosperity. These instances are rare. The general upshot of the business after all these years is failure. Indians are not well managed by the Government; they are cheated by contractors and agents, and they have every reason to say with Sitting Bull, that "the white Americans are liars and thieves." If we do not care for the good opinion of the red-skins, we ought at least to have enough respect for the public faith to deserve a better reputation than that which the fugitive Sioux Chief has given us in British America. It seems a great shame that in this single branch of the public service we should have made so little progress that a great scandal or a great blunder is possible at any time. Affairs go on in the slip-shod way which was familiar to our grandfathers. Is it not possible that there is statesmanship enough in the country to put the Indian service on as intelligent and satisfactory a footing as the postal service, for example? There was a time when private enterprise served us better than the Government in the transportation of letters, money, and packages. Now, the postal service puts to shame all the transportation companies. But, if any private corporation or business firm were to manage its affairs with such disastrous and disgraceful results as those which flow from the Indian service, it would be wound up forthwith for the benefit of its creditors. The present

Administration, during the first half-year of its existence, has taken hold of a few public questions with a certain amount of boldness and originality. It is to be hoped that it will find time, by and by, to mitigate the long-standing grievance in Indian affairs. This has been asked of each successive Administration ever since we can remember. But it is a demand which is as imperative now as it ever was.

A Great Official Scandal

January 8, 1878

The report of the special commission appointed to investigate the workings of the Indian Bureau, which is printed in *The Times* to-day, is not cheerful reading. Any candid person will be certain to say, after looking through it, that the condition of the Indian service is simply shameful. It has long been notorious that rascally agents and contractors have connived to cheat the Indians. As the Indians cannot, as a rule, understand figures or written words and characters, it is easy to impose upon them. It now appears that a ring has long existed in the Indian Bureau at Washington for the express purpose of covering up these frauds and facilitating others. It may be said that dishonest contractors, agents, and middle-men have camped in the Department of the Interior and have made themselves absolutely impregnable to investigation. Bureau clerks deliberately suppressed charges and evidence against the thieves. They also wrote out the reports and accounts of derelict agents, and then passed them as correct. One of the most venial forms of fraud practiced in the Indian Bureau was to audit and approve accounts of those agents who had previously formed a conspiracy with the employes of the bureau. Of course, the report of the commission does not make these charges in plain language. It states the facts, however; the conclusion is obvious. Though a ring is called a "group," people know just what is meant.

The circumstances under which this investigation was ordered are these: Last Spring, charges were preferred against S. A. Galpin, Chief Clerk of the Indian Bureau. Secretary Schurz appointed a commission of inquiry, consisting of an Army officer, the Chief Clerk of the Interior Department, and a gentleman selected from the office of the Attorney-General. Galpin's case was soon swallowed up in the multitude of corruptions disclosed by the inquiry. But, although all the charges against Galpin were not sustained by evidence, enough was found to justify the Secretary in dismissing him with a letter reflecting severely upon his official character. This Galpin appears to have been the chief of the Bureau Ring, or, as the Commission euphemistically puts it, "the group" in the office. Charges and specifications sent to the Indian Bureau were taken possession of by this man and locked up in his desk. A regular system of suppression of everything prejudicial to the interests of swindling agents and contractors was maintained in the Indian office. The excuse in the case of Galpin, as given by himself, was that he knew that the charges were false, or that he had forgotten to take them out of his desk. It thus appears that official documents were not registered, numbered, and distributed in the office, as required by the regulations, but were made the personal property of the "group" of which Galpin was chief. Moreover, these clerks kept up a vigorous private correspondence with agents, contractors, and employes of the Indian service, leaving it to be inferred that dishonest men were regularly informed of all that concerned them and their affairs. Their correspondence was kept from the files of the office, but the information derived therefrom enabled the plotters to influence the official acts of the Indian Bureau so as to harmonize with the covert understandings arrived at by these writings.

If it be asked what kind of a Commissioner could have managed the Indian Bureau while these tricks were being played in it, we may find an answer in two significant facts: The officials and employes of the Indian Bureau did not cooperate with the Commission in its attempt to get at the bottom facts, but they sometimes hindered the inquiry; the late Commissioner, (Smith,) under date of March 26, 1877, declared that he knew no custom or practice in the Indian Bureau that could properly be termed an abuse, unless it was, perhaps, the disposition of the clerks to enlarge their leaves of absence. The report very forcibly says that—

"The absence of regulations, system, and method; the suppression of charges and specifications; the carrying on of semi-official correspondence; the careless disposition of papers and records; the relinquishment of authority, or delegation of official power to another; the loss or disposition of valuable papers; the unwarranted and officious opposition to the Board of Indian Commissioners; the unfitness for their respective positions of the Chief Clerk, Correspondence Clerk, Annuity Clerk, and others; the persecution of the chief of the Medical Division; the incompetency of the chief of the Accounts Division, the inefficiency of the acting chief of the Land Division, the habitual lack of circumspection in the Finance Division, the uselessness, without instructions, of the force of the Civilization Division, and finally, the general demoralization of the force of the bureau throughout, did not afford the data from which the late Commissioner could find abuse."

This paragraph we have just quoted is the general indictment of the Indian Bureau. Many of the details will be found in the report elsewhere printed. It is sufficient to say that every conceivable form of fraud has been committed by the Indian Ring, and that the Ring consisted of men in the office of the Indian Bureau, as well as out of it. There were frauds in weighing and counting cattle issued to Indians, frauds in goods and supplies, frauds in receipts and accounts, and frauds in the management of Indian trust funds. This latter item, indeed, seems to have been the groundwork of a most outrageous abuse. The proceeds of the sales of products of Indian labor in the hands of agents were, by a juggle with official decisions, kept out of the Treasury, diverted from the hands of the Indians, and probably stolen at last by the harpies who managed this branch of business. The candid reader, after going carefully through the report, will conclude that the whole Indian service needs a thorough reorganization. Secretary Schurz has probed its corruption to the bottom. He has showed firmness and courage in his determination to turn to the light the abuses which have for years pervaded the Indian service. It is a mortifying exhibit which is made. It now remains with Congress to provide for such a reorganization as shall protect our Indian wards from the oppressions of bad men, and prevent the recurrence of similar scandals.

ᥱ Why Indian Wars?

July 16, 1878

The discovery of the wholesale robberies committed at two Indian agencies in Dakota is undoubtedly a severe blow to the reputation of agencies conducted under the oversight of religious organizations. More than this, the scandal thus created will strengthen the popular feeling that the Indian service will be safer in the hands of the War Department than under its present management. The Indian Agent at the Crow Creek Station, who seems to be the chief offender, was appointed eight years ago, during Gen. Grant's Administration. He was selected by the Advisory Committee of the Episcopal Church, that organization having several agencies in Dakota assigned to its charge. Under the plan adopted during Gen. Grant's administration neither the President, Secretary of the Interior, nor Indian Commissioner could be held directly responsible for the Indian Agents who represented the various religious bodies. They were nominated to the Executive by committees or councils of the Churches represented by them. Of course, it happened sometimes, as in this case, that a weak or bad man was selected. But, generally speaking, the system worked well, and such offenses as those charged upon Livingstone, the Crow Creek agent, have been rare.

It is said that Livingstone began his dishonest operations in 1870, when he was first appointed. He and his partners have had a long term of immunity. Many different Commissioners of Indian Affairs, and at least two Secretaries of the Interior, have failed to detect their nefarious operations. The present administration of the Indian Bureau has brought to light a system of robbery which is remarkable for its audacity and its intricacy. The ring at the Crow Creek Agency took possession of the post and managed affairs for their own special and private benefit. These agencies usually have a trading-post, the owner of which is licensed by the United States Government. His business is separate and distinct from that of the Indian Agent. Indians and others buy of the trader. But the agency is the depot for the disbursement of rations, supplies, annuities, &c., due the Indians from the Government. The Indians do not in all cases live upon specified reservations. They are scattered in the vicinity of the agencies, to which they resort once a week, or less often, for their rations. They are encouraged to raise cattle and to grow such crops as can be readily sold in the region or used for their own sustenance. The Indians at the Crow Creek and Cheyenne River Agencies cultivated hay, oats, corn, and potatoes. They also owned over 100 head of fine cattle.

It is easy to understand how a dishonest agent, under this complicated system of supporting the agency Indians could cheat the Government and its wards. The thieves at the Crow Creek Agency took the agricultural products from the Indians, sold them, and pocketed the proceeds. Or they bought these products from the Indians, paying for them in rations belonging to the Indians, and then charged the Government for the articles thus purchased, receiving pay therefor on prepared vouchers. And, finally, these articles, on which two or three fraudulent profits had been made, were sold to traders, steam-boat men, and passing teamsters. In many instances the fruits of the Indians' industry were taken possession of by the agent, turned over to the post-trader, and by him resold to their lawful owners. The annuities sent to the Indians by the Indian Bureau were confiscated by the Livingstone Ring; the same thing was done with the rations; and, for the purpose of securing as many rations as possible, the number of Indians was over-stated. The latest census received from Livingstone put the total number of his wards at 1,223. The amount of money voted for this agency during Livingstone's administration was $170,000. But, of course, this sum represents only a part of the plunder. The Ring supported themselves and supplied their hotel from the products of the Indian farms about the agency and from the agency farm.

It has been generally supposed that the settlement of a region near an Indian Agency or reservation increased the chances of detection of dishonest practices. But it is also true that the temptations to defraud the Government and the Indians are more numerous as trade and commerce surround the trader. The Crow Creek Agency is on the east bank of the Missouri, 230 miles above Yancton, on the old Winnebago Reservation. It is the post through which supplies are sent to the Lower Brule Agency and the Brule Military Station, and is on a traveled road to the Black Hills country. An agricultural settlement like this, on land and water thoroughfares, afforded advantages to an enterprising trader, with a stock supplied by the Government, which were not to be despised. And it is simply said of Livingstone that "he stole all he could."

It is noticeable that while this man was defrauding and oppressing the Indians he professed great interest in their welfare. In his latest report to the Commissioner of Indian Affairs, Livingstone recommended that Congress should at once extend over the Indians the jurisdiction of the United States courts, in order, he said, "that Indians should understand that they could not commit crimes and go unpunished." This philanthropist should not fail to have a taste of the medicine which he recommended for others. To a great extent, this case resembles many others. The Indians at Crow Creek are Yanktonai and Minnekonjo Sioux. They belong to a family of aborigines from which we are constantly receiving reports of uneasiness and discontent. If the operations of men like the Crow Creek agent are duplicated with anything like frequency among other groups of Indians, it is easy to understand why they are restless and discontented. They do not receive fair treatment from the Government. Sometimes Congress fails to do its duty; sometimes contractors cheat in quantity and quality of supplies; and often it happens that the agent robs the Indian and the Government with impartial hand. Frontiersmen provoke and maltreat the red men, encroach upon their reservations, drive away and destroy their game, and even steal their cattle and scanty crops. And there are people who wonder why we have Indian wars!

✑ An Important Office

February 9, 1880

The fact that the Administration of President Hayes has been an exceptionally pure one serves to deepen the regret with which all good citizens regard the recent scandals in the Indian service. Generally speaking, the President has been fortunate in his choice of subordinate officers, so far as their probity is concerned. In pleasant contrast with preceding Administrations, this term of the Presidential office has not been agitated by any great scandal. The most persistent efforts of the opposition have failed to fasten upon any officer of the Government any enduring stain. And it is noticeable that the allegations against the man who has just been dismissed from the Indian Commissionership were made by friends of the Administration, not by its unfriendly critics. Perhaps this may account for the languid interest which the Democratic papers have evinced in the matter, now that it has been brought to a head by the dismissal of Mr. Hayt. It seems to be conceded that an investigation which results in the purification of a public office, and which has been set on foot by the party in power, has no interest to the party on the outside. It is only when party capital can be made by an attack that the fierce virtue of the Democracy is aroused. There is small chance for accumulating party ammunition to be used in the next campaign in the treatment which the dismissed officer has just received from the Administration. Mr. Hayt has been convicted of duplicity and misdirection in office, and he has been removed by the President and Secretary of the Interior.

Nevertheless, the manner of Mr. Hayt's original appointment was unfortunate and unpromising of good. It should serve as a warning to men high in authority and intrusted with the power of appointment. Mr. Hayt was a member of the Board of Indian Commissioners during Gen. Grant's Administration. In that capacity he made a vigorous attack on the Administration of Commissioner Smith, then at the head of the Indian Bureau. This was resented by the President, and, very soon after the accession of the late Hon. Z. Chandler to the office of Secretary of the Interior, Mr. Hayt was obliged to withdraw from the board. There was nothing on the surface of this which was discreditable to Mr. Hayt. But it was most unfortunate that he should have seemed to profit by the campaign which he was represented to have undertaken in the interest of honest government. He should not have been asked to take a place which he could have justly claimed that he had had some share in making vacant. Nor was it true, as was lately asserted by

Secretary Schurz, that Mr. Hayt was a man of large means, to whom the modest salary of Indian Commissioner was no object. Doubtless, the Secretary had been led to believe that this was true; but, nevertheless, it was not the fact, and the sequel has shown the folly of putting into a responsible place, requiring assiduous attention and rare tact, a man who was over head and ears involved in his own business, and unable to give the great interests committed to him a tithe of the care which they required.

But the unfortunate mistake of the President was that he allowed Mr. Schurz to dictate an appointment of which he (the President) knew nothing. If there is any officer of the Government, below the rank of a Cabinet Minister, who is charged with the weightiest of public responsibilities, that officer is the Commissioner of Indian Affairs. He is charged with the disbursement of many millions of dollars annually, and his duties bring him into contact with schemers and men who are seeking opportunity to plunder the Government and its Indian wards. He must not only be wise and shrewd to detect and prevent fraud, but he must be removed far above temptation to profit by any of the opportunities which he sees almost daily passing through his office. And yet, this officer, of whom so much is expected, and who has largely in his hands the power of making peace or war possible with the Indian tribes, is paid the small salary of $3,000 a year. Undoubtedly, Mr. Schurz thought that he, at least, knew Mr. Hayt when he gave him the appointment of Commissioner of Indian Affairs. The sequel has proved that he did not know him. The Bureau of Indian Affairs has been in a state of chaos ever since the late commissioner went into it. And if the President has any feeling of mortification at the inglorious termination of Mr. Hayt's career in office, he may reflect that he did not know anything about Mr. Hayt when he allowed him to be appointed. It was well known, when that selection was made, that the President was reluctant to make it, and that he did make it, finally, against the wishes of his immediate friends, and without being informed himself as to the appointee's qualifications.

It is evident that the vacant office will not be filled readily. It is a most difficult position to occupy. Notwithstanding the efforts of many of the higher officers of the Government to purify and keep pure the Indian service, it is to-day the most prolific source of corruption and fraud. It seems as there was something in the atmosphere of the Indian Office which demoralizes any man who breathes it. From time immemorial, or at least ever since there was an Indian Bureau, nothing pertaining to the office has long escaped the taint of corruption or suspicion. The place is sought for by men who want it only for evil purposes. The Commissioner, once honestly installed and honestly trying to do his duty, is beset by sharpers, as well as embarrassed by a public sentiment which is against every Indian contractor as a suspected thief. Let him do his best, and he will not be able to prevent wholly the frauds and impositions which are practiced on the Indians. To crown all, he is set to carry out a "policy" which is not worthy of the name, and which varies with every wind that blows. If we may call that a policy which consists of weakness and wickedness alternating, year by year, then we may well pity the officer who is intrusted with its execution, under the laws of a Congress easily terrified by civilized ruffians into committing any injustice which may be demanded for the time. And whatever else the President and the Secretary of the Interior may not do, let us hope they will find a Commissioner of Indian Affairs who will honestly attend to the important duties of his office. No such man can be obtained by sending out a scout with a lasso.

ᗡ The Zunis and Their Lands

May 30, 1883

We are glad to learn from the statement which Senator Logan has given to the public that he had no interest whatever in his son-in-law's attempt to establish a cattle ranch upon the lands of the Zuni Indians in New-Mexico. It is now clear that for some reason he reconsidered his original determination to get possession of these lands, although, we regret to say, the latter part of his statement indicates that this change of mind was not caused by the discovery that the taking of the lands would be an act of great injustice to the Zunis and might bring them face to face with famine. It was in December last that the Senator made known to the Washington correspondent of *The Times* his intention to take the lands around the Nutria Springs. A correspondent in or near Santa Fe—said to have been that enterprising and intelligent ethnologist, Mr. Cushing, who voluntarily went into exile in the Zuni pueblo for the purpose of learning the history and traditions of that ancient race—had declared, in a long letter published in a Boston newspaper, that the Senator had undertaken to become the owner of these lands, which the Indians had cultivated for centuries, and which had been excluded from their reservation by a surveyor's error, recently discovered. When the Senator's attention was directed to this statement, and to the plea made by the Santa Fe writer in behalf of these peaceful Indians, he replied: "I think I will take the land if I can get it." The Senator's reply was reported in a dispatch published in *The Times* on the following morning, Dec. 13, 1882, as follows:

"If it was public land he [Senator Logan] saw no reason why it should not be pre-empted. He had looked at the land, and he thought he would take it if he could get it."

So it appears that he changed his mind, for it was his son-in-law who attempted to take the land, and he was not concerned in the transaction. The President, however, learned that the land had been omitted from the reservation by an oversight, and that it was needed for the support of the Indians, who supposed that they owned it. He at once corrected the error, and in this way prevented the establishment of the ranch.

It is said that the Zunis owe the preservation of their land to Mr. Cushing. If this be true, then he is a philanthropist as well as an ethnologist, and he deserves the praise rather than the contempt of such men as Senator Logan. In his work at the Zuni pueblo this young man has surely shown bravery, self-denial, industry, enthusiasm, and other qualities which that intrepid soldier cannot fail to admire. It must be that Mr. Cushing has been misrepresented to the Senator, and that an accurate knowledge of his character and labors would remove the unfavorable impression which the Senator has received. There is something of the hero in a young and well-educated man who becomes a "white Indian," eats "the vilest food ever known to a human being," and lives "in the midst of the most nauseating and offensive stench," for the sake of science alone.

If we did not know that the Senator had no part in the cattle ranch enterprise we might be led by a part of his statement to suppose that he was in sympathy with those who tried to get the lands, and even with persons who regard our Indian treaties as compacts that white men are not bound to respect. The Senator thinks that the Zunis have too much land, and he says so in a series of argumentative questions. He apparently regards their privileges as far greater than those of white men who try to locate land near their "sacred soil," as he calls it. The Indians, and especially the Zunis, seem to be regarded by him as nuisances and highly favored interlopers who stand in the way of white men who desire to pre-empt or buy land. The Zuni reservation is a very small one; it is only a dot on the map. Each Zuni's share is very small in comparison with the share of an inhabitant of the Indian Territory or of an Indian in one of the large reservations. The Senator's plan of distribution, if applied to all Indian reservations, would release millions of acres to those who are in search of cattle ranches, but it could hardly be adopted without ignoring our treaties, and we cannot believe that the Senator would recommend the violation of these.

✏ Another Queer Order

April 11, 1885

At the next session of the Senate Mr. Teller will probably be urged to explain a little transaction in Indian lands which has attracted the attention of certain gentlemen who believe that the Government ought to deal fairly and honestly with its Indian wards. Like one or two other transactions concerning which he has been requested to enlighten the Senate, this took place just before he and his chief went out of office.

Telegrams forwarded from the West on March 2 announced that hundreds of squatters had taken up claims on the Crow Creek Reservation in Dakota, having learned that it was to be thrown open for settlement. It was also said that the most valuable portions of the reservation had been taken by a syndicate of politicians who had for several days had private information about the Government's intention. On the same day the fact that the reservation had been thrown open by Executive order was made known in dispatches from Washington. It now appears that the President's order, issued under Secretary Teller's advice, was dated Feb. 27. There were in the reservation about 635,000 acres, of which 500,000 were taken from the Indians by the order, which had been issued without warning. Nothing had occurred to prepare the Indians or their agent for this action of the Government, and it caused great surprise and dissatisfaction, because the reservation had been regarded as one protected by treaty. Protests were forwarded by the agent and others to Secretary Lamar. The order was suspended, and after a careful examination of the facts Attorney-General Garland has pronounced it to be illegal and void.

In procuring this order Secretary Teller not only ignored Congress and all persons who were interested, officially or otherwise, in the matter, but also found it convenient to disregard the views previously held by the department and by Congress concerning the nature of the Indians' title. The Indian Rights Association, of which ex-Attorney-General MacVeagh is President, declares that the order was prepared in great haste, that no official notice of it was given to the Indian Bureau, and that not the slightest hint of the department's intention was given to either of the Congressional Committees on Indian Affairs. It seems to have been planned in secrecy because Congress and the department had regarded the lands as covered by the Sioux treaty of 1868 and not subject to Executive order. Two years ago a commission appointed by Secretary Teller undertook to induce the Sioux to relinquish for a consideration 11,000,000 acres of their great reservation. The Crow Creek Reservation adjoins this, and is understood to have been included in it by the treaty of 1868. The commission's labors were not satisfactory to Congress, and after an investigation had shown some disagreeable facts Congress endeavored to provide by legislation for a fair and honest trade with the Indians. The bill in question was approved by the Administration, but after it had passed the Senate Mr. Teller suddenly and unexpectedly procured the Executive order which would take the lands without compensation or the least regard for the Indians' treaty rights.

As a result of this remarkable action the Indians or the squatters must suffer. The order, if enforced, would leave the Indians in possession of thousands of acres of worthless land out of which they could not get the allotments in severalty which they desire to take. It would deprive them of their pasture land and cut off the support of the agency cattle. These Indians have always refused to join other bands of Sioux in their attacks upon settlers. On the other hand, if it is revoked, the Government will have great difficulty in removing the squatters, who ought not to be forced to pay a heavy penalty for an Executive blunder. The Secretary has succeeded in making trouble for a great many persons. It is not probable that this was his sole purpose. There may be other more fortunate persons to whom the order has been a blessing. Perhaps he will disclose his real motive and object when he explains this transaction next winter.

✏ The New Indian Policy

July 25, 1885

The President has promptly acted in accordance with the recommendations of Gen. Sheridan. The ranchmen who have for two years controlled nearly 4,000,000 acres of the Cheyenne and Arapahoe Reservation have been warned by Executive proclamation that they must depart with their herds within forty days. The Indians have been temporarily placed under the management of the War Department. Agent Dyer, who has defended the lessees, and under whose administration of affairs the Government has been issuing rations for 2,800 Indians who do not exist, retires and is succeeded by Capt. Lee, of the Ninth Infantry. The rights of the Indians as well as the lives and property of settlers on the border are to be protected. The impulse that led the President to send Gen. Sheridan to Fort Reno was born in sound common sense. The results of the General's investigation show what can be done by a just and clear-headed man.

"The cattle leases are void, and the Government has the undoubted right to remove the cattlemen and their herds." This declaration made by the President after consultation with the members of his Cabinet lets daylight into a carefully designed and diligently fostered plan to give greedy ranchmen a foothold upon Indian lands in all parts of the West, and in this way assist those who covet the reservations set apart for the Nation's wards. The laws relating to the admission of white men to reservations and forbidding the making of contracts and leases are expressed in plain language. When Secretary Teller was asked by the Senate to explain under what authority the leases had been made he tried to show that the statute declaring that "no lease of lands from any tribe of Indians shall be of any validity in law or equity," unless made "by treaty or convention," as provided by the Constitution, had not been violated, by asserting that a lease of grass was not a lease of lands. According to his interpretation the ranchmen who have inclosed vast tracts in the Indian Territory with wire fences, and who maintain possession of this land by means of armed cowboys, have been merely enjoying a lease of grass. It was not his duty to try to find holes in the law. The practice of allowing such leases to be made with uncivilized persons who are unable to guard their own interests in a bargain was a dangerous one. It would inevitably lead to such disturbances as this one which has caused so much alarm. But the Interior Department under Mr. Teller was more intent upon securing Indian lands for Western men than upon strictly following the spirit of the law and avoiding Indian outbreaks.

Whatever shall be the final result of the arrangements made for a settlement at Fort Reno, the action taken will direct the attention of Congress to the land leases and the encroachments recently made upon this reservation and others. "The Indian," says Senator Dawes, who is familiar with all phases of the Indian question, "is approaching a turning point in his destiny. The hunger for his lands was never so great, and the determination to appropriate them was never so strong. Capital and cattlemen are reaping enormous profits from the ranches they have been permitted, under the form of leases, to appropriate to their own use without the interference of law or its officers. The interpretation of these leases has been turned over to the arbitrament of the cowboy's revolver on the one side and the Indian's Winchester rifle—purchased with the distributed rental—on the other, till the land is filled with terror and the army alone is able to keep the peace between them and protect the life of the innocent settler. There is not left to the Indian the undisturbed enjoyment of an acre, no matter what his title." If all Indians were fitted by education and inclination to take and hold land in severalty, the problem might be peacefully solved. Unfortunately, many years must pass before thousands of them can, under the most favorable circumstances, be prepared for that step.

∽ The Indian Commissionership

June 12, 1889

It was announced in our Washington despatches yesterday that Gen. Thomas J. Morgan of Rhode Island had been appointed to be Commissioner of Indian Affairs, *vice* Mr. John H. Oberly, resigned. This announcement, like many others proceeding officially from this Administration, is deceptive in effect and in intent. It is true that Mr. Oberly resigned his post, but he did so after he had been informed of the President's purpose to make a change, the information being given according to a statement of Mr. Harrison's quoted by the Springfield *Republican*, in order "that you may take such action in anticipation thereof as you may think proper." Plainly, if Mr. Oberly had not resigned he would have been removed, and the course of the President must be judged as if he had been removed. Gen. Morgan is described by the *Republican* as "a gallant soldier and a good man," but he was appointed because he was a Republican in party politics, and he would not have been appointed if he had not been a Republican. Mr. Oberly was displaced because he was not a Republican; had he been one he would have been left in office. In other words, the very difficult and important office of the Indian Commissioner is regarded by Mr. Harrison as a part of the spoils system, to be disposed of as partisan spoils, and under no possible circumstances to be filled by "the discriminating test of fitness" alone.

This is not so flagrant or so shameless a case of subjection to the spoils idea as the replacement of Mr. Pearson in the New-York Post Office by Mr. Van Cott, because Gen. Morgan is not a mere professional politician, but it is a distinct violation of Mr. Harrison's own pledges and of the pledges of his party and a complete violation of the principles of sound administration. Mr. Oberly is a man who has proved his special fitness in every way for the work of the Indian Bureau. He has had experience; he has been tried and pronounced by the Indian Rights Association—the most competent and exacting judges in the country—to be beyond all doubt qualified. He is a Democrat, but so far from being a partisan ready to advance his party at the expense of the service, he is an ardent and unflinching and practiced opponent of partisanship in Indian affairs, not only ready, but determined to drive party politics wholly from the service. To pretend that he was turned out because it was feared that his Democracy would interfere with his usefulness is to pretend what no one familiar with the facts will believe, and Mr. Harrison or Secretary Noble least of all. If there be any danger of injury to the service from the partisanship of the incumbent it will be infinitely greater with Gen. Morgan than it would have been with Mr. Oberly, because the latter has shown himself absolutely and even defiantly independent of all partisan influence, while his successor cannot but be hampered by the knowledge that it was his partisan connection that secured his appointment in the place of a man certainly as able and far more fitted by special experience for the duties of the office.

We regret, in connection with this matter, to be obliged to call attention to the attitude of Senator Dawes of Massachusetts, who has some reputation as a friend of the Indians. In a letter to the *Republican* Mr. Dawes said: "If Mr. Harrison thinks that the best instrumentality to lift [the Indian service] out of the filth and up to its highest possibilities is one whose whole soul is consecrated to the advancement of that political party under whose management that depth has been reached, so be it; the responsibility, so far as I am concerned, shall rest with him." This is Mr. Dawes's way of saying that Mr. Oberly ought not to be retained. There is a complicated variety and a nauseating amount of falsehood and hypocrisy in this statement that could only be achieved by a thorough-going Republican partisan. Doubtless a Democrat of the same type could lie as boldly, but he would not claim that he was doing it in the cause of morality and philanthropy. In the first place, with the exception of the last four years, the Indian service has been under Republican control for nearly thirty years, and the filth in which it has been sunk has been Republican. In the next place, Mr. Oberly's "whole soul is" *not* "consecrated to the advancement" of any political party, and Mr. Dawes knows that it is not. He knows, or he ought to know, for it is the truth, that since he has been in the Indian office, and while he was Superintendent of Indian Schools, and also while he was in the Civil Service Commission, Mr. Oberly was wholly devoted to the advancement of honest and pure and faithful public service, and to the eradication of partisan influence, direct or indirect, from all appointments, promotions, or dismissals in that service. Mr. Dawes's statement is a deliberate misrepresentation in general and particular of the facts, made with the intent to deceive and to cover an entirely unjustifiable act with the cloak of a pious purpose. It is quite in harmony with the course of this Administration in several—though not all—directions, and it makes the change in the Indian Commission seem more inexcusable than it would have seemed if it had been made in dogged silence.

⮌ The End of the Indian War

January 17, 1891

The President and the Secretary of the Interior are the two men who ought to feel most relieved and most grateful that Gen. Miles has succeeded in averting the general Indian war that has been so long and so seriously threatened. For these two are the men immediately responsible for the threat, and upon them would have rested the frightful responsibility for the great battle that a week ago everybody expected to be fought. Mr. Harrison showed some sense of his responsibility, though by no means an adequate sense. He showed it, in the first place, by sending Gen. Miles by telegraph a silly admonition to "avoid bloodshed," as if Gen. Miles could not be trusted to avoid, if it were possible, a battle in which his own blood was liable to be shed, while that of the President was not in the least danger of effusion. He showed it, in the second place, by issuing an order removing, at the request of Gen. Miles, five of the agents whom he had appointed at the request of politicians and putting in their places men recommended by Gen. Miles. The five agents removed were conspicuous among those representatives of the Interior Department whose incompetency or rascality had brought on the state of mind on the part of the Indians that threatened to result in war. After issuing an order removing them, however, the President revoked that order, except as to one agency. At that agency Gen. Miles could assure the Indians concerned that they would be honestly treated and the faith of the Government kept. With regard to the four other agencies, respecting which he had made similar recommendations, which the President had taken steps to carry out by issuing an order to that effect, the General could give no assurances, for the reason that Secretary Noble raised a "point of etiquette," which prevailed with the powerful mind of the President, and made the retention of the old agents "a personal matter." That the sensibilities of Mr. Noble might be soothed, the President in effect forbade Gen. Miles to assure the Indians dependent upon these four agencies that their treatment in the future would be any better than the treatment in the past, against which they had revolted and to which they had declared in words, and in actions that speak louder, that they would die rather than submit.

Mr. Noble, for his part, has not exhibited even the disquiet shown by the President, but has made it evident that his responsibility for the threatened slaughter did not make him at all uncomfortable. The very great credit due to Gen. Miles for bringing to an early and peaceful end what threatened to be a terrible campaign is all the greater because he really had no help at all from Washington. The one thing that appeared to be indispensable to turn the Indian war into an Indian peace was that Gen. Miles should be able to assure the Indians that hereafter the promises of the Government to them should be kept and not broken. If he had made such an assurance the Indians would doubtless accept it, for the experienced among them, untutored though they be, are yet aware that the officers of the army differ from the agents of the Interior Department in two important particulars. They do not tell lies and they do not steal.

Without being able to make such an assurance, and to give the pledges of its genuineness that would have been furnished if the order revoked by the President had been in force, Gen. Miles has ended the war, with great credit to himself and with no thanks at all to Mr. Harrison or Mr. Noble. But assuredly the matter ought not to end here. When the President of the United States takes the ground that the sensibilities of the Secretary of the Interior are more important than the lives of six or eight thousand white men and of three of four thousand Indians, it is high time that somebody in authority should institute an inquiry. But nothing of the kind has come from the majority in either house of Congress. The inquisitive Senator Dawes is silent and the curious Senator Hoar operates his curiosity in other directions. The Indian trouble is composed temporarily, and we have time to consider what is next to be done. If nothing is done, and the thievish or incompetent agents go on in their old courses, the trouble will surely come up again, and will be far more difficult to allay by peaceable means. Congress has now an opportunity to put our Indian affairs on a decent and rational basis, and the neglect of this opportunity will surely be visited upon the country hereafter. Meanwhile there is some comfort in the announcement that a delegation of chiefs is to go to Washington and have a pow-wow with the great Father in person. Pow-wows of this nature have very seldom come to anything in the past, but the coming pow-wow ought to be an exception. Heretofore the Indians have undertaken to tell their own stories with only the help of an interpreter, and they have not made the most of them. This time it is to be hoped the Indian Association will provide them with counsel who will gather the facts of the case and present them in detail. Such a statement, if made by a lawyer of only moderate ability, would not only be deeply impressive to the country at large, but it would also have the effect, to borrow the language of statesmanship, of putting the Great Father "in a hole."

Costly Economy

June 22, 1894

The Board of Indian Commissioners, in the recent debate on the Indian Appropriation bill, received highly significant expert testimony as to its value. The Hon. Dennis T. Flynn of Oklahoma declared that "there is scarcely a matter ever broached in Congress, or in the department, with reference to the Indian Service that these people are not around nosing in." Mr. Flynn did not intend this as complimentary testimony to the value of the service of the Commissioners, but it is. The Commissioners, we may remark, are a body of highly-respectable business men, interested in the honest and effective application of a sound and humane policy to the Indians, who are appointed practically as Inspectors, who have performed their duties with zeal and patience and skill, and without any salary. The only expense incurred by the Government in return for the advantages thus secured is the paltry sum of $5,000 appropriated annually for the traveling expenses of the Commissioners. This appropriation Mr. Holman, through an entirely mistaken idea of economy, proposes to withdraw.

If any large corporation, exposed to carelessness and peculation in its business, should try to economize by discharging men who, at a small cost, had reduced this risk to almost nothing, its next year's accounts would show the folly of such saving. Congress is asked to do just this thing as to the Indian Commissioners, and it would be equally foolish. But there is more in the matter than this. The Commissioners guard not only the pecuniary interests but the honor of the Government. The waste and corruption in the Indian Service which their vigilance and practical knowledge of business have prevented or corrected are not merely or chiefly wrongs to the taxpayer. They are far more serious wrongs to the Indians, who are the wards of the Government. Such wrongs have very permanent and important consequences. Much of the bloodshed and violence and rapine of our "Indian wars" have been due to just these causes. And now, when these are relatively improbable, the waste and corruption which the Commissioners fight so successfully would retard or defeat the efforts of the Government gradually to convert the Indians into civilized and self-supporting people. Such a result would be costly even if the $5,000 were really saved, which it would not be, but as many hundred thousands lost. Every consideration of honor and humanity demands that the work of the Commissioners—which, we may add, is highly appreciated by the Interior Department—shall be continued and extended.

11 Indian Culture and Politics

The Interior Department will naturally be at a loss for a precedent in treating the application of the Sioux Indians for permission to erect a battle monument in memory of heroes of their tribe. The American Indians are not a monument-building race, and such effigies and columns as now exist to perpetuate the valor and virtues of any chief or brave were erected by Indians who had become civilized, and generally through the influence of the whites. The Sioux can scarcely be called a civilized tribe. . . .

—*New York Times*
June 19, 1897

D
URING THE DECADES in which the Indian problem was a matter of priority for the *Times*, its editorial writers rarely appeared to take a serious interest in the Native American cultures. They might accord an Indian culture a positive account if it compared favorably in some way with that of white civilization. Otherwise, they tended to ignore it and leave it shrouded in mystique, as the domain of savages. The fact that the *Times* felt comfortable in classifying tribes as "civilized" and "non-civilized" or "wild" was in itself revealing. These classifications were common in the terminologies of various government agencies and were never questioned by the *Times*.

The *Times* editorial writers hardly expected politics among the Native Americans, except among those "civilized tribes" who had acquiesced to the government, put down their arms, and taken up residence in the Indian Territory. Here, the Indians practiced a brand of politics the *Times* understood—politics rife with corruption. But politics among the Native Americans elsewhere got barely a passing glance. When the chiefs competed for attention, that was "aboriginal politics," scarcely meaty enough for serious editorial attention.

Similarly, culture among the "civilized tribes" seldom was deemed noteworthy. The native cultures in this setting had tended to fade, as the Indians became more like the white neighbors by whom they were surrounded. These tribes gained more attention by having lobbyists in Washington than they did for their native customs. Surely, like their newly freed black brethren, they had their eyes on a higher prize: a coveted seat in the United States Congress. That was cultural advancement the *Times* editorial writers could reckon with. The *Times* tended to fall into the same pattern even when taking the longer view of Native American history. The revered Six Nations were most important because of their political structure. It seemed logical to the *Times* editorialists that these were tribes of more sagacious Indians, further advanced in the arts of civilized life than others among the seventeenth-century natives.

Culture among the "wild" tribes was more likely to gain at least passing mention. In what surely was not a calculated policy, *Times* editorial writers frequently made derogatory references to aspects of the Native American cultures such as food preferences and dress—obvious, if superficial, differences that set the Indians apart from most men and women of white European heritage. Passing comment, often in a broader context intended to be favorable to the Indians, helped create or perpetuate damaging stereotypes.

Intentional or not, a disdain for Native American cultures typical among whites during the period showed up regularly in *Times* opinion pieces. The first of the following editorials is an example. Instead of viewing the Paris Exposition as an appropriate showcase for the Indian cultures, the *Times* took the position that the Native American was "not a particularly creditable specimen of humanity." It feared that a display of native culture might be an embarrassment.

Native religion, for the most part, was a topic avoided on the editorial pages of the *Times*. The Indians were pagans, after all, and little was known about their religious beliefs and ceremonies. But there were occasional expositions of such mysterious religious rites as those of the Zunis, when these could be authenticated by scholars. There was also a general assumption that contact with Christian missionaries was beneficial to the natives. In this vein, the *Times* applauded the work of Catholics, Quakers, and those of other denominations who established Indian schools.

The *Times* obviously felt it had a valid reason to delve into Indian social institutions such as slavery. A brief editorial-page item in 1883 noted that the existence of slavery among the Navajos in Arizona had only recently been discovered and that the tribespeople were "very much surprised to hear that slavery on American soil is illegal" and their slaves would have to be set free.

In time, as the Indians advanced toward a level of sophistication the *Times* editorial writers believed essential for full national participation, the editorial columns paid more attention to their progress. They noted the social and political entities through which the Native Americans conducted their own affairs, even if imperfectly, so long as these approximated recognized systems of white culture. These fell under the same editorial scrutiny the *Times* habitually focused on traditional entities of white governments. For example, when the Chickasaw Supreme Court decided in 1889 that white men married to Indian women of the tribe would no longer be allowed to vote in Chickasaw elections, the *Times* took issue. "The white husbands have too large interests in the farming and cattle business of the Chickasaw Nation to submit to the present decision without a hard struggle," it declared. The following year, after the Secretary of the Interior had validated the Chickasaw court decision—a requirement that showed just how little true self-determination was allowed the "civilized tribes"—the *Times* noted that the white men in question still were expected to pay a head tax. Taxation without representation was bad under any circumstance, the newspaper said, but taking away the ballot from taxpayers who once enjoyed it was even worse.

In some instances, the *Times* inadvertently demonstrated the level of mystique that, in the minds of whites, encompassed Native American cultures. The ghost dance and the so-called messiah delusion were cases in point. Neither phenomenon was well understood, and both terrified white society. Both were relatively extensive movements that crossed tribal lines and clearly signaled the possibility of Indian unification. As the *Times* understood very well, the Native Americans were fierce warriors even in disarray; united, they still had the potential to be a powerful force. Besides, in an editorial approach based on a we/they perspective, the fervor the Indians brought to the messiah delusion and the ghost dance clearly set them apart as different from their white neighbors on the frontier.

The uneasiness with which the *Times* viewed the messiah delusion was apparent in a brief editorial-page item in December 1890. The *Times* believed its old nemesis, Sitting Bull, had deliberately fanned the flames of the Indians' visions of race revival. His apparition was rumored to be about at night, it said, gliding from hilltop to hilltop in the Bad Lands and motioning the Indians to follow. Sitting Bull's ghost thus had picked up where the old chief left off at his death, suggested the *Times*, resuming the business of mischief making. "Such a vision, if once seen, may appear again and again to their feverish imaginations," the *Times* asserted, "reinforcing the Messiah delusion; and so the implacable and unreconstructed son of Jumping Bull may supplement the work of his life with a certain posthumous leadership."

The *Times* editorials that follow deal with Native American cultures and politics from a variety of perspectives. But for all the attention devoted to them, these were subjects on which the newspaper never developed a consistent editorial direction.

⌁ A Questionable Enterprise

December 27, 1866

What is the particular object for sending to the Paris Exposition a collection of Indian savages, with their war paint and feathers? They can scarcely be called products of American *industry*, nor are they in any respect the legitimate results of our peculiar institutions. This Exhibition is intended to illustrate the progress made by all the nations of the earth in art, science, modes of life, and the various processes and products of labor:—what bearing upon these objects this assortment of Indians is expected to have, we find it somewhat difficult to imagine. Very likely they will excite the curiosity of a good many Europeans, but that is no reason why they should be included among the products of American labor. The American Indian is not a particularly creditable specimen of humanity in his best estate, and when he comes to be exhibited side by side with an American bar-room, we fear that he will excite a good deal more surprise than admiration.

The managers of the American Department of this Great Exhibition must not let it degenerate into a show of curiosities. Whatever can properly be done in that line may safely be left to Mr. Barnum or some of his enterprising imitators. If we are to do the country any credit or service at Paris, it can only be by showing the world what has been done in the legitimate development of labor in all its departments, in a country where individual enterprise is left wholly unfettered. An exhibition of Indian war-whoops and gin-cocktails may be very amusing, but it is certain also to be very disgusting.

⌒ Freedmen in the Indian Territory

April 25, 1870

Of all the negroes to whom the war brought freedom, none, perhaps, were more miserable or oppressed than those of the Indian Territory. When emancipation came, it brought to them no change for the better. The Indians were, of course, compelled to release them from bondage, and nominally did so. But the reality of bondage remained. Their former masters became their enemies. There was no longer the motive to tend them as useful animals. Equality created hatred, born of jealousy, before impossible; and, while the nation gave to the negro a new social status, the Indian Territorial authority removed from him no legal or political disability whatever. Especially was this the case with those slaves which were owned by the *quasi* united tribes of Choctaws and Chickasaws. Manifestly this condition of affairs could not be allowed to continue.

An attempt was made in 1865, by a treaty, to secure some equality of local rights to these negroes. The two nations ceded "the leased district" to the United States, in consideration of which $300,000 was invested by the latter for the nations at five per cent. The principal was to be paid to them when they had given the negroes equal rights with themselves, and those who were residents forty acres each of the ceded land on the same terms as the Indians. If, however, any of the negroes desired to move out of the Territory, $100 was to be paid to each from the $300,000. If, further, the nations failed to fulfill these conditions within two years, the entire sum was to revert to the benefit of such negroes as wished to remove, those remaining having no interest therein. There were other provisions by which the ex-slaves were protected in respect to their labor and civil rights generally. With the execution of the treaty the matter ended. No subsequent action was taken by the two nations.

The negroes naturally complain of this, and demand some arrangement for their safety and welfare. They consider themselves full citizens of the nations with whom their lives have been passed, and, regarding the Territory as their proper home, prefer to remain in it. Conventions to urge these claims were, however, prevented by the Indians, who tore down the printed notices, and threatened the lives of any who should venture to attend; and they actually did arrest one colored man. Meetings were held in other localities in spite of these intimidations, and three delegates appointed to lay the case before Congress. But the delegates were too poor to go to Washington, and when Senator Carson, of Arkansas, was able to leave his State for the purpose of representing them, Congress had adjourned.

The circumstances certainly entitle these poor freedmen to consideration by the Government. Their wrongs are felt all the more bitterly that many of them fought for the Union, and moreover that those who did were excluded from the treaty of 1865 by their absence on military duty, which enabled the Indians to call them non-residents. Whether what the negroes now seek can be wisely granted is another matter. Continued residence among the Choctaws and Chickasaws would subject them to worse cruelties after their forty-acre allotments were secured than before. The general opinion of those who appear to understand the subject best, is that a country should be set apart for them in the leased district, where they could be all together, or in some other locality. At all events the question remains, whether these Indians are to oppress a loyal class of people, or whether the Government shall interfere and force a settlement which will insure peace, and protect the negroes in their homes and industries. There should be but one reply, and that is that justice must be done without further delay.

⌒ The Indian Council

June 19, 1871

The "new departure" of the red men is, when considered as a chapter in human progress, perhaps a more momentous event than the great political juggle which the Democratic pale-faces have been seeking to accomplish under that title. Mazzini the other day ridiculed the idea of the French Communists going back to the Middle Ages for a political idea, and asked why they should have stopped short of the patriarchal unit of government—the family or the tribe. In the Indian effort to form a self-governing community, we have an illustration of exactly the reverse of the latter alternative. The patriarchal organization which our race left behind them on the steppes of Asia finds its duplicate on the Western plains. The most advanced of the political systems of the world finds itself face to face with the most primitive whence it has been evolved, and the tribe is suddenly compelled to adapt itself to the township, the electorial district, and all the institutions which these bring with them, or submit to the terrible certainty of decay and ultimate extinction. The "five nations" of the Indian Territory number less than sixty thousand, but they present a conclusive proof that the red man can be civilized, and they are the only medium through which we can hope to reclaim the wild tribes of the plains. Their country comprises "one of the richest and most fertile regions in the United States," is 382 miles long, 208 miles wide, and contains 70,456 square miles. It has been described as containing fifty millions of acres of land, and as being equal to seventy States of the size of Rhode Island, and about one and a half of the size of New-York. For every man, woman and child in the Indian Territory there is thus, at present, an area of not much less than one thousand acres, so that the Territory can undoubtedly sustain with very great ease the six millions claimed for it by Gen. Sherman, and is as large a field as could possibly be desired on which to work out a great political and social experiment.

The Territorial Constitution on which the General Council at Okmulgee is at present deliberating is in many points merely an expansion of the existing political usages of the "Five Nations." Among the Cherokees, for example, there exist already an upper and lower Legislative Chamber returned by nine districts, and elected after a fashion essentially representative. The new Constitution aims at effecting a fusion which shall be first political and then social. Its probable results were thus described by Gen. Sherman: There will be no longer Creeks, Choctaws or Cherokees; all the titles of the tribes will be merged in one people, and all executive, legislative and judicial functions shall be consolidated in one centre. It is precisely at this point that the true Indian problem is touched, and from it the difficulties in the way of the acceptance of the Territorial Constitution will be found to arise. We have long since discovered that a radical error was committed in dealing with the Indian tribes, as with independent nations. We are more slowly becoming awake to the fact that in doing our best to strengthen the tribal organization of the Indians we have made no less decided a blunder. If the Indian is to survive on this continent at all, it must be by elevating himself to the social, industrial, and political level of the white man. With time and opportunity, it is pretty obvious that he can do this. It is equally certain that the maintenance of the authority of the Chiefs and their belongings forms one of the most potent obstacles to Indian progress. Among the semi-civilized tribes, this is specially obvious. We intrust to the Chiefs for distribution, a large proportion of our bounty, or of the returns of funds held in trust by the Government. The nominal head of the tribe thus becomes vitally interested in resisting that certain decay of his authority and importance which results from the adoption of civilized usages. Nothing brings out the independence of the individual so strongly as our republican freedom, while nothing is more inconsistent with its legitimate exercise than the perpetuation of a kind of dignity which has no significance apart from barbarism or warfare.

To the provisions of the Constitution which was drafted in December last for the new Territory of Oklahoma we have previously adverted. They do not differ in any marked degree from the type which prevails in the other States. It was expected that before the present meeting of the General Council the new Constitution would have been formally accepted by the various tribes in the Territory. The Indian seems, however, to be as jealous of his distinctive tribal organization as any old German Duchy was of its mimic Court and its solemn farce of State administration. It is easier to control the outward semblance of deliberative and representative bodies than to grasp the new idea of a coalesced nation on which they rest. It is requisite to bear in mind that the Indian tribes have historical memories whose force we are very apt to underrate. For example the Cherokees, no later than ten years ago were said to have numbered 25,000, while at this moment they do not contain more than 16,000 souls. Ascending by ever widening gradations like this, through the decades of a couple of centuries, we begin to find ourselves in the presence of a veritable nation whose seven great clans are still represented on the seven-pointed star of their State seal, and whose original wealth is but faintly reproduced in the four millions of acres of land which they hold in fee simple, and the four millions of dollars of trust funds on which the Government pays them an annual interest. A competent authority states that previous to the war the Cherokees "owned immense herds of cattle, one individual alone owning 20,000 head. Others owned 15,000, 10,000 and so down to 300, and the man who owned less was considered a poor Indian." Of other tribes similar statements might be made, and they are of immense importance in helping us to estimate the difficulties which arrest the completion of Indian union as well as the greatness of the wrongs whose memory still begets distrust of our intentions toward the red men.

☞ The "Six Nations"

June 28, 1873

On the 13th of June was held what may prove to be one of the last great ceremonies of the greatest Indian organization ever known to white men on the North American Continent. It consisted in an election of chiefs by the Tuscarora Tribe, the last of the famous confederacy known as the "Six Nations." The event took place on the reservation of the tribe, which is a tract of six miles wide by four miles long, situated in the town of Lewiston, N.Y. Since the last Grand Council, held twenty years ago, the Tuscaroras have lost, by death and accident, nine chiefs; and the Council convened on the 13th, met to mourn over the dead, and to select candidates to fill their places from among the living.

There are many reasons why the "Six Nations" hold an exceptional place in American history, and why their deeds, even in decay, should bespeak interest and honorable record. The original Five Nations—the Mohawks, Oneidas, Onondagas, Cayugas, and Senecas—received the Tuscaroras as a sixth member of their union in 1712. Paramount among all the tribes of the Continent for courage and prowess in war, these aboriginals were likewise beyond all other red men in sagacity and in the arts of civilized life. It is highly probable that, but for the advent of the whites, these five races would have anticipated ourselves in extending their rule over the whole Continent. Known by the general name of "Iroquois," they actually originated for themselves a substantial reproduction of the Achaean League, or, more strictly, an anticipation of our own national confederacy. Each tribe was within itself independent, but was bound to all the others for purposes of war or common interest. All such questions were discussed and settled by a sort of Wittenegemote, or Congress, commonly held at Onondaga. So far has the traditional influence of this fact extended through the generations, that, to this day, the "court language," so to say, of the "Six Nations" is that of the Onondagas, and at the late election the speeches were made in that tongue. The old Roman policy of encouraging other nations to become incorporated with themselves was pursued by the Iroquois with much success. But they had other merits not always possessed either by the Romans or the modern copyists. Their sachems lived in the utmost simplicity, received no salaries, and gave away alike their shares of the spoils of war and the perquisites of peace. Such was the strength and prestige of their consolidation and wise management that they were feared and respected from the Atlantic to the great lakes. One Mohawk, it is said, has often put to flight a whole party of Indians from New-England or the South. Another peculiar characteristic of the Iroquois, astonishingly at variance with the usages of other tribes, was the great deference paid by them to women. The matrons had a regular power in the State, were represented in the public councils, and actually had a veto influence in the declaration of peace and war. Here, again, the traditional customs of the Confederacy were respected in the late election; the candidates for Chiefs having been designated by women, and duly ratified by what is called the "Chiefs' Council."

It is not strange, considering the skill, vigor, and manly superiority in general, of these celebrated red men, that Fenimore Cooper should have so frequently chosen them to be the heroes of his unrivaled romances of the forest and prairie. The race of which Hiawatha was the Washington, and which can boast Logan, Red Jacket, and Shenandoah, certainly had qualities deserving of permanent respect and commemoration. Their number now is very few; but they have a still further distinction to add to those which set them apart from other nations of the Continent, in the singular fact that they still occupy a portion of their old hunting-grounds, and have not deserted, or been driven from, the graves of their sires. There are only 300 Tuscaroras at Lewiston, but, with the deputations from the other tribes of the confederacy, 600 united, on the 13th, in the festivities succeeding the election. Everything, we are glad to observe, passed off with the utmost dignity and decorum. There was first an elaborate song of lamentation for the chiefs who had gone to the "happy hunting-grounds" since the last grand council. This occurred in the open air, around the traditional council fire, which sent up its thin spirals of blue smoke through a copse of maples. The pipe of peace was smoked, and the company then marched with much solemnity to the "long house," a true Indian structure, fifty feet by twenty, built of poles, bark, and withes—no white man's tool having been used in erecting it. Here the lament was again sung, strings of wampum were produced, and a long series of emblematic and memorial ceremonies performed, ending in the formal ordination of the new chiefs. This done, an Indian banquet followed on a large scale, to which, in turn, succeeded a game of ball by the "bucks" of the different tribes, and the whole wound up at night with a grand war-dance, in full old-fashioned paint and regalia. Among the delegates from other tribes present was Gen. Parker, President Grant's former chief of staff, and the ceremonies were closely observed by many spectators of distinction among the "pale-faces." It is well that it should have been so; for such a scene, on such a scale, is not likely to be witnessed often again; and there is a deep and melancholy interest in watching these last memorable observances by the remains of tribes once so exceptionally strong and famous, and in recollecting that these last scions of a noble race still set up their lodge and build their council fire, like their forefathers, by the blue waters of Lake Ontario.

ᔐ Oklahama

May 19, 1874

The long-suffering Indian is determined to come to the front. The guttural accents of his anguish-stricken appeal for a place in Congress are heard even in the National Capital. The war paint and the immemorial feathers have been laid aside. The noble red man no longer covets his neighbor's scalp as the most desirable of earthly possessions; his haughty eye is fixed upon a more brilliant prize. He dreams of nought save a maiden speech in the Federal legislative halls; his stoicism and impenetrable calm have vanished before eager desire and wild excitement. The immense success of the negro as a legislator—especially in South Carolina—has served to stimulate the red man's pride and ambition. It is not impossible that in course of time we shall have an Indian in Congress; there would be something at once grand and pathetic in the spectacle of a descendent of the proud aborigines defending the rights of his fading race against the final and fatal domination of the white man, who has usurped the ownership of the soil. But before the red man can attain Congressional honors, a few barriers which he has heretofore insisted on keeping between him and the Caucasian must be thrown down.

That part of the American domain at present known as the Indian Territory, and inhabited mainly by Indians partially or wholly civilized, contains seventy thousand square miles, or a larger area than the New-England States; is bounded on the north by Kansas, the south by Texas, the east by Missouri and Arkansas, and the west by Texas and New-Mexico. Its climate is magnificent; its fertility superb. It has sometimes been called, possibly without exaggeration, "the garden spot of the continent." Surrounded on every side by States and Territories of the Union, it is yet as alien and independent as any country of Europe. For more than forty years it has been the home of the Cherokees, Choctaws, Chickasaws, Creeks, and other remnants of noble and warlike nations, who were moved "beyond the Mississippi" from their lands in Florida, in Alabama, Tennessee, Georgia, North Carolina, and other Southern States. Binding and comprehensive treaties were made with these nations in 1837, and renewed in 1866 guaranteeing them the lands in the Territory forever. They hedged themselves about with safeguards against the white man. They found that they must make a bold moral stand against him, and they made it. Bitter feuds developed between the parties who had agreed to cede the lands east of the Mississippi, and to whose influence was due the removal to the "Indian Territory." To-day the lands there are held in common; no individual can sell anything beyond the improvements on the acres which he occupies, and no white man can settle among the "nations" unless he marries an Indian woman, and virtually forswears his allegiance to the Government of his own race. The members of the uncompromising faction take a savage pride in thus guarding their independence and maintaining their autonomy; and they relentlessly destroy, if they can reach him, any one of their race who may make overtures to the white man for an opening of the territory to white settlement. They have adopted many civilized forms in their Government, have shown a disposition to follow the arts of peace, to support schools, and to improve their lands; but they do not wish to become citizens of the Union.

Nevertheless, those Indians who think that the elevation of the "Indian nation" into a territorial government to be called "Oklahoma"—the purchase of their lands from the various tribes, the overthrow of all the obstacles to white immigration, and the final admission of the rich and fertile division as a State—would be a wise and beneficent measure for the Indians as well as the whole south-western country, are growing in power and have a voice in Washington. They have capable and accomplished advocates of their cause, they have lands which would render them rich for life were they marketable, and they have political ambition. The railroad, too, has pierced the jealously-guarded country of the red man; and in its wake will follow that turbulent and aggressive current which he has never been able to withstand. The bloody vendetta which began in 1839 between those who favored compromise and co-operation with the white man, and those who sternly refused any fellowship with him, may be revived, and the sixty or seventy thousand people now scattered over the vast area of the Territory may yet be convulsed over the momentous issue. The white man can afford to wait patiently. He can see many reasons why the Indians would be vastly better off as citizens of the United States than they now are; but it best becomes him to allow them to decide for themselves whether they will still maintain their haughty isolation, or will finally adopt the sentiments of those who wish, for the red as well as for the black man, a place in Congress.

↜ Aboriginal Politics

June 4, 1875

Nobody need suppose that the Indian Chiefs now negotiating at Washington are such untutored children of Nature that they have no knowledge of politics. Indian politics, it is true, differ somewhat from the variety known among white men. But in all essential particulars, the points of similarity are striking and numerous. At home, the rival chiefs may be more outspoken in their jealousy of each other than when in Washington, where a common exigency unites them. But, even in their talks with the President, Secretary, and other officials, their petty rivalries are apparent. Of the leaders, Red Cloud represents the Ogallalla Sioux, and Spotted Tail the Brule Sioux, while Sitting Bull appears for the Northern Sioux, who have only a contingent interest in pending negotiations. The nominal chieftain of the Ogallalla Sioux is the Old Man Afraid of His Horses. This chief is very old and infirm, and as he can no longer lead his braves upon the war-path or in the chase, nor bring into camp large spoil to divide, is practically displaced by Red Cloud, a vigorous Indian now in his prime. Red Cloud is a redoubtable warrior, of fine presence, great natural abilities, and endowed with a certain eloquence which makes him influential in aboriginal politics. He leads the braves on the war-path, and has performed many daring exploits in the face of the enemy, (both white and red,) which have fired the admiration and ambition of the young men. He easily disputes, by right of suffrage, the sway of the partly-superannuated Old Man Afraid of His Horses. The hereditary chief of this branch of the tribe is, or should be, the Young Man Afraid of His Horses, who is now in Washington, and who is the son of the Old Man, &c.,

above mentioned. This young brave, who is in some sort an Indian Edward the Black Prince, is likely to give Red Cloud a hard fight for the chieftainship of the Ogallallas, if his life is spared, which is by no means certain, as Indian politicians have a way of getting rid of rivals which repeats the history of mediaeval times in Europe. Spotted Tail is Chief of the Brule Sioux, and is now chiefly anxious to distinguish himself as a diplomatist for the admiration of his people at home. So far, he has succeeded admirably, and has proved himself able and shrewd. Sword is one of Red Cloud's first warriors, and is son-in-law of that chieftain.

It is easy to see how, with their free system of politics, the chiefs of Indian tribes are continually surrounded by intrigues and cabals. Whenever there arises an occasion which calls the head men to Washington, there is bitter strife to see who shall go. The opportunity is one which may make or unmake a chief, or an aspirant for chieftainship. Once there, these wily politicians resort to precisely the same arts that are thought to be the disgrace of American legislation and politics. Each aboriginal statesman desires to cut a good figure—not in the newspapers, for his constituents do not read the newspapers—but in the eyes of the watchful followers who will report to the home lodges all that is said and done with an accuracy that will make impossible any "cards" of denial or explanation, or "statements," from the men who have assumed the honors and responsibilities of leadership. Spotted Tail seems to have excelled in this sort of diplomacy, to the discomfiture of Red Cloud, whose eloquence is more in the *ore rotundo* manner, say like that of Gen. N. P. Banks. His rival in the palaver now going on, Spotted Tail, shows great wit and shrewdness. Some of his hits remind one of the genial Congressman, S. S. Cox. For example, when the "Big White Chief" pictured to the sardonic band the beauties and attractions of the Indian Territory, and kindly advised them to move into that terrestrial paradise, Spotted Tail replied that he and his people were born in their present home; that they desired to be buried there; and, if the Indian Territory was so desirable a country, why should not the Great Father send there his white children who were anxious to get into the Black Hills? Red Cloud, on the other hand, has made at least one ignominious failure. And when he failed to make a good point where he had an opportunity, his friends explained that it was owing to "too much whisky." Of course, this lapse was a welcome chance to the Young Man Afraid of His Horses, who heads the opposition to Red Cloud.

Possibly some of our readers will recollect politicians at Washington and Albany who have needed similar friendly excuses to be made for them when their constituents have asked troublesome questions.

In a very sensible manner these politicians of the wilderness have accomplished all they really wanted. The cession of the Black Hills is postponed for the present; but the question will be taken up when the chiefs meet Government Commissioners in the Sioux country. But they now secure the absolute cession of so much of the State of Nebraska as lies north of the Niobrara River and south of the present line of their reservation. For abandoning hunting privileges south of the Niobrara, they get $25,000 in cash, which is to be divided between the Brules and the Ogallallas. This gives the Indians a natural boundary for the lower edge of their reservation, and leaves Western Nebraska fully open to white occupation, though it will not be available for some time to come. These politic chiefs, however, prefer to bring the matter to their followers before they sign the agreement. In just that fashion the President would send a treaty to Congress before it was executed. Public opinion among the Sioux, however, manifests itself in other ways than in memorials to Congress and newspaper articles. News travels from village to village; every intruder is known and described, just as Prof. Marsh is "The Bone-hunting Chief" among the Sioux, who know nothing of paleontology. And, to save bloodshed, the Indian diplomatists take the papers home with them. They feel that they have done a good stroke of business, and they go back to play a little demagogism with their dusky constituencies.

↩ [Untitled]

January 26, 1881

A Denver dispatch to yesterday's *Times* reports a number of murders by the Apaches in New-Mexico. These Indians, whose number is estimated at from 9,000 to 10,000, have always been more or less troublesome to the settlers in their neighborhood, and are regarded as extremely treacherous and malignant. Although native to the Territory where their late depredations have occurred, their raids extend far into the States of Chihuahua and Sonora, and they stay there part of the year. Ever since the arrival of the white race in Mexico the Apaches have been in constant warfare with them, though it is said that the Spaniards found them proud and independent, but peaceful and well disposed. The aboriginals were so badly treated by the invaders, and so repelled by the unwise missionary efforts to convert them, that before the end of the seventeenth century they made common cause with the Pueblo savages to drive out the enemy. The missions were destroyed, the priests massacred, the mines seized, and every Spaniard caught was put to death. The Pueblos were finally subjugated, but the Apaches could not be overcome, and to this day they defy all Governments and every form of civilization. For many years these warlike, indomitable people have not been united. They carry on hostilities in small guerrilla bands or marauding parties, and although their power has been broken, they continue to be a terror to travelers, settlers, and the local authorities. The State of Chihuahua for a long time paid them a bounty to prevent their inroads, but to no purpose, of course. They accepted the bounty, and continued their outrages. They are the Arabs of the continent. Mounted on small ponies of great endurance, they sweep over the plain, hunting the antelope, wolf, deer, or settler with equal zest. They are very skillful with the bow and arrow, but of late have learned to use fire-arms with fatal effect. All the women ride like men, and are sometimes mistaken for them. Many of the latter have recently adopted the Mexican blanket and sombrero, while the women generally wear a short petticoat, and let their hair stream over their bare shoulders, but cut it short when mourning for their husbands. The younger children go nearly naked. Those under 2 years are carried in a basket by the mother, and strapped to it in a standing position, the basket being fastened to the saddle when the mother is on horseback. The men usually daub their faces with vermilion, and grease their bodies before they go to fight, which they do with horses in rapid motion, being never themselves at rest. The chiefs can have any number of wives, and exercise no sort of moral restraint. But a woman found guilty of adultery is tortured to death in the most ingeniously horrible manner. The Apaches often torment their foes, but never scalp them. Them seem to believe in one God, and the spirit of Montezuma is blended in some way with their religious aspirations. They have, like the Jews, a repugnance to the hog; they dread the rattlesnake, respect the bear, which they never slay, and revere superstitiously the owl, eagle, and all birds completely white. The Apache tribes are among the most diffused on the continent, embracing many known to us as yet only by name. They are very interesting ethnically, and very dangerous personally.

⌐ A Boston Revival

March 31, 1882

If Col. Olcott and Mme. Blavatsky had staid in the United States, instead of going to India in search of the true faith among the Brahmins, they might have found a religion more truly bric-a-brac than anything they will discover in Bombay. As it is, Boston has secured this inestimable boon, and is at this moment in possession of a faith as ancient, if we may believe the missionaries, as the American continent. This cultus has been imported from the far West by a band of Zuni Indians, who live in New-Mexico. The Zuni religion is a delightful form of paganism, much more pagan, in fact, than that of the ancient Greeks, or even than of the earliest Phoenicians. Precisely what the Zuni faith consists of no non-Zuni person can tell. The delightful mystery which envelops this antique religion constitutes its chief charm. No sensible person would care much for a creed, confession of faith, and ritual which could be understood by everybody. If it were not for its being a peculiarly rococo and early-twilight religion, Boston would not have cared a rap for the Zuni development. Every aesthetic person knows that the further back in the world's history we go, the better do things become. Boston has something better than early English or even the Italian Renaissance. It has the Zuni religion.

How long the Zuni Indians have maintained their strange and mystic ritual may be estimated from a single statement: When the Zuni faith was first revealed to man, one of the conditions imposed upon the patriarchs of the tribe was that they should go to the sea side every month and bring home a quantity of sea-water for incantation purposes. As the region now known as New-Mexico was then near the borders of what is now known as the Atlantic Ocean, this was an easy task. But, as all geographers and other scientific persons very well know, the American continent has been steadily rising from the sea, ever since its foundations were laid. It has been estimated by a well-known scientific person that the continent has risen three-quarters of an inch during the last five centuries—without making any allowance of the strata of tomato cans and hoop-skirts formed along that portion of the Atlantic sea-board frequented by Summer visitors. If the student of theology will calculate the time required, on this basis, to raise from under high-water mark that portion of the American continent which lies between the Atlantic Ocean at Boston and the country of the Zunis in New-Mexico, he will ascertain with tolerable accuracy the age of the Zuni faith. And this calculation is now being worked out by several Harvard Professors, who will, in time, give the result to the world, showing that the Zuni variety of paganism is so very aged that the Hindu faiths now being imbibed by Olcott, Blavatsky, and the other Theosophists may be considered as modern inventions.

As years passed by, and successive generations of Zunis came and went, and centuries and eons rolled over their heads, the Atlantic Ocean grew more and more remote to the Zuni ritualists. They had been in the habit of starting for their monthly supply of sea-water immediately after breakfast, and of getting back with the sacred fluid in time for a 12 o'clock dinner. The journey grew longer, and some of the Zunis grumbled a good deal over the necessity for these long pilgrimages. Nevertheless, no orthodox Zuni could possibly think of worshiping in the simple faith of his fathers without a fair supply of salt water. Mere salt and water would be no more efficacious than a three-foot gas burner on a consecrated altar where real candles are prescribed by the ritual. It was in vain that the precious store was hoarded. In course of time it would waste, and it is reported that the Zuni youth, profanely thinking that any liquid so carefully guarded must be good to drink, became surreptitiously inebriated on one of the few remaining bottles left in camp. Then, after the lapse of about five centuries, during which the Eastern sea had been pushed half-way back to the coast of Europe from New-Mexico, the last few drops of consecrated brine were gone, or nearly gone.

At this emergency appeared on the scene Prof. Cushing, a zealous student of ethnology and theology. He saw his opportunity. Being desirous of learning the history of the Zuni tribe, its faith and its literature, he offered to get for them a supply of the much-desired sea-water, provided they would make a Zuni of him. The simple people agreed to this proposition, the only conditions being that the Professor should bring in a scalp and marry a Zuni woman. Nobody knows where the Professor secured his scalp, although there are ugly rumors concerning the mysterious disappearance of the hair of a "subject" in the Boston Medical College. To marry a Zuni woman he flatly refused, and this part of the contract was waived, as they say in law. Last Tuesday Prof. Cushing and his band of Zuni ritualists were taken to Deer Island, in Boston Harbor, by the Mayor and Common Council, accompanied by the Rev. Phillips Brooks, Collector Beard, several Harvard Professors, and a steam-boat load of "citizens generally." There were incantations, delightfully pagan ceremonies, and a general ducking all around. Prof. Cushing was initiated into the thirty-third degree of the Zuni faith, and may now learn the sacred epic, which is never written out, and which may be rattled off orally in twenty-six hours. The ceremonies over, the Zunis were bundled into wagons, with their demijohns and bottles, and the City Government of Boston and the Faculty of Harvard College went home with the delightful consciousness that they had assisted in preserving one of the oldest and most truly bric-a-brac forms of heathenism known to man.

✍ The Indian Messiah Delusion

November 20, 1890

The strange excitement now prevailing among a dozen or more Indian tribes, notably among the Arapahoes of Wyoming, the Northern Cheyennes of Tongue River, and the Sioux of Pine Ridge and other agencies, is probably without a parallel in the history of the aborigines. The influence which has been exerted at times by the "Dreamers" is familiar, as also is the ordinary potency of their "Medicine Men." But the present widespread delusion is that a so-called Messiah of the red men is now somewhere in the mountains of Nevada preparing to bury all the white race under the earth and leave the red race on top. This idea, which seems to have originated about a year ago, and to have attracted the attention of army officers only last Spring, has been steadily spreading, until now it has taken possession of tribes hundreds of miles apart. It appeals to all classes—to the restless youth, to the religiously disposed, who mix it with the instructions of the missionaries, and to those who are filled with race hatred, like mischief-making Sitting Bull.

The picture which is drawn by the preachers of this new delusion appeals very strongly to the race feeling of the red men, and particularly to those who oppose civilized life. Never has unadulterated native Americanism been carried further. The aborigines only are to be left in the land. The buffalo will appear again, the plains will be stocked with horses, and the dead Indians will be restored to life. Under prospects not more vivid and promises not more grand the Arab Mahdi of the Soudan was able to rally his people to arduous campaigns and bloody battles. It is the opinion of army officers that the Indian Messiah, too, is not a figment of the imagination, but a living personage. According to some accounts he is a white man; according to others, a Pah-Ute Indian, living at Walker Lake, in Nevada. Some Indians speak of having visited him last Autumn and repeat what he said.

The result of this delusion among the red men is very much what it might be among whites, and, in fact, what historically it has been in such cases. They are taken up with talk about the future, perhaps neglect their crops, and, it is said, in some instances have torn down their houses and sold the logs. If the old pastoral days are to return, and if the earth is to be the common property of all, with no gold or silver coin, but plenty of game and fish to be had for the taking, labor seems useless, and even a house and lot mere incumbrances. The ghost dances are pursued with great assiduity, and, indeed, dancing is closely connected with this delusion. But, of course, the main fear of the settlers on the borders of the reservations is lest the excitement shall lead to the warpath and to endeavoring to advance unduly the progress of events by beginning that annihilation of the white race which is so confidently predicted. It is true that those who have seen the Indian Messiah say that he expressly commands not only industry and sobriety, but living at peace with the whites. But it is with this as with some other religious injunctions and tenets—the followers take what suits them and overlook or distort the rest. Kicking Horse, having heard about visiting this Messiah in the woods, improves on the story, and makes his pilgrimage through a hole in the sky. Indeed, the Indian story now current may be a mass of embroiderings on the original teachings of this mysterious prophet, whoever he is. That it has been wrought in here and there, not only with scraps of the Christian faith, but with the practical grievances which each tribe has—complaints against agents, lack of food, and what not—seems clear.

Yet the officers of the army who are most capable of judging do not look for any general war as the result of this excitement. Here and there disorder may occur, especially if it finds a basis in some practical cause of complaint, but no concerted uprising is expected. The season itself is now against any such undertaking, as the snow will soon be on the ground. Gen. Miles, while not underrating the seriousness of the situation and the signs of disorder, expects to bridge over the interval until severe Winter weather by the precautions now taken. Bodies of troops have been sent to the Sioux agencies from various posts, and these, with the garrisons near by, should be able to keep order and guard against any serious hostilities.

✍ [Untitled]

January 29, 1891

The alarm started in Northern Minnesota among the settlements bordering on the Chippewa reservations is entirely natural, considering the recent events in Dakota, but there is good ground for trusting that no trouble will occur. The Chippewas of that region, it appears, are engaged in a series of dances. The dance, however, is an institution which has existed among the red men for generations, and, since there is a good deal of dancing that is wholly peaceful, the inference that hostilities are about to break out seems hardly warranted as yet. The Chippewas themselves speak of the dances as being of a religious character, in which case they may not prove much more menacing to peace than the saltatorial exercises of the Shakers, and even less so than those of the big Injuns at a Tammany ball, where firewater flows freely. The fears of the settlers have properly received consideration from the State authorities; but it must be remembered that these Chippewas of Minnesota have within a short time agreed to make over to the Government, for opening to settlement, about four million acres of land. To do this, many of the bands will have to leave their familiar homes and take small allotments on one of two reservations. Indians who agree to so important a real estate transaction, and who have so good a peace record as the Chippewas, are entitled to some presumptions in their favor. Now that the settlers in the region of the dances have had rifles and ammunition furnished to them by the State, they may feel easier.

✍ Indian Reservation Courts

March 6, 1891

The Indian Appropriation bill has among its provisions an item for the so-called "Courts of Indian Offenses." The Judges in these tribunals are Indians exclusively, and in some cases there are other court officers who also are Indians. It may surprise many people to learn that these courts are in operation at nearly thirty agencies and that there are nearly one hundred Indian Judges regularly employed. Their salaries can hardly be called extravagant, the maximum being only $10 a month, while a large part of them get only half that sum. Their income was still further cut down until of late, as the appropriation of Congress only allowed the courts to be held eight months in the year; but now they are held all the year round, the regular sessions being twice a month. Each court consists of three Judges, nominated by the Indian Agent and appointed by the Commissioner. In a few cases a smaller or a larger number constitutes a full bench.

The Courts of Indian Offenses originated about eight years ago, in the desire to restrict and, as far as possible, abolish certain barbarous customs of the red men, such as the dances in which wounds are inflicted and the practices of the medicine men. The jurisdiction was naturally extended to intoxication, the sale of liquor in violation of reservation rules, larcenies, injuries to property, and various other offenses. They also have a certain jurisdiction in civil suits where Indians only are parties. At one agency we find that twenty-six cases were tried during the year; at another, sixteen; at a third, seventy-six, of which forty-eight were civil and the remainder criminal; at a fourth, ninety-one criminal cases, besides many settlements and adjudications involving property. Wife-beating, assaults, and disorderly conduct were among the prominent offenses, and were usually punished by fines or imprisonment. Not until the year 1888 did these tribunals receive recognition from Congress in the form of a small appropriation for the pay of the Judges, which has since been doubled. Up to that time the courts had shuffled along in a singular way, the Judges either getting nothing at all for their services or paying themselves out of the fines which they collected. Sometimes the Indian police also served as Judges, which was a practice rather hard on the accused. The payment of salaries now enables the Interior Department to appoint Judges who do not belong to the reservation police force, and thus to secure a greater degree of impartiality in decisions. Care is also taken that the persons selected shall be, as far as possible, men of influence in the tribe and intelligent and fair-minded.

While this system of courts is necessarily crude as well as limited in scope, it can hardly fail to have a good effect in accustoming the red men to the settlement of their disputes and grievances by law instead of by violence. Although the decisions of the Judges are subject to the review of the agent, yet they seem to be very generally approved, and it is evident that the Indians must have more confidence in justice as dealt out to them by influential and respected members of their own tribes instead of by a man of a different race who cannot even understand their language or communicate with them except through an interpreter. Some of the Judges speak English and others do not. As will be understood, these courts do not have jurisdiction of the gravest offenses, like murder, nor even of less serious ones in which a white man is a party. But they serve to settle promptly and without going beyond the limits of the reservation such minor offenses as would ordinarily come before a Justice of the Peace. They can hardly fail to diminish any sense of arbitrary government which might come from the decision of such cases by the agent, and their educational value must be important. In some instances regular records are kept of the principal cases, and a strict order is followed in the presentation of evidence, while the decision of the court is always reached by retiring for consultation. Such a system, combined with that of Indian police on the reservations, should in time accustom the red men to that "home rule," in accordance with law administered by themselves, which is at the foundation of citizenship.

↢ [Untitled]

January 16, 1892

The revival of the ghost dances among the Cheyennes and Arapahoes and some smaller tribes of the Indian Territory hardly seems to be a cause for apprehension. No doubt these performances are exciting, and whenever large gatherings of the aborigines are thus engaged there is a possibility that their frenzy may take the form of raiding upon neighboring ranches. But there is just now no evidence of hostile intent on the part of these saltatory enthusiasts. A delusion like that of a year ago as to the arrival of a miraculous saviour for the red men and the imminent ushering in of a golden age, could not be expected instantly to vanish. Among the Sioux it received a rude and apparently a decisive shock, because, being joined with certain practical grievances which led to a hostile attitude on the part of many bands, it brought on the armed intervention of troops. The virtues of dancing in garments supposed to denote a spirit garb to protect the wearers from the deadliness of bullets were not made apparent, as matters turned out in Dakota. But in the Indian Territory there is no such test of the prevailing delusion, and it is only natural that those who once put faith in it should continue for a time to do so. The failure of the hopes on which it is based will assuredly come, and meanwhile the authorities can afford to be patient, though watchful.

Indian Culture and Politics

ᶜᵔ The Choctaw Troubles

September 15, 1892

The election recently held in the Choctaw Nation has led to a fierce dispute over the count, has cost the lives of several men, and has arrayed the two parties in arms. An appeal, however, to the United States authorities has been answered by Agent Bennett, who at the last accounts had succeeded in binding the leaders of both parties to disband and disarm their followers, and to submit their dispute to the law for settlement.

Close elections with controversies over the count and an impulsive rushing to arms have become familiar incidents in the experience of the red men with parliamentary government and popular suffrage. A few years ago the struggle in the Cherokee Nation between the Nationalists, led by Bunch, and the Downing party, led by Mayes, threatened to produce civil war. The killing of the editor of the Tahlequah *Telephone* stimulated a rush of both parties to adjudication by the shotgun. Fortunately United States authority intervened, under urgent action by the Interior Department, and after the allegation of ballot-box stuffing had been investigated and the votes had been counted under the supervision of a United States officer, Mayes was declared elected as Chief and all opposition disappeared. Shortly afterward in the Chickasaw Nation a disputed election for Governor occurred. The two candidates, William L. Byrd and William M. Guy, submitted their respective claims to Secretary Vilas, who gave a temporary decision for the former, pending judicial action, and that decision was confirmed. At the next election the contest was so hot between Byrd and Sam Paul that the Governor had out his militia at the polls, while the Indian police and United States Marshal were also on hand. This contest passed without bloodshed, and Byrd was re-elected. Two years ago, among the Choctaws, W. W. Jones, the present Governor, was elected by the Progressives over Smallwood, the candidate of the Nationalists, but the latter refused to make a fight on the count. This year the ballot seemed to show that Jones was re-elected; but some of his opponents assassinated several of his party and brought about the present state of affairs.

Yet the wonder, after all, is perhaps not that there is so much election rioting among these tribes, but that a pacific and lawful settlement is so promptly agreed upon. In every instance the arrival of a duly accredited rep-

.resentative of the United States Government on the scene is a signal for an end to the appeal to arms, and in every instance after an agreement has been made as to the method of counting the votes in the presence of the National Council or Legislature there has been a peaceful acquiescence in the result. All this is promising for the time, probably not far distant, when these Indians will, as American citizens, take part in national elections. And it would be a great mistake to imagine that the Cherokees, Choctaws, and Chickasaws have nothing more at stake in their hotly-contested political canvasses than the personal ambitions of leaders or the division of the spoils of office. They are concerned with practical questions as fundamentally important to them as any that are discussed in the Presidential contest. The Cherokees have for years had under consideration the proposed sale of a great part of their lands to the Government. The Chickasaws have had prolonged controversies over the status of the freedmen among them and of white men who have married Indian women of the tribe. The Choctaw Council has had disputes with a local railroad over alleged violations of the law, has undertaken some queer legislation to dissuade the people of the tribe from taking the oath of allegiance to the United States, has sought to eject intruders from the reservation, and has aimed to regulate Choctaw citizenship. This question as to what constitutes citizenship is all the more important both to the Choctaws and Chickasaws in view of the well-known appropriation of about $3,000,000 by Congress—more than two-thirds allotted to the former—for the transfer of their title to the Cheyenne and Arapahoe lands.

The present may be considered a turning point in the political history of the civilized tribes. The time seems to be near when they must decide upon their future destiny, in view of the advance of white settlements all around them. They are expressly exempted from the operation of the severalty allotment law; yet when they see tribes which they have been accustomed to regard as wild Indians, either near by or on more distant reservations, accepting allotment, the question arises as to how long they shall refrain from it. In a larger sense the question involved is whether the tribal relations shall be loosened, or whether the wall of race separation created by old treaties shall be kept up and strengthened. Certainly such political issues as these are enough to make the election contests among the civilized tribes as hot as we sometimes see them.

⌒ The Iroquois at the Fair

July 11, 1893

The Indian chiefs who have arrived at the World's Fair, representing the Iroquois or Six Nations, have as one of their number an interesting man named Solomon O'Bail. He is a grandson of that celebrated Seneca half-breed who was known in his time as the Corn Planter. The Indian warfare of the Revolution had not more than one or two distinguished leaders who, in point of services, surpassed the Corn Planter.

It is unlikely that we shall ever greatly enlarge our knowledge of the Iroquois, the most interesting of all the aboriginal owners of North America. It is true that unpublished material relating to the Revolution exists in such collections as the Sparks of Harvard College and the Draper of the Wisconsin State Library; but the publication of it could scarcely shed further light on what is of most interest in the subject—those intellectual and physical endowments out of which the supremacy of the Iroquois arose.

The Corn Planter's talents may in part be ascribed to the white blood that coursed through his veins; but this was not true of those earlier leaders by whom the fabric of the Iroquois League was reared. When that League was formed, the white man had not made acquaintance of the Iroquois, if, indeed, Columbus had yet made acquaintance of the American Continent. Solely by the Indians themselves was the structure of the League originated. Under the strength of its organization their wonderful work of conquest was carried on. They at one time had subdued the greater part of the eastern half of North America. So early as 1608 Capt. John Smith met Mohawk Indians in Chesapeake Bay, and was informed that they "made war upon all the world." From their splendid vantage ground about the headwaters of the rivers of this State the Iroquois were able to penetrate to any part of the country, and prosecute successful conquests wherever they chose. To them the highway was easy either to Dutch settlements on Manhattan Island, to French settlements on the St. Lawrence, or to the villages of other Indians as far south as the Carolinas or westward to the Mississippi River.

Much as geographical advantages did for them, the secret of success lay largely elsewhere. It was in fact the League itself which gave them their greatest power over all other tribes. In that union there was a degree of strength which no other Indian organization could hope to equal. Prof. Freeman, in his historical account of federalism, which has just been republished, praises federalism in its best form as "the most finished and the most artificial product of political ingenuity." Writing as he did during our civil war, and in a belief that the Union would not be preserved, he nevertheless was deeply impressed with the fact that the Union had endured for more than seventy years. This was "as long as the greatest glory of Athens," and "not far short of half the duration of the greatest glory of Rome." To the elements of federalism in the Roman Commonwealth he ascribed much of Roman greatness—the duration of her independence and the wide extent and loyalty of her allies.

No one who studies the political structure of the Iroquois League can fail to observe that it was essentially a federation of powers. It answers to Prof. Freeman's definition of the federal system as one which "forms a single State in its relations to other nations, but which consists of many States with regard to its internal government." At Onondaga, where were held the councils of the League, had been set up the capital of this ancient American federation, which endured, not as did the one of Greece, for less than a hundred years, but for perhaps half a thousand years.

Prof. Freeman takes away from the Americans who created the federal system of the United States none of the glory that belongs to them as originators. They were not conscious imitators of the founders of the Achaian League and they shine not with borrowed light. But the red men also worked without a model. They were the authors of their own powerful institutions. When Prof. Freeman remarks that "the lawgivers of Achaia and the lawgivers of America are entitled to equal honor," the praise belongs not alone to Washington and his associates, for, like them, the lawgivers of the Iroquois, out of their own minds and experience, created that formidable political union by which an imperial domain became subject to the Indians of New-York.

Index

Index

Index

Index

Index

Seventh Cavalry, 108, 137, 167, 271
Seventh Infantry, 150
severalty allotments, 23, 54, 83–85, 90–91,
   193, 288–90. *See also* lands, Indian
Seymour, Horatio, 44
Shawnees, 5, 134, 182
Shenandoah, 330
Sheridan, Gen. Phil: authorizes extermination, 238; foresees Indian war, 151, 158;
   Indian lands policy of, 313–15; winter
   campaign of, 65, 136–38; on work of Indian Commission, 67–68; mentioned,
   7, 27, 37, 180, 272, 294. *See also* Piegan
   massacre
Sherman, Gen. William T.: on cause of Indian wars, 28, 190–91, 213; heads peace
   commission, 236; supports reservation
   policy, 135–36; views on Indians held by,
   76–78, 106, 134–35, 152–53, 156; white settlers and, 256, 265; on work of Indian
   Commission, 67
Shoshoni, 152, 165
Siletz Reservation, 84
Sioux: hostilities by, 3, 5, 56, 135–36; injustices to, 31–32, 305–7, 312–13; lineage customs of, 47–48; linked to Messiah
   delusion and ghost dance, 165, 339–40,
   343; military operations against, 5,
   149–51; missionaries among, 181; visit
   Washington, 8, 187–89, 268–69; mentioned, 37, 73, 76, 177, 259, 290, 321. *See
   also* Black Hills; Brave Bear; Custer,
   Gen. George A.; Red Cloud; Sitting
   Bull; Wounded Knee, battle of
Sioux Nation, xix
Sioux Reservation, 85, 86
Sissetons, 46–47
Sitting Bull: Canadian exile of, 112–17,
   120–22; death of, 14, 124, 296; defends
   views, 285–86; linked to Messiah delu-

sion, ghost dance, 323–24; vilified by
   Times, 9–10, 95–96, 257, 339; mentioned,
   7, 13, 88, 93, 109, 244, 291, 302. *See also*
   Black Hills; Little Big Horn, battle of
Six Nations, 179, 322, 329–31. *See also* Iro-
   quois League
Sixteenth Infantry, 118
Sixth Cavalry, 118
Sixth Infantry, 150
slavery among Indians, 59, 322–23, 325–26
Slim Butte, 10
Slow Bull, 93
Smith, Commissioner E. P., 72, 172, 279,
   304, 308
Snakes, 1, 142, 190, 220
Society of Friends, 67
Socorro County, N.Mex., 118
Solid Muldoon, 286
South Carolina, 3, 331
South Dakota, 46–47, 85, 210
Southern Pacific Railroad, 122
Spokanes, 190
Spotted Tail, 8, 10, 31, 103, 188, 269, 333
Springfield Republican, 315
Standing Bear, 21, 222
Standing Buffalo, 103–4
Standing Elk, 10
Standing Rock Agency, 291
Stanton, Secy. Edwin M., 260
Stephen, Fitz James, 231
Sturgis, Col. Samuel D., 108–9, 272
Sully, Gen. Alfred, 5, 172, 176, 215, 216
Sunderland, Rev. Dr. Byron, 85
Supreme Court, U.S., 38–39
Swaine, Col. P. T., 224
Sword, 334

Tahlequah Telephone, 344
Tall Bull, 211
Tecumseh, 30, 184

Robert G. Hays teaches agricultural communications and journalism at the University of Illinois, where he has won international awards for both his teaching and his contributions to mass communications research. His articles have appeared in a number of newspapers, magazines, and academic journals. His books include *Country Editor, State Science in Illinois, Early Stories from the Land,* and in collaboration with Gen. Oscar W. Koch, *G-2: Intelligence for Patton,* an important addition to the history of World War II. He and his wife, Mary, live in Champaign, Illinois, and have two sons.